A
BASEBALL
Gaijin

A BASEBALL *Gaijin*

CHASING A DREAM TO JAPAN AND BACK

AARON FISCHMAN

FOREWORD BY
Don Nomura

SPORTS
PUBLISHING

Sports Publishing books may be purchased in bulk at special discounts for sales promotion, corporate gifts, fund-raising, or educational purposes. Special editions can also be created to specifications. For details, contact the Special Sales Department, Sports Publishing, 307 West 36th Street, 11th Floor, New York, NY 10018 or sportspubbooks@skyhorsepublishing.com.

Sports Publishing® is a registered trademark of Skyhorse Publishing, Inc.®, a Delaware corporation.

Visit our website at www.sportspubbooks.com.

10 9 8 7 6 5 4 3 2 1

Library of Congress Cataloging-in-Publication Data is available on file.

Jacket design by David Ter-Avanesyan
Front jacket photograph: Kyodo / Kyodo News Images
Back jacket photograph: Getty Images

Print ISBN: 978-1-68358-477-3
Ebook ISBN: 978-1-68358-478-0

Printed in the United States of America

A pair of recently departed relatives who were perpetually supportive of me and this project, Jerome Behar and my maternal grandmother, Alice Nemon. This book is also dedicated to my amazing father, Joel.

CONTENTS

FOREWORD BY DON NOMURA

Most people first associate me with Hideo Nomo, and I wouldn't have it any other way.

I'm very proud of my role in helping Hideo make baseball history. When he signed with the Dodgers in February 1995, he inched closer to becoming the first Japanese-born player to play in the major leagues in thirty years. Then, on May 2, he did it, holding the rival Giants to one hit over five scoreless innings, attracting the attention of millions on both sides of the Pacific.

Hideo's so-called tornado delivery was certainly striking, but he was darn good too. That first season, he won NL Rookie of the Year, started the All-Star Game, and placed fourth in Cy Young voting. Hideo was not on loan from his Japanese team, as was the case with Masanori Murakami in the 1960s. Rather, he planned to become the first player from Japan to leave Nippon Professional Baseball on a permanent basis and forge a long MLB career. Of course, Hideo was able to accomplish that, and as a result his journey from Japan to the majors has rightly been credited for opening the door for Japanese players to come to the majors.

I don't even think brave would be the right word to describe Hideo in deciding to head to the States. Instead, I would say he was determined. Absolutely determined. Let me explain. At the time, Mac Suzuki was my only client, and a friend of Hideo's introduced us. Early in our first conversation, it was clear that his mind was already set. He basically said,

"Nomura-san, I'm gonna play in the major leagues next year, so just get me over there." In other words, he knew he was doing it, and it became my job to figure out how that would work, legally and contractually.

The reason "brave" seems misleading or wrong is that Hideo was supremely confident in his game and basically tunnel-visioned with what he wanted to do, with what he felt he had to do. As far as I could tell, he had no fear or anxiety about the move from a cultural or baseball perspective. It didn't seem to matter to him that he spoke virtually no English and had only ever lived an Eastern lifestyle. Those were not even conscious obstacles to him. His goal, his motivation was to play in the big leagues. Everything else was secondary.

Maybe, at twenty-six, he was too inexperienced or naive to anticipate how difficult some of those cultural adjustments would be. Regardless, we hatched a plan, and he was fully on board. I told him, "You have to learn the language. You'll have an interpreter, but I want you to go out with the players, talk with them, get to know them." It turns out he quickly got close to fellow starting pitchers Ramón Martinez, Chan Ho Park, and Ismael Valdéz, all through the speaking of English, which was the first language of none of them. Mike Piazza became a good friend too. Most of all, though, I think then–Dodgers owner Peter O'Malley's embracing of the role of a fatherly figure ensured that Hideo felt comfortable in every aspect of life, from living quarters and team travel to on-the-field matters and everything in between. It wasn't as if Hideo didn't receive significant support from others; he did, and it was invaluable. But all the support in the world would not have mattered if he were prone to giving up and returning to Japan when circumstances became difficult.

My point in touching on Hideo's story of overcoming challenge after challenge to make history is to highlight the singular importance of setting a goal, as lofty as it might be, and going after it with everything you've got, no matter the sacrifices you have to make. Hideo's sheer determination reminds me of that of Tony Barnette, my client whose inspirational story occupies the forthcoming hundreds of pages. Tony, a white

American choosing to go to Japan in the hopes of revitalizing his stagnating career and one day achieving his lifelong goal of pitching in the major leagues, is in some ways quite different from Hideo and his path. But in my decade getting to know Tony, it's clear he has that same mentality, and that's what kept him going and going whenever he suffered a setback, big or small.

Tasked with penning this foreword, I'm happy to set the scene, but I didn't exactly have to tell you about the man's unrelenting resilience. This quality in Tony will become quite apparent as you go along for the ride, through all of Tony's ups and downs, in Japan and the States. Some of his experiences will probably make you laugh, and I assume others will make you cry. But I challenge you, the reader, not to feel inspired after vicariously experiencing Tony's exhilarating transformation from minor-league pitcher to elite NPB closer to successful Texas Rangers reliever. I don't think you can.

I'm not sure if you're the same way, but whenever I meet people like this, I instantly develop a respect for them. While it is an objectively admirable quality, I think how I feel about Tony, Hideo, and others I've encountered like them just as much comes from how that one, integral quality reminds me of myself, what I went through, and how I came out on the other side despite immense and onerous challenges.

Growing up in Japan, a one-race nation, I always felt like an outsider. My father was a white, Jewish American, so at the very least I looked different than my peers. He told me from very early on—I was probably not much younger than six or seven—that as a minority, being half-Japanese and half-American, I had to work much harder than my peers. "Don't forget that," he'd say. "The only way you're gonna be accepted is you gotta work two, three times harder than the guy next door."

Even though I was always athletic and dabbled in various sports, before age twelve, there was no way I would've ever become a baseball player or eventually gotten into the baseball player representation business. That was when the man who would eventually become my stepfather, baseball legend Katsuya Nomura, came into the picture and changed the direction of my life. From that point on, it was all baseball, all the time. We're talking twenty-four hours a day, seven days a week, 365 days a year.

As I got older, I continued to attend a K–12 American school in Japan, but through his connections, my stepdad was able to secure me a spot with one of the top high school baseball programs. There, I would train for the next four summers as well as another month each of those winters. I couldn't play on their team because I wasn't a student, but the experience changed everything for me. At my regular school, baseball was much more laid-back. Conversely, at Kindai High School in Osaka, the whole system was like nothing I'd ever experienced.

Kindai was like a military camp. We practiced from 9 a.m. to 10 at night. Every player had to shave his head. You were never allowed to talk back to the coaches. "Yes, sir" or "No, sir" was how we were expected to speak to them. So whatever they said, there was no questioning. You just had to do it. That's how strict it was.

I remember the boys and I exhausted after taking hundreds of ground balls, not having a drop of water that we could drink. So we'd sneak into the bushes and drink the water from the river and the rice paddies. It was so incredibly tough, but those who made it through were bonded together. Although I was an outsider, these guys embraced me as one of their own. Fifty years later, I still go out with some of them today.

I completed the program with the knowledge that "If I could make it through this, I could make it through anything." When I started, there were about 170 guys of my age. Three and a half years later, sixteen of us had survived without quitting. The experience was eye-opening and often difficult to endure, but I didn't want to quit and have to go back home because, to me, that would have shown weakness. I wanted to make sure that I hung in there and followed what the other guys were doing. I probably didn't know it then, but the grueling training was profoundly shaping the strong-willed, resilient adult I would become.

Six years later, when I was released by the Swallows' minor-league affiliate and came to the United States, I was shocked to find that being a former professional baseball player meant nothing as I pursued work. People wouldn't hire me because I didn't have the requisite education. After a little while, I sent my wife and young daughter back to Japan, while I worked three jobs and basically made myself homeless in order to save money. I lived in my car for almost a year.

In my mind, there was only one way to get out of the rut. That was to work hard. I figured with twenty-four hours in a day, if I could sleep maybe four, five hours, I could probably put in a good eighteen hours of work and make something like $3.50 an hour. This was my routine: I started my primary job at 9, worked there till 5, and then went to my boss' home, where I helped her first-grade son with his homework for a couple hours. That second job paid no money but provided me a free daily dinner and a place to shower each night. Then, I was off to sleep in my car for five hours (on a good day) before beginning my third job at 3 a.m. at a motel in downtown LA. Every Saturday night, a friend allowed me to use his shower, crash on his couch, and spend my whole Sunday there. Then it was back to the weekly grind. I was on a mission.

These details may sound bleak, and you may be wondering how I kept going this way for so many months. I truly believe I was able and willing to do all of it because of my aforementioned foundational experience with Japanese-style baseball. To this day, I still thank my manager from back then, Yoshio Toyoda. He and the program instilled in me that if there is a goal important enough to achieve (like, earning enough money to bring my wife and daughter back to LA and make a real life for ourselves), then I am going to do everything in my power to do just that, no matter the sacrifices. So I have to live in my car? So what! Three jobs? No problem.

I don't want to overly simplify or glorify Tony's decision to come to Japan in the first place. When we had our first discussion, he made it clear he had very little interest in going overseas. Pitching in the major leagues was his primary focus, and at that point, he was on the cusp of achieving that, knocking on the door at Triple A. Then, a couple hours later, I got a call from his father, Phil, who asked if the roughly $500,000 I cited was realistic. He seemed skeptical. Granted, half a million dollars was (and is) a lot for a twenty-six-year-old who had never signed a big-league deal. Indeed, it was the going rate for gaijin starting pitchers at the time. From my perspective, once Phil spoke to Tony again about the opportunity, Tony's eyes were truly open to what it could do for him.

If the significant increase in salary made Tony much more willing to leave for Japan, you'll notice that it was the people and their support, the rich culture, the delicious food, and the overall infrastructure behind him that made Tony want to stay for years.

Like Nomo in Los Angeles, he wasn't going it alone in Tokyo. Critically, his interpreter, Go Fujisawa, quickly became a good friend on top of an invaluable language and cultural resource. Tony's partner, Hillary, provided a wealth of love and support throughout the decision-making process and the many years they were in Japan (as well as before she joined him). Teammate Aaron Guiel served as an incredible mentor and friend. Then there was the expat community, including friends like Canadian sportswriter Rob Smaal and the English-language bloggers at TokyoSwallows.com. From a baseball perspective, coach Tomohito Ito had the biggest impact on Tony's success over there, while managers Junji Ogawa and Mitsuru Manaka gave him a chance to shine in their own unique ways. The Swallows fans completely embraced Tony, especially by Year 2 and on, and he felt the same way about them. Of course, his family back home was in his corner throughout the six-year experience, and that meant the world to him.

Again, all these wonderful, amazing circumstances can be in place, but a gaijin will ultimately fail if he doesn't come in humble, open-minded, and willing to work his butt off. I've seen it before, from both sides. I've had clients who would constantly complain about various restrictions or obligations, like "Why do I have to practice on an off day?" or "Why do I have to wear a suit to that event?" That kind of thing. Sadly, guys like that will never succeed in Japan or anyplace else.

Tony was not that guy. Quite the opposite. Like anyone, he had his complaints that he'd express to me privately. This happened at various stages, like when he was repeatedly demoted for his poor play during Year 1 and when he suffered serious injuries later in his Japanese career, just as he seemingly was on the cusp of returning to the majors. But the important thing about these complaints was that he always took responsibility. For example, when he had to wake up very early to commute to the minor-league facilities in Toda, he'd always couch his valid complaints with "This is what I have to do. This is what I get paid for." He never portrayed himself as a victim. Instead, he perpetually displayed gratitude for the opportunity. I just knew he would do everything in his power to live up to the high expectations he and others had for him.

If you ask me, Tony had this competitive, unrelenting spirit in him all along. It was how he was raised. It was what he was taught. So I don't credit his Japanese experience for creating it in him. I do think, though, that the circumstances, including all the trials and tribulations he faced, highlighted what he was made of and brought those attributes to the surface for all to see.

Realistically, Tony was never one of the most talented players in baseball. He didn't throw 100 miles an hour. He's not six-foot-five. He isn't built like a rock. But what made him a big leaguer and a successful pitcher was his determination and a strong-willed mind. In that respect, he reminds me of another client, Masato Yoshii. He never threw hard either and was a sponge, absorbing information whenever and wherever he could. Like Tony, Yoshii's hard work, his curiosity, and his creativity, supplemented by his talent, combined to create a long career. Now a manager with the Marines in Japan, these qualities will probably make him successful in his latest baseball challenge too.

As one proud agent, I invite you to appreciate Tony's journey as documented in copious, vivid detail throughout the rest of these pages. While Tony's baseball achievements are not unprecedented, the unconventional route he took to get to the major leagues, spending six years in Japan and debuting with the Rangers at thirty-two, provides real hope for minor-league pitchers thinking of taking their games to Japan with a burning desire to one day pitch in the big leagues. But even if you're not a pro athlete or aspiring to be, and most of us aren't, there are real gems to be discovered from immersing yourself in Tony's tale.

Enjoy!

PROLOGUE
(TOM CRUISE + KEANU REEVES) / 2

The guy was just on me at all times.

The eleven-hour flight from Los Angeles has arrived at its destination, Tony Barnette's new home. As the six-foot-one white man with long black hair steps off the plane and into Tokyo's Narita International Airport, the cameras begin flashing. The Japanese media are waiting specifically for him and a couple fellow American pitching imports.[1] It's an awfully novel feeling for a man who was largely anonymous the previous season in Triple A with the Arizona Diamondbacks' Reno Aces.

Born in Alaska before spending the bulk of his childhood in a suburb of Seattle, Washington, the twenty-six-year-old is certainly no seasoned international traveler. It's his first trip outside North America, let alone to Asia.

There's no translator yet, but greetings and questions fly at him in Japanese and broken English. He smiles, taking in as much of the scene as he can. Trying to avoid doing anything stupid, he's frozen in the moment.

He goes through customs, where the official stamps his passport and collects his embarkation card. After retrieving his three stand-up suitcases—he'll be living out of those for the foreseeable future—and loading them onto a cart, he continues through a set of doors. A slim man with short, black hair and long sideburns named Go Fujisawa is holding a sign that says "Mr. Barnette." Also twenty-six, Go will become Tony's lifeline in the days, weeks, and months ahead. Educated at Indiana State University, he's a Japanese-English interpreter employed by the Tokyo Yakult Swallows to work with the team's English-speaking pitchers. After a brief second stop to speak with media members, they're off to the hotel in Tokyo.

Meanwhile, in Arizona, where it's still morning, sixteen hours behind Japan time, Tony's girlfriend, Hillary Jones, has just gotten to work at her marketing job. She runs her first Google search in Japanese and sees a number of airport arrival photos. Initially, she thinks the media throng must be mistaking him for someone else. They are not.

When she returns home, she is thoroughly amused by the *Sponichi Annex*'s treatment of her boyfriend in its morning newspaper. Two pictures accompany an article: A large photo of Tony wearing a standard white *hachimaki*[2] while holding a rice ball in one hand and a baseball in the other, as well as a smaller photo of him walking into the airport terminal. On the right side of the story, a math equation appears, declaring Tony a cross between actors Tom Cruise and Keanu Reeves, followed by the word *ikemen*, which is a newish term that translates to "good-looking guy" or "metrosexual." Clearly, the Japanese media have a unique way of welcoming foreign players.

Five thousand, eight hundred miles away—but for all intents and purposes, a world away—he begins to get to know his translator. Within days, thanks to Go's apparent omnipresence, Tony likens him to a shadow. As he would later explain, "The guy was just on me at all times, making sure that I knew everywhere I needed to be, when I needed to be there, and what I needed for that situation." During the car ride to the hotel, Go starts to describe what Tony will need to know over the coming days and beyond.

Following a brief stop to unload luggage, the duo brave the Tokyo evening rush hour, allowing for Tony's first exposure to the city's internationally renowned transportation system. The train is so packed that neither man can move more than a few inches in any direction. They're on their way to meet new teammate Jamie D'Antona, who happened to play in the Diamondbacks organization while Tony did. Although the two never shared a clubhouse, they have previously met and are familiar with each other.

The Swallows' lead interpreter and Go's immediate superior, Koji Kondo, has arranged reservations for the party of three at a nice *yakiniku* restaurant. Tony's first experience with *yakiniku*, which translates to "grilled meat" and bears strong resemblance to Korean barbecue, is love at first sight. The conversation is a success too, flowing freely among new friends. D'Antona had played for Yakult the previous season, so he's able to enlighten Tony on the team, Nippon Professional Baseball (NPB), and the Japanese experience more broadly. After dinner, Go leaves the Americans, who take comfort in each other's camaraderie as they stroll the streets.

After a marathon of a day, sleep is calling Tony's name. When he wakes up the next morning, it will be January 27, 2010, with spring training scheduled to start in five days.

From Tokyo, the team will fly to Okinawa, the fifth-largest Japanese island, located approximately 400 miles south of mainland Japan. Without snow and boasting warmer winter temperatures than the other prefectures, Okinawa is an ideal training spot.[3] There, Tony will debut as the Swallows' newest foreigner. By rule, each NPB team is permitted to field a maximum of only four foreigners (known in Japan as *gaijin*)— including no more than three position players or three pitchers—on its active top-team roster at any time. To open camp, he will be the only newbie among the foreigners, joining Korean closer Chang-Yong Lim, Canadian outfielder Aaron Guiel (who played five seasons with the Royals and Yankees), and the aforementioned American first baseman D'Antona.

He has to remind himself: The whirlwind of the past twenty-four hours did indeed occur, as surreal as it seemed. Just a few months earlier, at his family's Thanksgiving dinner in Washington, Tony would never have guessed that he'd be playing baseball in Asia the following season. Then, his big-league dreams felt so close to being achieved. Those hopes would have to be placed on the back burner, hidden away for now. Rather, it was time to tackle the challenge of the present: surviving and thriving in a strange, foreign land.

In his bed in Tokyo, Tony closes his eyes and instantly falls asleep.

Notes

[1] Both men arriving with Tony will be pitching for the Chiba Lotte Marines. Like Tony, it's Bill Murphy's first time in Japan, though Bryan Corey pitched for the Yomiuri Giants in 2004.
[2] A traditional Japanese headband.
[3] Before any given season, at least nine of the twelve NPB teams hold part or all of their camp in Okinawa.

CHAPTER ONE
WHY JAPAN?

"Once he made the decision, he was all in on it."

Tony did not seek out this Japanese experience. It found him.

It all started with a simple text message, a mere seven and a half weeks before his airport arrival. It was one of his Triple-A teammates, Bobby Korecky, asking if he could pass along Tony's contact information to a Japanese agent with whom he'd been working. Tony quickly assented without giving it much thought. "I figured we'll hear what he has to say."

He was coming off a mixed 2009 campaign, in which he led the Pacific Coast League in wins and starts, but also posted a 5.79 ERA with 62 walks. The underwhelming earned-run average could partially be explained by the PCL's higher-altitude stadiums, which long made it a high-scoring league.[1] Still, his performance lagged behind that of many of his peers. He wasn't excelling, at least yet. Regardless, he expected the Diamondbacks or some other organization to value his ascent up the minor-league ranks, where Tony had gone from a tenth-round draft pick to a formidable Triple-A starter in just three and a half seasons.

Just as he received Korecky's text, the Rule 5 draft was fast approaching. Held on the last day of baseball's annual winter meetings, which take place in early December, the Rule 5 draft was created to prevent organizations from stockpiling major-league talent in their minors. If a player is not on his organization's 40-man roster and has played in the minors for a certain length of time,[2] he becomes eligible to be selected by any team. The drafting team, however, must keep the player on its 25-man major-league roster for the entirety of the season. Otherwise, he's offered back to the original team. With Tony's fourth minor-league season in the books, he'd become Rule 5 eligible, allowing him to assess how highly the Diamondbacks and/or other teams valued his current ability and future potential.

The first contact from agent Don Nomura felt slightly strange because many of the details could not yet be divulged. "They told me they were interested, and we just kind of talked about it for a little," said Tony, who then called to update his American agent, Dean Steinbeck. Quickly, they realized that the two agents' offices were a block apart in the Los Angeles area. Their proximity allowed for a productive in-person meeting, while Tony stayed with his girlfriend in Arizona.

Hillary had started dating Tony a year earlier while he was playing in the Arizona Fall League. The daughter of Ken Jones, who pitched professionally for six seasons but never quite made it to the big leagues,[3] Hillary knew how crazy and unstable professional baseball life could be. Although she was born two years after Ken quit baseball and returned to school, she grew up hearing plenty of stories.

The Rule 5 draft came and went without Arizona protecting Tony.[4] No other organization selected him either. Although Tony had been climbing the minor-league ladder, he had just turned twenty-six and apparently, in the eyes of Arizona and others, still wasn't ready to be a regular major-league starter.

"I had asked the Diamondbacks what they saw of me," he said, "and they basically told me I'm not in their immediate plans and, if anything, they see me as a fill guy, just come in and fill a spot here or there." Essentially, the "fill guy" is a player promoted to the majors in the event of an injury who is afforded little playing time or margin for error. Specifically, the Diamondbacks envisioned, at best, Tony as a spot starter or bullpen piece for a limited time. It's not uncommon for a spot starter who's only been promoted due to a big-league injury to be demoted right after his start, even if he pitches well. That highly coveted spot on the 25-man roster can then be given to an extra pinch-hitter or bullpen arm until the vacant rotation spot comes up again.

The Diamondbacks made it clear that while they would be happy to see Tony return—most likely as a nonroster invitee to spring camp before beginning the season in Triple A—they also would not try to stop him from going to Japan.

So it was up to Tony. A rushed but intensive decision-making process began in which he would solicit the advice of "baseball minds who knew a little bit more than I did about the situation." Over a week and a half, he spoke with as many people as he could.

Reaching out to Mel Stottlemyre Jr. was a given. The man had played an integral role in his development as a pitcher. First, he was his rookie-ball pitching coach in the summer of 2006, Tony's first year as a professional. For the next few seasons, he served as the organization's pitching coordinator, allowing him to oversee the progress of all of Arizona's pitchers. By the time Tony got to Triple A, Stottlemyre had been named pitching coach for the big-league squad.

Both were from Washington state and genuinely liked each other. Plus, Mel hailed from a successful pitching family and knew the ins and outs of the business. His father, Mel Sr., won 164 games over a storied eleven-year career with the Yankees—Mel Jr. and his brothers grew up at Yankee Stadium, cavorting with all-time greats—before serving as a pitching coach for 23 more seasons. Mel's younger brother, Todd, pitched in the majors for fourteen years and won two World Series rings. Although

injuries limited Mel Jr. to a lone major-league season, he had been studying the art of pitching his entire adult life.

Potential new teammate Aaron Guiel would be another valuable
resource. By this point, the outfielder could reasonably consider himself
an NPB veteran, having logged three seasons with the Swallows. The two
shared an agent in Nomura, who set up the conversation, recommending
that Tony hear from a fellow North American about life in the league and
Japan. In turn, Guiel could get acquainted with a prospective teammate.

"I didn't know Tony, but for my agent, I was more than happy to do
it," recounted Guiel. "Plus, getting to know a guy before he comes over
is pretty key. So to sit and talk with Tony, and just kind of give him some
advice and see where his heart and mind was at was important for me."

He relayed the details of his own circumstances and resulting decision three years prior. With injuries to big-name stars Gary Sheffield and
Hideki Matsui, the Yankees acquired Guiel from the Royals in July 2006.
In New York, he saw regular action and performed serviceably, but he was
turning thirty-four that October, and demand for him as a major-league
mainstay was nonexistent.

He spoke of a five-year major-league career that was the epitome of
unstable. Over those seasons, he averaged just over 61games at the highest level, shuttling back and forth between Triple A and the big leagues.
Following Guiel's first call-up in 2002, he played 277 more games in
Triple A for both the Omaha Royals and Columbus Clippers. With a
wife and two young kids, Aaron Guiel craved much more structure for
his family.

According to Guiel, that offseason, he could have signed a major-
league contract with the Phillies or Rockies as a fourth outfielder, but he
was not confident that either option would land him in the majors for
good. "That's a tough job to keep," he said, "and people recycle that job
all the time."

But even if he'd been guaranteed that he would stay in the majors all
season, he was concerned his playing time would have been erratic: "If

you play well, you stay in the lineup. If you don't, you're on the bench. It's really difficult to have a good, solid year that way." So, he opted for Japan. "I was tired of being an extra guy. I went over to Japan for a lot of different reasons. Mostly, it was stability."

Money, which often intersects with stability, was another critical factor. "Japan was [offering] twice the money," said Guiel. "It was time for me to just go. I had played in the major leagues for parts of five years. We had reached that goal, so in my heart I was at peace with it. And I wanted to set myself and my family up. I was able to walk away, go to Japan, and not look back."

Of course, Tony hadn't reached the major leagues, adding another difficult dimension to the whole calculus. After he wasn't selected in the Rule 5 draft, the Swallows sizably increased their offer to $500,000—roughly twenty-six times the $2,100 per month, before taxes, he was making in Reno. To further entice the American right-hander, Yakult also offered performance incentives and a vesting option, an optional second year that would become guaranteed if he were to reach certain statistical benchmarks.

He was tempted to go, but he needed to make sure he was making the best choice. He huddled with family over the holidays.

"I'm saying, 'By signing this contract, what am I giving up, if anything?'" said Tony of his thought process. "'Am I trading in my dreams for a paycheck? Am I potentially pursuing my dreams of being a professional baseball player even further? Am I using this just as a springboard to get back to the States?' All these questions are flying around my mind that just really couldn't be answered."

"Tuffy" Rhodes is widely celebrated as one of the most impactful gaijin in NPB history. Drafted in the third round, seventeen-year-old Karl Derrick Rhodes was seemingly on the fast track to stardom, already debuting for the Astros at twenty. On Opening Day 1994, the lefty homered thrice off Dwight Gooden. Despite his tantalizing potential, Rhodes never stuck on any of the three big-league teams for which he played over six seasons. After 1995, he moved on to Japan, where he ultimately achieved icon status, slugging 464 home runs, learning Japanese, and playing past his forty-first birthday. Rhodes never did return to the majors. After he elevated his game to new heights in 1999, at least one organization reached out. But by then, he was on the wrong side of thirty, and no MLB situation could even remotely match the pay or reverence his new home afforded.

Hawaiian two-sport athlete Wally Yonamine[5] was the first American to play professional baseball in Japan after World War II, ultimately spending many years there, playing and later managing. Within a year, Negro League veterans were the next Americans to appear in NPB. A decade later and a few seasons removed from their MLB days, former stars Don Newcombe and Larry Doby became the first former big leaguers to appear, playing 1962 together with the Chunichi Dragons before returning home to retirement.[6]

Throughout history, many fringe major leaguers have spent the remainder of their careers in Japan, with varying degrees of success. In the mid-1970s, Charlie Manuel left for Japan, where he spent the last six seasons of his playing career[7] following a forgettable MLB stint. He excelled, leading the Swallows to their first championship in 1978 and appearing in the next two Japan Series with the Kintetsu Buffaloes.

A number of more notable former big leaguers ventured to Japan in the twilight of their careers, hoping to squeeze out a little more money when their services were no longer desired in North America. Approaching thirty-six, former MLB superstar Andruw Jones made the journey, registering two mediocre seasons with the Rakuten Golden Eagles. One of Jones's 2014 teammates was two-time World Series champion Kevin Youkilis, who at thirty-five would log just 21 NPB games before retiring from baseball altogether.

The previous year, Jones won an NPB title with former MLB third baseman Casey McGehee. Only thirty years old, he performed well enough to land a big-league contract with the Marlins.[8] Pitchers Colby Lewis and Ryan Vogelsong similarly took great advantage of their NPB experience to boomerang back to the majors, as did Scott Atchison and left-handed specialist Pedro Feliciano.

Cecil Fielder used his lone season with the Hanshin Tigers, 1989, to transform his major-league career. The husky twenty-five-year-old had played four seasons with Toronto, but he wanted to play every day. When Hanshin gave him that chance in 1989, he capitalized on it.[9] Upon returning to the States, Fielder signed with the other Tigers and proceeded to launch 95 home runs over the next two seasons, finishing second in AL MVP voting each time.[10]

Alfonso Soriano was another multi-time All-Star who spent an early part of his career in Japan, although his NPB tenure unfolded quite differently. As a teenager, he participated in the Hiroshima Toyo Carp baseball academy in the Dominican Republic.[11] By 1996, the young Dominican was playing for their farm team in Japan. Due to the organization's failure to recognize his potential and a contract dispute, Soriano played just nine games with Hiroshima before going on to star with the Yankees, among other teams. Ultimately, he enjoyed a long, successful big-league career that included over 2,000 hits and 400 home runs.

Gaijin like Fielder and Soriano, players who returned from Japan to go on to achieve massive success, were extremely rare. Merely returning to the majors was not easy. Between 2000 and 2009, 298 qualifying gaijin appeared in NPB games.[12] Approximately one-quarter of them appeared in the major leagues at any point after their NPB stint. Specifically, the return rate for the 167 gaijin pitchers was only slightly better, at nearly 26 percent.

Getting back to the big leagues was one thing. Sticking was quite another. Regardless of whether a returning pitcher had stumbled in Japan or performed decently or even well, the odds of him lasting in the big

7

leagues for long were not great. Over one-quarter of the returnees failed to log more than ten post-NPB MLB appearances, and more than half made fewer than 36 such outings.

For all the pitchers whose MLB returns were brief and flawed, more than a handful of hurlers found a way to record productive big-league seasons after their disastrous NPB stints. The list includes Justin Miller, Bryan Corey, Chris Resop, Héctor Carrasco, D. J. Carrasco (no relation), and Kameron Loe. Each of the latter two struggled as Fukuoka SoftBank Hawks starters but returned to the majors as reliable relievers for multiple seasons thereafter.

Notably, only forty-four of those 298 NPB foreigners came in without any MLB experience. From that group, just eight would ever reach the majors after their time in Japan. That's a tad over 18 percent, an even worse return rate than a generic gaijin over the same period. Out of the only four pitcher returnees without previous big-league time, three of them barely made their mark, logging fewer than 20 MLB games apiece. The outlier, Venezuelan reliever Rafael Betancourt, debuted at twenty-eight[13] and went on to pitch twelve years for Cleveland and Colorado.

Of course, Tony would be one of those guys to have never played in the majors before arriving. If the twenty-six-year-old left, he'd be a few years younger than the 29.5 gaijin average over the preceding ten-year period. He saw his relative youth as a plus, but he also understood the daunting picture the broader numbers were painting.

Two weighty questions arose: First, how did he like his odds? Second, and potentially more important, even if he didn't feel good about those odds, was he or could he be at peace with the prospect of never achieving his unshakable goal of becoming a major-league baseball player?

During these trying days, Hillary primarily just listened. Intuitively, she sensed the toll the decision was taking: "He felt like maybe he was trading the chase for the big-league dreams to go to Japan, so that was I think the main struggle he dealt with." She vowed that they would remain committed to each other no matter what he decided.

Phil, a longtime salesman for a large stationery company, was in New Orleans for a conference when his son first mentioned the opportunity in Japan. The man who never let young Tony grow out his hair was always passionately supportive of his endeavors and goals, long hair notwithstanding. As a former military brat who moved constantly, whenever his dad was re-stationed, he knew that one's city or residence could be temporary. But to him, family was permanent.

They spoke frequently as Tony wrestled with his decision. "At the end of the day, this is your call," he told him. "I'm not gonna tell you, 'Stay here.' I'm not gonna tell you, 'Go there.' Because I don't want you looking back five years from now blaming me because I told you to do one thing or the other." Tony characterized their discussions similarly, noting, "Whenever my dad has given me advice over the years, I think he's done a very good job of never forcing his personal opinion or belief onto me." Instead, Phil would pose questions to try to highlight the pros and cons so that Tony could critically weigh his options and make his own best decision.

Phil Barnette loved sports, particularly baseball. Therefore, so did his three sons.

As the youngest of the brothers, Tony's competitiveness and desire for inclusion spurred him to raise his level of play. If he wasn't good enough to play with his brothers and their friends, he wouldn't be allowed to tag along. It was that simple. This applied to baseball, basketball, and any other game played in the neighborhood.

Cory was four years older than Tony; Randy was two. When Tony was nine, he and Randy teamed up for Federal Way Little League's Major White Sox. Naturally, Phil coached the squad.

As Phil got promoted from district sales manager to regional marketing manager to eventual national director of training, he spent increasingly more time away from home. When he was coaching his sons, he handled the travel by leaning on quality assistants. As they got older, Phil transitioned into a different type of supportive role, entrusting their coaching to others.

In fifth grade, Tony's teacher asked him what he wanted to do when he grew up. "I want to be a professional athlete," he told her. An enormous Seattle SuperSonics fan, he had his eyes on the NBA. "I remember her telling me, 'The odds are very slim. You need to have a backup plan.' And I remember very vividly just thinking, 'This lady's crazy. I'm going to the top, baby!'" He was indeed dominating the courts and fields at Rainier View Elementary, but what a bold prediction for a ten-year-old.

Of course, the supremely confident kid's prediction would ultimately prove correct, but not in basketball, his first love. Understanding his superiority in baseball and overall lack of size, he quit playing basketball after ninth grade and turned his athletic focus to baseball year-round. That same year, he dropped wrestling as well.

The singular focus allowed for accelerated growth. In tenth grade, he made varsity, where he garnered very little playing time. But Tony was permitted to "double-dip," as they called it, alternating between watching his varsity teammates from the dugout and starring for the junior varsity team. Around age fifteen, he began to show incredible improvement while playing for Triple Play Baseball, a club team that attracted some of the area's best talent.

However, at the time of his high school graduation, he stood five-foot-ten and weighed 160 pounds. He went undrafted and drew virtually no interest from four-year colleges. He expected as much given his lack of size and considerable room for improvement. In Tony's mind, major-league baseball teams and universities didn't understand what he could do on the mound. Like his fifth-grade teacher, they were simultaneously doubting and fueling him.

Determined as ever to make a living playing baseball, he enrolled in Central Arizona College. Known for its strong baseball program,[14] the community college is located in Coolidge, roughly halfway between Phoenix and Tucson, the state's biggest cities. After two strong seasons in Coolidge, Tony felt surprised and insulted when there were still no major-league takers, especially after seeing junior college teammates who had been relegated to the bench get chosen over him.[15] Despite the setback, he jumped at the opportunity to transfer to perennial baseball powerhouse Arizona State. "Okay, well, ball's still rolling," he thought. "If Arizona State still wants me, then things are still good because it's Arizona State."

After suffering through a dreadful junior season for the Sun Devils, he, in his words, "came out of my shell and started doing really well" the next year, boasting a 6–1 record along with a team-leading 70 strikeouts in just under 55 innings. Scouts gradually began to take notice, but usually they came to see a bigger-name prospect. In fact, Tony credits one such outing for changing everything.

On a Friday night in May, scouts descended upon Tempe to watch a promising Oregon State pitcher named Dallas Buck. Although he was projected to be a first-round draft pick, major-league teams were concerned about his elbow. While Buck pitched decently, scouts in attendance were treated to a seven-inning, ten-strikeout masterpiece by Arizona State's starter, one Tony Barnette. The Sun Devils won 10–3, and Tony had stifled an offense spearheaded by future pros Cole Gillespie—a third-round pick that year—and Darwin Barney. A month and a half later, the Beavers would go on to win their first of back-to-back national championships.

That June, the home state Diamondbacks selected Tony in the tenth round, legitimizing his fifth-grade prediction.[16] "I'm pretty much 100-percent positive that that game alone got me drafted," he said.

Hearing his name called marked a huge moment, but as tens of thousands of draftees throughout history can attest, the work was just beginning, and he had an uphill climb. After their rookie-ball season together, Mel Stottlemyre Jr. didn't sugarcoat things. "He told me straight up when we were in spring training: 'You don't have time to screw around. You're already, what, twenty-three, trying to get a Single-A job, where most twenty-three-year-olds, we're trying to push them up the organization, up to Double A, Triple A by now.' So he made it very clear that being at my age, at the level I was at, I needed to put a fire under my ass and get going, so to speak."

Tony did work his butt off and moved up the minor-league ladder—from Missoula to South Bend to Mobile to Reno. Still, age factored heavily in Arizona's contentment to let him leave.

As mid-December approached, Tony was running out of time. A final decision needed to be made as the Swallows filled out their roster. They were more than happy to pay the $200,000 the Diamondbacks were requesting in exchange for relinquishing their rights. They just needed to know if he was in.

Hillary remembers the moment she learned that Tony would indeed be taking advantage of the offer. After returning home from a final exam, she saw him "sitting on the floor of our apartment with his hands over his head. I could just see the decision wearing on him. I think he had made the decision that day to go to Japan. And I don't think he ever made that decision easily, but once he made the decision, he was all in on it."

He notified his American agent, who worked out a representation framework. It was determined that if he ever returned to the United States, he would work exclusively with Dean Steinbeck. And as long as he stayed in Japan or went elsewhere in Asia, he'd work only with Don Nomura. Nomura's assistant flew to Phoenix, where Tony signed the contract.

"I do remember the look on his face when he said he was going to Japan," said Hillary. "It was just like, 'Oh, my God. Here we go.'"

Notes

1   Between 2005 and 2009, Pacific Coast League teams scored an average of 5.1 runs per contest, while teams from the International League averaged 4.4 runs per game. During the same period, National and American League teams averaged 4.6 and 4.9 runs, respectively.

2   Four years if the player is signed at nineteen or older; five years if signed before age nineteen.

3   Double A was the highest level Ken Jones reached.

4   In other words, Arizona did not place him on its 40-man roster.

5   Yonamine played running back for the San Francisco 49ers in 1947. After the season, he broke his wrist playing amateur baseball and decided to leave football behind.

6   Interestingly enough, Newcombe, a longtime pitcher, only pitched once for Chunichi, nearly exclusively playing outfield and first base. At the plate in Japan, Newcombe actually performed markedly better than Doby.

7   At thirty-six, for the Kintetsu Buffaloes, Manuel batted .325 with 48 home runs and 129 RBIs. Twenty-four years later, the Buffaloes merged with the Orix BlueWave to become the Orix Buffaloes, which they remain to this day. In the United States, Manuel is best known for skippering the Phillies to consecutive World Series in 2008 and 2009; they won the first.

8   At thirty-four, after three years split between the Marlins, Giants, Tigers, and the Giants' and Tigers' Triple-A affiliates, McGehee returned to NPB, where he'd finish his career playing for the Yomiuri Giants.

9   Before 1989, Cecil Fielder bet former teammate Fred McGriff (now a Hall of Famer) that he'd hit more home runs than him. Fielder would win the bet despite playing in 56 fewer games.

10   All but thirty-one of Fielder's 319 career major-league home runs came after his only season in Japan.

11   The Carp established their Dominican baseball academy in 1990. Other notable members included former Mets outfielder Timo Pérez and Alejandro Quezada, who was the first player acquired by a major-league team via the posting system. Quezada, now known as Alejandro Díaz, never surpassed the Double-A level.

12   Gaijin who played in Japan before ever appearing in an MLB organization's minor-league system were excluded from the dataset.

13   Partially explaining Betancourt's late blooming, Boston originally signed him as an infielder and exclusively played him there for his first three minor-league seasons before putting the right-hander in its Low-A bullpen.

14   Central Arizona College has produced more than a dozen major-league players, including Ian Kinsler, Doug Jones, Dan Wheeler, Tom Pagnozzi, Rich Harden, and Scott Hairston.

15   "Even to this day, I take offense to it, to be honest with you," said Tony more than a decade and a half later. "I knew I was good enough to go to the next level. I just didn't understand why nobody else was seeing it."

16   Interestingly enough, Dallas Buck was Arizona's third-round pick in the same draft. Despite the early buzz surrounding his potential, arm injuries continued to plague Buck, who never surpassed Double-A ball and did not appear in the minors after 2011.

CHAPTER TWO
WELCOME TO NPB, ROOKIE

I remember all of a sudden getting over there and feeling completely alone and realizing there's a massive body of water between you and your family, your car, your comfort zone, everything.

On a Friday night in the bustling city of Tokyo, "In Bloom" blared through the Meiji Jingu Stadium speakers as Tony trotted to the mound for his highly anticipated NPB debut. Located in the heart of downtown, the stadium attracts thousands of businessmen who come directly from work to drink beer and watch baseball with their colleagues and friends.

Although Tony was Yakult's sole new gaijin and naturally its most notable offseason acquisition, manager Shigeru Takada decided to ease him in. Rather than have him start on the road against the defending champion Yomiuri Giants—the New York Yankees of NPB, thanks to their national appeal and unparalleled success over nearly six decades—or against the talented Chunichi Dragons,[1] Takada opted for patience. This gave Tony the chance to make one *ni-gun* or minor-league start before debuting at home against the unintimidating Yokohama BayStars, who were coming off a 51–93 campaign in which they were offensively inept.

His handpicked song energized him. Nirvana, the legendary grunge band from his home state of Washington, also added a familiar, American flavor to the stadium. He hoped his baseball career would soon be in bloom, blossoming for all to see.

From the opening pitch, any first-game jitters could not have been detected by the 13,038 fans in attendance. He dealt comfortably, retiring BayStar after BayStar as if he'd pitched in the league for years as opposed to never before. By the time Tony was done, he'd pitched seven shutout innings, allowing three hits and three walks. Fellow right-handed foreigner Chang-Yong Lim earned the save, helping Yakult edge Yokohama 1–0.

The Jingu Stadium home crowd enjoys a tradition seen nowhere else in Japan or anyplace on Earth. Every time the Swallows score, their fans erupt in a summer festival song, "Tokyo Ondo," while raising and lowering their miniature umbrellas in unison. Yes, umbrellas. There are clear pink and green mini-umbrellas sold at the stadium for ¥1,000 apiece.[2] Notably, award-winning writer and Swallows fan Haruki Murakami credited attending a 1978 game for spurring him to pen his first novel.

When soccer-loving Brit David Watkins first came to Japan in 2001 to teach English and escape his unfulfilling corporate finance job, this fascinatingly bewildering exercise helped draw him in. As a diehard, lifelong Aston Villa fan, he couldn't bring himself to find a new soccer team to support; Japan had neither the cultural enthusiasm for soccer nor the high level of play. Instead, he sought a Japanese substitute that could mimic soccer's historical importance in the UK. Despite being rather bored with cricket growing up in Warwickshire, he quickly developed an incredible passion for Japanese baseball, specifically falling for the Swallows. In 2008, with friends, he created the English-language fan website TokyoSwallows.com.

"It's a really endearing thing," Watkins said of the run-celebrating ritual, "and it's one that really baffles people when they come over here. People kind of go, 'Hey, why does everyone got these little umbrellas?'

And you're like, 'Just wait. Don't worry.' And then they end up scoring, and everyone stands up and starts dancing. It's quite a sight." From the home dugout on the first-base side, Tony believed it looked like "jellyfish bobbing in the water."

The accompanying dance is fairly well known throughout Tokyo and utilizes simple choreography in case a new fan is unfamiliar. A tiny but critical section called the *ōendan* leads the way. Boasting trumpets and flags, this group of around ten to fifteen volunteers with special access is based in a cordoned-off area in the middle of the right-field bleachers but also dotted around the outfield to help lead the cheers.

The great umbrella tradition traces back to the late Swallows superfan Masayasu Okada. Nicknamed "Uncle Yakult," he became a fan in the franchise's third year and advocated for using household items to enhance one's cheering experience while saving money for the game ticket itself.[3] The dreadfully performing Swallows struggled to attract fans, so those in attendance waved around umbrellas to boost the perceived turnout. Later, as attendance improved, they switched to mini-umbrellas in a nod to corneal safety.

Thanks to Tony's stellar debut performance, he was named "Hero of the Game," an honor bestowed upon a standout player, or pair of players, for the winning team of every NPB game. Following celebratory hand-shakes with teammates, he was directed to a designated spot near home plate, along the first-base line, and handed a sign. Koji Kondo, the gaijin hitters' interpreter, joined to help him navigate the ensuing interview. Moving forward, Go Fujisawa would aid Tony with all interviews, but like Tony, he was making his debut. Accordingly, Kondo showed how it was done as Go watched from the dugout.

Team staff set up a portable backdrop. Yakult's mascot, Tsubakuro, a black swallow with a red face and yellow beak, waited nearby in a blue Swallows helmet, clearly in a jovial mood. Throughout the interview, Tony held in front of his chest an advertisement for a team sponsor. Clutching a microphone audible to the crowd, the interviewer began, as Kondo whispered bullet points, informing Tony of the gist of each question. This limited lag time in his responses. Following each answer, the veteran interpreter took the microphone and translated his words into Japanese. Then, Tony posed for pictures, still holding the sign.

Later that night, it was time to celebrate his first victory in Japan. He met Canadian sportswriter Rob Smaal and Rob's American friend at Legends Sports Bar in the Roppongi district. Smaal had met Tony during spring training and did not want to let him party alone. The three sat on the deck, enjoying pizza and beer while reminiscing about Tony's masterful performance.

Smaal and Guiel met at a batting practice in 2007. Nearly twelve years separated them, but their backgrounds happened to share a couple striking details. Both hailed from Vancouver Island in Western Canada and, in Nanaimo, had once played for the same Little League coach, Dick Simpson, whom they adored. The sentimental connections didn't stop there, as they quickly learned that Guiel's grandmother lived across the street from Smaal's parents for years, the epitome of a small world.

When Guiel arrived, Smaal had already been living in Japan for some time. After graduating from the University of British Columbia in the early 1980s, Smaal briefly taught computer science and coached basketball. He then ventured to Japan to serve as a sports editor for the *Japan Times*. He returned to Vancouver for a few years to write for a nightly sports highlight show while also filing stories for various wire services. In advance of the Nagano Winter Olympics, the *Japan Times* asked him back "to beef up the sports section." Smaal happily accepted, returning in 1995. By 2010, he was still in Japan, albeit writing and editing for the *International Herald Tribune*,[4] also known as the *Asahi Shimbun* in Japan.

He loved the country for its culture and the career opportunity it afforded him, but most important of all, it was where he met his wife.

Smaal's recreational hockey team, the Tokyo Canadians, a group largely consisting of Canadians with a few Americans and Japanese sprinkled in, held an annual fundraiser, typically at the Canadian Embassy. They'd raise money with a few hundred people in attendance. Yoko Higuchi attended one, and the rest is history. With Yoko and, later, two kids by his side, Tokyo was even more solidified as Rob's second home.

He made a habit of getting to know English-speaking players, particularly those who played for the hometown Giants or Swallows, becoming good friends with pitchers Seth Greisinger and Marc Kroon. Before long, Smaal and Guiel grew close too, as did their families. The two golfed and occasionally saw concerts together.

"It's a unique situation in Japan where there's not that many [English-speaking] people over there," said Guiel. "You form long-lasting friend-ships, and he was one of my favorite people." The feeling was mutual. "He's really genuine," said Smaal, "authentic, easy-going, no attitude. He's a really good guy."

In 2009, Guiel introduced Smaal to D'Antona, and the next year he provided the outfield assist with Tony. Smaal and Tony didn't yet know each other well. However, the spring-training encounter, followed by their night at Legends, marked the beginning of what would become a fruitful relationship. Making friends so easily, so far away from home, would prove immensely important, particularly given how challenging Tony's Japanese experience promised to become.

The day after Tony's airport arrival, in which he generated comparisons to Cruise and Keanu, the interpreters retrieved him from the hotel and took him to the stadium to meet the team. Two-plus months out from his first NPB start, it was one of the informal days when the players gradually filter in, begin workouts, pack their bags, and prepare for spring training in Okinawa.

A smattering of players introduced themselves, but it was all kind of a blur as Tony recollected years later: "I couldn't even tell you who was the first guy I met that day. I do remember after they showed me my locker, maybe like ten minutes later, they took me to meet the coach." Shigeru Takada, generally referred to as "Takada-san," consistent with the Japanese honorific title, was the manager. He was a traditional, hierarchical manager, and a man of few words.

When Guiel first arrived three years earlier, he benefited from playing for an approachable manager. Atsuya Furuta was also a veteran catcher, allowing for much more open communication than is typical of a traditional relationship between NPB coach and player. A stereotypical *senpai-kōhai* relationship, derived from the high value Japanese society places on respecting one's elders—and authority figures more generally—can effectively create a "big barrier between coaching staff and player," according to Guiel. The presence of player-manager Furuta, he argued, eroded the usual hierarchical interactions so commonplace in Japanese baseball.

"You could talk to him as easily as any other teammate, and then sometimes you forget that he's the manager," said Guiel. "He was a great source of information. I thought it was a great move because it helped players like myself get comfortable along with some of the younger players. That open dialogue was there."

Takada had once been a player himself, but his final season on the field came three decades earlier. He was to be respected as a manager should, with neither that ideal nor really anything else up for discussion.

For thirteen seasons, Takada played outfield and third base for the Yomiuri Giants, who won the Nippon championship each of his first six years there.[5] More recently, before being hired to helm the Swallows, Takada served as Hokkaido Nippon-Ham Fighters general manager. In his final two seasons, Nippon-Ham appeared in the Japan Series twice. In 2010, the sixty-four-year-old was set to begin his third year with Yakult.

The initial late-January encounter between Takada and Tony was brief but instructive as to how their relationship would unfold. According to

Tony, "He basically said, 'Welcome to Japan,' and 'I expect big things from you.' That was it. All he said to me. He then walked off. And then the next time was after my first start. He just said, 'I'm proud of you. Keep it up.'" Otherwise, they never spoke, which was merely how Takada operated. He believed players should show obedience to their manager and that if they have something to say or ask, they should go through an assistant coach. The manager and player should directly interact as little as possible, he thought.

By the end of the week, the team had flown to Okinawa, where it would begin spring training. The island, which is best known internationally for its heavy and controversial presence of the US military, hosts, as of February 2021, some 30,000 American military personnel and 31 bases.[6] Okinawa was also the birthplace of Dave Roberts,[7] the speedy former outfielder revered in Boston for helping the 2004 Red Sox reverse the so-called eighty-six-year curse. As manager, he later led the Dodgers to their first championship in over thirty years.

Although there would be months to get acclimated before the regular season commenced, Tony found himself disoriented from the beginning and very much struggled with a prevailing sense of uncertainty. In his experience, spring training had always brought unfamiliarity, but this was different: "Well now, not only do you not know who's who, but now nobody really even speaks your language.

"I really didn't have a game plan. I had a plan, and then I got punched in the mouth. The reality of everything had set in, and then I was kind of just floating there, trying to do the best I possibly could with what I had. And it really wasn't that much. I didn't really have much to go off of."

For a gaijin new to Japan, according to Guiel, no level of preparation can fully ready you for the unique experience: "There's no mountain. There's nothing you can do to completely prepare for it." When he first landed in early 2007, media members mistakenly swarmed a random businessman, thinking he was the left-handed-hitting Canadian. Guiel observed the scene, as a feeling of isolation was already hitting him. He distinctly remembers "all of a sudden getting over there and feeling completely alone and realizing there's a massive body of water between you and your family, your car, your comfort zone, everything."

The Swallows spring-training camp was run very differently than the Diamondbacks camps with which Tony had become familiar.[8] Unlike the customary routine at major-league camps, efficiency did not seem to be valued in Okinawa. Instead, perception, seniority, and submitting to authority were placed at a premium.

"I was used to the American way," said Tony. "You get in, you get your work in, you go home. You don't just sit around and waste time." He and Dominican right-hander Eulogio "Frankie" de la Cruz[9] were doing just that, working efficiently until early afternoon before leaving for the day. They soon discovered that the approach rankled their teammates.

According to Tony, "We just kind of learned that in Japan everybody hangs around. They waste time, and it doesn't really matter. You see young guys checking corners as they're leaving to see if they can sneak out without a team captain or one of the older guys seeing. It was pretty funny. I learned to pace out my days because in spring training early on it's not so much how much work and how much time; it's how much work is perceived that you've done."

"The nail that sticks out gets hammered down" is a popular Japanese proverb. As an unquestionably collectivistic society, individuality and creativity traditionally rank very low as desired qualities. Conversely, conformity is emphasized. Within organizations, such as baseball teams and white-collar businesses, it is not only expected, but also essentially required, for everyone to be on the same page.

"We stick out as it is," Tony said of gaijin. "There can only be four of us, and the expectations of the foreigners are so high, so if you're doing things that are disrupting the team or whatever in any way, it's going to stick out even more."

The Japanese even have a word for the harmony, balance, and cohesion achieved when individuals sacrifice their personal interests to further a communal goal: *wa*. It's treated as an integral element of Japanese society and inspired the name of best-selling author Robert Whiting's groundbreaking 1989 book on Japanese baseball, *You Gotta Have Wa*. Japanese players who have violated a team rule, and consequently upset team *wa*, must apologize to their owner, manager, and teammates. In youth baseball, contrite players will typically return to their team with a buzz cut in order to atone for their mistake.

With rare exception, NPB teams set a collective pregame stretch time. It precedes batting practice and applies to all hitters regardless of when they're assigned to take their BP swings. These sessions are typically divided into four or five groups, creating a scenario in which batters in the later groups, usually the starters, could have to wait as many as forty minutes before stepping to the plate. For Japanese teams, there is social value in aligning players' schedules like this. Something as innocent (and efficient) to Westerners as customization of player schedules, however, is seen as a threat by the Japanese clubs, who fear it would threaten to disrupt team synergy and run the risk of promoting selfishness.

Aaron Guiel even saw such collectivism play out at restaurants, where he remembered facing challenges when, for example, he tried to slightly modify a sandwich order. *Japan Times* baseball writer Jason Coskrey, who also came over in 2007, did not have the same struggle. As someone who "hates tomatoes," he couldn't remember a fast-food restaurant not abiding by his request to omit them.[10]

Still, the Japanese unquestionably have a highly structured society. "They don't like to deviate," said Guiel. "They don't like to accommodate." David Watkins added, "Japanese people don't really like an overabundance of choice a lot of times, I think. They like things to be simple, and they don't like to be put on the spot. They don't like to go in and be asked like a million things because it kind of throws them off-kilter a little bit."

To illustrate the point, Watkins stated that in British Subway restaurants he and others would list the vegetables they desired, whereas in Japan, customers had to note which particular items they did not want or else it would be assumed they wanted them all. "I think over in the United States, we want variety," said Guiel. "We kind of have an entitlement, like 'I'm gonna have it how I want it 'cuz I'm paying the bill.' Over there, there's an acceptance of things, and I don't think it's a factor. We would complain high and low about the whole thing, whereas the Japanese just simply don't. They accept it. There's a oneness to how everybody is."

In Okinawa, the team ran like a well-oiled machine, as it was designed to do. But that didn't mean all of its parts felt comfortable. Hillary lovingly shipped her boyfriend Tagalong Girl Scout cookies, his favorite kind. Despite the gesture, Tony found it exceedingly difficult to adapt or relax. Maybe moving into the Tokyo apartment that the team fully furnished would be the catalyst. He desperately craved a sense of normalcy. Maybe leaving Okinawa and returning to the big city would provide that.

Within baseball circles, Nippon Professional Baseball is referred to as "Quadruple A" because it's considered a step below Major League Baseball but superior to Triple A. NPB's twelve teams are evenly divided into two leagues. The Swallows play in the Central League, where pitchers hit for themselves. Meanwhile, the Pacific League uses designated hitters. Games that are deadlocked after 12 innings end in a tie[11]—blasphemy to a traditional American baseball fan, but completely normal in Japan.

All NPB clubs are owned by corporations involved in business outside of baseball and are named accordingly.[12] For example, the Yakult Corporation, which manufactures and sells a probiotic milk beverage similar to yogurt, owns the Swallows. The Giants are owned by Yomiuri

Shimbun Holdings, the country's largest media conglomerate that most notably owns two newspapers and the Nippon Television Network, and online retail giant Rakuten owns the Golden Eagles.

Since 2007, each league's top-finishing team, considered the pennant winner, has earned a bye into the final stage of the Climax Series—the Japanese equivalent of the championship series—where it awaits the winner of the best-of-three opening Climax Series between its league's second- and third-place teams.[13] In each stage, the team with the better record hosts the entire slate of games. In fact, regular-season record is so highly valued that during the Climax Series' final stage, the host team, fresh off a bye, begins with a one-game advantage.[14] The winner of each Climax Series final stage then faces off in the Japan Series to determine a champion.

To borrow another American sports analogy, the Swallows and Giants can be thought of as the NBA's Clippers and Lakers, respectively. Like the Clippers and Lakers in Los Angeles, both teams represent the same metropolitan city and have experienced very different fates over their histories. Between 1950 and 1990, Yakult managed four winning seasons. Four! Over the same period, Yomiuri won seventeen Nippon titles and finished a mere two seasons with a losing record.

By Tony's arrival, Yomiuri had won 21 championships compared to Yakult's five. Although the competitive imbalance hadn't been quite as stark in recent decades—the Swallows won four titles between 1993 and 2001—the inferiority complex remained intact for most of the franchise's fans. Jingu Stadium routinely ranked near the league cellar in attendance, whereas the Giants' mammoth Tokyo Dome perennially found itself at or near the top.[15] Despite both playing in Tokyo, their respective fan bases and level of cachet differed drastically.

This predominant underdog aspect of being a Swallows fan really appealed to Watkins back when he was looking for a team to get behind. British people, he argued, tend to root for the underdog. Asked why that is, Watkins responded, "Maybe because we're a little, insignificant country that somehow managed to just bully their way to being an empire. Maybe it's that. I don't really know, but we tend to always kind of identify with the underdog."

While the Giants have been immensely popular since the 1950s, there exists a decent-sized segment of fans—Watkins called it a "movement"—who consider themselves "Anti-Giants." They may disparagingly refer to Yomiuri as "Gomiuri," with *gomi* meaning "garbage" in Japanese. How a non-Yankees baseball fan might regard the Yanks as the "Evil Empire," these Anti-Giants fans feel similarly about Yomiuri, whose historical dominance makes them sick.

One of these fans sat beside Watkins at his first NPB game, and Yomiuri wasn't even playing. Watkins stood up to root for the home Swallows but had no idea he was in the road cheering section. A mistake like that can turn the crowd against you in a hurry, even if your team is home. "This one guy took me under his wing," he recalled, "and was hugging me and stuff and saying, 'It's okay. I'm with you. I'll support you because I hate the Giants. You're okay. I'll protect you from the mob.'"

In NPB stadiums, Jingu included, the home cheering section begins in the right-field bleachers, where most of the *ōendan* sit. The left-field bleachers, where Watkins accidentally sat, are reserved for the visitors.[16] By his estimation, most stadiums enjoyed a 4:1 home-to-visiting-fan ratio, whereas Jingu's had long been much lower.

Yakult didn't always market directly to its own supporters. "What made fans angry with the organization a lot of times," said Watkins, "is that because they end up filling, say, 50 percent of the stadium with opposition fans, they cater to those fans almost as much as they do the home fans. Instead of trying to expand the amount of home fans, they didn't really bother with the marketing, and they just were content to bring lots of opposition fans into the stadium." There was the time the organization allowed an unofficial Hanshin goods store to open down the road when the Swallows didn't even have their own team store in or around the stadium.

"Jingu's a tough place to be a home team," Tony confirmed. "Other teams travel so well." In the mid-to-late aughts, including 2010, the Tigers were the best example. Watkins remembered their fans occupying much of Jingu, even encroaching into Swallows territory: "They would just come and sit in the right-field bleachers and take up seats of the Swallows fans, which caused fights and a lot of ill feeling. So the Swallows have that feeling of 'It's them against us.' Even in our own stadium, these guys are treating it as their own, and it leads to a quite unique mindset among Swallows fans."

This very mindset likely steered many away from ever becoming Swallows fans, while at the same time reinforces the special connection loyal Swallows supporters feel toward their team and one another. They belong to a small but exclusive club, which David Watkins joined soon after moving to Tokyo. While they may have generally been regarded as nonthreatening losers, the Swallows were Watkins' lovable losers.

Tony's debut win improved Yakult to 5–2. As baseball fans know universally, hope springs eternal despite what a team's lackluster history may suggest. At the very least, it signaled a fun start for a long-suffering franchise. A week earlier, they had opened the season by taking two of three from the vaunted Giants.

The rookie's next two starts produced two more Swallows victories. On April 9, he didn't exactly bring his A game but battled through six innings to defeat the formidable Tigers. In the sixth inning, on pitch number 102, he surrendered his first NPB home run on a changeup to Craig Brazell,[17] who pushed the ball narrowly inside the left-field foul pole.

"I remember both of us arching our backs, wishing it to one side of the pole or the other," said Tony. "We had a good laugh about it the next day." He felt he made a quality pitch but that the strong American got just enough of it, taking advantage of Kōshien Stadium's unique dimensions.[18]

He quickly recovered, striking out the next batter on a slow curveball and retiring two of the next three to leave with a 4–3 lead. Yakult would win 8–3.

He had struck out just three guys and allowed 12 base runners. In retrospect, the shaky victory was likely an ominous sign of struggles to come, but Tony followed the start with a one-run, four-hit gem over seven innings. Although he received a no-decision, the Swallows came away with a 2–1 win.

In mid-April, at least on paper, he was sitting pretty with a 2–0 record and 1.80 ERA. The apartment was nice, located in the Minato ward, just ten walking minutes from Jingu Stadium, but he felt homesick and alone. Of course, those problems were much easier to ignore when Yakult was winning and he was pitching well. As soon as the team's and his personal performance began to plummet, the feelings of isolation and alienation magnified.

"Away from the field, everything just sucks because you go home and it's just you in your apartment and all you have to do is think about the struggles that you're going through on the field," said Tony. "And then the next morning, you wake up and you're thinking about the struggles and how to fix them, and you try to fix them, and then it doesn't work, so you go back home. It's just a frustrating process."

Tony likens pitching in an NPB stadium to putting on a loud concert. Only in the metaphor, he is not performing onstage; he's more of an audio engineer. "Everyone starts screaming, and it's not for you because you're the pitcher."

Although the batter and pitcher are essentially on an island performing for the audience, NPB crowds typically only make noise when their team is on offense. For example, at Jingu, all Swallows supporters rise to their feet while their team hits. The *ōendan* serve as conductors, leading the cheers. Each Swallows batter has a personalized cheer song with associated choreography, which was written and distributed by the *ōendan* prior to the season.[19] A few of the more established hitters even have customized flags fans like to wave in encouragement.

Some players' songs and choreography illuminate their strengths. The cheer for power-hitting outfielder Wladimir Balentien, who will join Yakult in 2011, includes "Paint a rainbow into the stands," an artful way of imploring him to hit a home run. Then, the fans use their arms to motion what they hope will soon be the ball's trajectory, landing somewhere beyond the left-field fence.

They fall completely silent every time their opponent starts batting, right as their pitcher's work begins. The only crowd sounds? The visiting contingent exhorting its offense. "Pitchers don't get nothing," Tony said, not complaining as much as informing. "It's your walk-out song and then a pat on the butt, and go to work."

According to David Watkins, there are pitcher cheers, but they are more the exception than the rule: "You might get like a little chant when you come on, like saying 'good luck' essentially. And if you're struggling, then they'll pitch up for about twenty seconds with kind of like a '*Ganbare, Ganbare, Baw-Net-Toh*,'[20] for example, which would be like [a] 'Do your best, do your best, fight, fight' type thing. But yeah, mostly the pitcher is alone." At least the eight teammates playing defense around the pitcher provide good company.

Over his next four starts, Tony's ERA ballooned from 1.80 to 5.61 as he gave up 22 runs in 17.1 innings. His confidence suffered. Simultaneously, his manager, Takada, was also losing faith.

In a start against the Orix Buffaloes, he was replaced with no outs in the fourth. The move confounded him: "That kind of blew my mind as to how short the leash really was at that point for me. I didn't understand how that worked here [in Japan], but that's the way they were doing it, and it was really frustrating."

In Japan, the manager notifies the umpire of the pitching change, while the pitching coach makes the trip to the mound—unlike the protocol in the States, where the manager gets the ball from the pitcher. In that particular game, Tony had already allowed three runs in the opening three innings. When he struggled with his control to begin the fourth, Takada decided it was time to send the pitching coach out there.

Faltering starting pitchers are generally removed from games earlier than in the major leagues. Given that their games are lower-scoring, NPB managers tend to place a higher value on each run. That's why you'll see much more bunting in Japan as opposed to the big leagues, where managers would rather play for a bigger inning than sacrifice an out to try to manufacture a run. "It's definitely a whole different world," said Rob Smaal. "There's baseball, and then there's Japanese baseball. They're almost two different sports."

The dud against Orix was nothing compared to his previous start against the mighty Giants. Pitching in Tokyo Dome, also the location of the Japanese Baseball Hall of Fame, before a crowd of over 44,000,[21] Tony's night nosedived before the seats could even get warm. It all started innocently enough with an infield single by Hayato Sakamoto. The ensuing sacrifice bunt and single set the stage for feared cleanup hitter Alex Ramírez to face Tony for the first time.

Hailing from Venezuela, Ramírez had spent parts of three seasons with Cleveland and Pittsburgh from 1998 to 2000. Ten years later, Ramírez was a popular NPB veteran and a bona fide star.[22] First, he played for the Swallows, for whom he hit .301 and averaged 30 home runs and 107 RBIs over seven seasons. Then, he went to the Dark Side, signing with Yomiuri, where he managed to take his game to another level, winning back-to-back Central League MVP Awards right away. In 2010, he would go on to hit 49 home runs and drive in 129 runs.

With teammates on the corners, Ramírez launched one into the seats. Tokyo Dome went crazy, as Tony tried to keep his emotions in check. From there, the inning continued to devolve. After inducing a fly out, he allowed a double and subsequent home run. He would retire the eighth batter, but not before he had given up five first-inning runs. It all happened so fast—in a matter of 18 pitches and less than 15 minutes.

The third inning wasn't pretty either. After the sixth run scored on a walk and two singles, the long-haired right-hander's night got worse when Sakamoto drilled a three-run homer. Tony got the next batter to ground out, mercifully ending his night after three innings and nine earned runs.

The relative rareness of the NPB three-run home run did not apply to these Giants, who went on to hit a league-leading 226 long balls in 2010, while the other eleven teams averaged 125. Tony had faced a star-studded lineup that was clearly much better prepared than he was. Due to the standard NPB schedule—each team played the five others in its league 24 times apiece—he would be seeing this Yomiuri lineup again soon.

Notes

1   The Dragons finished the 2009 season at 81–62–1.
2   Depending on exchange rates, ¥1,000 (1,000 yen) has roughly equaled $10. Since the start of 2021, the yen has progressively weakened. On January 1, 2024, for example, ¥1,000 equaled $7.10.
3   In addition to the umbrella, Uncle Yakult brought a frying pan to simulate the effects of a drum and has been credited for pioneering the use of megaphones at NPB games, an idea he derived from seeing them used at MLB games.
4   The *International Herald Tribune* has since been rebranded the *International New York Times* and, most recently, *The New York Times International Edition*.
5   None of those 1968–1973 teams had a gaijin on them. Tapping into the country's postwar nationalistic spirit, Yomiuri proudly touted its "pure-blooded" roster for years despite the presence of half-Taiwanese home-run king Sadaharu Oh beginning in 1959. From 1958 through 1973, Yomiuri won thirteen pennants, all without a single gaijin.

6   According to *The Nation*, "Okinawa prefecture accounts for just 0.6 percent of Japan's land mass but contains more than 70 percent of the country's US-occupied territory." Additionally, Okinawa Island hosts about half of all US military personnel in Japan.

7   Roberts's Japanese mother, Eiko, met and married his American father, Waymon, a marine stationed on an Okinawa military base.

8   Tony was a nonroster invite to the Diamondbacks' major-league camp in 2009 and also appeared as a "JIC" (Just-in-Case injury alternate) a year earlier.

9   De la Cruz did not make the opening-day roster and wound up spending the bulk of the year at the *ni-gun* level, logging just nine, mostly uneven, outings with the top-level Swallows. He then signed a minor-league deal with the Milwaukee Brewers and by mid-August 2011 was back in the majors for a fleeting moment. Tragically, de la Cruz suffered a fatal heart attack in 2021, mere days after his thirty-seventh birthday.

10   Jason Coskrey also recalled that whenever he ate out with the late, great *Japan Times* columnist Wayne Graczyk, restaurants honored his friend's idiosyncratic requests.

11   Between 1995 and 2017, a Japan Series game couldn't be declared a tie until it had gone 15 innings. But since 2018, Japan Series games (Games 1–7) also follow the 12-inning tie rule.

12   Although the Matsuda family (privately) owns about 60 percent of the Carp, Mazda is the franchise's largest single shareholder. Two-thirds of NPB teams are also named after their locations, whereas the Giants, Tigers, Dragons, and Buffaloes are not.

13   Between 2004 and 2006, the Pacific League shortened its teams' schedules to 135 games and implemented a similar-looking two-round postseason format. Meanwhile, the Central League maintained its regular-season schedule length, opting to send its pennant winner directly to the Japan Series, where it would await the winner of the PL playoff.

14   In other words, since implementation in the 2008 playoffs, each league's pennant winner must win only three final-stage games in order to advance, whereas its opponent must win four. Understandably, only five of the 30 pennant winners since have failed to advance to the Japan Series. (This excludes the 2020 pennant winners, who did not have to play in a best-of-seven final stage.)

15   In the Central League, throughout the 2010s, Yokohama Stadium kept Jingu company at the bottom of the annual attendance rankings, while the Tigers' Kōshien Stadium placed next to Tokyo Dome at the top.

16   The visiting contingent typically extends into foul territory and/or center field if its size demands more room.

17   The left-handed-batting first baseman Brazell would go on to hit 47 home runs in 2010.

18   Hanshin's historic stadium, which opened in 1924, twelve years after Fenway Park, features two foul poles just 312 feet away from home plate. Reminiscent of Fenway's Pesky's Pole in right field, the foul poles' proximity to the plate allows for the occasional unimpressive batted ball to sneak by for a homer.

19   This does not apply when pitchers step to the plate. Instead, the stadium plays the same generic song for all of the team's pitchers. For all the cheer songs, which typically change

from year to year, fans can get a sheet full of lyrics from the *ōendan* at the stadium or find the words online.

[20] "Baanetto," with a prolonged first vowel pronunciation, is the Japanese way of saying "Barnette."

[21] More than 15,000 fewer fans had attended Tony's home start against Hanshin six nights earlier.

[22] Ramírez's colorful home-run celebrations sometimes included the team mascot, something his home crowd naturally ate up.

CHAPTER THREE
FRIENDSHIP AND ISOLATION

Oh, my God. Everybody's looking at me like, "God, why doesn't this guy speak Japanese?"

Tony had never been homesick. He had attended junior college and ASU for two years apiece, living in a different apartment every year, before experiencing the nomadic life of a minor-league baseball player. In the minors, he lived in Montana (Missoula), Indiana (South Bend), Alabama (Mobile), and Nevada (Reno), all in a matter of three and a half years. But above all, his parents' divorce when he was seven years old set a critical early tone for his on-the-go life that so sorely lacked a stable home base.

When Phil and Jackie Barnette separated, they allowed their three boys to decide where to live. "Naturally, as kids," said Tony, "when you're young and confused, you don't know what the hell's going on, you decide to flip-flop a lot. You want to hang out with Mom. You want to hang out with Dad. You move with one. You move with the other. Then back and forth."

In the years following their divorce, both parents moved frequently. They always remained in Washington but at times lived far from each other. For his part, Phil moved from Juanita, where the family had been living, about 30 miles south to Federal Way, also a suburb of Seattle. Later, he moved a few more times within Federal Way.

One time, Jackie moved to southern Washington's Vancouver, close to Portland, Oregon, and 145 miles south of Federal Way. Tony moved in with his mom that summer but "instantly regretted that decision" once he started school in the fall.

"I didn't like the kids I was going to school with," he said. "There wasn't really sports. There were after-school intramurals that were clearly unorganized, and that just was not what I needed." Students were required to choose from one of two electives. "What do you mean I have to do band or choir? I hate both of them," he remembered thinking.

After a month of begging and pleading, Tony's parents let him move back to Federal Way, where he had friends and wasn't forced to take band or choir. More importantly for his future, he resumed playing baseball upon his return.

"If I never moved back," he wondered in retrospect, "then who knows if I actually would have ended up in sports?" Phil doesn't believe he would've, given the coaching and competitive infrastructure already in place for Tony in Federal Way. In Vancouver, "he would have had to start that entire process over," argued Phil.

When his dad swiftly remarried, an eight-year-old Tony could not wrap his mind around the development. The routine moving ceased by the time he entered high school, culminating a period that would profoundly shape his nomadic lifestyle.

He had grown accustomed to—even comfortable with—moving at least a couple times each year, but in Tokyo, for the first time, Tony felt uneasy in his new home. The ample geographic distance, the sixteen-hour time difference, the language barrier, the on-field struggles. All those factors combined to create this sense of "maybe I'm not where I'm supposed to be."

The guys had March 14 circled on their calendars for some time. A couple weeks before opening day, back when Tony's professional life seemed much simpler, legendary rock band AC/DC would be performing in Saitama. Tony, Aaron Guiel, and Jamie D'Antona hatched a plan: They'd play in Yakult's afternoon exhibition before venturing over to Saitama Super Arena in time to rock the night away. Tony would also be hosting his very first guest in the form of girlfriend Hillary Jones, who had time off for spring break. Ambitiously, she planned to fight jet lag and join Tony, his teammates, Rob Smaal, and Smaal's expatriate friend at the concert.

Because starters typically don't play entire exhibition games—and Tony wasn't scheduled to pitch—the trio thought they might be permitted to leave early. When they were denied, "We thought, 'Okay, that's fine. We still have lots of time,'" said Guiel.

Then, the baseball gods intervened. "The game just dragged and dragged and dragged and dragged," Guiel said. Once it ended, Hillary and the players took a taxi to the train station. In rush hour, they boarded a bullet train—a crash-course introduction to the Japanese subway system for Hillary, which she described as a "very surreal moment"—and quickly realized they'd be quite late to the venue, which was more than an hour away.

Smaal, who was already in his arena seat, called D'Antona, had him put his phone on speaker, and proceeded to add some spice to their interminable transit. They listened the rest of the ride, imagining what was happening onstage. Arriving halfway through, they still enjoyed the concert. The raucous crowd implored the band to stay on for an encore, and AC/DC obliged, performing "Highway to Hell" and "For Those About to Rock" before walking off.

Smaal was most impressed by Hillary's stamina: "We all said to Tony, 'Wow, that's a keeper, a girl that would do that.'" On the train ride back to the apartment, Hillary gave in to her international jet lag and fell asleep. She would have slept for the next two days if she weren't visiting Japan for the first time.

"I know they want to be understood," said Go Fujisawa of the gaijin he assisted. "I know they want us to understand them. Even if they look like they're doing well, they should have something they're concerned about. And to find that thing is my job."

He was born on May 2, 1983, in Tazawako, a small, quiet city[1] in the mountainous prefecture of Akita. Go's parents, a banker mom and a father who worked as a public officer in Tazawako's city hall, let him and his older brother roam free. "I was kind of wild," said Go, with a laugh, fully conscious of his buttoned-up professional persona. With his friends, he would often head to Japan's deepest lake, Lake Tazawa, where'd they play and explore. Other times, he swam at a nearby river while his dad and brother tried to catch fish.

He played baseball and was a pretty good pitcher by his account. While many of his peers dreamed of playing professionally, he aspired to play for the national team. "It was a kid's dream," said Go, so he never fleshed out exactly what he'd do for work. He just knew that members of the national team had to be amateurs and thus could not play baseball for a living. "I didn't really know about jobs. There wasn't much around me. It was a really small town." He felt he "had only three choices," to be either of his parent's professions or maybe a baseball player since he had so much fun playing.

But Go wasn't just physically active. He was a thinker too, voraciously reading a wide variety of comic books and novels as long as they were in Japanese. Young Go never read in English, although in junior high he was taught the language three hours each week. "I'd say I've never enjoyed studying English," said the Japanese-English interpreter, dead serious.

As high school neared its end, he hadn't thought about moving away for college. He had already been guaranteed a spot on the local college's baseball team, and Akita was all he'd ever really known; as a boy, he had rarely ventured to Tokyo. During his senior year, Go was recommended to try out for the team of Nihon, a private university in Chiyoda, Tokyo. By then, elbow and shoulder injuries had drastically limited his effectiveness,[2] and he did not make the team. He was content to quit the sport.

The failed tryout in Tokyo did, however, significantly shift his mindset regarding college. "I noticed that in the future I have to learn new things which I could never learn in the local area," he said. "The tryout just opened my eyes." Opportunities seemed endless in the big city. So Go Fujisawa, boasting a funny accent and unfamiliar dialect, headed for the bright lights of Tokyo. It was his next big adventure.

He majored in economics at Nihon and worked as a tour assistant for Hato Bus, a sightseeing company known for its trademark yellow buses with the company name plastered in red block letters. He and his boss routinely talked baseball, so she connected him with one of her contacts in the sports business world, Yoshi Hasegawa, an assistant to a sports agent at CSMG Sports.[3] This connection would prove monumental in crystallizing his postcollege career plans.

He looked up to Hasegawa, who he learned had acquired his master's in the United States. "He already got a job in MLB, and that was my final goal," said Go. "I was just trying to do the same thing." Once those seeds were planted, a determined Go set his sights on bringing his plan to fruition.

Following Hasegawa's road map, he applied to Indiana State University and was accepted into its two-year Sports Management and Recreation program, where he began in the fall of 2006. The first year kept Go so busy that sleep was often an afterthought.[4] He didn't make much progress with his English. There was no time.

The next summer, Hasegawa helped him land an internship with the Swallows, where he met Masayuki "Michael" Okumura, the head of their international scouting department. When Go returned to the States within a couple months, he had another internship waiting for him, an opportunity to work under his mentor, Hasegawa. The demanding Chicago-based position involved assisting a handful of CSMG Sports' major-league clients, including Tomokazu Ohka, Kenji Johjima, Akinori Iwamura, and So Taguchi. By the second semester, the three-plus-hour commute barely mattered as he was taking only one Monday-night class and could spend the rest of the week in Chicago or traveling for work.

Admittedly, the job "wasn't fun, just tough," and initial difficulties with English factored heavily. In retrospect, Go's certain that having to interact with people and solve problems in real-world situations enabled him to learn the language, and relatively rapidly. It was a sink-or-swim situation, and boy, did Go swim! "I wasn't shy," he said. "I was kind of scared to talk to people in English, but once you start working you have to push yourself to do it. They were counting on me. If I couldn't do anything, they cannot do anything."

He once traveled to Texas to help Kazuo Fukumori acclimate after the Rangers rookie spent over a decade pitching in Japan. At twenty-four, he was tasked with a slew of important errands, including helping his compatriot find a house and set up a bank account. Another time, he had to navigate the language barrier at an Arizona motel front desk and get his client a replacement room key card.

Fairly new to the country, language, and culture, Go was a sponge, absorbing something daily. It was also his first experience working with pro athletes. Not much longer than a month into the internship, his successful language acquisition dawned on him: "One time when I got home and went to bed, I just realized maybe I could speak English. Maybe I could understand what people are saying."

Go expected to remain in the States to look for work following graduation. But in April 2008, he received a surprising call from the Swallows. He hadn't formally applied for anything, but Okumura wanted him back, working for the organization. Naturally, Go jumped at the chance. He notified Hasegawa, who allowed him to return to Indiana to complete his master's. Eschewing graduation, he packed his things and headed to Japan, starting with Yakult in mid-May, a day after his return. By June 1, he was officially brought on as a full-time staff member.

As an assistant director of foreign affairs/international operations, he worked as the minor-league team's interpreter. As opposed to the Swallows' *ichi-gun* or top-level team, which employed a separate English translator for hitters and pitchers, the *ni-gun* squad utilized a single person for all gaijin.

Beyond translating, his responsibilities included preparing and editing contracts for international players, developing a new scouting theory based on existing data, finding international talent using the new approach, and convincing (or at least trying to convince) management that its finite budgetary resources should go toward signing particular international guys. Go was instrumental in adding a video component to Yakult's international scouting process. He also played a significant role in bringing aboard Jamie D'Antona, whom he discovered while interning for CSMG. Awfully young and brand new to the job, Go was quickly proving Okumura made the right decision to hire him.

On the road, Go and Koji Kondo accompanied the four foreigners to restaurants.[5] Accomplished closer Chang-Yong Lim spoke virtually no English. His Korean-Japanese interpreter, whom he'd bring to these dinners, barely spoke more than that. Occasionally, Lim would ask Tony, Guiel, and D'Antona a variety of questions, sending them through a sort of game of Telephone from Korean to Japanese to English, and vice versa for the responses. In turn, they'd question their teammate, who joined Yakult in 2008 after nine seasons in the Korean Baseball Organization.

Lim long had aspirations of playing in the major leagues and knew learning English would ultimately benefit his life and career.[6] Although he was not a gaijin, speedy outfielder Norichika Aoki sometimes tagged along for the same reason. Recording his first 200-hit NPB season at twenty-three and, five years later, going on to bat .358 in 2010, it was certainly no stretch to envision the left-handed batter landing in the majors soon.[7]

At these gaijin gatherings, which occurred much more frequently before the players' families arrived for the year, Go built rapport with the guys and dispensed cultural wisdom. Tony valued his insight, but otherwise while they were away from the field he did his best to refrain from contacting him.

"He's not with me at every beck and call," Tony said. "If I really needed him, I could call him and have him talk to somebody, but I try not to be a bother because he's got a life outside of the field too. He's got a wife,[8] so you don't want to bother him at nine o'clock at night when you're looking in the grocery store, trying to figure out where the spaghetti noodles are. I wanted to figure it out by myself. I couldn't be dependent on somebody else the whole time."

So he tried to solve most problems on his own. Sure, there were minor off-the-field victories from time to time, but by and large that first year felt like one massive struggle.

Navigating Japanese supermarkets, all while managing to eat healthfully, was one area in which Tony had difficulties settling into a constructive routine. "You're looking for, let's just say, low-fat ground beef, and all three shelves look like ground beef, and you don't know exactly which one's beef, pork, or whatever else it could be," he said. "You just kind of shy away. So then it's saying, 'Ah, screw it. I'm going to go over to McDonald's. At least I know what that is.'"

The vast language barrier left him feeling alienated from those around him. It also provided Tony newfound understanding and empathy for non-English speakers in the US.

"When you're sitting in the United States and you get in areas where people are like, 'God, I wish they would just speak English. Why don't they just speak English?' And all of a sudden you get on the other side of the fence, and you're sitting there, looking around the store, and you're like, 'Oh, my God. Everybody's looking at me like, 'God, why doesn't this guy speak Japanese?' It's really hard to explain, to put into words all the frustration and all the trials and tribulations you go through moving to a new country without knowing the language."

Every night, regardless of if or how he pitched, an empty apartment awaited him. Hillary was in Arizona, finishing her senior year of college and working at a marketing company. Albeit geographically distant, she was unflinchingly emotionally present.

Tony's struggles to adapt to Japanese baseball and off-the-field life drew he and his girlfriend of over a year closer. Despite the sixteen-hour time difference, she adjusted her schedule to ensure that she'd be there for him in his biggest time of need. Over those first few months, they spoke daily. Hillary woke up by 6 a.m. to Skype with him before she left to work. Before Tony went to sleep, he also would regularly call Hillary during her lunch break. Those pre-bedtime/lunchtime calls usually lasted ten minutes, at most, but they did remind Tony that he wasn't going through these challenges alone.

"She was definitely my sounding board," he said. "I really didn't have a lot of people who could relate to me while I was over here." Guiel, D'Antona, and Go were all happy to listen, but he hadn't known them for long and felt much more comfortable confiding in Hillary. Plus, he preferred to limit his complaining around the team: "I bitched at Hillary a lot. She was really good at listening, just sitting there, letting me rant and rave a little bit. That way, I wasn't doing it in a place that was inappropriate."

In his younger days, Tony wasn't adept at avoiding "inappropriate" displays of emotion at the ballpark, sporadically kicking over tables, toppling trash cans, and as most pro athletes tend to do, cursing. He considers himself to be an intense, fiery competitor, a quality he overwhelmingly views as an asset. At the same time, he has taken strides over the years to better control his temper. In 2010, this endeavor was still very much a work in progress.

There were at least a handful of angry instances in the dugout or clubhouse where Go strategically chose not to translate into Japanese exactly what Tony had said. "That was his first year as a translator too, and I trusted him," said Tony.

Player outbursts are viewed differently in Japan. The culture fosters a more deferential attitude among its players that results in fewer outward emotional displays. Over NPB's history, teams have fined, suspended, demoted, or released a number of Americans due to such behavior.

Rusty Ryal, Tony's minor-league teammate, experienced firsthand the strict discipline teams can impose on unruly gaijin. Playing for Yomiuri in 2011, his first NPB season, Ryal "wanted to do things his own way all the time," according to Rob Smaal, which led to frequent clashes with coaches and management. He wasn't producing at the plate either.

Ryal's frustrations came to a head late that season when he left his team's dugout without permission. He was subsequently fined,[9] and the longtime Giants general manager delivered a stinging public statement that read in part: "It's a disgrace for a competitive professional athlete to do such a thing." Despite the GM publicly granting Ryal a second chance, he never again appeared in an NPB game.

Early the following season, the Chiba Lotte Marines curiously demoted their own gaijin—their cleanup-hitting DH no less—for reasons ostensibly unrelated to performance. On consecutive April nights, Josh Whitesell hit the opposing catcher on his backswing, sending Hikaru Ito and Toru Hosokawa off early.[10] Standing a sturdy six-three, his swing undoubtedly had considerable force, but he swears there was no ill intent, as he "wasn't doing anything other than taking my normal swing."

To Whitesell, the move was inexplicable. He was just ten contests into his debut season with Lotte and a gaijin for whom the organization had exceedingly high hopes.[11] In a cruel twist of irony, he learned of his demotion the day of his thirtieth birthday and would not rejoin the *ichi-gun* roster for another three months.[12] The Marines likely wondered what they were missing the preceding months when Whitesell launched six homers over his first nine games back and kept drilling the ball en route to the Pacific League's August MVP Award.[13]

Other times, team (or league) discipline was much easier to understand. On July 31, 1998, a fifteen-year-old Go Fujisawa was watching

TV when he witnessed an unforgettable gaijin outburst. Incensed, after a costly home run immediately followed a borderline pitch not going his way, Giants pitcher Balvino Gálvez fired a baseball at home-plate umpire Atsushi Kittaka, narrowly missing him. The Dominican was suspended for the remainder of the season. Following 1998, however, Yomiuri re-signed Gálvez because he'd done well his first three seasons there and it needed the pitching help. While he never returned to the majors, he likely would have if not for another on-field outburst.[14]

Despite his first-season struggles, Tony successfully avoided any blow-ups that would necessitate management involvement. During Whitesell's first NPB stop, as a Swallow, Guiel regarded him as much more intense than Tony. But it was a "manageable intensity," said Guiel. "Josh would lose control sometimes. The Japanese guys don't really like it all that much, but Josh just had high standards."

Whitesell possessed an abundance of power, but he struck out often. His feast-or-famine hitting could lead to frustration. According to Guiel, Whitesell quickly learned how to conceal his anger whenever it bubbled up: "If he went into the tunnel down below and he needed to blow off some steam, he might break a bat, he might kick something, but he would never infringe on anybody else that was around him."

Tony, too, was well aware that where one showed emotion really mattered. He knew that destroying a water cooler in plain view of the TV cameras would embarrass the team and himself, whereas ducking into the clubhouse to throw something or curse would likely go undetected during a game.

Guiel didn't witness much of the pitcher's anger: "When he first got over there, I don't want to say he was quiet, but he wasn't very expressive with his emotions, and I think it was a positive thing because it let the team know that he wanted to be a part of it. And so when things weren't going well, they were very patient with Tony. It was this let's-work-together attitude rather than let's put this kid in his place."

Tony didn't quite recall such a mature version of himself, but he suspected Guiel's impression likely mirrored what his coaches and other teammates saw. Thanks to the daily therapeutic Skype calls with Hillary and Go's occasional softening of his words, he was effectively disguising his frustration. It still wore on him though.

Much to Tony's dismay, pitchers bat in Central League competition. "When I was a starter, I hated hitting," he admitted in a June 2014 appearance on the *Japan Baseball Weekly* podcast. "I thought it was a giant pain in the ass, to be honest with you. Especially [if] you come in after a bad inning, give up a couple runs, and you're sitting there and you're trying to cool down, they're like, 'Hey, you're leading off.' You're like, 'Okay, great. Let's fail some more.'"

As a hitter in 2010, Tony had a difficult time, accruing 13 strikeouts in 21 at-bats. His two hits were mere singles, though Tony did manage to successfully execute three sacrifice bunts and draw two walks.

Beginning in Triple A,[15] he felt particularly confident in his bunting ability, largely thanks to Brett Butler, his manager with Reno. Butler was certainly someone to trust on small-ball matters, having compiled 147 career sacrifice hits, including a league-leading 24 in 1992. "Everyone's like, 'It's just bunting,'" said Tony, "but bunting's hard, man."

In Double A and Triple A, the night's starting pitcher typically arrived by 3 or 3:30 for batting practice[16] and would begin practicing bunt after bunt. He'd then take a round of swings before returning to the clubhouse for some rest and relaxation.

At all professional levels, when it comes to hitting expectations for pitchers, there aren't a lot. Bunting ability is essentially it. "Every pitcher kind of prides himself on not looking like a complete idiot," said Tony. Probably even more motivating, "Your pitching coach and your manager will jump your ass if you don't get bunts down."

When not bunting, "you really just hack away," he said. "You get up there and just basically go with the old adage that my dad used to teach me: 'Swing hard just in case you hit it.'" Over three seasons, spanning his last two years in the minors and his inaugural NPB campaign, Tony batted .160, with one extra-base hit, in 75 at-bats.

Given his lack of power,[17] it was no surprise when Tony vividly remembered his lone professional double several years after it occurred. Facing a hard-throwing righty, Esmil Rogers, whom he expected to throw fastballs to a fellow pitcher, he focused on making contact, hoping the pitch's speed would do the bulk of the work. And he connected in front of the home Reno crowd!

"It was like the best day of my life," he joked. "The ball hit off the top of the wall. I was rounding first just wishing it out [of] the park." Despite the ball nearly clearing the fence, he was certainly not about to fall into a celebratory home-run trot. "Pitchers don't have home-run trots," noted Tony. "I was going at about 85 percent, not turning it on just yet, because I knew that if it did fall into play, I was stopping at second. There's no way I'm trying to stretch it into a triple. As a pitcher, you just go station to station. You keep it simple."

Besides the hard-hit double, Tony's night featured two additional hits, both line-drive singles, including one with the bases loaded that drove in two. So, 60 percent of Tony's hits in 2009, and all of his RBIs, came on a single August night against the Colorado Springs Sky Sox. Tony would never drive in another run as a professional.

In his 2014 podcast appearance, he expounded upon the added complexity of being a Central League starter: "In the PL, pitchers can just worry about pitching. They don't have to worry about strapping on a helmet and getting up there, taking their licks against 90-mile-per-hour fastballs and sliders and splits. Because, to be honest, [then teenage Fighter Shohei] Ohtani's the actual only real hitter on a pitching staff. Everybody else may have been a hitter at one point, but that skill has completely diminished over time."

The nature of the gaijin quota cultivated close relationships among the foreign players. "When you're there, and there's only four non-Japanese guys," said Guiel, "you look out for each other. You root for each other."

After eagerly assisting Tony as he weighed going to Japan, Guiel's work wasn't done once they became teammates. Despite various factors that limited each player's time around the club and the two playing completely different positions—hitters and pitchers rarely practice together—he helped Tony as much as possible.

He certainly felt the love, dubbing Guiel a "good mentor" on Japanese baseball. "Off the field," said Tony, "you can't really ask for a nicer guy to be around. We would go to dinner, breakfast. When you're in a foreign country with only a few people that you're similar to, you tend to spend a lot of time with those people."

Wherever his career had taken him, Guiel had been regarded as a compassionate, high-quality teammate, and the longer he played, the more information he could impart to the younger guys. Beginning NPB season number four at thirty-seven, he was oozing experience.

According to Rob Smaal, "Aaron's the kind of guy, definitely, that when new guys would come in—he'd been there a while, he knew the system—he would give them advice, not on how to pitch or how to play baseball, but on how to get along over there with the management, teammates. And a lot of guys don't do that, right? They don't make that effort."

Part of Guiel's approach simply stemmed from the concept of paying it forward. When he was an NPB newcomer, Adam Riggs, whom he had played against for years in the minors, and Alex Ramírez served as "perfect teammates" to the Canadian uninitiated into Japanese baseball.

Riggs boasted a two-year NPB head start, which he drew from when consulting with Guiel on his decision to come to Japan.[18] "As soon as I arrived, he showed me the ropes," he said. Most notably, he quickly learned the heightened importance of body language amid stubborn language barriers. Riggs always appeared cheerful regardless of whether he was healthy or hitting well. This attribute, he noticed, endeared Riggs to his teammates. Accordingly, Guiel vowed to always keep a positive demeanor no matter the circumstances.

Ramírez was actually two years younger than Guiel but had already amassed six full seasons of NPB success. His clout within the organization was unmistakable, as Yakult's hitters in the final batting practice group were permitted, upon Ramírez's request, to arrive later than their teammates, a rare bending of the collectivistic rules. His massive production proved more than convincing for Swallows brass, allowing Guiel to reap the benefits of the policy. Ramírez's engaging, charismatic personality assuredly helped his cause too.

Outgoing and prone to making friends wherever Yakult traveled, his biggest impact on Guiel's acclimation came socially. Ramírez spoke English well and possessed many other qualities that could significantly aid an English-speaking gaijin like Guiel. "His Japanese was passable," according to Guiel. "He knew restaurants. He knew people. He was instrumental in helping me adjust to life off the field." Plus, he'd accumulated an encyclopedic knowledge of NPB pitchers and catchers and was more than happy to impart intel to his teammates.[19] In their lone season together, they combined to produce 64 home runs and 201 RBIs.

By the time Tony arrived, the man whose teammates called him "AG" had reached the peak of his pranking prowess. Guiel believes the habit had a positive effect on the clubhouse, particularly the gaijin: "You're trying to play little jokes on each other just to keep the atmosphere light because sometimes you get homesick. It grinds you down."

On one occasion, while rehabbing with the *ni-gun* team, Guiel eyed first baseman Shinichi Takeuchi's unattended car keys. Guiel didn't own or drive a car in Japan, so here was his chance to drive while simultaneously pranking a teammate. He grabbed the keys and, with another teammate, drove a quarter of a mile down the road. "He was scared," said Guiel. "We weren't gonna crash his car, but still probably not the smartest thing. We used to have fun with those guys because sometimes especially the younger players in Japan get so serious and so focused that they forget to loosen up."

Sometimes, Tony was a target of Guiel's antics. Soon after his arrival, Guiel welcomed him with a surreptitious half-inch layer of wasabi in his hamburger. If Tony ordered coffee and made the mistake of getting up, he'd likely return to find Tabasco sauce in his beverage.

Although he wasn't loud or particularly expressive, Tony "makes sure to get you back," said Guiel, who described him as a "straight-faced prankster. He's the quiet little assassin." One of his go-to pranks involved putting A535, a pain relief cream, wherever he could, whether he snuck some in a cap, sock, or even a teammate's jockstrap.

More frequently, they'd team up to prank their more staid Japanese teammates. "When you've got guys like Tony and I playing little tricks, they have a tendency to not take themselves so seriously," said Guiel. "It keeps the atmosphere real fun."

Jamie D'Antona was the 2010 Swallows' third and final English-speaking gaijin at the season's outset. His route to Japan could not have been more different from either of the other two. Following a celebrated three-year career at Wake Forest, where he batted .354, slugged .677, and drove in 242 runs in 172 games, the six-foot-two, 215-pound corner infielder earned a 2003 second-round selection by the Diamondbacks. Unlike Tony and Guiel, who were drafted in the 10th and 21st rounds, respectively, D'Antona became a pro with instant, through-the-roof expectations. By 2004, he and first-round draftees Conor Jackson and Carlos Quentin were nicknamed the "Three Amigos" due to their obliteration of minor-league pitching.

Ahead of 2009, *CBS Sports'* Eric Mack ranked D'Antona as Arizona's fourth-best prospect but wondered where he could fit on defense. During the previous season, he struggled defensively, particularly at third base where he spent most of his time, though he also played poorly across the diamond at first. He atoned for that by batting .365 with 21 homers. He appeared in the Futures Game at Yankee Stadium and played in the Triple-A All-Star Game and won its Home Run Derby.[20]

He was first promoted in late July but managed just three singles in 17 big-league at-bats. As the 2008 calendar year wound down, D'Antona determined Japan was preferable to bouncing back and forth between the majors and Triple A. That offseason, he had to undergo surgery to repair the cartilage in one of his knees. So, it was understandable when Arizona obliged D'Antona's request by releasing him, freeing him to leave for Japan.

Once Guiel and D'Antona became teammates, they clicked right away. D'Antona was strong-willed and opinionated. Guiel most admired his sincerity. "Whenever you had a discussion with him, you were never really put off because he was always well-thought-out." And they had plenty of deep discussions. Guiel, who was nearly a decade older, felt the youngster was "mature beyond his years."

D'Antona, a "big teddy bear" to Guiel, liked to goof around off the field, showing an offbeat tendency to work behind the counter at places the team frequented. According to Jim Collins's book on the 2002 Chatham A's of the Cape Cod League, *The Last Best League: One Summer, One Season, One Dream*, D'Antona liked to spontaneously help in the kitchen then too.

At Legends, where the gaijin often spent summer nights, Smaal distinctly recalled D'Antona serving drinks and cleaning tables. Of course, he wasn't getting paid. One particular episode stood out: "Some guy walked down the street with a mug of beer, and Jamie chased him down to get the mug back. It cracked us up that he chased a guy down the street to get a beer mug back for the bar. Like, who cares, right?"

Teammates enjoyed his quirky behavior. Unfortunately, he came to Japan with knee issues that only worsened over his two seasons there.[21] If not for D'Antona's ailing knees, Guiel envisioned a seven-to-ten-year

NPB career for the slugger, consisting of 30-plus homers per season. In addition to his body failing him, the authenticity Guiel so admired may have disturbed Swallows management. "With Jamie, what you see is what you get, take it or leave it, and he doesn't really care," said Guiel. As Smaal phrased it, "He would kind of buck the system somewhat. He wasn't as willing to toe the line. I don't want to say anything negative about him, but he was less likely to do things their way as opposed to doing things his way."

Over Smaal's many years watching gaijin come and go, he learned the critical importance of adapting and accommodating. Gaijin who failed to or refused to do both typically did not last long.[22]

Notes

1. In 2005, Tazawako merged with the town Kakunodate and the village of Nishiki to form a city called Semboku.
2. When fully healthy, right-handed-throwing Go's fastball was clocked at 135 kilometers per hour in high school, or approximately 84 miles per hour.
3. In October 2008, the Octagon sports agency acquired the bulk of CSMG, including its entire baseball division, around twenty of its employees, and more than 140 of its clients.
4. It was not unusual for Go to eat and sleep in the library instead of going back to his apartment. He joked that he was "commuting between school and the library."
5. Sometimes they broke into two groups and ate at different places, the pitchers with Go Fujisawa and the hitters with Koji Kondo.
6. In 2013, Lim ultimately made good on that dream, making six relief appearances for the Chicago Cubs.
7. Aoki would first appear with the Milwaukee Brewers in 2012. On a local San Francisco Giants telecast in 2015, with his interpreter by his side, Aoki accidentally uttered, "Shit," before laughing and covering his mouth. Throughout the rest of his MLB career, he'd share the podium with his translator, despite reportedly progressing a great deal in his English speaking and comprehension since 2012.
8. Go actually didn't marry Mari until March 1, 2012, but they had already been dating by the 2010 season.
9. The sum was believed to comfortably exceed ¥100,000, which translated to approximately $1,300 at the time.

10   Ito left to the hospital on a stretcher. Fortunately, he was not severely injured, and neither was Hosokawa.

11   In announcing the signing, the team president said he expected 30 home runs before adding, "We hope he can spark our offense."

12   In May, the two players who platooned at first base badly struggled, combining to bat .188 with just two extra-base hits, yet Lotte stood at 26–15–5 by month's end, so Whitesell stayed put. At least that was Whitesell's theory as to why he didn't get promoted much sooner. By the end of June, the Marines still occupied first place and preferred not to rock the boat by allowing Whitesell to return.

13   The stellar August followed by a solid September earned Whitesell another one-year deal with the Marines worth $850,000, although, in retrospect, he wishes he'd instead signed a two-year contract for more stability.

14   Just days from his thirty-seventh birthday, various media reports expected Gálvez to make the Pittsburgh Pirates' 2001 opening-day roster . . . that is, until he stormed off the field after a disagreement with his pitching coach. He then packed his bags and left practice without saying another word. Instead, Gálvez played that season, his final one, in South Korea.

15   Double-A and Triple-A games would not feature any designated hitters if both sides were NL-affiliated teams. Since the 2022 season, there's been a universal DH, meaning every minor-league team always uses a DH as does every major-league team.

16   The Swallows' starting pitcher of the night wouldn't take batting practice on the field, but he could hit in the cage if he wanted. Tony never did.

17   Playing home games at Hank Aaron Stadium in Double A apparently did not rub off on Tony's bat.

18   Much like Aaron Guiel would do for Tony, Adam Riggs encouraged him to call if any questions arose. Former Winter Ball teammates George Arias and Derrick White also spoke with Guiel as he compiled more information about his potential Japanese experience.

19   Ramírez's baseball intelligence helped him accumulate a gaijin-best 2,017 NPB career hits and get hired as the Yokohama manager in advance of the 2016 season. In 2017, Ramírez led Yokohama to its third Japan Series in franchise history.

20   It took two tiebreakers in the final round, but D'Antona ultimately edged defending Triple-A Home Run Derby champion Mike Hessman. Coincidentally, Hessman also ventured to Japan, where he struggled in 2011, his lone season with the Orix Buffaloes.

21   Those would also be the final two years of D'Antona's professional playing career after a Marlins 2011 spring-training invitation didn't work out.

22   Although having too much organizational depth seems like a good problem, NPB teams typically don't like to pay more gaijin than they need. Yomiuri, which could always afford to, is one notable exception.

CHAPTER FOUR
TONY LOVES HILLARY JONES

I remember specifically thinking pretty immediately, "Whoa, he's really different."

While the fraternal atmosphere cultivated by Aaron Guiel helped to ease some tension, Tony saved the deeper issues for his partner in Arizona.

"The only person that I could really bounce my frustration off of was Hillary," he said, "so she was there as well as she could be for me, to try to help me keep a sane mind throughout the entire process. She really never gave me advice. I never really went looking for advice. It was more me saying, 'This is what I'm frustrated with,' and kind of getting it off my chest, and she was great at just kind of sitting back and letting me vent."

It wasn't as if he was saving all his frustrations for her. At dinner, he and Go would occasionally talk about what he was going through—granted, with less depth and emotion—and Tony found him to be "very understanding." Still, she served as his rock.

The original plan had been for Hillary to visit him periodically, while continuing to work in Arizona for the rest of 2010. The plan changed after her unforgettable spring break trip, where she had an amazing week of discovery and felt closer to Tony than ever before. At that point, said

Hillary, "it seemed pretty daunting to be separated for the whole season." It was also becoming increasingly difficult for both to navigate the sixteen-hour time difference. "It was like, 'If we're gonna stay together, I think we should just be together.'" She didn't make a decision directly after returning, but as her graduation approached, moving to Tokyo full-time began to seem like a real option.

Her parents and sister were in Arizona, as was the job she'd worked since her sophomore year at Arizona State,[1] but she was willing to leave it all to be with him. Some coworkers thought it would be unwise for her to leave to join a professional-athlete boyfriend on another continent, though her immediate family was extremely supportive. Specifically, her mom told her, "At the end of the day, if it doesn't work out between you and Tony, you got to travel to Japan, and that's awesome." Hillary also reasoned that she could likely return to the company, given the amicable split and her three solid years spent there.

She loved exploring new cultures, too. Just twenty-two, she had already gained some worldly experience. At nineteen, following her freshman year, Hillary spent a semester in Barcelona. Her "first time being away from the bubble of my family," as she put it, was "definitely uncomfortable. It was a little shock to the system, which ended up being really beneficial. I really think it started an appreciation for getting out of my comfort zone." The experience opened her world to new possibilities, allowing her to feel what it was like to thrive in a new environment.

While studying abroad, whenever she had a free day, Hillary loved to board a train by herself and venture out of the big city. Once, she hiked up Montserrat, a multi-peaked mountain range in Catalonia. At the very top—where she reached via gondola—she took in memorable views, including many of the beautiful and historic Abbey of Montserrat.[2] That summer, she enjoyed sampling the various beautiful beaches of Sitges, a town just southwest of Barcelona. Another time, she went to a cava winery, where she enjoyed tasting varieties of the Spanish sparkling wine, which closely resembles champagne.

The sites she viewed and the people she met only fueled her curiosity. Upon returning to school, Hillary knew that would not be the end of her international travels if she had anything to say about it. She went on to minor in Spanish and receive an international business certificate at Arizona State.

After further considering her options as March 2010 turned into April and then as May loomed around the corner, it was settled. Tony's short walk home from the stadium would no longer culminate in an empty apartment. Hillary even missed her college graduation in order to hurry over to Tokyo. She was on her way.

When Hillary describes her upbringing, "They were always there" repeatedly comes up in reference to her parents.

"When I got out of elementary school, she was always waiting under a tree in front of the school to walk home with me," she said of her mother, Kim, who, for a decade, did accounting work for a pool-cleaning business run by her brother. The job gave her the flexibility to spend ample after-school time with her two daughters. During every one of Hillary's high-school golf competitions, she and Kim walked the course together.

Ever the athlete, much of young Hillary's time was consumed by sports. All four years, she played softball, soccer, and golf for Millennium High. With softball and soccer, she had the good fortune of briefly playing alongside her sister when Casey was a senior and she was winding down her freshman seasons and the varsity teams were promoting players from JV. Even better, with golf, the sisters were teammates all season long. Like Tony, with his older brothers, Casey's athletic passion and ability drove Hillary to perfect her game.

Softball was her favorite from a social standpoint, chanting with her teammates from the dugout and communicating in the field. Her best friend, Bridgette, starred as the team's ace, while Hillary patrolled center field.

She probably enjoyed playing soccer the most. Primarily a defender because "I wasn't very fast, I wasn't very good at scoring," she switched positions early senior year when the team's elite goalkeeper went down with a knee injury. "Hey, you play softball. Can you dive?" her coach asked. "Not really well," she responded. "Do you want to be the goalie? You're probably one of the tallest girls on the team." "Yeah, let's do it." Hillary had fun despite admittedly having "no idea what I was doing."

Her best sport, golf, earned her a couple partial athletic scholarships from small universities around the country, which she spurned to attend Arizona State, her parents' alma mater,[3] on a full-ride academic scholarship. Missing golf right away, Hillary managed to golf one season for a local community college until the situation became untenable.[4]

When Ken took a job with the city of Tempe a year earlier, a statute obligated the family to move within the city limits. Hillary's mom then took a job with ASU as an accountant. Kim's workplace was situated literally across the street from Hillary's freshman dorm. "She could see our parking lot from her work," she said. "I'm pretty sure I got a text from her one time like, 'Hey, where are you? Your car's not in the parking lot.' But they definitely gave me my space. It was nice to have them close. It was really close, but it was nice. I got to go home for a meal every once in a while."

They were always there. After his baseball career ended, Ken went back to school, yet that didn't prevent him from coaching his daughters' teams or volunteering as an umpire at their Little League. Neither did going to night school to get his master's degree.

"They were just present for all that stuff," said Hillary, who knew Tony similarly needed her presence. For months, her emotional support via Skype was invaluable, but it surely had its limitations. It had been embedded into her psyche from an early age that one has a duty to unequivocally support one's loved ones. There was absolutely no way Tony was going to be left alone.

They first met at a Diamondbacks game through mutual friends in the summer of 2005. Tony was between his junior and senior years of college. Meanwhile, Hillary was gearing up for her senior year . . . of high school. Due to the forty-five-minute commute from Tempe to her high school, most of her friends were Arizona State students.

One of those friends knew Tony and his good buddy Jason. Upon their first encounter, "I immediately had a crush on him," she said, "but I was seventeen." Over the following weeks, they talked semi-frequently.

At the height of AOL Instant Messenger, Hillary often used AIM to converse with Tony after school or softball practice. She felt sparks, while also believing that for Tony "there was nothing there" beyond platonic, albeit entertaining, banter. "He pretty much showed zero interest. I had a huge crush on him. I was like, 'Man, he just doesn't like me.' That was pretty much the extent of it."

"Now he'll say, 'I wasn't gonna show any interest because you were seventeen, of course,' but he didn't tell me at the time. Now, looking back, it makes sense, but at the time, I was like, 'What the heck?'" They sparingly kept in touch over the ensuing years through an occasional text message or social media post. Over time, Tony had a couple girlfriends at various minor-league stops, while Hillary had a few college boyfriends.

It wasn't until more than three years after the Diamondbacks game that they began to get close. By then, Hillary was an ASU student, a junior, and Tony was back for the Arizona Fall League as a Diamondbacks prospect.

The chance meeting happened at a Tempe Halloween party, where Tony asked Hillary to go out with him. She declined but never believed her feelings had dissipated. Rather, she had a boyfriend and remained focused on her academics with final exams approaching. "He thought

I was playing hard to get, but I really wasn't," recalled Hillary. "I just was actually busy. I took my classes pretty seriously."

There was one other reason. "I was kind of hesitant to date a baseball player at the time," she said. "You know, because he was only there for Fall League. That doesn't sound very permanent."

Putting aside the nomadic lifestyle of the typical baseball player, she quickly realized he wasn't like most jocks. "When I first met Tony, I remember specifically thinking, pretty immediately, 'Whoa, he's really different.' I don't want to throw baseball players into a bunch—maybe just guys in general when I was young—just the tough guy kind of mentality. And he was, especially for a baseball player, just really honest and genuine. I remember it being almost shocking, so it was really refreshing."

His fun, free, self-deprecating nature intrigued her. "That's what I like about him," she added. "He's just like a two-year-old in a grown man's body. He doesn't really care about what anybody thinks. And if you like him, great. If you don't, great. That's who he is."

After Hillary declined his offer, a persistent Tony kept asking, ultimately leading to a group date at Chili's, with Hillary's best friend, another Hillary, brought along as a sort of buffer. The fairly platonic lunch date went well, but Tony's In-N-Out chocolate milkshake delivery—one for each Hillary—weeks later "might have won me over," Hillary admitted years later.

But there was still the boyfriend, whom Hillary had been dating for six months. At twenty-one, she had the judgment and wherewithal to realize her connection with Tony was notably stronger and not something she should fight. So she spoke with her boyfriend.

"It was such a weird conversation because I was like, 'I've always been in love with this other guy, and he's acting interested now.' I was pretty honest about it. I was like, 'I feel like I need to pursue that.' And he was awesome about it. He was like, 'Hey, if you feel that way, you should pursue that.' It was probably the most mature breakup of all time."

About a week after they began dating, Tony left for Washington to spend the offseason with his parents before leaving for Triple A in Reno. Both would grow accustomed to sharing a long-distance relationship, but nothing would compare to the Tempe-Tokyo distance they would be forced to navigate the following year.

Notes

[1] "I kind of had to mourn the loss of the company," said Hillary. Although she wasn't in a role that she felt would be fulfilling in the long run, she loved the company, respected its leadership, and saw a potential for upward mobility.

[2] Founded in the eleventh century, the monastery was rebuilt over one hundred years ago and still functions today, housing over seventy monks.

[3] Hillary's sister and Tony are also proud Arizona State alumni.

[4] In order to be eligible for the team, Hillary signed up for four online classes, to which she paid just enough attention to pass. With her busy academic schedule, she couldn't even practice with the team. Her coach didn't mind, and neither did she. After one season, the arrangement became too difficult to handle.

CHAPTER FIVE
TOILING IN TODA

I fell into that dark place, professional athletic purgatory, where things aren't going your way. You start pointing fingers why they're not going your way, and you end up realizing you haven't pointed a single finger at yourself.

Ditching the graduation cap and gown in Tempe for a baseball cap in Japan's most populous city, Hillary made it in time to attend Tony's disappointingly short start against Orix. The couple hadn't seen each other since Hillary's visit two months earlier. Now, they'd be living under the same roof. Because they weren't married, she had a short-term visa that would allow her to stay up to ninety days.[1]

She admittedly overpacked, much like Tony months earlier. "We had no idea what to expect," she said. "We took way too many winter clothes when it was mostly hot the entire time." She also brought a full bag of toiletries, thinking certain preferred items might not be sold anywhere in Tokyo. In retrospect, they largely were. "Out of ignorance, we just didn't know."

Despite his buoyed spirits from Hillary's arrival, he continued to appear overmatched on the rubber. In his next start, he and Yakult fell to the Marines. In a disastrous first inning in Chiba City, Tony allowed five runs by way of a marathon two-out rally that featured three doubles, three walks, and a single. This time, Shigeru Takada left him in, and he rose to the occasion, totaling 132 pitches while allowing just one run over five more innings of work.

Silver linings aside, his ERA was subpar (5.61), and the team was losing at an alarming rate. In-season managerial changes were rare,[2] but Takada's days were numbered. With Yakult sitting in last place at 13–32–1 and losing nine straight and fifteen of its last sixteen, he resigned the following Wednesday.

Starting shortstop Shinya Miyamoto, who, at thirty-nine, had seen it all over sixteen-plus NPB seasons, was refreshingly transparent about his guilt: "We were awful. I felt there was more we could have done as players. After he returned from the press conference, I apologized to him. He just wished me luck. All I can say is that I feel really awful and that I'm sorry." Nori Aoki similarly took responsibility, telling a *Sponichi Annex* reporter, "We couldn't put up the numbers."

Despite the public support for their departed manager, Tony claimed, years later, that many of his teammates did not actually like Takada because of his disdain for interacting with players. "From my understanding, a lot of the organization wasn't really on the same page as him," added Tony. Plus, Swallows fans were unhappy, he contended. "People thought he was a good general manger and good in the scouting department, but managing baseball just was not for him."

Indeed, Takada could never remotely match the success he achieved as a general manager. In the late 1980s, he managed Nippon-Ham for four unspectacular seasons, never once finishing higher than third in the Pacific League.[3] After returning to the Fighters, from their front office he quickly led them to two straight Japan Series appearances in 2006 and 2007. A decade later, as GM, he'd steer the Yokohama DeNA BayStars[4] to the Japan Series.

Aaron Guiel played for him for parts of three seasons yet barely knew him. He felt Takada's aloofness might have hampered the development of the younger Swallows: "He could've done better to create a connection with the players. Some of the younger players felt intimidated. Tony got a raw deal in that circumstance, and I don't think there was the openness to bridge that."

Swallows writer David Watkins took issue with Takada's in-game management style, which he felt was outdated. "It was relying on maybe the way the game was played back when he played," Watkins opined. "It wasn't good."

One of the bench coaches, Junji Ogawa, was assigned to take over the reins. His personality and leadership style, according to Tony, provided a breath of fresh air: "He's personable. He'll sit there and joke with you. He'll come by and ask you how you're doing that morning. He's the complete opposite of what the other guy was. Everybody likes him, and he's a good baseball man."

Ogawa's first game as manager halted Yakult's losing streak, but not how an American baseball fan might think. Short on pitchers and with Tony momentarily out of the rotation, Ogawa summoned him to pitch the 11th inning (and later, the 12th). Although he loaded the bases with two outs in the 12th, he was able to induce an inning-ending ground out. In the bottom half, the Swallows stranded two runners, effectively triggering a 3–3 tie. Well, at least they didn't lose.

Never the best sign when a starter is brought in for relief duties, the move further confirmed that Tony's poor play had done serious damage to his standing with the team. He was back in the starting rotation on June 4 against Seibu and pitched extremely well for five and two-thirds innings before he began to unravel. Still, the team won 12–6, as he earned his first victory since April 9.[5] Batting third, Guiel hit 3-for-5 and drove in five runs, highlighted by a three-run, fifth-inning homer.

The good vibes quickly expired when Tony was sent down to the minors. Although the likelihood of a team demoting one of its well-paid gaijin may seem low, it's quite common if the player is struggling badly enough. In recent years, some of NPB's most highly paid players—guys paid considerably more than Tony—including Tony Blanco, Alex Guerrero, Garrett Jones, Gaby Sánchez, and Vicente Padilla, were demoted after producing underwhelming results. And by then, similar moves had been happening for decades.

Tony felt blindsided, but with the benefit of hindsight, he's certain he deserved it: "I may have thought I was surprised, but I wasn't." He knew as well as anyone how poorly he had been pitching. If only that made the demotion any easier.

From each organization's pool of no more than seventy players, it fields an *ichi-gun* team and a *ni-gun* affiliate, the terms meaning "first troop" and "second troop," respectively. At any one time, the *ichi-gun* roster may not exceed 28 players, including three "inactive" spots.[6] When a player is demoted, he has been "deregistered." Unlike the major leagues, most clubs don't have multiple levels of farm teams.[7] Tony was sent to the Toda Swallows, Yakult's *ni-gun* squad located in Saitama, the prefecture that envelops the northern boundaries of the Tokyo prefecture. Each of the twelve organizations owns its minor-league affiliate, which in all cases, beginning in 2011, uses the same name and uniform design as the parent club.[8]

"It's usually pretty [straightforward]," Tony explained of the demotion process. "It's not even a thing. Literally, they just send a translator, you go to the office, and they say, 'Hey, we're sending you down. You need to get better.' 'All right, sweet.' It sucks every time you get sent down, but it's pretty unemotional from their standpoint. Every once in a while, they would give me a little piece of advice on something they thought I needed to get better."

Playing in Toda meant that his ten-minute walk to Jingu Stadium would be replaced by nearly an hour of travel consisting of two train rides and a taxi trip into the *ni-gun* facilities. First, he'd walk to Gaiemmae station. That was the easy part. From Gaiemmae, Tony would take the Ginza line to Shibuya, one of the busiest commuter rail stations in the world. There, he'd switch to a JR East train[9] and utilize the Saikyō line, getting off at Toda station. Finally, a cab would take him to the field.

His entire routine had to change. Instead of sleeping in and walking to Jingu by early afternoon, he suddenly had to wake up around 6 a.m. to arrive on time.[10] In bustling downtown Tokyo, people on their way to work packed into the subway like sardines with little to no sense of personal space. Shibuya station was the worst.

Tony likened it to navigating Los Angeles freeways during morning rush hour: "Getting on the subway at 7, 8 in the morning is just like hopping on the 405 or I-10 at 6:30, 7 in the morning. Best of luck to you."

Within days, Tony became "extremely pro" at minimizing the discomfort of his commute by strategically boarding the subway as far from staircases and escalators as possible in a quest to secure a seat for himself. "If you hesitate, it's gone," he said. "If you want to sit down, get in there. Don't be afraid to cozy in right on next to people. There's no bubbles. Get comfy."

Guiel had spent plenty of time in Toda due to a 2008 elbow injury and his back, which began ailing a couple seasons later. There, he periodically played in games. He also received medical treatment and worked on his body through conditioning and weightlifting. Often, the days were long.[11]

Rehabbing from injury could certainly feel like a grind—and was becoming more so as 2011 progressed—but Guiel could properly put into perspective where he stood in his career and how far he'd come. In the face of incredible adversity, he had traveled a long, strange, and winding journey to get to Japan, let alone the big leagues in the first place. The act of making his way through it all engendered an unmistakable gratefulness to still be playing in the latter half of his thirties.

He was born in 1972, the middle of three boys. At ten, his parents divorced, and he moved with his mom and brothers to Vancouver Island, British Columbia, near Victoria. His father was barely around and not much of an athlete. Guiel's maternal grandfather, Lloyd Gilmour, who gave him his first baseball glove, filled the void. Gilmour had a rich sports background from which to draw. He'd spent nineteen years as an NHL referee[12] after a logging accident derailed his professional hockey career.[13] Gilmour, whom *Sports Illustrated* once labeled the "NHL's best official because he is virtually an invisible man on the ice," left the game in 1976, though Guiel still holds fuzzy memories of seeing him on TV.

Gilmour then moved to Nanaimo with his wife and opened a restaurant, where Guiel's mother worked as a cook for over a decade. He was Guiel's role model, serving as a steady presence and perpetual motivator. He encouraged his grandsons to play sports, including golf, hockey, and baseball, and attended their games.

Despite the family connection and growing up in hockey-crazy Canada, Guiel was more interested in soccer, rugby, and baseball. "In Canada," he said, "the major leagues isn't a door that you feel is open, so you play everything because you want to be a well-rounded athlete, you want to enjoy your summers, and you just like playing everything." A late bloomer, he estimates he didn't realize he could potentially play professionally until after high school. Upon graduation, the acclaimed National Baseball Institute[14] offered him a spot, but he turned down the Vancouver-based traveling team. He wasn't convinced there was a path that would lead to a pro career. Instead, he enrolled at Kwantlen College and worked in his family's business,[15] not returning to baseball until the following year with the NBI as a representative of Kwantlen.[16]

Guiel's consistent performance managed to grab the attention of the California Angels, who selected the nineteen-year-old in the twenty-first round of the 1992 draft. Later, a second year with the NBI convinced the

Angels they should sweeten their signing bonus offer in order to avoid losing Guiel to the 1993 draft.[17] By 1996, he had reached Double A, where he was excelling before tailing off. This required him to start the next season in Midland again. No problem. He proceeded to slash .329/.431/609.

But just as the twenty-four-year-old lefty felt confident in his soon-to-be upward mobility within the organization, he was reminded of the harshness of the business and how everything can change in an instant. That happened in August when Todd Greene, the Angels' starting catcher, fractured his wrist, and they decided to deal Guiel in return for a catcher they could slot in immediately.[18] "I felt like my progress with the Angels had been all for naught," he said. Just like that, he was headed to the Padres, where he felt more highly touted prospects Mike Darr and Gary Matthews Jr. nipping at his heels on the organizational depth chart.

Somehow, through 1998's first two months, Guiel managed to hit .260 in Triple A without being able to "pick up the spin on the baseball" as a result of double astigmatisms that were causing his contact lens to blur his vision. As the condition deteriorated, the decision was made to have LASIK surgery, sidelining him for two months that were well worth the layoff. Upon his return, Guiel hit .372 over the season's final six weeks. But when he followed with a subpar year, again in Triple A, the Padres cut bait.

In late spring training, the Athletics brought him in. Disappointingly, a failed physical—it revealed a pinched nerve in Guiel's shoulder[19]—triggered an instant release without Oakland seeking a second opinion or allowing him to play for a lower salary. Faced with the possibility of having to take the season off or play independent ball, he contacted an agent friend, who presented another opportunity. The friend connected him to the Mexican League's Oaxaca Guerreros, who took him instantly. Guiel flew directly from Phoenix to Oaxaca, beginning an adventure unlike anything he'd ever experienced.

He played extremely well, delivering ample power at the plate. The experience was quite isolating, though. Guiel missed his girlfriend. No teammate spoke English. There wasn't one English-speaking TV station either. His dial-up internet connection was poor. When they played in Nuevo Laredo, he used the opportunity to travel across the border to Laredo, Texas, and download as much music as he could. "I would stay the night there so at least I could get a little taste of being back in the US."

A few months into the season, as he readied to board a routine team flight, his phone rang. It was his agent. The Kansas City Royals were interested. Guiel learned the Royals were not, however, prepared to pay any money to buy out his contract. So he went with the Guerreros to their destination. But during the two-hour flight, the same friend who facilitated the signing helped him avoid paying a buyout by stipulating that if he ever returned to the Mexican League, he would have to play for Oaxaca. Now, Guiel had to retrace his steps back to Mexico City. And so continued a frenetic day of travel that included an eight-hour Greyhound bus ride from Mexico City to Oaxaca[20] and culminated in his arrival in Edmonton, Alberta. What's more, he played the very next day for the Triple-A Omaha Golden Spikes.

Guiel was twenty-nine when he finally made his major-league debut in June 2002. He started hot[21] but cooled down considerably within a couple weeks. He bounced between Triple A and the majors over the ensuing years. Not even two years after his debut, he encountered another major roadblock when his left eye again stopped seeing the ball clearly. The embattled hitter needed another LASIK surgery and could only muster a career-worst .156/.263/.296 line with the top team. Post-surgery, the Royals gave Guiel over a dozen August starts, but he continued to struggle mightily. He needed months off to recover to full health.

The path was never easy. In Guiel's rookie NPB season, his output of 35 home runs belied his initial difficulty with acclimating to Japanese pitching. Over the opening month, he specifically struggled to adapt to the league's larger strike zone. He had always considered himself a patient hitter, but he no longer could afford to be. This altered his approach and led to a significant performance decline[22] until he cracked the code in late April. He also believes he initially underestimated the impact of lifestyle changes away from the field. Once he grew more comfortable, he improved as a batter. Even though Guiel's Toda appearances were all considered rehab stints, he could very much relate to Tony's 2010 doldrums.

It would have been easy for Tony to stew in anger while commuting to Toda. At times, he did. He also used technology as a welcome distraction, whether he was reading, watching movies, playing *Angry Birds*, or doing something else on his iPad. Providing some solace, he traveled with Jamie D'Antona or Guiel when either was also headed there.[23]

The Toda facilities were unbearably hot. "I can't even tell you how hot it is," Tony said. "It's so humid, and you're just sweating. You're running. You're sitting in the sun. You're just like, 'God, get me out of here!'" There wasn't any escaping the sun with the team only playing day games on artificial turf. First getting demoted with summer approaching, more sweltering days were certainly on the horizon.

Unsurprisingly, *ni-gun* day games in small cities did not attract many observers. Home games typically drew no more than a few hundred fans. Road affairs often attracted more. Still, the measured attendance rarely exceeded 1,000 unless Toda was playing in Yokosuka, the home of Yokohama's affiliate, or a couple other larger stadiums. Hillary attended an away game, where she saw "maybe a hundred people at the most." Guiel added, "Some of the [*ni-gun*] facilities you go to are maybe, maybe high-school quality."

At any level, pitchers like to pitch. Only Tony was rarely afforded that opportunity. In Toda, his arm was rested in case the *ichi-gun* Swallows suddenly needed a spot starter. Thanks to a rainout and the regularly scheduled post-Interleague break, they didn't, giving him just six innings of *ni-gun* work over a three-week period. He was beyond frustrated and developing an unhealthy attitude for anyone, let alone a baseball professional.

"Honestly, I was having a pretty big pity party for myself at that time, looking back," he said. "'Poor me, oh, poor me. This is bullshit. Blah, blah, blah.' I fell into that dark place, professional athletic purgatory, where things aren't going your way and then all of a sudden you kind of start pointing fingers why they're not, and you end up realizing you haven't pointed a single finger at yourself. I was showing up to the minor-league complex, working, stretching, playing catch, throwing bullpens, and it was just so monotonous. I was getting so tired of it that I didn't even want to work out."

With the new routine, he would usually return to his apartment around 1 p.m., the same time he used to leave for the field while with the top club. Often, he'd then stay in for the rest of the day. During this period, Hillary noticed a sizable increase in his video-game consumption.

"I probably did play more video games," Tony admitted. "That way, I could just waste more hours. I probably should have spent more time with Hillary, but I was so tired. I was so gassed. I was so ready just to leave Japan at that time. I was over it." According to Tony, "It was also a way of socializing with my friends back home."

Guiel could relate: "Being away from friends, being away from family, being away from our dream of playing in the major leagues, those all wear on you. And when things don't go well on the field, you start to feel like a downward spiral is happening, and you try to find something other to grab on to that allows you to see the light at the end of the tunnel."

Feeling sorry for himself and sinking in proverbial quicksand, Tony determined he had to revisit the times in his life when the odds seemed most stacked against him yet he remained resilient and ultimately emerged victorious. He had to in order to find that "light at the end of the tunnel."

"I finally pulled my head out of my ass and got it back on my shoulders where it belonged and started working out and realizing, 'You know what? I remember when I was at Arizona State. I was almost done with baseball there too. I thought everyone had given up on me.'"

Not everyone had, but many were beginning to. In 2005, after transferring from Central Arizona, he badly struggled on what was easily then the biggest stage of his baseball life. No longer pitching in Coolidge against smaller and weaker junior college batters, the stakes increased significantly in Tempe. In retrospect, Tony is certain he wasn't ready for university academics, and at the time it was obvious that head coach Pat Murphy would only make things more difficult. He had been recruited by Chris Sinacori and Jay Sferra.[24] But when he got to campus, he learned that Sinacori had been replaced as pitching coach with Jack Krawczyk, whose coaching Tony and some fellow pitchers would deem inadequate.[25]

From the start, Tony and Murphy clashed. "We were oil and water," said Tony. "I think we just butted heads the whole way." Twice, Murphy told him in front of the team that he should take him behind a dumpster and shoot him, adding the second time that no one would miss him. "He got personal with this shit." Although Murphy had not yet reached his coaching peak at ASU, he had enjoyed a decade of success there and the accolades that came with it. He had his way of doing things. From Tony's perspective, that didn't involve much teaching: "Pat kind of just expected people to know what to do and if you didn't do it, then you were worthless to him. Either you were already a star or 'I'm gonna make you do a bunch of crazy-ass drills and if it doesn't work, then you're just no good.'"

At the higher level, Tony showcased a gift for striking out batters. Unfortunately, he also surrendered lots of hits.[26] At one point, after falling out of the starting rotation, he was removed from the Sun Devils' traveling roster. That first year in Tempe, he allowed 71 hits in 50 innings. A 4–1 record belied his 7.02 ERA.

Early the next season, he and a few teammates were essentially considered alternates. They wouldn't even participate in practice, instead arriving afterward to play catch and then go home. Tony strongly considered asking Murphy to redshirt him for the season so that he could transfer to a Division-II school, where he'd actually pitch. He contemplated the idea and spoke with his dad about it, but fortunately he never quite got there.

"What did I do at that point? I was like, 'Okay, so here's what we're gonna do: We're gonna go start lifting heavy again. We're gonna try to get bigger, try to get stronger, and we're gonna start trying to throw as hard as humanly possible.' It was like, 'If I'm gonna go out in this game, I'm gonna go out on my terms. I'm gonna throw as hard as I possibly can until I blow out.'"

One night, he and the other practice players were tasked with throwing live batting practice to the team. "They're like, 'Just throw fastballs,'" said Tony. "I'm like, 'All right.'" Sick and tired of his current situation and carrying a boulder-sized chip on his shoulder, Tony unleashed his fury on his teammates. There was no chance he was going to groove meatballs down the middle, so he reared back and threw as hard as he could, alternating indiscriminately between four-seam fastballs and two-seamers and moving the ball on the inside and outside edges of the plate. "I've never been an overbearing power pitcher, but I had fuzz on it," he recalled. "I was just absolutely carving these guys up."

After he jammed teammate C.J. Retherford on one, the third baseman started yelling at him. Tony yelled back. Soon, they were cursing at each other. "And I just turn around. I'm like, 'Give me another ball.' And I see Murph and Esmay[27] just kinda looking at each other, just having one of those moments like, 'What the hell's happening right now?' And I just kept throwing as hard as I could for I don't know how many pitches. Then I ended up walking off the field."

Not long after, ASU was in Surprise, Arizona, for a weekend tournament. Tony had been pitching better. In a team meeting, Murphy singled him out, saying, "Something's got into Barnette," before asking him what changed. Oh, man, did Tony have an answer for his head coach!

"I do not know what hit me," he reflected years later, "but I was completely over it at that point. I had had enough, and I was just so mad that I said, 'I stopped giving a fuck. I just don't care.' I was like, 'I do not care what anybody in this room thinks of me anymore. I don't care what Murph thinks, I don't care what Esmay thinks,[28] Sferra. All the guys in this room right now, I do not care what any of you think of me anymore. I do not care.' And I just kinda sat down." A shocked Murphy mumbled something like "All right, well that's that then," and adjourned the meeting before it got any more awkward.

After the cathartic incident, Tony began to turn his performance around. "In hindsight, I had a moment of clarity 'cuz I walked out of that meeting without worrying if anybody was looking at me or caring what anybody was saying. It was just like I finally felt free of it." Given all the obstacles, he doesn't think "there was any reason I really should've made it out of Arizona State." Tapping into memories of how he did would help him escape the Toda rut in which he was so deeply mired.

There was another defining moment that came to mind. He'll never forget the time manager Clint Myers[29] wanted him to redshirt his freshman season at Central Arizona two and a half years before his breakthrough at Arizona State.

Months away from his nineteenth birthday, Tony arrived there motivated, itching to prove he'd been overlooked by Division-I schools. He started fall workouts with boundless energy and optimism. One day, his right knee gave out in practice. X-rays revealed a piece of bone had broken off the knee. Although the piece of bone had likely been dislodged years earlier, the orthopedic surgeon believed, he needed surgery to remove and reattach the problematic piece.

Following surgery, he rehabbed as hard as he could. It marked the first serious injury of his career, and he was determined not to let the setback derail his freshman season. Despite a valiant effort, Tony was falling behind the other pitchers. When it came time for cuts, Myers wanted him to redshirt. The move would've allowed the manager to use Tony's spot on another player, while preserving his freshman eligibility and deferring it by one year.

The proposed move made perfect sense from the manager's perspective, particularly if he wasn't going to be able to play much or effectively. But Tony already despised the idea the instant it came out of Myers's mouth.

Never shy, he was honest with his manager right away. "I said, 'I don't want to get redshirted. I do not want to. I need to play, and I'm gonna play.' It was one of those times where you kind of stand up for yourself. I remember me and him stared at each other for a good, like, thirty seconds." When the stare down concluded, Myers told Tony to discuss the matter with pitching coach Eric Doble. Whatever decision those two came to, Myers said, he would support.

The conversation with Doble went much the same way, although quite a bit quicker. "Do you want to redshirt?" Doble asked. "Absolutely fucking not," an adamant Tony replied. "All right. You're not gonna redshirt then. I'll use you. I'll need you." His resistance to redshirting paid off in a significant way. Myers eased him in by way of a limited bullpen role. Tony performed so well that he soon found himself excelling as a key member of the starting rotation.

Thus, in the unforgiving Toda heat, away from the glare of the media and the attention of thousands of cheering Tokyoites, Tony relearned to take pride in the daily grind. He was struggling mightily, to be sure, but he reminded himself of the two biggest times he overcame adversity. Each time, while he had to put forth the requisite physical work, the beginning of a seismic turnaround came from a steadfast refusal to back down from an imposing challenge. On each occasion, Tony's attitude was the first and most important tool in his arsenal. It was at this point in which he vowed to do everything in his power to regain control of his professional baseball career.

Precisely three weeks after his last *ichi-gun* appearance, Tony was given another opportunity to start. The rust clearly showed. To make matters worse, he had a special audience there to witness it. Phil Barnette, with wife Susanna and her son, Jesse Dunbar, had flown in to watch his son pitch in Japan for the first time.

Jesse had been an only child when his mom married Phil, instantly inheriting three older brothers at the age of five (Tony was eight). While differing interests largely kept Jesse and Tony from spending quality time together as kids, on that trip, he could tell something was bothering Tony. According to Jesse, "I don't think he directly said that, but he did feel uncomfortable because everything is so different from what he's used to. I think he had a little bit of culture shock."

Tony's poor pitching and "culture shock" notwithstanding, Jesse loved the weeklong trip, his second time seeing Japan, despite not getting the opportunity to explore as much as he would have liked due to injuries limiting Phil's (knee) and Susanna's (back) mobility. Team responsibilities mostly kept Tony occupied, while Hillary showed her guests around and helped them navigate the Tokyo transit system that she had just learned herself. Other than a couple sightseeing adventures, Hillary accompanied the group at her apartment or their hotel, which were located a couple subway stations apart. One night, Tony joined them at an upscale Brazilian restaurant.

On the mound, Tony was locked in. He had to contend with the 2010 Tigers, which represented a Herculean task for most pitchers, let alone one fresh from the farm. While Yomiuri was easily NPB's most powerful offensive team, Hanshin had its most reliable hitters, topping all clubs with a .290 batting average.[30] If the Giants' historical dominance resembled that of the Yankees, the Tigers' paucity of championships coupled with their large and loyal fan base brought to mind the Cubs.[31]

Three Central League teams are located in the Kanto region, an urban metropolis that includes the Greater Tokyo area but also stretches from Saitama down south to Kanagawa and on its eastern end touches part of Chiba. They are the Tokyo teams, Yakult and rival Yomiuri, and Yokohama. Because the region is so densely populated and attracts workers from various parts of Japan, the other Central teams informally adopted their own Kanto home stadiums. Specifically, the Tigers had long considered Yakult's Jingu Stadium to be their home away from home, and Friday night was no exception with Hanshin coming to town playing stellar baseball.

"All I could hear were Tigers songs and chants," said Hillary, who sat with Phil, Susanna, and Jesse. She also remembered hordes of their fans banging together yellow thundersticks all night. Although Hillary and company were technically seated in home territory, the overflow Tigers faithful had spilled into their section. One boisterous Hanshin fan sat in front of them.

From one through nine, no one was an easy out, as Tony was quickly realizing. An all-too-common occurrence that nightmarish season, he got into trouble early. He opened the night with a walk. Following a sacrifice bunt, the next three batters singled. When all was said and done, seven earned runs were charged to Tony, including four from the opening frame. He failed to get through the third inning.

As Tony fell apart, his father was growing increasingly frustrated from his seat. "Phil kinda started yelling towards Tony," said Jesse, "and the man in front of us was looking back at Phil a little bit angrily. Phil started shouting louder at one point, and the guy hit his [thundersticks] harder and harder, and then Phil stormed off because he was so upset about how Tony was doing."

Batting third for Hanshin, Matt Murton was also playing his first season in Japan.[32] But his acclimation unfolded much more seamlessly, as he would go on to register a historic season. Batting .349 with 91 RBIs, the outfielder's 214-hit output would break a record set by twenty-year-old Ichiro Suzuki in 1994 when the legendary lefty compiled 210 hits and batted .385 for Orix.[33]

Boston's 2003 supplemental first-round pick had spent parts of five seasons with the Cubs, A's, and Rockies, most prominently as an everyday left fielder with Chicago in 2006. Seeing his playing time wane and growing dissatisfied with the up-and-down lifestyle of a minor league–major league tweener, Murton elected to take his game to Japan. Like Guiel and so many former big leaguers who made the same call, stability was the primary motivating factor.

In six seasons, the redheaded righty became a bona fide NPB legend by recording 1,020 hits. Ahead of 2016, at age thirty-four, he decided to try to return to the big leagues before it was too late and managed to hit .314 for the Triple-A Iowa Cubs. But with his skills dwindling, the Tigers' Toledo Mud Hens released him the following April. Before the next season, he retired to take a front-office job with the Cubs.

After the Hanshin shellacking, Tony was sent back down, the Friday night start a fleeting reprieve from the heat and the cramped hour-long train rides.

The next *ichi-gun* opportunity took another three weeks to materialize, and again went horribly. The fearsome Giants teed off, scoring seven runs off Tony, winning 14–8 in front of 44,748 observers.

Looking back, Tony divided his season into two distinct buckets: when he faced the Giants or Tigers and when he faced anyone else. Not one to make excuses, it wasn't good enough for him that he pitched fairly well against most other opponents. The nature of the NPB schedule necessitated playing teams within one's league, including Hanshin and Yomiuri, particularly often.

Six of his 15 NPB starts (40 percent) came against Hanshin or Yomiuri. In those starts, his performance suffered remarkably, as he allowed 35 runs in 25.1 innings for a 12.43 ERA. Over the remaining appearances, including the relief stint against Rakuten, he posted a 3.31 ERA in twice as many innings. All nine home runs Tony allowed were slugged by Hanshin or Yomiuri, too.

The entire months of June and July found him shuttling back and forth between Toda and the *ichi-gun* level. Finally, in August, he made four consecutive *ichi-gun* starts. Three came against a non-Hanshin, non-Yomiuri opponent, and Tony finished the season with a sub-6.00 ERA by the thinnest of margins at 5.99.

The season typically runs until early October, but Tony was no longer needed at the *ichi-gun* level after August 22. The Swallows had no hope of reaching the playoffs, so they decided to lean on their younger players. As a result, he spent the rest of August and much of September in Toda. A week and a half before the regular season ended, he was allowed to return to the United States, where Hillary was waiting for him.[34]

"Once they told me my season was done, I packed my bags and got home as fast as I could," he said. Virtually all signs pointed to Tony's Japanese experience as a one-season failure.

Notes

[1]   A couple months after her mid-May arrival, Hillary reset the ninety-day visa timeline by taking a trip to Honolulu, where she met her mom, Kim, for a short vacation. It was Hillary's first time visiting Hawaii.

[2]   Between 2001 and 2019, more than 10 percent of MLB managers stepped down or were fired during a season. During the same period, either was true of less than 4 percent of NPB managers. But in-season managerial moves were becoming less rare, as Takada's resignation marked the third consecutive year an NPB manager resigned midseason.

[3]   Between 1985 and 1988, Takada's Nippon-Ham Fighters won 235 games, lost 255, and tied 30 times. In two-plus seasons managing the Swallows, Takada's winning percentage was slightly worse, with 150 wins, 178 losses, and six ties.

[4]   Once the BayStars were bought by the Software company DeNA following the 2011 season, the organization adopted the Yokohama DeNA (pronounced like DNA) BayStars as its name.

[5]   Over Tony's previous seven starts, he went 0-4 with three no-decisions.

[6]   Thus, only 25 can be used, and the inactives aren't allowed in the dugout. Two of the inactive spots have typically been reserved for the starting pitchers from the previous and following games. Ahead of the 2019 season, NPB increased the number of inactive spots to four and expanded the *ichi-gun* rosters to 29.

[7]   However, a few clubs do have a *san-gun* ("third-troop") team, which plays against amateur and unaffiliated minor-league teams. In 2023, the Hawks added a *yon-gun* (fourth-tier) team.

[8]   The 2010 season was the last for the Shonan Searex, Yokohama's *ni-gun* team since 2000. Orix's *ni-gun* affiliate was the Surpass Kobe for nine seasons through 2008.

[9]   Short for the East Japan Railway Company

[10] Toda played morning and afternoon games, sometimes as early as 10 a.m.

[11] For a morning game, he had to leave home by 7 a.m. Typically, he arrived back by 3 or 4. Some days, Guiel was lucky to return by 1. On rare occasions, he played the entire game, did a full workout, and received full treatment, not getting home until as late as 5.

[12] Most notably, Gilmour officiated two memorable games: A contest between the Soviet Red Army and the Philadelphia Flyers in 1976, and the quirky Game 3 of the Stanley Cup Finals the preceding year, which featured heavy fog and a Buffalo Sabres player killing a live bat with his stick.

[13] At the time of the accident, Gilmour was a teenager in the New York Rangers organization. He was also a skilled baseball player.

[14] Prolific left-handed slugger Matt Stairs played for the NBI a few years earlier.

[15] Guiel's dad's side of the family bought and sold houses and multifamily apartment buildings.

[16] Kwantlen, like all other schools that NBI players attend, did not field its own baseball team.

[17] The Angels originally offered a $5,000 signing bonus shortly after Guiel was drafted. According to Guiel's recollection, the following May, the offer was increased to approximately $35,000.

[18] The catcher was Angelo Encarnación, who stole two bases and recorded seven hits in 17 at-bats, but after 1997 he never again appeared in the big leagues.

[19] Guiel's shoulder never bothered him the rest of his career.

[20] After returning to his apartment in the early-morning hours, Guiel slept for a few hours before he had to pick up his final paycheck from the team office and head to the airport.

[21] Over Guiel's first six MLB starts, he recorded 10 RBIs and reached base on 15 of 28 plate appearances.

[22] During Guiel's first three series, he went 3-for-24 with 11 strikeouts and no RBIs. By the 20-game mark, he was batting .185 with 22 strikeouts and just five RBIs.

[23] D'Antona's Toda experience overlapped with Tony's the final three weeks of July, whereas AG and Tony were both there from late August through the first half of September. Naturally, Tony would cross paths with them at the facilities, allowing him not to be the only gaijin around.

[24] Sferra, a longtime assistant under Murphy, served as recruiting coordinator, as well as outfield and first-base coach. His son, J.J., was also a starting outfielder on the team.

[25] Krawczyk lasted only one season and quit coaching after that. Jeff Mousser took over as pitching coach.

[26] No teammate logging at least 20 innings allowed more hits per inning than Tony.

[27] Tim Esmay was the team's bench and third-base coach. Ultimately, he took over the head-coaching job when scandal-plagued Murphy was forced out ahead of the 2010 season. Beginning with the 2024 season, Murphy serves at the manager of the Milwaukee Brewers.

[28] After the episode, Esmay pulled Tony aside to ask if he was okay and if they were okay. Tony apologized, assuring that he had nothing against Esmay and that the coach just got caught in the "crosshairs."

[29] Immediately before leading the baseball team as head coach, Myers coached Central Arizona's softball squad. Once his coaching tenure in Coolidge ended, he opted to return to coaching softball and in Year 3, 2008, led Arizona State to a national title. They won again in 2011, and

in 2016 Myers's Auburn Tigers fell one win short of what would've marked his third Division I national championship. A season later, he resigned amid scandal.

30   The other five Central League teams held averages between .255 and .268 for the season.

31   Another similarity between the teams: like the Curse of the Billy Goat allegedly plagued the Cubs from 1945 until 2016, the Curse of the Colonel allegedly derailed the Tigers' championship hopes between their first title in 1985 and their curse-breaking 2023 championship.

32   Eleven months earlier, while both players were in Triple A, Murton was the player who retrieved Tony's double off the right-field wall.

33   Since, left-handed outfielder Shogo Akiyama broke Murton's single-season hits record, notching 216 in 2015 for the Seibu Lions. Akiyama later played two subpar seasons for the Cincinnati Reds before returning to Japan in 2022. But in the process, he made history as the first Reds player to be born in Japan.

34   Nearly three weeks earlier, Hillary had returned to Arizona.

CHAPTER SIX
GOODBYE, JAPAN?

That's pretty disheartening when your entire life you've strived to be a professional athlete, and then one day it's just taken away from you. Just blink of an eye, just gone.

"The writing was on the wall," said Tony. "Numbers-wise, I didn't live up to the expectations that I had or that the team had for me. My impending release was going to happen. It was just a matter of when." As expected, a few weeks after he returned to Arizona, his agent relayed that the Swallows would not be re-signing him after his rocky 2010 campaign.

To add injury to insult, over the season's last three months, he was hampered by a sharp pain in his right foot. On the morning of a scheduled start in Hokkaido, he got up and could barely stand on it. Without even taking an X-ray, the team doctor curiously diagnosed him with gout, despite the lack of any of the condition's most common risk factors.

A frustrated Tony looked back on the episode: "God. Unbelievable. These freaking doctors, they take my blood, they take all this stuff. All my levels come back normal, and they're like, 'Oh, well, it looks like gout. All these tests, they don't say it's gout, but I'm just gonna give you gout medicine. Good luck.'"

The pills didn't work in the slightest, although anti-inflammatory drugs served as a temporary solution. Insoles also mitigated the pain, as he played through the injury the remainder of the season without a diagnosis that made any sense. As soon as Tony saw a podiatrist in Arizona, the medical mystery was solved. He had a hairline fracture on the bottom of his foot and was advised to stay off it as much as possible while it healed. According to Tony, he's never had a related problem since.

Writer Rob Smaal, who witnessed his own Japanese medical misdiagnosis, as well as those of others, argued Japan has a long way to go in this area: "It's bizarre [for] a country with such high technological standards and advanced technology. If any big-name Japanese player pulls a knee or something, it's right on a plane over to the US basically."

Although Aaron Guiel acknowledged that medical care in Japan was "top-quality," he strongly preferred to see an American specialist for anything other than minor ailments. "We trust the doctors in the States just a little bit more," he admitted. Accordingly, the Swallows allow their gaijin to seek second opinions there. "Elbow, shoulder, back, we're gonna go where we trust because if the surgeries don't go well, our careers are pretty much over." Jim Allen, a baseball writer who formerly wrote columns for the *Daily Yomiuri*, attributes the disparity in care more to NPB teams cutting costs than the medical technology lagging behind in any real way.

While Tony was struggling with his foot and overall pitching, Yakult was playing exceedingly well. Team performance under Shigeru Takada and Junji Ogawa was like night and day. Following Ogawa's May promotion, the Swallows won 59 of their last 98 games, managing to finish above .500 at 72–68–4. He presided over four winning streaks of five games or more, including an August run of ten consecutive victories.

Just days after Yakult's final game, the Swallows rewarded him with a two-year, ¥70 million contract to stay on as manager. Ogawa reminded Guiel of his first skipper in Japan, player-manager Atsuya Furuta. "[Ogawa] was very personable. It was surprising how much he seemed to be aware of our situation. He knew if our family was at the game. He knew our mannerisms. He was self-confident, but yet he didn't put up any wall. He just seemed like a real guy, and he was easy to be around."

"A lot of the younger players, they were able to play loose and free," added Guiel, "because they didn't feel like they were going to be scrutinized or looked too closely upon after a bad game. I think sometimes when you become a coach and a manager, you do forget how hard this game is. Furuta and Ogawa-san didn't forget."

Ogawa didn't physically move into the manager's office until a couple weeks after the season concluded, instead working out of the coaches' locker room for nearly five months. The unique setup may have aided communication with his coaches, though after the move he told reporters his open-door philosophy would remain in place.

The midseason turnaround must also be credited to the front office's acquisition of American first baseman Josh Whitesell. From the day he joined the Swallows through the end of the season, they compiled a .636 winning percentage (48–27–2).

On June 3, he batted cleanup for the Syracuse Chiefs in Buffalo, New York.[1] The very next week, he was in Japan, and two weeks after that, he was playing left field at Jingu, "with the fans cheering behind me, drums blasting, and I was looking around like, 'Wow, this is interesting. This is like a European soccer game atmosphere kind of thing.'"

Back in 2003, Montreal selected the six-foot-three slugger in the sixth round out of Loyola Marymount University. The burly lefty would not appear in the majors until five years later as a September call-up for the first-place Diamondbacks. The Dodgers overtook Arizona for the NL West crown, as Whitesell, who had been dominating Triple A,[2] garnered just one start and nine plate appearances.

The following season, he was promoted from Triple A and demoted back down three times. The erratic playing time, Whitesell believes, featured prominently in his failure to hold on to a major-league spot: "I'm a timing and rhythm kinda hitter that relies on getting consistent at-bats and feeling comfortable at the plate. When I'm not getting those consistent at-bats, I'm not gonna be able to get you the same performance." Over 108 big-league at-bats in 2009, he batted .194 and slugged .287, a far cry from his production as a minor-league power hitter.

In July, Whitesell's wife, Melissa, had given birth to fraternal twins, a girl and a boy. This led the first-time father to begin seriously exploring a move to Japan, a career route he'd heard mentioned by many a minor-league teammate over the years. "I needed to feed my family," he said. "The money was 100 percent the initial motivating factor." So, after the season, he switched agents expressly because he wanted a representative with strong ties in Japan. Arizona moved on from Whitesell, but by the end of the calendar year, the Nationals had signed him to a minor-league deal. NPB was still an attractive option while he continued his pursuit of a big-league job.

Beginning the season in Triple-A stadiums in Syracuse, Moosic, and Allentown, he was not fond of the East Coast weather. Having grown up in North Carolina and Southern California, he liked it much warmer. Though the cold wouldn't fade for another few weeks, his offense began to heat up as April drew to a close. By the time Yakult acquired him, he was batting better than .300 with respectable power. Behind the scenes, of course, his agent had been working on securing his departure.

Once Whitesell arrived, he started settling in to his team-supplied apartment, in the same complex as closer Chang-Yong Lim. Because he flew in on a tourist visa, he couldn't participate in official team activities until he obtained a work visa, which required flying to South Korea. In the meantime, he did individual workouts, attended a couple games, and watched more games on TV to acclimate himself to NPB and its teams. Once he had his work visa, he began practicing.

Feeling a sense of urgency to inject Whitesell into the heart of their batting order, the Swallows decided to give their newest addition a *ni-gun* start. But just one. Essentially a dry run and an opportunity to shake off the proverbial dust that could have accumulated from not playing any games the past three weeks, he batted leadoff. After five plate appearances with Toda, he was deemed ready to join the *ichi-gun* Swallows.

Although Whitesell, once a hard-throwing pitcher, tore his labrum as a college freshman and subsequently had to resort to a sidearm throwing motion in the field, Yakult put him in the outfield for his first two NPB appearances. Unfortunately, the injury had rendered him a subpar out- fielder. After experimenting for those games and one other,[3] the organiza- tion exclusively started him at first base or DH, the only places he played throughout his minor-league career.

Following the *ni-gun* tune-up, he was back in action in Tokyo at 2 p.m. the next day. In his inaugural at-bat, a ground out stranded run- ners on the corners. However, he made sure, in the eighth, to memorably introduce himself to the Jingu fans by pulling a slider into the seats. The solo homer came two batters after Yasushi Iihara's home run transformed a 2–1 Swallows deficit into a 3–2 lead. The next inning, Lim retired Hanshin 1-2-3 to secure the victory.

Naturally, the home-run boys were honored as Heroes of the Game. Wisely, Iihara left the presentation a tick early to avoid the towel full of shaving cream headed for Whitesell's face. Courtesy of Jamie D'Antona, Whitesell now had shaving cream all over, yet he laughed, quickly wiped his face, and continued with the interview.

For the 2010 Swallows, Whitesell amassed a stellar slash line of .309/.399/.591 in 68 games.[4] Although he didn't play enough games to qualify for various league awards,[5] his OPS (on-base + slugging) ranked second only to Central League MVP Kazuhiro Wada. Meanwhile, just four hitters in either league posted a better slugging percentage.

A natural hitter, Whitesell did not have to alter his approach much to adjust to the Japanese game. A month and a half in, he confidently told the *Daily Yomiuri*'s John E. Gibson, "It's just doing what you know how to do. I've been swinging a bat since I was five years old, so it's the same game. You know the nuances are different, but just go out and take good at-bats, and when you get good pitches to hit, don't miss."

The only real adjustment, he said later, was learning the "biased" gaijin strike zone, which notoriously expanded for foreign batters and shrunk for foreign pitchers. It was initially so maddening because Whitesell had long prided himself on his knowledge of the strike zone as evidenced by his elite walk rate throughout his career. But because he had such strong plate vision and discipline, the learning curve was not steep and he walked regularly.

Despite joining Yakult in late June and playing fewer than half of its games, he tied for second with 15 home runs, just one shy of the team lead. Particularly helpful was Whitesell's suddenly seamless ability to hit fellow lefties.[6] As a pro, he had never excelled to such an extent against left-handed pitching.[7]

Although Tony was sent to Toda the day of Whitesell's NPB debut and wouldn't return for weeks before ultimately being demoted for good in late August, he appreciated having him in Tokyo. They'd played together in Reno the previous year and considered each other good friends. One season earlier, 2008, saw a Whitesell-D'Antona pairing tear it up at the Triple-A level for the Tucson Sidewinders. When Yakult acquired Whitesell, D'Antona was struggling at the plate[8] while continuing to battle chronic knee problems.

D'Antona rarely started in July or August since Whitesell had become the superior option at first base. The two Americans shared an agent, creating somewhat of an awkward situation. With only four gaijin spots per team in a league without a DH, they played the same position. Essentially, Whitesell took D'Antona's spot. For their part, both players swear there was never any animosity. When Whitesell endured a challenging September, D'Antona garnered some starts, although given Whitesell's overall output and the state of D'Antona's knees, Yakult was happy to move on from D'Antona at season's end. For his efforts, Whitesell earned upward of $400,000 and was re-signed for one year and $1.1 million plus incentives.

Conversely, no case could be made that Tony played any role in the club's turnaround. Yakult planned to cut ties with him. He had no problems with this given the way the season transpired. What scared him most was the lack of interest from major-league organizations.

When he received word that he wasn't going to be retained by the Swallows, he started making calls. He reached out to former teammates and coaches from the minors, and he contacted executives from several organizations, including the Diamondbacks. Those calls were feelers. So early in the offseason, before the annual winter meetings, everyone said they'd get back to him as soon as they knew more. But once they did, not a single team expressed interest.

"All the pictures from that offseason," said Hillary, "he just looks so sad, and he has these big, dark circles under his eyes. It just sucked the life right out of him." Soon after they heard from Yakult, Hillary and Tony got a dog. At that point, they figured he'd be playing, if anywhere, in the United States the next season. Therefore, it would be much easier to transport a dog to their next destination.

Hillary adopted Po, an unknown type of pit bull mix, from a Phoenix animal shelter. "He was my first little baby," said Hillary. According to Tony, Po was "definitely Hillary's dog" from the start,[9] but he supplied enough love to go around. Fittingly, the dog named after Jacopo, the main character's most loyal friend in *The Count of Monte Cristo*,[10] managed to lighten Tony's emotional burden to a certain extent.

"That's what pets are for, man," he said. "They're friends, and they don't say anything. You can sit there and be a miserable SOB, and they're gonna still hang out with ya. Nobody wants to hang out with you when you're down in the dumps and all that. But dogs and cats, they'll hang out. They don't care."

Po was a good dog, but existential human problems persisted. For two and a half months, Tony increasingly worried about his uncertain future. He didn't know if he would have to play independent baseball. A dreaded and often desperate destination for professional baseball players, independent teams are unaffiliated with major-league organizations, and they are considered to yield a lower level of play than their minor-league counterparts. Even worse, he wondered if he would have to quit baseball entirely.

"It was really hard to deal with mentally, just because the only thing I'd done was play baseball throughout my life," said Tony. "I had worked random offseason jobs just to pay rent and pay the bills, but when you're an athlete and you've done nothing but basically play baseball your entire life, there's that transition period of moving into the real world and getting a real job. That's pretty disheartening when your entire life you've strived to be a professional athlete, and then one day it's just taken away from you. Just blink of an eye, just gone. And then you have to mentally prepare yourself to work a desk job or do whatever you're going to do for the rest of your life."

Well before he proudly informed his fifth-grade teacher, he envisioned himself as a professional athlete. Not only did "pro athlete" still embody Tony's self-image, but also he remained confident that he had a number of productive years left in the tank. Still, whether any team was going to come to the same conclusion was an open question.

Adding to his anxiety, he had just purchased a house in Litchfield Park, Arizona, a small city 20 miles northwest of Phoenix. The 3,200-square-footer on a one-and-a-half-acre lot came with a swimming pool, an essential in the scorching Arizona desert. "It added in a lot more stress to the picture," said Tony. "I'm sitting there, saying, 'Great. Now I've got a mortgage and no job.'"

Aside from the understandable second thoughts after such a sizable transaction, losing the house was never regarded as a legitimate possibility. Given the $500,000 Tony made in 2010, neither he nor Hillary was worried about their ability to afford house payments for the foreseeable future. "We bought that house knowing that if he never played baseball again, we would be able to afford it," said Hillary. "We're very cautious that way."

The house-hunting process began from Japan thanks to an online portal their realtor friend set up. From there, they compiled a list of suitable options. While Tony was toiling away at the facilities in Toda, Hillary's Arizona visit sold them on a particular house.

She called right away. "Tony, this is the house. This is the one. This is perfect." He'd never stepped foot inside the house but had seen pictures of every detail, and he trusted Hillary. Amid a rush of excitement and a handful of competing offers, he gave Hillary the go-ahead to sign on the dotted line. "We both felt that this was the house that we're probably going to die in," he said. By mid-October, they moved into their new digs.

For a month, Tony took a break from training to decompress. It had been a draining season in Japan, both physically and mentally. "I tried to relax as much as I could," he said, "and just kind of almost reflect on the season and what had gone wrong. But I totally hadn't written myself off as a baseball player. I continued working out. I continued my throwing programs and stuff of that nature, just in case the next opportunity were to present itself."

Every offseason, dating back to his Arizona State days, Tony trained at the then–Fischer Institute of Physical Therapy and Performance in Phoenix. The world-class, state-of-the-art facility, founded by Brett and Stephanie Fischer in 1997, long catered to professional baseball and football players. For years, three-time Cy Young winner and eight-time All-Star Max Scherzer was the gym's most notable frequent visitor. NFL defensive backs Tyrann Mathieu and Darrelle Revis also trained there.[11] Hall of Famer Randy Johnson rehabbed at Fischer to bounce back from an injury-plagued 1996. The following season, teenage Tony watched as "the Big Unit" registered 213 innings and a second-place Cy Young finish for his beloved Mariners.

There, Tony followed a regimen designed specifically for him. Usually lifting five days per week, he'd do legs one day, followed by an upper-body day before resting on Day 3. Then, the cycle repeated. Critically important for him, the facilities included an indoor pitching mound.

Even though Chris Sinacori, one of the men who recruited Tony to ASU, never formally got to coach him, the former pitcher[12] routinely stopped by Fischer during Tony's postcollegiate offseasons. There, he made quite a mark on Tony, who dubbed Sinacori "probably one of the most knowledgeable pitching coaches I've ever encountered in my life." He especially appreciated Sinacori's ever-present positivity and his ability to "keep stuff simple."

Throughout his adult life, Tony has understood the importance of taking care of his body ahead of the long grind of a baseball season. "I just want to get a good base for the rest of the season," he said, "because as the season goes down, with every pitch you throw, with every day that you run, your body's going to break down little by little. I try to get as strong as I can in spring training and obviously in the offseason training so that I can try to maintain that as long as I can through the season, so that my body doesn't break down on me."

By mid-December, he was resigned to the likelihood that he would be playing in an independent league the following season. Stateside interest was nonexistent, yet he wasn't ready for his baseball career to end.

A week before Christmas, Tony received a phone call from his agent that was just as perplexing as it was promising. According to Don Nomura, the Swallows were considering a few scenarios in which they would bring back his client for another season. He advised patience while he lobbied Yakult.

A few days after Christmas, Nomura delivered a gift via another call, during which the possible good news was cemented: The Swallows indeed agreed to re-sign him. After a dreadful season that included multiple demotions to the minors, Tony would be given another chance by the same team for which he struggled mightily. When Nomura told him, he reacted with excitement, awe, and confusion all wrapped up into one: "Holy shit. What? Why?"

He was then informed that his annual salary would be cut in half, a fact that didn't bother him one bit. His baseball career was resurrected from the dead that night. That was all that mattered. Of his substantial pay cut, he even felt lucky, explaining, "At that time, they didn't need to know that teams in the States had already turned me down. Otherwise, they would have paid me a lot less." Despite the reduced pay, Yakult included a vesting option, as it did in the 2010 contract, which would allow Tony to return for 2012 provided his 2011 performance meet certain statistical goals.

Tony believed Yakult's early-season managerial change factored heavily in producing the opportunity: "I think he [Ogawa] saw that there were flashes of greatness. I showed that there was a lot of good in me. It's just there were times where I kind of imploded. So I think he took a chance on me, thinking that he saw something that the other manager didn't see."

Tony's professionalism and maturity amid a difficult individual season may have also been instrumental, according to veteran mentor and friend Guiel. "When he was a starter and he had some failures, I thought he carried himself very well," he said. "I think those are the key reasons why that door stayed open, whereas a lot of other foreigners, that door closes."

It was later revealed that the second chance—with Yakult and in Japan—nearly did not come to fruition. While Swallows decision-makers evidently saw something in him, it also took a notable Korean pitcher, Young-soo Bae, failing his physical to give Tony the opportunity to fill one of the team's four coveted gaijin slots. At the time, South Korean newspaper *JoongAng Ilbo* reported that Bae was a Hepatitis B carrier and that an elbow surgery he needed in 2007 was denied when blood tests on his liver concerned doctors.[13]

As 2011 approached, Tony was twenty-seven and had just endured what seemed like years of stress amid myriad ups and downs. Of course, all the craziness—from the initial Japanese contact to the decision to play there to the massive on- and off-field challenges to the purchasing of the Arizona house to his Swallows release to his eventual and improbable re-signing—had happened in thirteen months' time, yet 2010 was ending with optimism and hope.

He felt assured in his ability to bounce back from his rookie struggles in Japan. Most Americans who had struggled like that had not previously been asked back. He was grateful for the chance to return and firmly believed all the difficult times could be drawn upon as fuel to make him stronger, better.

A new year and a new season awaited as he continued his training in Arizona. In just about a month, he would be flying back to Tokyo in an effort to make 2010 a distant memory.

Notes

[1]   A twenty-one-year-old Stephen Strasburg earned the win for the Chiefs that day. Five nights later, he'd make his major-league debut, beating the Pirates and striking out 14 over seven innings.

[2]   Whitesell batted .328/.425/.568 for Tucson and ranked second in the PCL with 110 RBIs in 127 games.

[3]   It was a July 11 tilt against Chunichi. Additionally, on July 4, Whitesell moved from first base to left field for the game's final inning to accommodate a teammate who pinch-hit and remained in to play first.

[4]   Whitesell's numbers would have looked even better if not for an uncharacteristically poor September. He was slashing .346/.451/.679 through the end of August but hit just .190 with seven RBIs in 17 September starts.

[5]   To qualify, one needs 3.1 plate appearances per team game. Therefore, Whitesell's 268 plate appearances fell well short of the requisite 446.

6   Against lefties in 2010, Whitesell batted .371 and slugged .597 in 74 plate appearances. Whitesell's theory as to why? Japanese left-handers tend to throw more over the top than their American counterparts. "When the arm angle's coming from a little bit higher slot," he said, "it de-emphasizes the difference between facing a righty and a lefty."

7   As a minor leaguer, Whitesell held his own against lefties with .278 batting and .436 slugging, but he undoubtedly was superior against right-handed pitching with respective averages of .302 and .530.

8   D'Antona was batting .219 and coming off a month of May in which he drove in just six runs out of the cleanup spot.

9   According to Tony, Po would cling to Hillary and "lose his mind trying to find her" if she left. Other than Hillary, Po wouldn't allow anyone to walk him.

10   *The Count of Monte Cristo* is one of Tony's favorite books and movies.

11   Every year, the institute also offered a pre–NFL Combine training camp for prospects. Ahead of the 2014 draft, in which the Raiders would select Khalil Mack fifth overall, Tony crossed paths with the talented linebacker at Fischer but didn't yet know who he was.

12   Sinacori, a six-foot-four right-hander, never got past the High-A level and quit playing the game by twenty-six.

13   When the Swallows deal fell through, Bae returned to South Korea, where he pitched through the 2019 season. Three days after winning his eighth KBO championship, his first with the Doosan Bears, Bae announced his retirement at the age of thirty-eight.

CHAPTER SEVEN
MARCH 11, 2011

I felt like the entire world just started shaking.

"It was a normal day," Tony wrote on his blog,[1] in reference to March 11, 2011, which began typically, unexceptionally. The Swallows were slated for a 1 p.m. exhibition contest in Yokohama. After breakfast, he grabbed his baseball bag and caught the train. Not scheduled to pitch, he squeezed in a throwing session shortly after the game started. Then, he went into the training room to stretch before icing his right arm. He subsequently changed clothes and got in some cardio and lifting. To cap off his workday, he hopped in the shower. "Everything was pointing toward a great day," he wrote.

In the middle of Tony's shower, relief pitcher Kenichi Matsuoka opened the door and attempted to communicate. Matsuoka, whose phone had just sounded an earthquake warning, tried to pass the message along but spoke virtually no English. "He's looking at me," said Tony, "trying to find the words to say, but he couldn't, and then he just started motioning his hand back and forth. And I'm like, 'Okay. What's that mean?' And the next thing you know, boom, the room started shaking very, very much."

He had to get out of the shower and to a much safer place. "I just kind of freeze," he said. "I'm almost riding it out." Upon turning off the water, he slowly and gingerly left the shower. By this time, Go Fujisawa, who had been multitasking—getting in touch with his girlfriend[2] while looking for Tony—located him. Given the ongoing shaking that showed no sign of abating any time soon,[3] Go feared the building might collapse. With urgency, he told Tony, "Get some clothes on! Get out of here!"

With his eyes fixed on the ceiling, Tony obeyed, grabbing the closest clothes he could find, which included Josh Whitesell's shorts.[4] Living in Japan most of his life, Go had experienced a number of earthquakes. Instantly, he knew this one was markedly different. When it hit, "I felt like the entire world just started shaking or something," said Go, who had been in the locker room socializing with pitcher Kyohei Muranaka. "I have never experienced those kind of shakes from the first moment."

When the earthquake was first felt in Yokohama, at 2:46 p.m., six innings had been completed. The Swallows led 3–1, Shingo Kawabata stood at the plate, and Aaron Guiel waited on deck. Before the inning could begin, Guiel heard the word *jishin* uttered by a radio announcer. He knew it meant "earthquake" and braced himself. Seconds later, the shaking commenced and the game was halted immediately, as Guiel walked to home plate and then moved toward the pitcher's mound, where players, staff from both teams, and media members began to congregate. Once Tony was clothed, he ran to the middle of the field, joining the others.

With his cell phone, Tony called his apartment complex's front desk, asking them to notify Hillary that he was okay and would be back as soon as he could.[5] Guiel reached his wife through Skype, briefly describing the developing situation and asking her to tell their kids that he was safe. He passed around his phone in case any teammates needed it to reach their loved ones. Earlier, when Go was able to connect with his girlfriend who was at work, he had one simple message for her: "Go back home as soon as possible. Stay there. Do not move."

Hillary wasn't home, about ten minutes away, walking down Omotesandō Street, which overlaps both Minato and Shibuya. It's a popular shopping area that houses various high-end fashion stores and is lined with beautiful, grand zelkova trees. On a Friday afternoon, it was packed with people. Initially, she thought the earthquake was no big deal, but then it "got stronger and stronger and stronger."

Then, she observed all the reactions around her. "What I realized about earthquakes in Tokyo is that people just go about their business, and nobody really seems alarmed by them. So when that big one hit and people around me were screaming and panicking, freaking out, then I realized it was probably much bigger than usual for them." To keep from falling over, she grabbed on to a light pole. Once the shaking stopped, a phoneless Hillary ran home to get in touch with Tony.

At the apartment, all the phone lines were down. Just as Hillary began to craft a Skype message for Tony, there was a knock at her door. All residents were being advised to leave their apartments and go to the lobby. There, an employee relayed Tony's earlier message, calming Hillary's nerves substantially. Still, she watched the chaotic TV footage and couldn't help but worry.

"I'm watching these waves sweep over the land with fire and cars, taking everything with it, and it was all in Japanese so I can't really tell where the footage is coming from," said Hillary. She knew Tony was playing on the coast, which was unsettling. Fortunately, he was south of Tokyo and the tsunami was affecting northern Japan, a fact Hillary didn't learn until moments later. "It was still horrifying to watch."

While the teams, reporters, and stadium staff stood on the field, the fans[6] remained in their seats as instructed. At 3:03, the game was officially canceled. Then, at 3:08, twenty-two minutes after the initial earthquake, an aftershock of 7.4 magnitude rocked the stadium, causing the stands and light towers to sway from side to side. "I think that made people more afraid," Yakult's manager said later that day. Wherever possible, fans clung to nearby railings. Seven minutes later, an aftershock shook the bleachers again, this time registering a 7.9. Stadium crew had already begun to visit the crowd section by section in an effort to facilitate the fans' transfer from their seats to the outfield, where they'd be safer. Meanwhile, other workers were erecting barriers to cordon the teams off from everyone else. By 3:22, the first fan reached the field.

At 3:26, the third large aftershock struck at 7.7 magnitude. Fortunately, Yokohama Stadium was a designated evacuation site because of its apparent safety in the case of disaster. What's more, the field was considered the safest part of the stadium. Soon, people from nearby who hadn't even attended the game were brought onto stadium grounds, on the exterior concourse, just inside the gates.

A few minutes into the initial quake, it was obvious no ordinary earthquake was occurring. Yet none of the Swallows knew that a deadly tsunami had been triggered and was on its way to Sendai. Tony remembered the vibe on the field in those early moments: "Everyone was nervously smiling, kind of joking around, just trying to ease the tension of the game being canceled and all that."

Then, an image of the main Japanese island, Honshu, appeared on the big-screen monitor beyond the fence in straightaway center field, and the players' moods grew more somber. The graphic used red, yellow, and green shading to indicate where scientists expected tsunami landfall and estimated how high the waves would reach in various areas. As soon as Go saw, he sought to comfort young pitcher Yoshinori Sato, who hailed from the Sendai region and still had family there.[7] A little later, the screen showed live images of small waves hitting a Japanese city. The tsunami and its catastrophically devastating effects were about to come into much clearer focus.

After an hour and a half on the field, everyone was permitted to leave. Yakult players and staff headed to the clubhouse to regroup and determine their next moves. As the players filtered into the locker room, there was a typical level of chatter.

Once the TVs were turned on and showed the tsunami hitting land, everyone fell silent. "You saw the fear and the scared looks on people's faces," said Tony, describing the scene. "Everyone's looking around like, 'Oh, my God,' because there's some guys that that's where they were born, that's where their families were. It was sheer hopelessness on their face. I couldn't imagine watching the water just ravage that city, knowing that that's where your house is, that's where your family is." From the clubhouse, Tony called Hillary—marking the first time they were able to speak since the earthquake hit hours earlier—and let her know that, while it could take a while, he'd be on his way home shortly, in a car with teammates.

David Watkins, the Brit who cofounded TokyoSwallows.com, was at a work meeting in Tokorozawa[8] when the quake rattled Japan. Meanwhile, his seventeen-month-old daughter, Emma, was home with her grandma. With his boss' permission, Watkins left to begin a half-hour bicycle ride back home. He stopped only a few times when the first couple aftershocks struck,[9] rushing home to his daughter.

Arriving just before 3:30, Watkins was none too pleased to see Emma sitting directly in front of a large, wobbling TV, observing an "apocalyptic kind of scene," his mother-in-law in the kitchen. He picked her up and turned off the television. He'd have to wait much longer to be reunited with his wife.

At the field, after the players were released, Go prioritized making sure the gaijin had a ride back to Tokyo, the logistics of his own transportation a distant second. For trips to Yokohama, the Japanese players typically drove their own cars. With the subway and most highways closed and taxis not in operation, the gaijin needed to find a teammate to take them back. Fortunately, second baseman Hiroyasu Tanaka was up to the task.

All gaijin except for Chang-Yong Lim,[10] including Tony, Wladimir Balentien, Whitesell, and Guiel, squeezed into Tanaka's car as he followed Shohei Tateyama. If the veteran pitcher had not known the area so well, Tony believes the group would not have made it out of Yokohama that night, like a chunk of his teammates. Because of the closures, a forty-five-minute drive took upward of three and a half hours. Along the way,

Tony texted pictures of damaged buildings. "That wait for him to get into Tokyo felt like forever," said Hillary.

Go didn't leave Yokohama until the next day. He'd been so preoccupied with helping the gaijin that he was "kind of stuck at the stadium" by the time he tried to leave. Fortunately, the chief athletic trainer, Katsuhiko Kobayashi, was still around and had a car. Joined by fellow interpreter Koji Kondo and the conditioning coach, Jun Takahashi, Go and the trainer attempted to drive back but abandoned the futile idea within an hour. Cutting their losses, they slept at JT's parents' house in a city near Yokohama.

Others, like Jason Coskrey of the *Japan Times*, wound up staying overnight in Yokohama Stadium due to the shutdown of the public transit system and the lack of available rooms in nearby hotels.[11] Walking home to Kichijoji[12] would have been an "insane undertaking" for Coskrey, who, along with more than a handful of fellow reporters, slept in the tiny, cramped stadium press box. Still, they had a roof over their heads, and BayStars staff brought tea and a snack, accommodating their guests as best they could.[13] Some lay across multiple chairs. Meanwhile, Coskrey leaned over a table, resting his head there. He didn't leave the stadium until the following morning when most of the trains were up and running again.

Sportswriter Rob Smaal had his own unnerving experience. Earlier in the day, he had lunch with Giants pitcher Seth Greisinger[14] before the two met Smaal's wife and two-year-old son, who were accompanied by family friends at a nearby park in Hiroo, in central Tokyo. Greisinger then headed to his sixteenth-floor apartment, where he'd experience the massive shaking. Smaal went a different direction to take the subway home. When he got to Ebisu station and began putting money into the machine, "the whole wall started moving." A week earlier, he'd had a hernia operation. He wondered whether the prescribed medication was causing him to hallucinate.

Smaal went back outside and, evidenced by swaying buildings and pieces of glass and metal falling from them, quickly realized the shaking earth was indeed an objective reality. He couldn't get ahold of anyone, and neither trains nor taxis were running. He needed a plan of attack. Miki, the family friend, and her husband, Patrick,[15] lived relatively close, so Smaal headed there. Nobody was home. He took a seat beside their front door, on a staircase, wondering, waiting. Within an hour, Yoko returned with Miki and the kids. A few hours later, Patrick came home. The Smaals would stay a couple nights until they could safely return home.

Watkins was having a decidedly more difficult time reuniting with his wife, whose phone died long before they could be together again. Near Tokyo Bay,[16] Hisae could see fires outside her work window. With virtually everything shut down, leaving such a densely populated area proved next to impossible. Early on, she was able to send several messages, the last of which saying she was working her way home and hoped someone could pick her up along the route.

Day turned to night, and Watkins had not heard from her since. He stayed awake, perusing Twitter and various news sites until she walked through the door around 5 a.m., allowing him to breathe a mammoth sigh of relief. "She was super-scared," he recounted. "She said she thought she might never see her family again." A kind colleague had driven Hisae home after she'd walked half of the way.

The following weekend, the Watkins family boarded a *Shinkansen* bullet train for Nara.[17] They sought to steal a few nights of sound sleep and to simplify Emma's feeding regimen, which had been complicated by rotating blackouts that periodically rendered it impossible to refrigerate breast milk.

Hordes of people were urgently trying to leave Japan, although plane flights were delayed due to the backlog created by the shutdowns of Narita and Haneda airports for much of Friday. And of course Sendai Airport was under water and nonoperational.[18] "The few days following," said Smaal, "it was chaos. It was crazy. There was a mass exodus. A lot of the expats were fleeing in droves, the guys working for banks. I don't blame them. People were worried. They didn't know what was going on. They weren't worried about buildings crumbling down on them or another earthquake or another tidal wave. They were worried about the radiation. There were all these talks about Chernobyl going on, right?"

Initially, Hillary pushed back on the idea of leaving alone. "Tony was talking about sending me home, and I was thinking, 'Well if you're staying here, I'm staying here,'" she said. Tony's agent called and made a convincing case for why it would be much easier to evacuate Tony, if it came to that, if she was already back home. Nomura's argument made sense, but she still leaned toward staying. Tony and Hillary decided that she would leave if and when nuclear sites were melting down.

As Tony was readying to leave for his first practice since the earthquake, news reports documented the rapidly worsening nuclear situation. Although a full-blown meltdown was not announced,[19] Hillary was ready to go. Right then and there, she went online, booked a flight that would be leaving Narita Airport that afternoon, and left her apartment with a single backpack of items. She arrived to see lines wrapping around the terminal. Two and half hours later, she was finally through the security checkpoint, grateful not to have missed her redeye Delta flight.

Nearly everyone on the flight was Japanese, including a number of families taking their young children out of harm's way. By Sunday morning, Hillary had arrived in Portland and alerted her family and friends through Facebook, writing in part, "I am so thankful to be on stable ground. Stay safe, Tony!" Until a broadcast reporter had asked her what it felt like to be on one of the first Portland-bound flights out of Japan, Hillary had no idea that was the case.[20]

Because he was recovering from back surgery and on the team's *ni-gun* roster, Yakult allowed Guiel to return to Vancouver. There, he received treatment and, more critically, spent time with his family,[21] using the opportunity to reassure them that everything would be okay. Meanwhile, Tony stayed.

In Washington, Phil endured many a sleepless night worrying about his son's safety. "If I had my choice, he would've been on the first flight out of there," he said. "From a dad, you don't care about baseball; it's a sport. I just wanted him to be safe. At that point in time, 'safe' was being Stateside, not over there in Japan. Obviously he had a bigger grasp on what was going on than I did, but you sit over here in America and you're watching the news and you see the pictures on TV and you hear the 'radiation' word, and you're saying, 'Son, just get the heck out of there.'" Of course, Hillary wanted to be with Tony too, although she planned on returning to Tokyo within a few weeks.

Notes

[1]   Tony's blog, curated by yours truly, appeared on Patrick Crawley's long-defunct DavisSportsDeli.com. The particular post was published within four days of the fateful events of March 11.

[2]   Now his wife

[3]   The earthquake would last five minutes and forty-six seconds.

[4]   The shorts fit well enough despite Tony's smaller stature.

[5]   Hillary did not yet have a cell phone in Japan.

[6]   Attendance for the exhibition game was measured at 3,756.

[7]   Sato later used a phone in the press box to call home. They were safe. Similarly, teammate Kazuhiro Hatakeyama learned his family was safe in Iwate.

[8]   A bedroom community where the Seibu Lions play

[9]   He saw people looking up. Following suit, he noticed "all the wires were wobbling about."

[10] Like his fellow gaijin, Lim lived in an Oakwood luxury apartment complex, but his was located in the heart of the Roppongi district, less than a couple miles from where the others lived in Aoyama. Pitcher Seth Greisinger lived there too.

[11] For dinner, Coskrey was able to walk a few minutes down Minato-Odori Street to McDonald's before returning to the stadium. McDonald's and nearby convenience stores remained open and appeared largely unaffected because power was never lost.

[12] While Kichijoji is part of Tokyo prefecture, it's located outside of Tokyo's twenty-three special wards.

[13] At least five Yokohama players stayed overnight, too. Elsewhere, some fans and evacuees also remined overnight.

[14] Greisinger wasn't traveling with the team because he'd started two days earlier. Unlike in MLB, it is standard protocol across NPB to limit a starting pitcher's travel time if he's not going to pitch on a particular trip, regular season included.

[15] Patrick is the same American who joined Tony and Rob at Legends to celebrate the pitcher's first NPB win.

[16] Tokyo Bay is the largest industrialized area in Japan. More specifically, she was working in Tamachi.

[17] Nara is located next to Kyoto and just under 300 miles southwest of Tokyo.

[18] Limited Sendai Airport services would resume on April 13, but domestic flights and most international flights would not return until late July and October, respectively.

[19] A nuclear meltdown had occurred, but that fact was not publicly divulged for another two-plus months. More on this later.

[20] Her interview appeared on the now-defunct Northwest Cable News channel, catching the attention of various people in Seattle who knew Tony.

[21] They had originally been scheduled to fly to Japan on March 20. After the events of March 11, they immediately canceled the flight.

CHAPTER EIGHT

GANBARE, NIPPON— BEGINNING TO HEAL

Oh, my goodness! This is totally like Chernobyl Mach 2! The whole sea is gonna be infected!

The triple disaster of March 11, 2011, encompassed a 9.1 earthquake that triggered a massive tsunami, which, together with the quake, led to the Level-7 Fukushima nuclear disaster, history's second-worst nuclear accident after Chernobyl.[1] Collectively, it has become known as 3/11 or the 2011 Tōhoku disaster. Japan's most powerful earthquake ever recorded[2] generated forces more than five hundred times stronger than the 2010 earthquake that killed over 100,000 people in Haiti. Given the location of the epicenter, in the Pacific Ocean 43 miles east of the Oshika Peninsula, Tōhoku, Honshu's northeastern region, was horrifically battered by the ensuing tsunami. Specifically, three of the mountainous, historically poor region's six prefectures, Miyagi, Iwate, and Fukushima, suffered catastrophic damage.[3] In some parts of the 300-plus miles of impacted coastline, waves reached as high as 125 feet.

Residents of Sendai, Iwate's capital city, had only eight to ten minutes of warning, and even many who reached evacuation sites in time did not survive.[4] Officially, nearly 20,000 perished from the disaster, the vast majority from drowning, including the 2,553 still missing today. In addition to the human cost, survivors lost homes, offices, and farmland, along with critical city infrastructure such as bridges, roads, railroad lines, and hospitals.[5] Twenty-five million tons of debris was left. Early on, the government estimated between $200 and $300 billion of direct damage had been done, equaling 3 to 5 percent of Japan's GDP. When factoring in lost business activity and indirect costs like cleanup and the evacuation and relocation of people, private economic forecasts pegged the expected cost to be nearly double the government's figure.

The tsunami displaced hundreds of thousands. Most initially went to live in evacuation shelters under challenging circumstances before they could be accommodated with their own, less-than-ideal temporary shelter. All too often, multigenerational households separated due to financial and space concerns. Varying degrees of "survivor's guilt," depression, and PTSD tormented an untold number of survivors and first responders.

Social media, which was then relatively new, critically allowed people and groups to crowdsource radiation levels at a time when government-provided information was scarce and/or unreliable. Granted, the presence of social media accelerated the spread of conspiracy theories as well as good-intentioned inaccurate information. Given the starkly different coverage from the domestic and international media, it was difficult to know whom to trust. "You've got the kind of Japanese, NHK version of it," said David Watkins, "which was 'Things are kind of under control. Things are of course terrible, but don't worry about this too much.' And then you had the international news, which was like 'Oh, my goodness! This is totally like Chernobyl Mach 2! The whole sea is gonna be infected!'" Before TV networks could deploy their reporters to the scene, they broadcasted user-generated images and videos on a loop, which generally increased panic and fear.

Hailing from Akita, one prefecture west of Iwate, Go feared the worst when he couldn't reach various friends. Fortunately, they survived,[6] but the same wasn't true for some of his friends' friends or their family members. Go characterized himself as "less motivated" at work given all that had transpired. Baseball was, after all, just a game.

Without Yomiuri's permission, Brian Bannister left as quickly as he could on March 16. The first-year gaijin, whose father played in Japan,[7] had been pitching well until he retreated to the States, never to return again. Despite signing a contract worth $1.8 million two months earlier, he announced his retirement by month's end.[8] Rakuten's Juan Morillo was the only other gaijin to leave without coming back.[9]

In the quake's aftermath, the weekend's exhibition games were canceled. But by Monday, baseball returned to the masses, at least for a moment, as Yomiuri and Hanshin drew a capacity crowd of 30,000 spectators to Nagaragawa Stadium in Gifu City. Donation boxes were placed throughout the stadium, with all proceeds going to relief efforts. With the Japanese flag flying at half-mast, the day game ended in a 2–2 tie.

Naturally, the Japan High School Baseball Federation considered canceling the upcoming Spring Kōshien. In Japan, high school baseball, known as *kokoyakyu*, is huge. Twice annually, a country that loves baseball more than any other sport pays closer attention to the high schoolers than the pros. The annual spring and summer tournaments enjoy a rich tradition, dating back to 1924 and 1918, respectively.[10] Although the summer event is bigger, both hold a special place in the hearts of everyone who travels far and wide to compete or attend. They're also prime opportunities for scouts to discover young talent.

"The tournament is the closest thing Japan has to a national festival," wrote Robert Whiting in 2020, after the thirty-two-team, single-elimination spring invitational was canceled due to the coronavirus. "It is special." It's considered so sacred that before going home the players traditionally scoop up dirt from the infield as a cherished keepsake. Much to the relief of the masses, the JHBF didn't wait too long before giving the go-ahead for the 2011 *Senbatsu*[11] to proceed on March 23, its originally scheduled date. Its occurrence provided some semblance of normalcy.[12]

Of course, things weren't normal. Brass bands and any form of cheering were prohibited.

Although the *Senbatsu* was played several hundred miles southwest of the temblor's epicenter, its role in the early stages of recovery should not be dismissed. It couldn't bring back lives, quell radiation fears, or restore destroyed homes, but over its twelve-day run, its teenage competitors brought people together as millions tuned in to the national NHK broadcasts. While it may have provided a welcome distraction, it also subconsciously reminded Japan of its resilience. A catastrophic disaster was not going to alter the Japanese way of life.

Elsewhere in sports, the Japan Basketball League[13] quickly canceled its season and upcoming postseason. The rival bj league actually resumed play on March 19 despite three of its sixteen teams shutting down operations for the remainder of the season.

Just four days after the tumultuous events of March 11, NPB held league-wide meetings in an effort to decide what to do about a fast-approaching opening day. Since the two-league system began in 1950, it had never postponed its start due to a natural disaster, so this was a new scenario for the key decision-makers. It was also a weighty one. People had been killed, others were missing or displaced, property was damaged, including two Pacific League stadiums, concern persisted about leaked radiation, and rolling blackouts posed a challenge with regard to holding stadium events, especially at night.

Reports out of the Tuesday meetings revealed the Central League desired to keep its March 25 date, while the Pacific League hoped to push back its start by a few weeks. By Thursday, March 25 and April 12 were set as the respective starts.

Central League executives, with Giants chairman and de facto owner Tsuneo Watanabe leading the charge, argued that starting the season on time could lift the spirits of the public, providing a positive outlet during turbulent times. Proceeds earned could be sent to affected areas, they said. The Japan Professional Baseball Players Association[14] vehemently disagreed, believing both leagues should be postponed. "It's just too early," said Hanshin's Takahiro Arai, JPBPA chief players' representative.[15] "The players' consensus is that it is inappropriate to start the season." His well-respected teammate Tomoaki Kanemoto published a concurring column in *Nikkan Sports*.

Tony agreed, telling reporters, "My own personal opinion is that people need time to mourn. They need time to emotionally and mentally get their heads around the situation. I just think there are more important things than baseball going on right now."

On March 16, Yakult played its first game back in a Jingu Stadium devoid of fans. "Yesterday was pretty bizarre," said Tony, who pitched three innings in a win over Yomiuri. "It was tough to wake up in the morning and get focused for a game."

Over the ensuing weekend, it was decided the Central League would delay its beginning by four days, but pressure was mounting for the league to sacrifice more. Specifically, its players were unhappy, it was suffering from bad press, and Japan sports minister Yoshiaki Takaki and Renhō,[16] a state minister assigned to monitor electricity conservation, were pushing the league to conserve power. Within days, it became clear the Central League's position was untenable, and it was announced that both leagues would open on April 12. To accommodate a full 144-game schedule, the league rescheduled canceled games to October and set the Japan Series to begin November 12, a few weeks later than normal.

Various rule changes were implemented to conform to the new status quo. Although games could still run 12 innings, once three and a half hours elapsed, a game would not go into any further extra innings.[17] If a game had to be halted early due to a blackout, it would be called. For April, energy-conserving day games would be required of Yakult and the five other teams playing in areas of diminished power.[18] Come May, all teams could play at night.

On March 29, the "Japan Earthquake Relief Soccer Match" was held, pitting the national team against a J. League All-Star squad. All 38,000 tickets sold out in under an hour, and over $180,000 was reportedly raised. The following weekend, every NPB team played a pair of games to raise more funds for the relief effort.[19] All players wore black ribbons on their jerseys and observed a pregame moment of silence. Various Swallows collected donations in front of Jingu Stadium, including Akita native Masanori Ishikawa, who spoke to the crowd before first pitch.

To honor the victims and stand with the survivors, the Golden Eagles committed to wearing rectangular *"Ganbarou Tōhoku"* patches on their uniforms throughout the season. The other teams would place on their helmets a blue decal with white font that said *"Ganbarou Nippon."* *Ganbarou* does not precisely translate to English but can be understood to mean "You can do it" or "Come together."

The slogan *Ganbare Nippon* ("Stay strong, Japan") began appearing all over the country, including on skyscrapers and billboards, as bumper stickers, in TV commercials, and on social media profile pictures. Despite the turmoil, no rioting occurred, and looting was minimal. The positive, cohesive sentiment was supported by massive volunteer efforts spear-headed by nongovernmental organizations, nonprofits, and volunteers.

A number of citizens selflessly volunteered as firefighters despite losing their own family members or homes. Some even died while aiding their community on the front lines. Heroes were everywhere one looked. More than two hundred pensioners, all over sixty, volunteered to go into the Fukushima plant to spare younger workers from radiation exposure that could cause long-term health problems.[20] Elsewhere, countless public health nurses went above and beyond their expected duties in the most difficult of circumstances.

Ichiro Suzuki, a man worshipped in Japan, sprung into action. Within a week of the disaster, he'd donated ¥100 million[21] to the Japanese Red Cross. Daisuke Matsuzaka, another big-name MLB player, gave $1 million through the Red Sox' official charity.

Alex Ramírez added $1 million and didn't stop there. He'd already sent a truck with medical supplies to the Sendai area and was in the process of ordering roughly a thousand shirts that he'd sell before donating the proceeds. Fighters ace Yu Darvish and myriad others around NPB also dug into their pockets. Every team got involved in some fashion, and one of the country's two baseball Halls of Fame gave too. Through a new public-private partnership called Tomodachi, Major League Baseball committed to donating equipment and holding baseball clinics for youth teams in the Tōhoku area.[22]

Representing the NBA, late Lakers legend Kobe Bryant, whose father was in Japan when the disaster struck, recorded a PSA urging fans to donate to the Red Cross. Seven of his peers pledged to donate through the nonprofit Direct Relief International $1,000 per point for a designated game between March 25 and 27.[23] Thirteen additional players committed to donate a set amount.

Once Thursday, April 12, arrived, all games counted! One contest featured the only teams whose stadiums were damaged in the quake. The Chiba Lotte Marines could host the Golden Eagles because QVC Marine Field incurred only damage to its parking lot, which was fixed by then. Rakuten wasn't so lucky. Approximately eighty Eagles personnel were inside Kleenex Stadium when the massive earthquake hit. They summarily headed to the parking lot, where they called their families.[24] Within a day, structural damage was apparent, but it was unclear how soon the stadium could be ready to host games. American pitcher Darrell Rasner wondered aloud to *Daily Yomiuri* reporter Jim Allen: "Are we going to be one of those teams that doesn't have any home games?"

Days before the opener, manager Senichi Hoshino actually encouraged his Eagles to visit Sendai for the first time since the quake. "What we saw was unimaginable," said shortstop Kazuo Matsui. "At an evacuation shelter, even in those circumstances I saw all these lively faces. I had been struggling to find words to cheer them up a little, but in fact those people energized me." Similarly, the Marines took time to visit their prefecture's hardest-hit cities. Some players toured the tsunami-hit coastal city of Asahi, while a second group saw Urayasu, a town ravaged by soil liquefaction from the earthquake that figured to cost over $900 million to repair.

Because Kleenex Stadium wasn't ready, Rakuten couldn't make its highly anticipated return to Sendai until weeks into the season. Boosted by the return coinciding with the start of Golden Week, an annual series of national holidays beginning April 29, the atmosphere was "rather electric," according to then–Eagles executive Marty Kuehnert.[25] Behind future major leaguer Masahiro Tanaka's complete game, Rakuten edged Orix 3–1. US ambassador to Japan John Roos attended. In Jim Allen's postgame column, he called the game a "huge morale boost for the region" but acknowledged the "long grind" ahead.

About a week after 3/11, Rob Smaal's wife and son were able to leave, thanks to his savvy sister-in-law who facilitated their travel. Due to the difficulty in securing flights out of Japan, she got creative, booking them a trip that included connections from Tokyo to Fukuoka to Seoul to Vancouver to Calgary. Smaal, whose reporting duties prevented him from joining his family, heard alarming news over the loudspeaker at work: According to the government, levels of radiation in Tokyo's tap water had exceeded safety standards for infants to drink. At least Jake was already in Canada, he thought. They would return, but not for a few months.

Eventually, the Smaals planned on moving back to Canada, but the Great Tōhoku Earthquake accelerated their timeline. Shortly after Yoko and Jake came back, the small family learned it would soon be growing. With Yoko pregnant and Jake so young, the Smaals decided it would be wise to relocate amid radiation uncertainty. Their daughter, Jessica, was born the following January, and Rob was suffering from stomach problems that would not improve. By the end of June, they moved to Alberta, Canada.

"In some ways, that earthquake might have saved my life," said Rob, who five months later was diagnosed with stage four peritoneal mesothelioma and operated on after various Japanese doctors couldn't determine the problem. Over a decade, three hundred procedures, and a similar surgery[26] later, challenges persist, but Rob remains active and is feeling pretty good. "One of the top surgeons in the world that could deal with this kind of cancer I had just happened to be here [in Calgary]. I can't say I'm lucky 'cuz getting that disease, very few people get it, but just the way circumstances brought me here and into the hands of this guy who just sort of delivered me."

The tragedy dragged on as bodies were still being discovered. On April 27, ahead of Yoshinori Sato's start against Yomiuri, the Sendai native received heart-rending news: His high-school catcher who'd long been missing had been confirmed dead. One year his junior, he considered Izumi Saito "another big brother." Not too long before, they'd competed at the Summer Kōshien together. Despite his grief, the twenty-one-year-old chose to play, proceeding to pitch five innings of a rain-soaked affair. "I acted to the end with a strong heart that could not be broken," he said after the gritty effort. Dedicating the win to Saito, he signed the game ball and arranged for it to be shipped to the Saito family and placed in Izumi's coffin.

A few weeks later, Junji Ogawa juggled the rotation to ensure Sato could start one of Yakult's only two games in Sendai. He pitched brilliantly but was bested by Tanaka, who struck out 15 for the victorious Eagles.

As June was drawing to a close, a pair of upcoming games generated concern for some Swallows. They'd be facing the Giants twice in Fukushima prefecture, specifically in Koriyama, within 60 kilometers, or 37 miles, of the infamous nuclear disaster, where fear of radiation lingered.

When the 45-foot-tall tsunami hit the Fukushima Daiichi power plant, three nuclear reactors began to overheat. The height of the water was more than twice as high as TEPCO, the Tokyo utility company that runs the plant, had envisioned as a worst-case scenario. Generators stopped working, crippling critical cooling systems. Within five hours of the tsunami, one reactor had melted to its core, and by March 14, two more had suffered meltdowns, too. Disturbingly, TEPCO didn't disclose this information until May 24,[27] instead opting to downplay the situation's severity. The plant also incurred three hydrogen explosions on March 12, 14, and 15 because venting had not properly been implemented. Although the public had been privy to the explosions at the time, they were misled by TEPCO, which blamed Prime Minister Naoto Kan when in fact the utility itself erred by not obeying the government's instructions.

The government unquestionably made its share of mistakes too. Despite having a system to measure where winds are likeliest to carry radiation, it did not share any of that data with the public in those critical early days. Additionally, the government moved slowly in protecting its citizens from radioactive contamination in their food.[28]

Within a week of 3/11, the US Nuclear Regulatory Commission announced recommended evacuation or indoor sheltering for American citizens within 80 kilometers of the Fukushima plant. The Canadian embassy, along with that of some other countries, quickly followed suit. It wasn't until April 22 that the Japanese government formally designated all areas within 20 kilometers part of a "No-Entry Zone." Some 78,000 were evacuated. Evacuations from two more zones up to 60 kilometers from the plant[29] commenced in mid-May. By the Swallows' Fukushima visit in late June, 59,000 evacuees were still in limbo, staying in emergency shelters with no idea if or when they could return home.

"In principle, it's a great idea," said Tony of playing in Fukushima, "because people are suffering up there and if baseball can help cheer those people up or give them something else to think about other than the disaster, I think it's our duty as professional athletes. We should be giving back to the community any way we can. That's our way of showing that we do care, [that] we're not here to just make money. The fans are the ones that allow us to play this game."

"I don't really know how dangerous or not dangerous it is up there," he continued. "Right now, I guess I'm just taking the word of the team. I'm pretty sure they wouldn't put anybody in harm's way on purpose." Josh Whitesell cited similar benefits to the trip before touching upon his overarching fear: "On a personal safety level, it is recognized as the most devastating nuclear disaster in the history of our world.[30] I just want to make sure that me and my family are safe." To limit their time in the area, Yakult permitted Whitesell and Tony, among others, to arrive the morning of the first game and leave the following night, shortly after the second game.

The historic Kaiseizan Stadium hosted the games, marking the Giants' first Koriyama appearance since 1988. As one of the country's oldest fields, it once welcomed the 1971 Orioles and 1974 Mets on offseason tours of Japan and saw Sadaharu Oh play during his final pro season. Images from those trips lined the walls near the entrance. On the downside, the infield dirt appeared just as ancient, demanding periodic attention from dozens of groundskeepers and requiring the baseball to be replaced after every play in which it hit the dirt.[31]

Around 14,000 attended each game between the Tokyo teams. Wayne Graczyk, who covered the trip for the *Japan Times*, was surprised to spot very few masks. He did see one man wearing a dosimeter to measure radiation levels. Otherwise, he wrote, everything seemed normal, both at the stadium and around town. Playing as the visitors, the Swallows came away with a win and a tie before the teams moved to Tokyo Dome for the series finale.

Exactly one month later, the Swallows and Giants were in Fukushima again, but this time, even closer to the "No-Entry Zone" at Azuma Stadium in Fukushima City.[32] In less than two and a half hours, Yakult shut out Yomiuri, 2–0. The teams took the same 10:10 a.m. bullet train back to Tokyo to finish the weekend series with two games at Jingu.

By the second Fukushima visit, the nation was still reveling in Japan's exhilarating Women's World Cup victory over the number one–ranked Americans. In the quarterfinals, Japan drew the mighty Germans, who were hosting the knockout stage and coming off two straight dominant World Cup title runs.[33] Meanwhile, the Japanese squad, nicknamed *Nadeshiko* or "beautiful flower," had failed to advance past the group stage either time. Despite the long odds, they upset Germany in extra time. In the semis, Japan overcame Sweden with two second-half goals to draw Team USA in the gold medal match.

Team USA was a juggernaut. In 25 all-time meetings, Japan had never beaten the United States. Given the broadcast's 3:15 a.m. start, most wouldn't learn the result until they awoke, but diehard fans flocked to bars to watch Japan strive to become the first Asian team to win a World Cup. Each time the United States scored, Japan answered quickly, just when it needed a goal most.

Tied at two, a round of penalty kicks was needed to determine the Cup winner. Ultimately, twenty-year-old Saki Kumagai nailed the Cup clincher, top left corner pocket, out of American goalie Hope Solo's reach. That sent the Japanese players into pure elation as they piled on top of one another. Four months after one of the most painful moments in the country's history, a grieving Japan was feeling inspired again, at least for a moment.[34]

Of course, the country was still experiencing ample fallout from the disaster, including an ongoing reckoning concerning its nuclear state of affairs. In June, only nineteen of Japan's fifty-four nuclear reactors were online. In an effort to convince mayors and prefectural governors to approve restarting the idled reactors, METI Minister Banri Kaieda misleadingly assured the public on June 18 that all the nuclear plants had been checked and deemed safe.[35] Undermining this message in early July, the prime minister announced that Japan would follow the European Union model by making each reactor subject to a two-stage stress test before it could go back into use. Spurred by the damage inflicted by the Fukushima disaster, sentiment on nuclear energy was changing fast. Previously, local areas were typically happy to house nuclear plants given the revenue they attracted. By October, however, an NHK poll revealed that 80 percent of city mayors with reactors opposed restarting idled ones.

According to polling conducted by the major media outlets, public support for nuclear power declined precipitously from April to June, while an increasing slice of the public supported phasing out nuclear energy. Angry about the danger nuclear energy posed, people didn't just register their opinions through polls. The late Nobel Literature laureate Kenzaburō Ōe, among other influential figures, organized a citizens' campaign that collected more than eight million signatures for a petition opposing the government's plan to restart the reactors. The campaign took to the streets in force, as nearly 60,000 rallied in Meiji Park on September 19, Tokyo's largest demonstration since the 1960s.[36]

Through the brave actions of elected leaders, certain high-profile business leaders,[37] and the protesting masses, Japan was demonstrating that despite its unique geological predisposition to earthquakes, it could take meaningful steps to take control of its own destiny and usher in a brighter and safer future. If there ever can be a silver lining to a disaster of such horrific proportions, it is that, as well as how the Japanese people came together so beautifully amid incredible tragedy.

Notes

[1] On the International Nuclear and Radiological Event Scale, a major accident is categorized as a 7, the highest level there is. To date, only Fukushima and Chernobyl have been rated a 7.

[2] It was also the fourth most powerful anywhere in the world since 1900 when recordkeeping began. The Japanese call it by many names, including most prominently the Great East Japan Earthquake, the Great Tōhoku Earthquake, and the Great Sendai Earthquake.

[3] Fewer than one hundred people died from any other prefecture.

[4] Tragically, more than one hundred evacuation sites designed by local governments were inundated.

[5] A whopping 80 percent of hospitals in the three prefectures were at least partially damaged, and eleven were destroyed completely.

6   Go's friends were initially unreachable because they'd evacuated quickly without their cell phones.

7   Southpaw Floyd Bannister pitched for the Swallows in 1990 near the end of a 15-year major-league career.

8   Since retiring, Bannister, a longtime fan and student of pitching analytics, has held various coaching and front-office roles. Presently, he works in the White Sox front office after spending four seasons as the San Francisco Giants' Director of Pitching.

9   When Yokohama's Brent Leach left, he became NPB's very first restricted player (*seigen senshu*) despite the list's existence since 1998. Shortly after, Yomiuri put Bannister on the same list. This was one possible contributing factor to his decision to retire at thirty, as restricted players are prohibited from playing elsewhere, including outside of Japan. Leach, however, did return in July. Before an August game, he admitted he regretted his initial decision: "I should have stayed, but my wife was expecting a baby, and we kind of panicked." After eight starts, he was released and returned to the same Dodgers organization from which he came.

10 In fact, Kōshien Stadium began hosting the tournaments twelve years before the Tigers franchise formed and started calling the stadium home.

11 Japanese for "selection," Spring Kōshien is commonly known as *Senbatsu* because thirty-two schools from all over the country are invited to represent various regions.

12 Tokaidai Sagami High School of Kanagawa prefecture went on to win the tournament in dominant fashion, outscoring its opponents 46-11 over five games. Three of its hitters made it to NPB.

13 The 2012–2013 season was JBL's last when its eight teams joined the newly established National Basketball League. In 2016, the NBL and bj league merged to form the B.League, which operates today.

14 Founded in the mid-1940s, the JPBPA finally gained recognition as a union in 1985.

15 Arai took over as chief in 2008 for Yakult's Shinya Miyamoto, who served the previous three years. Before Miyamoto was another Swallow: Atsuya Furuta. Making his mark as leader, Furuta served seven years and orchestrated a memorable and successful two-day strike in September 2004, among other triumphs.

16 The politician's full name is Renhō Murata, though she's commonly referred to by her first name alone.

17 The game clock would continue to run in all instances, even in the case of a weather or stadium delay.

18 The affected teams, the Swallows, Giants, BayStars, Lions, Marines, and Golden Eagles, all played in eastern Honshu, areas powered by TEPCO.

19 According to reports, one return-to-play plan proposed by some veteran players called for charity day games to occur on every weekend in April, but management didn't support the idea.

20 The government thanked them for their selfless offer but wouldn't allow it.

21 The sum equaled roughly $1.24 million at the time. Ichiro's Seattle Mariners followed suit, as did the parent company of Nintendo of America, Inc., the majority owner of the Mariners.

22 For example, thanks to the effort, a repaired baseball field in Ishinomaki, Miyagi, was back in use by December 2012. The Yankees' Curtis Granderson attended the reopening.

23 Pau Gasol scored 26 against the Clippers, prompting Hall of Famer Magic Johnson to match the $26,000 donation. Playing against each other, Russell Westbrook and LaMarcus Aldridge combined for 48. In other designated games, Derrick Rose scored 24 and Al Horford notched 23.

24 By around 7:30 that night, all players were able to confirm that their families were safe.

25 Kuehnert briefly served as Golden Eagles general manager as the first gaijin GM in NPB history. He was demoted a month into their ill-fated first season, 2005. In the summer of 2018, when Kuehnert was named GM of the Sendai 89ers, he became the first-ever person (not just gaijin) to serve as GM in two of Japan's top pro leagues.

26 In February 2022, as Rob's tumors were growing and becoming particularly concerning again, surgeons removed a couple feet of his colon and parts of his stomach, among other things.

27 TEPCO also acknowledged that the earthquake may have caused some of the Fukushima damage, contrary to initial reports that only the tsunami was to blame. There's good reason to believe that TEPCO only disclosed any of this then because an international agency, IAEA, was on its way to conduct an investigation, and the utility was trying to get ahead of that.

28 For example, until unsafe levels of cesium were detected in beef on supermarket shelves in Tokyo and elsewhere, the government had merely been relying on voluntary shipment bans.

29 The two zones included a space 20 to 30 kilometers from the plant, labeled the "Emergency Evacuation Preparation Zone" and another area to the northwest of the plant, where winds carried the radiation.

30 Chernobyl is regarded as the most devastating, but Whitesell wasn't far off.

31 Following the first game, which he started for Yomiuri, Seth Greisinger called it one of the worst surfaces on which he'd ever played.

32 Like June 28 at Koriyama, the July 28 game had been planned before the Great Tōhoku Earthquake triggered the nuclear disaster and was subsequently allowed to proceed. The June 29 game at Koriyama was originally scheduled to be played in Utsunomiya, but Kiyohara Stadium was damaged in the quake, giving Koriyama a second game.

33 In the 2003 and 2007 Cups, Germany outscored its opponents 46-4.

34 The Japanese women had been ranked fourth in the world, but given the teams they beat, how they beat them, and the year in which it all occurred, their triumph undoubtedly symbolized something special.

35 A month later, it came out that METI had orchestrated a campaign to fabricate local support for nuclear energy. Under pressure as a result of the Ministry of Economy, Trade, and Industry's many costly post-Fukushima mistakes, Banri Kaieda resigned from his post in August.

36 In the preceding months, thousands had marched in support of the same cause in Tokyo on April 10, June 7, and July 11.

37 For example, SoftBank CEO Masayoshi Son put his money and reputation on the line to advocate for and expand the supply of renewable energy, and Rakuten president Hiroshi Mikitani quit the powerful Japan Business Federation in protest over its support for the energy status quo.

CHAPTER NINE
A RELIEVER IS BORN

We got free rein. It's cool when you're in a big city like that, and you kind of feel like you have it all to yourself.

The last time Tony started a game was March 8, 2011. It was a spring-training contest, days before the tsunami hit. That day, he was experimenting with a new pitch, a cutter. He gripped the ball like his four-seam fastball before "turning it just a hair" in his hand. He also adjusted his arm position in the hopes of increasing the pitch's movement. With those two minor tweaks, he had stumbled upon something special. "All of a sudden, I have this pitch coming out of my arm that was just an 'invisi-ball,'" said Tony.

Chunichi power hitters' inability to make solid contact quickly became evident. "This thing's magic," Tony thought. Ogawa and pitching coach Daisuke Araki noticed too. After the game, they pulled their American pitcher aside and eased into a potentially uncomfortable request. They were gauging how he'd feel about a possible shift from starting pitcher to reliever, a change for which bullpen coach Tomohito Ito had been advocating.

Growing up, Tony would always tell his dad, Phil, "A reliever's nothing more than a failed starter." As he ascended through the Diamondbacks' minor-league system, he started all but one of the 97 games in which he appeared. Naturally, he viewed himself as a starting pitcher. In his first NPB season, he pitched in relief just once. "It's a blow to your ego," said Phil. "I don't care how good you think you are."

Deep down, at twenty-seven, Tony may have still subscribed to the "failed starter" theory. The thought of no longer starting probably perturbed him on some level. But given Tony's dismal previous season, he didn't raise any misgivings. At this critical juncture of his career, ego took a back seat to pragmatism and survival. "I'll try anything now," he thought. "I couldn't have cared less where they put me as long as I was pitching." Hillary added, "He was kind of at their mercy. I don't think he was in a position to really say much about it. He just went with the flow."

Also ahead of the 2011 campaign, he jumped at the opportunity to switch uniform numbers from sixty-four to thirty-four. He wanted a fresh start, but there was more to it.

"Sixty-four, that's an absolute terrible number," Tony opined years later. "I hated it from the get-go. No offense, but it's very offensive lineman." Growing up, he associated numbers with the all-time greats who wore them. When presented with options, thirty-four was the obvious choice. Tony instantly thought of Hall of Fame pitcher Nolan Ryan, legendary Lakers center Shaquille O' Neal, and Raiders running back Bo Jackson.[1] "Thirty-four was way more of a Showtime number," he concluded.

The league made its own change before the season began. For the first time in its sixty-one-year history, every team would be using the same supplier for its baseballs. Mizuno won the contract and developed a uniform ball that had wider seams than previous NPB balls. As a result, run production diminished considerably.[2] It was a good time to be a pitcher in Japan.

By his second season in Tokyo, Tony had a bicycle, which sliced his already short commute in half and then some. The four-minute ride would be a welcome new wrinkle to his afternoon routine. At the clubhouse, he'd put on his uniform, then bike to the practice field a few blocks away. Theoretically, players could walk, but they preferred biking in order to avoid being stopped by fans.[3] "It was kind of awkward," said Aaron Guiel, "but you'd be in full uniform. Guys in the major leagues, if they saw what you were doing, it would seem quite strange. But it's just what you do."

One night after the teams' tsunami-delayed season opener, Yakult was back at Tokyo Dome. Back-to-back homers by Alex Ramírez and Yoshinobu Takahashi put the Giants up 3–0. By the seventh, it was time for Tony's first appearance in his new role, and just his second bullpen outing since four years earlier in Single A (South Bend).

As luck would have it, hitting-challenged pitcher Tetsuya Utsumi[4] was batting first. He unsurprisingly struck out looking. The next man popped out. But following a walk and a first-pitch single, trouble was brewing.

With two on, Ramírez stepped to the plate. Just over eleven months earlier, he victimized Tony with a demoralizing three-run homer. Tony had allowed nine runs, including five in the opening inning. He remembered. This time, however, he trusted his new cutter on a 1-1 count, jamming Ramírez, who rolled the ball back to him. Crisis averted. The cutter, a pitch he'd only begun developing in spring training, accounted for two of the three outs.

The ensuing Saturday, the electric blues guitar sounds of ZZ Top beckoned Tony into his first game back at Jingu. No longer a starter, he'd reasoned that "In Bloom" had to be replaced as his entrance song and "Sharp Dressed Man"[5] would do the trick. "They come runnin' just as fast as they can," the chorus began, "'cuz every girl crazy 'bout a sharp-dressed man."

He began the season as a middle reliever, typically pitching in the sixth or seventh. The next week in Hiroshima, the Swallows starter couldn't get out of the third frame, leaving them down 6–1. But they quickly trimmed the deficit. Behind 6–5 in the ninth, gaijin newcomer Wladimir

Balentien drilled a game-tying home run off closer Dennis Sarfate. Once Chang-Yong Lim retired three Carp, a tie was triggered, given the new post-disaster energy-saving rules.[6] Six and two-thirds scoreless bullpen innings made the improbable tie possible, with Tony contributing two.

The Swallows were building momentum, as was their newly converted reliever. Later that week, they were scheduled to host Yomiuri, but the three-game series was moved 100 miles southwest to boost attendance. With night games prohibited in April, team and league officials worried the Jingu crowd would be sparsely populated for the Tuesday–Thursday series. Away from home, Yakult still managed to sweep as Tony appeared twice more.

In the middle game, he preserved a 4–1 lead by striking out the side in a scoreless seventh, and power-hitting outfielder Balentien from the island of Curaçao added two homers to his growing total. The burly, six-foot-two slugger came over from the Cincinnati Reds organization, where he played Triple-A ball in 2010. In the preceding three seasons, he logged major-league time with the Reds and Seattle Mariners. Although he compiled 15 home runs, he struck out often and batted a lowly .221.

After delivering another home run in the series finale, Balentien had six in his first 14 NPB games. Tony, too, was on a roll. Three weeks in, he hadn't allowed a run. Rob Smaal wrote a column for the *Asahi Shimbun* in which he dubbed Balentien and Barnette the Swallows' "Killer B's."[7]

The first-place Swallows' typical Monday off couldn't cool them down, as they improved to 11–5–2 the following night. Balentien homered again. Tasked with holding a 3–2 lead, Tony failed for the first time all season, but the offense picked him up. The outlier aside, he was fitting in nicely in the pen.

"Just immediately," Hillary noticed, "he seemed like a totally different person on the mound." Looking back, Tony believes many, including pitching coach Araki, were responsible for his smooth transition, but he argues it was his bullpen coach, Ito, a former Swallows pitcher himself, who most critically prepared him. Araki would commonly delegate assignments to Ito, who would in turn work one-on-one with various pitchers.

Ito took a particular interest early in spring training, playing catch with him every day. Afterward, they'd discuss potential areas of weakness and how he could improve. "So whether it's mechanically or finger positions on balls—it didn't matter what it was—he always had something to challenge me for the next day," Tony said of Ito. "I loved it. I just ate it up."

He implored Tony to add a split-finger. Additionally, he emphasized how his approach had to change. "He was really getting on me to basically just go all out on every single pitch, leave nothing in the tank," said Tony, "just try to get away from the mindset of pacing yourself throughout a start and reminding me to basically throw as hard as possible. I'm only gonna be out there for roughly ten to 15 pitches at most; might as well just let it rip."

"When I went to the bullpen, I changed everything about the way I played baseball. They always say, 'Don't try to reinvent the wheel.' I went back, and I reinvented the wheel with myself. I knew that I had to do something drastically different with the way that I approached the Japanese game because it just wasn't working."

Tony's development of two pitches and his willingness to throw them often were instrumental to his improvement. In 2010, he threw a slider or changeup 38 percent of the time, two pitches Tony and his coaches felt had been ineffective. His four-seam fastball comprised 44 percent of his pitches.

During 2011, he reduced his four-seam frequency to 30 percent and, more dramatically and crucially, eliminated his changeup and slider altogether. This created the room for Tony to use his devastating new cutter at a 40 percent rate, while employing the new splitter nearly one-tenth of the time.[8]

Not yet one month into the season, Tony's team was increasingly relying on him to extricate it from difficult situations. Against Chunichi, number thirty-four replaced Yakult's starter who left with a 3–1 deficit and two on. Although Tony added further panic by walking Tony Blanco, he quelled the threat, striking out the next two Dragons.

Nevertheless, Chunichi iced the game when setup man Kenichi Matsuoka unraveled, allowing five runs. The disastrous performance resulted in Matsuoka losing his role to Tony. If Tony kept pitching well, he was told, he would remain the eighth-inning guy paving the way for the dominant Lim to close up shop.

Days later in Matsuyama,[9] Yakult was tied in the eighth. Again, Tony demonstrated the wisdom behind the saying "It's not how you start but how you finish." The first two Carp singled. As is customary in Japan, the next batter laid down a bunt to move the runners over. On the transfer from glove to throwing hand, Tony bobbled the ball, loading the bases.

Facing the bottom of the lineup, he opted for creativity, going to a split-finger fastball with which he'd been tinkering. He wasn't sure if the pitch was quite ready, but he knew his opponents wouldn't be expecting it. This was "the day it clicked," he said. For the first out, Tony deployed the splitter on a 2-2 count and got the batter to whiff at a pitch in the dirt. He sometimes called it a sinker because he gripped the ball like one but threw it with splitter action. It felt great out of his hand. "I gripped the sinker, and I just threw the shit out of it," Tony said excitedly. "I ripped it as hard as I could. I remember just throwing it, and this thing broke out of nowhere."

As veteran Tomonori Maeda, a pinch-hitter at this stage of his career, came up, Tony stuck with the splitter. He still vividly remembers the twenty-year pro's "What the hell was that?" reaction after missing the first pitch, which manifested in Maeda looking back at Swallows catcher Ryoji Aikawa before glaring at Tony. With two strikes, Aikawa called the pitch twice more. After a foul tip on the first, Tony struck out a swinging

Maeda, who was out in front again and looked back at the catcher, then stared Tony down before returning to the dugout.

To cap off the exhilarating inning, he fanned Hiroshima's shortstop on an outside fastball when he was likely thinking splitter. "I went off the mound just screaming, I was so pumped," recalled Tony. "And Aikawa sprinted right for the dugout, like just dead sprint." The Houdini act helped the Swallows finish with a tie.

Tony's repeated ability to stay calm under pressure was a new and welcome development. When negative plays occurred the prior season, all too often his performance deteriorated quickly. Time after time in 2011, though, this newfound mettle signaled that he could be counted on to deliver in tight games.

With Interleague play[10] set to begin, Yakult used its Monday travel day to fly an hour and a half north to Hokkaido. Hillary had been trying to reach Tony. By the time they were able to connect, the plane had landed. Tony was among his teammates, but she had to deliver heart-rending news that would shake his world at its core: His brother Randy had died suddenly in Arizona, weeks shy of his thirtieth birthday, leaving behind a three-year-old daughter and a promising career as a chef.

"I think he could tell as soon as I started talking that something was wrong," Hillary recounted, "and he was like, 'What? What happened?' I told him, and I don't even really remember much except for it was the immediate, 'Are you sure? Are you sure?'" Next, Tony instantly shifted to logistics. He'd talk with his coaches and get back to her with a plan.

First thing the following morning, Tony and Hillary were off to LAX— the thoroughfare needed for their journey—on a flight paid for by the Swallows. Just after they landed in Los Angeles, more heart-wrenching developments came their way: Tony's mom, Jackie, had suffered a heart attack and was in the intensive care unit.

It was her figurative "heart" and creativity Tony believes he inherited. Jackie, a longtime seamstress, and Randy, a cook, were the artistic ones in the family. Although Tony had never really possessed any traditional artistic skills, showcasing his natural passion on the mound, using it to his advantage, and learning when and how to reel it in demanded the ingenuity of an artist.

They flew to Phoenix. Upon arriving, Tony went directly to the hospital. His mother was the first person he saw, awake in her bed. "We tried not to [talk about Randy], you know? I just remember asking her, I was like, 'Mom, are you okay?' And she just instantly started crying and said, 'No.'"

And how could she be? Jackie Barnette had not only just lost one of her three sons, but she was also the person who found Randy lying motionless on her backyard patio. "I can't imagine having that image burned in your brain for the rest of your life," said Tony.

To this day, the family cannot be sure about what happened to cause Randy's premature death. All they know is that he was spending the day with his daughter at her grandma's house. Possibly to water plants, he went outside, where he collapsed from an elevated surface. He hit his head on the way down, tragically ending his life. There was some speculation that a previous baseball accident caused related brain trauma, but numerous tests failed to return a definitive cause of death.

"She was weak for a while, but she definitely got better," Tony said of his mom. "But mentally, I don't know how you deal with the loss of a child." Randy's death was jarring for his younger brother too. "It hit Tony really hard," said Hillary, "and it definitely hurt Tony that he wasn't around more. He was in Japan, so I think that makes it harder."

Randy was the middle of three Barnette boys, two and a half years older than Tony. Their special connection began as kids, according to Tony: "Me and him grew towards each other simply out of spite of my oldest brother. [Cory] picked on us. He gave us proper big-brother treatment. Me and Randy, we weren't big guys; my brother was always bigger than us. We had to rely on our speed and our wits and our humor to get the best of him, so we kind of formed a bond early on."

In adulthood, although the two didn't talk particularly often, they were always there for each other. "It was just something that whenever we were around each other, we knew," said Tony. "Every once in a while in life, you need that guy that'll keep your secret or that'll help you through something that's not exactly on the level." Randy would do that for Tony, and vice versa.

Phil likes to joke about Randy's evolution into an accomplished chef. He remembers when Randy called to ask how to boil an egg shortly after he moved away from home. Within years, he got to be very good at his craft.

Phil and his dad both loved cooking, but Randy's gift was more than a genetic trait. "It's kind of like Tony's passion for baseball," said Phil. "At some point in time, Randy just found this passion of being in the kitchen, and he just started working on it. He started with fast food, and he just kept going, going, going, working tirelessly twenty-four hours a day. He was always there early, always there late." Added Tony of his ability to make mouthwatering cuisine out of the most basic ingredients, "He was a genius in that."

Randy's memorial service was held on the following Saturday afternoon in Glendale. Between the funeral and grieving with loved ones, including his recuperating mother, Tony had much to occupy his time. Baseball could wait, as he took a couple of weeks with family before returning with Hillary to Tokyo.

"Yakult was really nice about everything," recalled Hillary. "They told him to take as much time as he needed in Arizona." Upon hearing the tragic news, the organization deregistered Tony from the *ichi-gun* roster. He could officially return as soon as May 26,[11] though Yakult made it clear there would be no rush.

Shortly after Tony left, a banged-up Aaron Guiel temporarily took his friend's roster spot. His back had been bothering him since 2010, when he was limited to 81 games. The Canadian then had endoscopic surgery, hoping to be ready by the start of 2011.[12] But considerable pain persisted, and by mid-May, the chronic lower back pain had become particularly troublesome.

His long-awaited return to the lineup on May 23 was cut short due to unrelenting rain. During the five-inning game, he grounded into a double play, stifling a potential Swallows rally, and was later grazed by a pitch[13] but stranded in scoring position.

While Guiel wanted as many at-bats as possible to find some sort of rhythm, his back rendered it difficult to log consistent playing time. He could swing without pain, he said, but not on consecutive days: "I'd feel fantastic for a day, and then the following day I'd go out, and it would be there. Then the day after that, it would be significant."

In light of the turf most NPB stadiums used as opposed to grass,[14] playing the outfield was even more painful than swinging. The surface produced a "constant pounding" that wreaked havoc on his ailing back. Hailing from the Central League, the Swallows couldn't ordinarily employ a designated hitter—an opportunity to semi-rest Guiel while keeping his bat in the lineup—although they had a few chances to use Guiel in the role during Interleague play.

On May 25, he batted third and had to play left field. He went hitless, with a walk, in four plate appearances. Three nights later, he pinch-hit in a critical situation. There were two outs in the ninth and no runners on, with Yakult trailing Seibu by one. Guiel's bat could have tied the game. Two years earlier, in such a scenario he would have struck fear into the opposing pitcher and potentially drawn an intentional walk. This time, he struck out. Sadly, at thirty-eight and severely hobbled, he was nowhere near the player he once was.

During Tony's two-week absence, Guiel registered no hits over three starts and two pinch-hitting appearances. With Tony's activation in early June, Guiel went back to Toda to try to restore his health and performance.

He returned to the *ichi-gun* Swallows in late August and, for a fleeting moment, was able to turn back the clock. In his third start back, Guiel came through with three hits, including a double for his first hit of the season,[15] a two-run double, and a single. The *modasho*[16] performance helped Yakult tie Chunichi, but it proved to be a mirage at this stage of his career. He'd finish 2011 with four hits in 29 at-bats, his only other hit coming on his final home run. Guiel's August 28 appearance was not a pleasant one, as he struck out all three times, including an incident where the bat slipped from his hands and nearly landed in the Kōshien Stadium crowd.

"I was really trying to come back and play at a high level, and it just wasn't working out," he said. "I felt like I could still play, but the back was a hindrance enough where maybe at the level I had grown accustomed to playing, it probably wasn't realistic. As a foreigner, they're relying so heavily on you for the team's success. The team didn't really put a lot of pressure on me, but at the same time they did need to have somebody ready to go for an everyday player. That last year, I knew the writing was on the wall."

On September 21, Guiel made it official, telling the organization he was retiring, with the three-strikeout night going down as his final game. He was permitted to leave with the season in progress, and within four days, he was back in Canada. Yakult had asked if he wanted to pinch-hit in a late September game, where he'd be honored. Not wanting to be a distraction to a team playing well and gearing up for the playoffs, he declined. The move also suited his personality. "I had never been the type of player that wants the spotlight and adulation," noted Guiel.

Retirement games are a time-honored NPB tradition. Scheduled for a late-season home game, essentially all retiring players are celebrated by their organization without regard to career accolades. If the player is no longer a regular contributor and his team's still playing for something, he'll likely only briefly appear.[17] Once the postgame Hero interviews have concluded, the honored player[s] makes his way to a spot in front of the pitching mound. A tribute video plays. Then the honoree delivers a farewell speech,[18] during which tears usually flow. Next, the *dōage* ritual, Japanese for "victory toss" or "lifting one in celebration," commences, in which the team exuberantly hoists the player into the air and back down, repeating the act a number of times. Finally, it's time for him to slowly circle the field, while waving and throwing balls into the crowd as the doting fans rain down colorful streamers. Throughout the lap, wistful music plays.

Guiel wishes he'd handled his retirement differently. "Just to disappear was probably not the perfect way to say goodbye," he said years later. "In hindsight, I would have liked to have had an opportunity just to thank the fans, thank some of the players, thank the coaches, just [in a] ceremonial [way], because I'd seen other players do it, and it's special not just for the player. A lot of those coaches work so hard to get you ready."

Before the next season, he would sign a largely ceremonial minor-league contract with the Royals, his primary big-league team. Guiel had no intention of playing again—he was too injured—but the contract allowed him to explore his aptitude for coaching despite all the organization's coaching positions already being filled.[19]

In five NPB seasons, all with the Swallows, injuries limited him to 441 games. He managed to slug .472, largely thanks to 90 home runs. While he hit for power, the contact wasn't always there—he struck out 385 times and batted .234.

Garrett DeOrio of TokyoSwallows.com reacted to the retirement by lauding the veteran's approach. "His numbers belie the positive impact he's had on morale over the years," he wrote. "Perhaps Guiel's biggest impact was that he came to Japan in the right way: He took things in stride, did what he could to get the job done, and endeared himself to the fans."

Over the years, Swallows fans thoroughly embraced Guiel. His batting cheer took the melody of "O Canada," his country's national anthem, but replaced the actual words with an exhortation for the hitter. Members of the home crowd, particularly in right field, brought miniature Canadian flags, which they waved in support of Guiel. He loved it all.

A month after he left, he got his retirement game. In the video that played halfway through Yakult's season finale, Guiel thanked the fans for their generous support throughout his Swallows tenure. After the game, a group of fans belted out one last "O Canada" Guiel cheer.

Although his Japanese career certainly had its ups and downs, there's no question in Guiel's mind that he made the right move at thirty-four to come over. "I really miss it," he said in 2013. "I played in some great places against some really good players, but playing in Japan was the highlight. I was able to walk away [from the majors], go to Japan, and not look back. And it turned out to be the best career decision I've ever made."

Management wanted Tony to pitch on the farm before rejoining Yakult, but back-to-back rainouts delayed any action. Since his departure, the Swallows had won two[20] of their first 10 Interleague games, largely unable to score runs. Although Balentien was off to a hot start generally, he'd been far less reliable with runners in scoring position. Meanwhile, Josh Whitesell had failed to replicate his highly productive 2010 half-season.

Early in the Swallows' fourth game, Whitesell had hurt his right shoulder on a violent home-plate collision. Consequently, he missed seven of the next ten games and started none of them. The absence provided Kazuhiro "Boo" Hatakeyama,[21] who was coming off a breakout 2010, a prime chance at taking both Whitesell's cleanup spot and the everyday first-base job.

In his first start in the new role, Hatakeyama homered twice. Although the portly veteran settled back in left field upon Whitesell's return, he'd virtually retain the cleanup position all season. Hatakeyama struggled at third base and lacked mobility in the outfield. But at first

135

base, his defensive failings could largely be hidden. The problem? Due to Whitesell's torn labrum a decade earlier, he essentially could only play first. Something—or someone—had to give.

Most troubling, Whitesell was striking out at the highest rate of his professional career.[22] Still, thanks to his overall production and Yakult's paucity of power hitters, Whitesell primarily held on to his starting role for a couple more months. By late August, Yakult briefly deregistered him.[23] Once he returned, though, he would start just thrice more. Years later, Whitesell pinpointed the 2011 season's diminished lighting as the primary factor behind his statistical regression, also citing difficulty adjusting to the league's new baseball and a lingering right shoulder injury.

After a few weeks of inaction, Tony's rust showed with poor outings on June 3 and 4. But the gaijin reliever quickly recovered, consistently and prolifically piling up productive outings. Notably, he appeared to shine brightest against his nemeses from the season before, the Yomiuri Giants. Yakult would finish 12–8–4 against Yomiuri, a critical mark given the teams' one-game separation in the final standings.

In the June-closing, three-game series that notably began in Fukushima, Tony notched a scoreless inning every night. In the middle game in the bottom of the ninth, he stranded runners on the corners by striking out Ramírez and retiring the next Giant. The game ended in a tie as would the next night's.[24] In the series finale, after Lim blew a two-run lead, Tony held the line in the 10th, again stranding the potential winning run in scoring position.

Five nights later, he was at it again, mystifying Yomiuri bats. In the eighth, with the game tied, he fanned the 3-4-5 batters, inducing a swinging strikeout on three different pitches: a cutter, curveball, and fastball, respectively. A badly slumping Balentien stepped to the plate with two outs in the ninth and the score still tied, and broke out of his funk with a sayonara single to left.[25] To secure the series sweep, Tony again held a tie score, setting the stage for another sayonara hit. At the All-Star break, the Swallows held first place, leading Hanshin and Chunichi by eight games apiece.

During 2011, Tokyo became home, as the nagging feelings of isolation faded away. Of course, Tony and Hillary sometimes missed *home home*, especially their friends and family, but Tokyo no longer felt foreign. For them, the city transformed from merely the location of Tony's workplace into their culturally rich home for eight months of the year.[26]

"Obviously Tony was doing better the second year, and so in terms of a routine, he and I were having a lot more fun exploring the city," said Hillary, reminiscing about a particularly special time of her life. "After his games, that's when we would go." The two would take off on their bikes as midnight approached and ride around Tokyo. "It was super-quiet," she said, "and nobody was out really."

These late-night bike rides helped them get their exercise in a fun and educational way.[27] And they provided Tony golden opportunities to decompress from the stress that comes with professional competition. For many high-level athletes, it's not as simple as flipping a figurative switch to return to normal life.

"Everybody does it differently," explained Tony. "Some guys internalize it, go home, shut everything down. I don't know. You see it in sports. Some guys drink. Some guys go out to nightclubs. [You've] just got to find what works for you, and that year, that started working."

The historic Imperial Palace, located in Chiyoda, Tokyo, was one of his favorite spots to visit on these bicycle trips. Even in rainy weather, they'd excitedly peruse the exterior of Emperor Akihito's[28] primary residence. In addition to the Imperial Family's private living quarters, the grounds also contain the main palace, an archive, museums, and more. The elegant palace, which was built on the site of the old Edo Castle,[29] is a grand testament to the world's oldest reigning dynasty, a fact not lost on a marveling

Tony: "We don't have these things that are so old and so enshrined in history like Japan does, like a lot of the places throughout the world. It's fun to see where people came from, where cultures derived from, and how they used to be ruled. It's history."

Tony and Hillary had such rich history accessible to them, a quick ride away, and their appreciation for Tokyo's hidden historical gems only grew over time. When walking alone one time, Tony spotted an ancient temple, "tucked away in the corner" between tall, modern buildings. He loved to explore and discover.

In their quest to grow better acquainted with their new home, they liked to experiment with different routes. They aspired to travel down every single Tokyo street, a lofty and admittedly unrealistic goal—there are far too many across the sprawling city. When the two would inevitably lose their place, all they had to do was find a nearby main street, stop by its train station, and pick up a map. "It was easy to get lost," said Tony, "but it was also easy to find yourself again." They didn't view getting lost as a problem. It was always much more of an adventure. "It seems like it's an endless puzzle of streets on streets," he added. "Every time you turn down a new one, you're gonna see ten more. That's why I always thought the delivery services were so impressive there."

Late at night, the typically busy streets of Tokyo were fairly empty. With fewer cars and people around, they didn't have to carefully navigate their way through traffic in a chaotic metropolis. The impromptu excursions were rarely rushed—Tony would not have to report for work until early the next afternoon—which contributed to their laid-back quality. "We got free rein," said Tony. "It's cool when you're in a big city like that, and you kind of feel like you have it all to yourself."

Aoyama Cemetery featured prominently in their rides. "It was always on our route because we would always detour to it," said Tony with a laugh. The 65-acre cemetery's beauty captivated them. Elegant cherry blossom trees line the streets winding through the grounds. During springtime, primarily between late March and early May,[30] the flowers known as *sakura* are everywhere.

In the daytime, many people are visiting loved ones' graves or embarking on various outdoor activities. At night, the cemetery feels more, well, like a cemetery. Hillary would sometimes find herself getting lost, imagining, "Who are these people?" and "What kind of lives did they lead?" The centuries-old gravestones[31] particularly intrigued her, as did graves honoring gaijin, like one of the first American doctors to work in Tokyo. "It was kind of dark I guess, but it was really pretty," Hillary said of the morbid hangout spot.

Every once in a while, Hillary loved taking the train from Shibuya to the Kamakura station, an hour south. From there, she'd rent a bicycle and ride along the beach, noticing local fishermen trying their luck.

During her first two years in Japan, Hillary did not own a cell phone. "It was kind of liberating," she said. Early on, Tony bought her a pink compass necklace to make sure she always generally knew where she was. Along with her apartment key, often on the same necklace, Hillary wore the compass out of necessity every day. But over time, the necklace became much more than a security blanket. It became Hillary's most cherished possession from her time in Japan and, to this day, hangs in a special place in her home.

Cell phone–free liberation almost came with a price. Once, Hillary lost track of time and nearly got stranded in Nikko, a small city in the mountains north of Tokyo. Trails off the main street led to waterfalls, and as one approached each waterfall, wild monkeys started appearing in large numbers. Eschewing the largest, most popular waterfalls, she visited the more secluded ones, moving farther and farther from the train station as the day progressed. Suddenly, she realized, it was getting dark.

"Oh, my God," she thought. "'I have to start running. There's nothing else. There's no taxis, no buses.'" She was a mile from the station and had to catch the last train of the day. Fortunately, Hillary did, but not without a serious scare. "I remember thinking, 'I don't know Tony's Japanese number.' I don't even know what I would've done."[32]

A notable family development made Tokyo feel even more like home. During the season, Tony's stepbrother, Jesse, moved to Japan to teach English full-time. Although "me being there had no bearing on him going," said Tony, Jesse naturally jumped at the chance to live and work in a country whose cultural exports he loved. As an impressionable kid in Federal Way, Washington,[33] Jesse became enamored by franchises like Pokémon and Dragon Ball Z. He loved anime, science fiction, and fantasy more broadly too. "That kind of stuff really captured my imagination," he said. Upon moving to the area, he occasionally stopped by his brother's apartment, about an hour south, and Jingu Stadium.

One of Tony's most dominant performances came against Chunichi, when he struck out the side, utilizing his increasingly feared cutter on eight of twelve pitches, including all three Ks. Between June 9 and the August 3 Dragons game, he pitched 22 scoreless innings, lowering his ERA from an already strong 1.93 to a virtually impenetrable 0.75. During the stretch, opponents failed to muster even one extra-base hit. Tony's diligent approach was paying off. After he put in the requisite work and felt validation every step of the way—from bullpens to live batting practice to game action—his confidence grew and success begot more success.

Complementing the increased confidence, Tony's new routine fit him like a glove: "When you're getting ready to go every single day, the routine gets to be so repetitive and like a sixth sense. You just wake up, and you do it. You don't even have to think about doing it anymore. One moment I'm sitting at my locker. I close my eyes, and next thing you know, I'm already on the table getting stretched out. And you don't even realize you went in there.

"I like being ready every single day. I like having to be alert and tuned into every single minute of the game. Sitting around [between starts], watching the game happen all the time and not being a part of it, it gets boring and it's easy to lose focus that way. Whereas for a guy like me, having to be ready almost every second is a lot better for my personality. It keeps me in tune. It makes me discipline myself on making sure I'm at the right place, at the right time, and not screwing around and letting my mind wander."

Leading up to the stretch run, in an effort to rest Tony, Ogawa held him out of the next five games, including a couple close ones. Rather than benefit from the break, he fell into his only slump of the season, as he allowed five runs and 12 base runners over his following three appearances. Meanwhile, a 7–15–3 August threatened to compromise the team's sizable first-place lead.

He recovered, pitching well over his next seven outings. Ironically, number thirty-four's worst showing of the season came against the Giants, whose bats he silenced in all 10 previous encounters. But on September 3, Yomiuri teed off. Unable to get through the inning, he was ultimately charged with four earned runs.

It was an exception to Tony's rule of brilliance, a blemish on an otherwise masterpiece of a season for a pitcher who ended the previous year nearly out of baseball entirely. Much more costly than the dreadful performance itself, it was quickly determined that Tony injured himself. He knew something was off. His right wrist wasn't exactly sore, but "something just didn't feel right" when he delivered pitches that evening. He tried to power through. Afterward, X-rays revealed a tiny fracture,[34] which would keep him out virtually the rest of the regular season.

By October 7, the Swallows were in the doldrums and the Dragons had overtaken them for first place for the first time since May. After hosting lowly Hiroshima for a weekend series, Yakult would square off with Chunichi four times at Nagoya Dome. Ahead of the critical series, the Dragons led the Swallows by half a game. With a dominant showing, either team could separate itself from the other.

Given Yakult's thin, overworked bullpen,[35] the series came at an inopportune time—toward the end of a grueling twelve-games-in-twelve-days stretch. Chunichi pounced, winning the first three. With one more game in Nagoya, the Swallows had to dig deep. First place was slipping away.

Standing in their way? Kazuki Yoshimi, who was enjoying a career year. Against a tired Swallows club, the right-hander went the distance with a three-hit masterpiece. Four and a half games back with only five remaining, for all intents and purposes, a first-place finish was no longer in the cards. On the bright side, barring disaster, they appeared headed for a top-three finish, which would ensure a playoff berth. Specifically, second place looked likely.

To provide two of their gaijin game action before the playoffs began, the Swallows registered Tony and Whitesell for the season finale. It was Tony's first *ichi-gun* game in seven-plus weeks. Whitesell hadn't played in seventeen days.

Following the twelve-day stretch, the Swallows took advantage of a lull in their schedule—three games over ten days—by winning two of their final three to stave off the Giants for second place. Yomiuri (71–62–11) finished a game behind Yakult (70–59–15), setting the stage for the crosstown rivals to meet in a best-of-three opening-stage Climax Series to be played at Jingu Stadium.

Notes

1. Jackson famously also played pro baseball, but he did not don number thirty-four on an MLB diamond, instead wearing sixteen, eight, and later, twenty-two.
2. By season's end, NPB scoring decreased from the previous season by over 25 percent. In the Central League specifically, home runs declined by nearly 44 percent, while the league batting average drop was much more modest.
3. If a player didn't own a bike, like Tony the previous season, there were usually plenty of extra ones lying around.

4   Utsumi batted .091 over the past four seasons, striking out nearly half the time. As the Giants' perennial ace, his poor hitting could be tolerated. In 2011 and 2012, he'd go on to win 33 games, sporting a sub-2.00 ERA each season.

5   The single debuted in 1983, the year Tony was born.

6   Because the first nine innings ran more than four hours, well past the new three-and-a-half-hour limit, no extra innings were played.

7   This was a play on the moniker inspired by the Houston Astros' hitting quartet of Jeff Bagwell, Craig Biggio, Sean Berry, and Derek Bell in 1996. A few years later, Lance Berkman joined the Killer B's, taking Berry's place. Later, for the 2004 stretch run, Carlos Beltrán hopped aboard.

8   It wouldn't be until Tony's 2012 season that he'd much more frequently use the splitter he was still perfecting in 2011, but more on that later.

9   Yakult was "hosting" Hiroshima at the neutral Matsuyama Central Park Baseball Stadium, known colloquially as Botchan Stadium after *Botchan*, a century-old novel still extremely popular in Japan. Matsuyama was the book's setting.

10 NPB Interleague play is a mid-May-through-mid-June tradition.

11 In NPB, there is no injured (or bereavement) list, but when a player is deregistered from an *ichi-gun* roster, he cannot return for ten days, retroactive to the last game in which he competed.

12 The 2011 season would mark the second and final year of the Swallows' contract with Guiel, which was paying the outfielder a total of ¥200 million plus incentives.

13 Over the course of Guiel's professional career, he'd always been hit by pitch strikingly often, although he rarely enjoyed reaching base that way. "I just was not very good at getting out of the way," Guiel said. "Never was." Remarkably, he was hit by pitch on approximately 3.9 percent of his career NPB plate appearances.

14 In the Central League, only the Tigers and Carp played on grass.

15 It took Guiel 20 trips to the plate to make it happen.

16 A *modasho* refers to a game of three or more hits for any NPB hitter.

17 In 2013, the mathematically eliminated Swallows gave retiring infielder Shinya Miyamoto a rare start and penciled him in at shortstop and in the second batting slot, two spots he hadn't occupied in years. The nineteen-year pro went 0-for-5 on the night but just missed connecting on an 11th-inning sayonara homer that would have gone down as a storybook ending to his career. Instead, Matt Murton caught the ball on the warning track. Still, Miyamoto was celebrated like a king after the game.

18 Family members, typically on the field not too far away, are mentioned without fail.

19 Guiel would go on to coach at the rookie-ball level all season. Although he considered it a "great experience," he ultimately concluded a career in coaching was not for him.

20 Yakult also tied one of those games.

21 Hatakeyama's teammates endearingly nicknamed him "Boo," short for the pejorative Japanese word *debu*, meaning something like "fatso" or "fat ass." Supposedly, he didn't mind.

22 On May 20, Whitesell struck out in all four chances. During the Interleague period, he led NPB in strikeouts despite not starting all of the games.

23   Deregistering Whitesell made room for Guiel to return.

24   The consecutive 10-inning ties marked Yakult's first back-to-back set of ties since 1987. Undoubtedly impacted by the new three-and-a-half-hour time limit, the Swallows would record 15 ties in 2011 and 11 the next year, when the time limit was still in place. Over the 2011 and 2012 seasons, NPB teams averaged 10.8 ties, nearly quadruple the 2.9-tie average over the four "time limitless" seasons immediately preceding and following (2009–2010, 2013–2014).

25   The game-winner marked Balentien's second hit in 13 games, ending a miserable 1-for-42 slump for the NPB rookie.

26   It was nine months per year for Tony, who spent Februaries in Okinawa.

27   "If I didn't lift at the field after the game," said Tony, "or if I'd thrown for three days in a row and hadn't got a lift in or something like that, it was a great way for me to get out and get some low-impact exercise. We'd both get a workout, we'd both get out, see the city when most people are sleeping."

28   Akihito took over the throne when his father, Emperor Hirohito, died in 1989. An elderly Akihito abdicated the Chrysanthemum throne in 2019, stepping aside for his eldest son, Naruhito, to take his place.

29   The castle was in use from 1457 to 1873.

30   Cherry blossoms typically start appearing at the beginning of February.

31   The country's first public cemetery, it opened in 1874.

32   "I probably would have just stayed in a hotel," continued Hillary, "but Tony would have freaked out if I had never called him and I never came home."

33   The state of Washington trails only California when it comes to number of sister cities with a Japanese counterpart. In 1993, Federal Way became sister cities with Hachinohe of the Aomori prefecture.

34   According to Tony, before X-rays were taken, the team doctor thought it was tendonitis and wanted to inject him with cortisone. Tony emphatically declined.

35   Tony was still sidelined, as was lefty specialist Kentaro Kyuko, who had been similarly terrific all season.

CHAPTER TEN
LET'S GET MARRIED

He stopped dancing, and he asked me to marry him. It was simple and lovely.

It was a nondescript night back in January, a couple weeks before 2011 spring training would begin. Tony and Hillary had just returned from having dinner with her parents. They were going about their normal routine in their new house . . . or so it seemed. Actually, Tony was finally ready to propose. For weeks, he'd been waiting for the right moment.

"I'd been thinking about that next step and all that," said Tony. Hillary had been too. "After that first year in Japan, she basically told me, 'I'm not gonna go chasing you around the world if we're not serious about this.'" He knew what he had to do but wanted to catch her off guard. This was the time.

He started dancing in the living room, and she followed suit. For them, this wasn't anything out of the ordinary. But then, with Matthew Barber's soft, acoustic "You and Me" playing, Tony suddenly stopped dancing and asked Hillary to marry him. "It was simple and lovely," she said. Hillary didn't expect it, at least not then. Upon hearing the proposal, she covered her mouth with both hands, tears welling up in her eyes. The answer was obviously yes, which she conveyed after gathering herself.

Spring camp in Okinawa is designed only for the players, with wives and children all but prohibited from attending. Thus, Hillary had an additional five weeks after Tony's departure to tie up loose ends in Arizona and prepare the house to be unoccupied all season. She'd also use the time to begin planning the wedding. November 11, 2011, 11–11–11, they decided, would be a memorable date for the event and would allow Tony enough time to return from Japan.[1] For the venue, they secured the picturesque Boulders Resort & Spa in Scottsdale, Arizona. Save-the-date notices were sent out to the couple's closest family and friends.

Then 3/11 changed everything. With the season delayed by two weeks, a November 11 wedding no longer made sense. Unwilling to risk a wedding without the groom—Yakult could still be playing then—they moved the ceremony back to December 3 and mailed new save-the-dates.

On Saturday, October 29, Game 1 was close. Tied at one, Yakult pulled ahead with two sixth-inning runs. A half-inning earlier, left-handed starting pitcher Kyohei Muranaka had come in. The brevity of the opening round allowed starters to pitch in long relief since only three men were needed in the rotation. Therefore, Junji Ogawa entered the postseason believing the Swallows had enough arms to get past the Giants and opted to rest Tony's wrist another week.

With Muranaka retiring one Giant after another, inning after inning, Ogawa planned to let him finish the game. A two-out, ninth-inning home run changed the calculus, as the lead dwindled to one. Fortunately, all Chang-Yong Lim required to seal the victory was one pitch. With the 3–2 win, Yakult needed only a win or tie to advance to the Climax Series' final stage.

Another tight one, Yomiuri clung to a 2–1 lead until Yoshinobu Takahashi clubbed a bases-clearing, ninth-inning double off Lim. In Whitesell's first postseason appearance,[2] he supplied a late RBI double, but the Swallows never drew any closer, falling 6–2. A decisive Game 3 was scheduled for Halloween.[3] The game's loser would be haunted all offseason, while the winner would be visiting the Dragons for a best-of-seven series with a Japan Series berth on the line.

Twenty-one-year-old Swallows southpaw Katsuki Akagawa, a playoff novice, was tasked with starting the all-important third game. Although it was rarely pretty, Akagawa did his job, extricating Yakult from numerous jams to pitch six and two-thirds innings of scoreless baseball. Most notably, the youngster stranded a pair of runners in the fourth and fifth.

Whitesell earned a rare start. Batting third and playing first base, he recorded a hit in two at-bats before a defensive upgrade sent him to the bench. The Swallows got on the board with a solo homer in the third, later adding a pair of insurance runs to take a 3–0 lead. Muranaka, the starter-turned-playoff reliever who had pitched so well two nights earlier, appeared again. Avoiding using Lim, Ogawa hoped Muranaka could pitch the last two innings. After a perfect eighth, Muranaka and company were just three outs from advancing.

After striking out Alex Ramírez, Muranaka grooved a 2-0 fastball down the middle. The mistake pitch landed in the heart of the Swallows cheering section. Suddenly, the score was 3–1, but no pitching change was coming. The next man grounded to third. Two outs.

When Muranaka fell behind in the count 2-1, TokyoSwallows.com cofounder David Watkins and his friends in the cheering section started a rare chant for the pitcher, encouraging him as he battled the hero of the previous night, Takahashi. The support for the pitcher was contagious. "The *ōendan* looked at us," said Watkins, "and they joined in and then all of the right field and the whole of the Swallows section were then led by us essentially in chanting for the pitcher, which is the first time I can remember that happening." Traditionally, NPB fans alternatively cheer loudly for the offense and remain quiet while their team is in the field. In the TokyoSwallows.com game recap, Kozo Ota wrote, "The sight of half the stadium chanting for Muranaka and drowning out the Giants cheers was moving and can't be adequately described in words."

With the crowd audibly behind him, Muranaka challenged Takahashi, who fouled off the offering to even the count. On the next pitch, Takahashi swung hard and whiffed, allowing the Swallows faithful to exhale. Yakult was moving on to the next round.[4]

The 2011 Swallows dominated Chunichi, starting 9–3–3, until the Dragons reeled off eight wins in their final nine encounters. By virtue of winning the Central League, Chunichi was awarded a 1–0 series lead before any games were played.

A healthy Tony Barnette was summoned early after Yakult's starter failed to get through the third inning. Making his playoff debut, he threw a smooth inning and two-thirds. Whitesell, who didn't start, grounded to third to end the game, the tying run stranded in scoring position. The narrow win gave Chunichi a 2–0 series lead, and Swallows archnemesis Kazuki Yoshimi's fingerprints were all over it.

Desperately needing a win, Yakult decided to promote nineteen-year-old Tetsuto Yamada and bat him leadoff.[5] Neither team could generate offense until Yasushi Iihara's unexpected eighth-inning homer[6] put Yakult up by a run. The next inning, Kazuhiro Hatakeyama singled in two to provide enough cushion for a 3–1 Swallows win.

The following night, the Swallows won again, evening the series with a 2–1 victory. In the contest, Tony again appeared early and went on to record seven outs. When he was inserted, Yakult led 1–0, but the Dragons had the bases loaded. After one of the inherited runners scored on a single, Tony buckled down and got a strikeout and ground out to minimize the damage. Then, a Nori Aoki single gave the Swallows a lead they would never relinquish.

The celebration was short-lived after Yakult dropped the next one, 5–1. During the loss, Yamada collected his first *ichi-gun* hit and RBI, but he also struck out with runners on second and third in a critical fifth-inning opportunity. Trailing three games to two, the Swallows absolutely had to win to avoid an early vacation, and guess who Chunichi was starting . . . Kazuki Yoshimi.

In the fifth, Chunichi's light-hitting second baseman disrupted a scoreless pitchers' duel with a two-run home run.[7] The ninth inning represented Yakult's last chance. Until then, only one Swallow had reached scoring position. Pinch-hitter Ryohei Kawamoto changed that by striking a leadoff double, but two successive strikeouts put the comeback in jeopardy. Then, Aoki singled to center, trimming the deficit to a run. Still alive. Alas, Hatakeyama fouled out to third, ending the Swallows' 2011 campaign while sending the Dragons to the Japan Series.

Fittingly, Yoshimi, who overpowered Yakult all season, was the one to end its otherwise robust season with eight strong innings in the series clincher. Starting Games 1 and 5 just four nights apart, the 2011 Eiji Sawamura Award runner-up[8] won twice, pitching 15.1 innings during which he allowed one solitary run and eight hits.

Whitesell didn't start or play in any of the final three games, likely signaling the end of his Swallows tenure. As for Tony, he finished his first season as a reliever strong, and the Swallows played the deepest into the postseason that they had since 2001. On the field, there was plenty to build upon for both player and team. Plus, in less than a month, it would be time for the skilled setup man to get married in Arizona.

"Two days, and you're out. It's that quick," said Hillary of the typical turnaround time between the end of Tony's season and his departure from Tokyo. This year, she'd already returned a little earlier to prepare for the December wedding. Tony's flight left on his birthday, just three days after Yakult was eliminated by the Dragons.

They lived in the same team-supplied, one-bedroom apartment each of the first two seasons. Yakult didn't set specific move-out dates, but because the team paid for the apartments, gaijin residents knew they couldn't remain year-round (not that they wanted to). Fortunately, the apartments came fully furnished, so no heavy furniture needed to be moved.[9] The morning of Tony's move-out, someone from the complex would conduct an inspection. Then, Go Fujisawa would come over to help, loading a team van with their belongings before taking Tony to the airport for his late-afternoon/early-evening flight.

Factoring in the time change, Tony's twenty-eighth birthday would last incredibly long. He left Tokyo around 4 p.m., flew over ten hours to LAX, and then finally boarded his connecting flight to Phoenix. Upon landing, it was still his birthday with ample time remaining for an authentic birthday dinner with Hillary.

The next month, they got married on one of the coldest days of the year at Boulders Resort in Scottsdale. It even snowed later that night, but the prospect of rain was the bigger concern. As Hillary and her bridesmaids got dressed in a hotel room, they could hear the unrelenting rain hitting the skylight above the bathroom. "They kept asking me," said Hillary, "'Do you want to move it inside?' And I was like, 'No, the pictures aren't gonna look good inside. I want it to be outside.'"

The weather cooperated, allowing the wedding group an hour break in the downpour to take care of business. The overcast weather even had an aesthetic benefit for Hillary, providing attendees "some pretty cool clouds for a pretty sunset in Arizona." And the view was already impeccable as the ceremony was held on a golf course overlooking hills made of giant boulders.

Hillary looked stunning in a white tube top strapless dress, although she was not well covered, and neither were her bridesmaids, who could be seen shivering during the 45-degree ceremony. "It was freezing," said Hillary. "I think I could hear my sister's teeth chattering while we were taking photos. We were already gonna keep it short, but we kept it even shorter to try to get everybody back inside."

Tony was much warmer in a black suit with a cornflower blue tie and a white dress shirt underneath. "It was a pretty dressed-down occasion," Tony said. "Maybe I'd go tuxedo if I had to do it over again, but it worked perfectly. The guys and the girls looked good. Everything looked great, and we all had a good time." At the reception, the newly married duo danced to Chris LeDoux's 1995 cover of "Tougher Than the Rest," a Bruce Springsteen original.

The small wedding—approximately fifty guests attended—primarily consisted of relatives, with a few friends among the group. Lacking a particular theme, it focused on the couple's burgeoning love and the resort's beautiful scenery. Hillary's freezing sister served as her maid of honor, while Jason Urquidez,[10] a former teammate from Central Arizona College, Arizona State, and the Diamondbacks organization, acted as best man.

Tony enjoyed having baseball buddies Drew Bowman and Ike Davis on hand too. The three all played for the 2006 Sun Devils. For nearly a decade following college, Tony and Davis, also a professional base-ball player,[11] worked out together every offseason at Fischer Sports. Unfortunately, Guiel and Whitesell couldn't be there, with the former recovering in Canada and the latter in California tending to twin toddlers while considering his next career move.[12]

For Tony, the "biggest controversy of the entire wedding" was a mix-up by resort staff that resulted in his parents and their friends receiving gifts meant for the bride and groom. Phil and his wife had driven down from Washington with close family friends. When the group returned to their suite after the wedding, they found a bottle of champagne and chocolate-covered strawberries, among other desserts, waiting for them. They enjoyed their good fortune, making sure to send Tony a picture of the gift basket the next morning, along with a tongue-in-cheek thank you. At breakfast, "Everyone's got their sunglasses on, working on like four hours of sleep," said Tony. "It was awesome." By the following Monday, he and Hillary were already in Maui for their honeymoon.

Notes

[1]   The Japan Series typically finishes by the first week of November.

[2]   In the narrow Game 1 win, Whitesell neither started nor pinch-hit, a clear sign he'd fallen out of favor.

[3]   Although Halloween is traditionally a Western holiday, the Japanese have increasingly embraced it in recent years. Trick-or-treating never caught on, but many like to wear costumes on the streets and at parties.

[4]   Yakult's series win snapped a four-year streak (2007–2010) of no Central team other than the Dragons and Giants meeting in the Climax Series' final stage.

[5]   Prior to the game, the teenage second baseman had never played at the *ichi-gun* level.

[6]   Iihara was coming off a homerless season in which he slugged just .165.

[7]   Hirokazu Ibata had hit one home run all season.

[8]   Rakuten's Masahiro Tanaka took home the award. Established in 1947, nine years before the Cy Young Award, the Eiji Sawamura Award honors the year's top NPB pitcher and is named after a dominant Yomiuri Giants (then the Tokyo Giants) right-hander who was killed in combat during World War II. Unlike in MLB, there is not a separate award for each league, but rather one for the entire NPB.

[9]   For items that were difficult to send back to the States, like a blender, for instance, the Swallows would accommodate their gaijin families by allowing them to store a few boxes at the field.

[10] Urquidez, a right-handed pitcher, never appeared in the majors, but he did rise as high as Triple A and most recently appeared in the Mexican Pacific Winter League in 2019–2020.

[11] In 2008, after three impactful collegiate seasons as a power hitter, including a strong junior year in the bullpen as well, the Mets made Ike Davis a first-round draft pick. He skyrocketed through the Mets organization, debuting in April 2010 and keeping the everyday first-base job the remainder of that season.

[12] When Whitesell was released, he knew he wanted to return to Japan. By year's end, he'd signed a one-year deal with the Chiba Lotte Marines worth $300,000 plus incentives.

CHAPTER ELEVEN
DOMINANCE AND DISCOVERY

That's what makes Mariano Rivera so damn effective.

The night after Chunichi bounced Yakult from the postseason, center fielder Nori Aoki asked the Swallows president to post him for MLB teams. By the following month, he was officially granted his wish. Since his first full season, the left-handed-batting Aoki's sustained success and durability increasingly intrigued teams on the other side of the Pacific. He'd earned seven All-Star nods and six Golden Gloves[1] in seven chances and remains the only NPB player to have notched 200-plus hits in two distinct seasons.

By posting Aoki, the Swallows gave major-league teams a four-day window to bid for exclusive negotiating rights. After the Brewers' $2.5 million bid won (and was approved by Yakult), they had one month to come to terms on a contract. If they failed, Aoki would return to Yakult, and Milwaukee would be refunded its posting fee.

Also in December, the Nippon-Ham Fighters tentatively garnered a record $51.7 million posting fee[2] in return for negotiating rights with gifted young right-hander Yu Darvish. Later, he and Texas agreed on a sizable deal that guaranteed that both Darvish and Nippon-Ham would be paid handsomely. A day earlier, with considerably less fanfare, Aoki and Milwaukee signed a two-year contract worth a guaranteed $2.25 million.[3]

For the better part of a decade, the Swallows regarded Aoki as a foundational piece. Suddenly, their prized center fielder was gone. For their troubles, they received $2.5 million, but they had a void to fill. Aware of Aoki's forthcoming departure, Yakult added American outfielder Lastings Milledge. At the time of his signing, he was excelling in the Venezuelan Winter League following a season he predominantly spent in Triple A.

Milledge was kind of a big deal early on, appearing in the 1997 Little League World Series and winning gold at the 16-and-Under World Youth Baseball Championships in Mexico. *Baseball America* ranked him the best sixteen-year-old in the country. Out of high school, the Mets made the Florida native a first-round pick, and by twenty-one he'd debuted in the majors. But underlying the tantalizing talent, there was often a concern about his behavior, on and off the field. Most recently, he'd gotten into a fight in a winter-league game after miming a celebratory grenade lob.

Naturally, Yakult hoped the still young outfielder had permanently put such trouble behind him. When Milledge's missed flight out of Tampa delayed his arrival by a day, Japanese media outlets ran with the story, speculating about the headaches his presence could cause. A team representative claimed he was not concerned.

The Swallows also added thirty-three-year-old Orlando Román, a versatile pitcher who had started, closed, and done everything in between.[4] The Puerto Rican could potentially serve as a workhorse, but his *ichi-gun* spot would have to be earned. Considering the four-gaijin quota and the presence of Milledge and Wladimir Balentien, along with Chang-Yong Lim and Tony in the pen, one would have to be the odd man out at any given time.

During the offseason, Yakult's vaunted closer started feeling soreness in his throwing arm that just wouldn't subside. Over the previous four seasons with Yakult, ever since coming over from South Korea, Lim had saved 128 games. Pitchers break down. It happens. He'd been pitching professionally since he was a teenager and always with a sidearm delivery. Going into 2012, Lim was thirty-five years old with a sore elbow. The Swallows needed a new closer.

Management approached Tony early in spring camp. "Lim is having elbow issues," they told him, "so we're probably going to start off with you as closer and see how things go." Tony was thrilled for the opportunity to earn the all-important closer role, however temporary it might be. He was not, however, surprised to be given the shot after bouncing back from a miserable rookie year and seamlessly transitioning into the setup role. In so doing, he demonstrated a level of consistency that impressed team decision-makers.

As a starting pitcher, his control was a major concern. After issuing virtually one walk every other inning in 2010, Bullpen Tony completely turned it around, walking a tad over one every four innings pitched. Simultaneously, he raised his strikeouts-per-nine rate from 7.9 to 10.3. His hits and runs allowed dropped precipitously as well.

Throughout the spring, Tony hadn't given Ogawa one reason to try anyone else, so he was tabbed for the closer's job. From the moment he first stepped onto the pitching rubber on March 30,[5] no doubt remained as to who would finish the season as the closer. Tony produced 18 consecutive scoreless appearances out of the gate. During the streak, which spanned fifty days, he never pitched more than an inning and efficiently averaged 12.5 pitches per appearance.

Tony felt his velocity increase since converting to a relief pitcher. In the new role, "You're definitely throwing harder," he said, "because you don't have to save your bullets." But pitch speed in a vacuum does not create a successful closer, especially for someone like Tony who never threw in the high 90s anyway. "Sure, you can throw more fastballs on any given night, but when closers come into a game, a lot of the time they're not getting guys out with their fastball." Deception, achieved by mixing up speeds and diversifying one's pitch repertoire, then becomes critical to upsetting the batter's timing.

"The real good closers have that nasty out pitch, those dirty pitches they can throw for strikes," said Tony. "That's what makes Mariano Rivera so damn effective. He's got those movement pitches besides his fastball that are nasty, and he throws them for strikes. So you really don't know what's coming when it's coming that hard."

Building off the introduction of a devastating cutter, which was the driving force behind his 2011 success, Tony used the substantial integration of a filthy splitter to take his 2012 arsenal to an entirely new level. Despite experiencing some nights in 2011 when the splitter was clearly working, like the memorable May 8 tie with the Carp when he escaped a bases-loaded jam, Tony threw it at a 10 percent rate. He needed more time to perfect it. Only then would the splitter become a consistent pitch he could go to more often.

It wasn't effective overnight. "I didn't introduce it right away, but I kept playing with it. I kept practicing with it. I kept moving the ball around, trying different things, and asking different guys about it. And eventually I came up with something that resembled a pretty damn good split."[6] By 2012, he felt good enough to use it on a quarter of his pitches.

After the 2012 season, a bullpen session at Fischer Sports would further propel his confidence in the splitter. Tony was throwing to Chip Gosewisch, his offseason trainer, while Eric Sogard[7] stood in the batter's box, just taking pitches. "That is nasty," Tony remembers Gosewisch saying. Sogard chimed in that the pitch looked like a splitter. Until then, Tony had always thought of it as a sinker and still sometimes refers to it as such. Its name notwithstanding, the interaction got Tony thinking, "I've really got to start throwing this more." So he did.

Both pitcher and catcher entered each save situation with a general understanding of how best to attack various batters using information gleaned from the scouting report. Longtime catcher Ryoji Aikawa was very quiet and even-keeled, nothing like the other catcher, young Yuhei Nakamura, who was much more excitable. Aikawa had been around a while, so not much needed to be said. Tony and Nakamura, however, would have long conversations about strategy. If there was something specific Tony wanted from Nakamura, he had to be explicit about it.

Emulating Mariano Rivera,[8] Tony typically liked to attack lefties early with an inside cutter. "I'll try to get them to swing," he said. "In Japan, they swing early, and they swing often. They try to ambush the fastball. So what I'll do is I'll run a cutter in on their hands and hopefully break a bat or get them to swing and miss or just screw up and hit a soft ball and roll something over. Sometimes I'll try to get them looking in, and then I'll try to bury a sinker away when I get ahead with two strikes to try to get them to chase out of the zone." Against righties, he usually aimed the cutter on the outer edge and the splitter—or "sinker" in his parlance—on the inside corner, mixing in fastballs and curves as well.

Since he was a little kid, Tony always seemed to possess a confidence about himself and his abilities, yet various struggles and setbacks over the years tended to cause the occasional doubt to creep in. As a new and dominant closer, Hillary observed, he was feeling assured as ever.

"Obviously in his role, it has to be a close game for him to come in, so it's a lot more intense," she noted. "But he loves that. The more stressful it is, I think he likes that." The intensity of the moment—the pressure that comes with being the pitcher counted upon to induce the opponent's final three outs—extended beyond the pitcher himself. His wife, it turns out, very much felt it from her seat, whether she was watching from home or the stadium. Two seasons earlier, she felt compelled to arrive on time to see Tony pitch the entirety of his start. Then, the intensity, for he and Hillary alike, was spaced over a longer period of time with breaks in between for the Swallows offense to take its turn. "Now, it's like so much energy just in five to ten minutes of him throwing," Hillary added with delight. "It's crazy." And if Tony didn't pitch on a given night, that was fine by them too.

On May 30, Lim returned as a setup man, hoping to avoid any further setbacks. Although neither inning was perfect, two consecutive scoreless outings to finish May seemed to bode well for his future health prognosis. Unfortunately, Lim was only able to appear seven more times before Yakult shut him down for the season.

"One day, he was throwing slow," said Tony. "He couldn't really throw anything." The day after a shaky outing against Yomiuri, the Korean reliever was deregistered and scheduled for Tommy John surgery.[9] The appearance would go down as the final of Lim's Swallows career.

On June 29, Tony headed from the clubhouse to the bullpen in the middle of the sixth as usual. As the Tigers clung to a 6–4 lead, he knew his team once trailed 5–0; he'd been monitoring the game on TV. By the end of the seventh, it was tied. Tony hadn't pitched in three nights, so he was pretty sure he'd be summoned for the ninth inning regardless of what happened next. He began to stir around the pen and throw to a catcher.

In the eighth, the Swallows manufactured a run to take the lead. Then, Ogawa picked up the dugout phone and called the bullpen, located in right-field foul territory. The bullpen coach answered, heard Tony's name, and nodded to him. Tony grabbed a towel to wipe away the sweat that had accumulated on his face and the back of his neck. The public address announcer made it official: "Pitcher Baw-Net-Toh."

This was his cue to begin walking briskly down the foul line. Within seconds, he entered into his trot, as his handpicked song, "Sharp Dressed Man," played throughout Jingu. Just before reaching first base, he crossed into fair territory. Soon after, he was greeted around the mound by pitching coach Daisuke Araki, who placed the baseball in Tony's glove, and then with the same right hand, patted him gently on the lower back.

Interpreter Koji Kondo, dressed in off-white khakis and a navy blue polo, joined them[10] in case the pitcher needed any translation, which he didn't.

Also there, Nakamura uttered a quick, straightforward encouragement—to the effect of "go get 'em"—with his glove covering his lips before running back to his position behind the plate. Tony reached down to grab the rosin bag.[11] He tossed it three times, hitting it with his open palm first and last, getting the back of the hand on the middle toss. He began to settle in by using his right foot to sweep dirt off the rubber. After a few kicks, from the point of each cleat into the dirt, Tony was ready to throw. As the infielders took grounders behind him, he delivered five warm-up pitches.

On a 2-2 count, he unleashed his little-used curveball, which Hanshin's left fielder missed for out number one. After the next two batters failed to reach, Tony had retired the side in order for his 19th save. Concluding his ritual, he lobbed the ball into the crowd for a fan to take home.[12]

One morning, pitcher Seth Greisinger's girlfriend, Joana, brought Hillary to a church in the Roppongi district.[13] It wasn't to pray. There, at the Franciscan Chapel Center, Joana and a diverse group—consisting primarily of expat women from various countries—made food for the homeless. Going every week had become a habit for Joana, who was pregnant and unaccustomed to not working or volunteering. Soon enough, Hillary knew she wanted to do it too.

Most often, they would make *onigiri* with *umeboshi* on top.[14] Nothing complicated, but they felt they were making a difference. Neither Hillary nor many others in the group considered themselves religious or even attended church. For them, the church program was merely a vehicle to foster their generosity and share it with the world.

The two American baseball pitchers' partners bonded over the commonalities in their backgrounds. Joana met Seth at a Washington Capitals hockey game, much like Tony and Hillary first encountered each other at a Diamondbacks game. Neither couple dated for over three years thereafter, with both reconnecting when serendipitous life circumstances brought them together. Both Hillary and Joana were summoned to Japan by the game of baseball and approached the experience with open minds and intellectual curiosity. Hillary always looked up to Joana, who traveled extensively,[15] fluently spoke four languages, and started her own non-profit called One Vision One World, which focused on building schools and homes for underprivileged children in Haiti.

Lastings Milledge's girlfriend, Depree Bowden, also made quite the impression on Hillary as "one of the most friendly people I've ever met." When the two strolled the streets of Tokyo, redheaded Hillary and the towering Depree, a former Division-I basketball player, found it impossible to blend in. Then again, that was part of the fun. "She was a show-stopper," Hillary said. Additionally, Depree's spontaneity and openness to adventure was a breath of fresh air. "I don't think she ever says no to anything," she added. One time, Hillary felt like walking home despite being five miles away. She was with Depree, who unsurprisingly agreed to accompany her. "She was just always game for whatever."

In Japan, Hillary's closest friends were Ken and Yuri. She met Ken, a Tokyo native about a decade her senior, at a Swallows game. Given his flawless English, they communicated effortlessly. "Becoming friends with Ken just totally opened a whole new side of Japan for us," said Hillary. He would take her and Tony to restaurants he enjoyed. Naturally, almost by osmosis, they picked up much about the culture by spending time with him. But learning was never the overarching goal. Whatever they did, they had fun.

Early on, Ken introduced her to a vivacious woman named Yuri, who fluently spoke English, Japanese, and French. Yuri joined them for dinner, and Hillary instantly felt at ease. "From the day I met her, it felt like I've known her forever," she said. "She lights up a room. She just changes the whole atmosphere."

Yuri, too, helped Hillary discover places she almost certainly would not have stumbled upon if left to her own devices, including an excellent *yakitori* restaurant located extremely close to where they'd been living for years. "Take a turn down a dark side street here and then take another turn," said Hillary, describing the hidden route. "Then walk down this set of stairs that you never would have noticed. It's this tiny place, but it's so good. Who finds something like that? It's something you never find."

In June 2012, TokyoSwallows.com was approaching its thousandth post since David Watkins, Chris Pellegrini, and Garrett DeOrio had launched the fan site four years earlier. In their inaugural post, DeOrio announced their presence and mission, while sprinkling in contextual details on Yakult's recent schedule and results. A photo of a scantily clad woman wearing a Swallows cap and a blue bikini top accompanied the text. In starting the website, they most fundamentally sought to connect with like-minded Swallows fans near and far, while hopefully bringing aboard new admirers too. Of course, the trio also started it as an outlet for their fandom, a way to write about their beloved team when few cared to hear their takes at home or their nine-to-fives.

The more readers, the merrier, but monetizing the website was never the goal, nor was it considered realistic given the fringe nature of the operation. The Swallows were then one of the least popular teams, and the website would be written entirely in English. In the early years, the enterprise gradually picked up steam, attracting a small but loyal following. The guys added a couple writers along the way and continued to diligently recap game after game before launching a monthly podcast in the summer of 2011 to complement the written coverage.

In celebration of their thousandth post, they wanted to thank their supporters and take a moment to enjoy what they'd created and grown. So they planned a party for Saturday evening, June 9. It would be a small, closed affair, reserved only for the writers and their supporters who took an early interest in frequenting the site and/or commenting below the posts. Pellegrini had one other person he wanted to invite: Tony, one of the team's most recognizable players by this point.

When rain caused Yakult's home game to be postponed, Tony suddenly had time in his schedule and thought it could be fun: "They extended the invite, and you're like, 'Well, let's go down there and say what's up to the people.'" Pellegrini wanted to keep it a secret in order to maximize the excitement of the closer's appearance, but also because he couldn't be sure Tony would actually attend.[16]

Tony, with Hillary, arrived minutes before 8. For Watkins, seeing Tony, a player he'd often written about yet never met was "super-exciting, but it was just really weird. I never imagined that that would happen." It felt surreal. Early on in their conversation, Tony wryly brought up something Watkins had written about him in 2010. "Something like 'And with that, the Tony Barnette honeymoon period is over,'" said Watkins, "and he just quoted it back to me and said, 'I remember when you wrote that.' It's like 'Wow. This is really strange.'"

The cameo was pretty laid-back. Tony and Hillary enjoyed refreshments and mingled with the crowd. It was a nice opportunity to meet the website's writers, all fellow expats. "They're just an interesting group," said Tony. "All of them from different backgrounds, different stories, all ended up in Tokyo and just get together and talk about a baseball team that's got highs and lows. Major highs and lows."

"How do you throw your nasty cutter?" someone asked. Why not show them since a baseball happened to be within reach, Tony thought. He spoke plainly and from the heart: "I don't know. I just hold it like this and just throw the shit out of it. There's really no secret magic. I don't put any spells on it. I practice. I found out how to do something pretty cool, and I just try to keep doing that, you know?"

Later, the assembled group participated in a lottery, which was giving away items signed by Tony. Fittingly, they asked the man himself to pick a couple winning numbers. Put on the spot, he chose the digits of his "Showtime" uniform number, three and four, before apologizing for his unoriginality. Within a couple hours, they went home with a memorable experience in tow.

"You don't think about it at the time," said Tony, "but Hillary and I, we're young people, we're just foreigners in Japan, we don't have many friends, and then all of a sudden there's these people that take an interest in what you do, that are fans of the game, and they invite you to come to a thing. It's like 'Okay, why not say yes to stuff?' That's one of those things that Hillary and I have tried to do over the years. I try my hardest, but I refuse to not be like a normal person."

Watkins found Tony to be personable and easy to talk to. Even his mere presence certainly was appreciated, validating the writers' hard work and enraptured attention over the years. "It was quite a good reward for what we'd been doing," said Watkins.

Upon Lastings Milledge's arrival, some members of the media said he resembled comedian Tetsuro Degawa, who happens to consider himself a Swallows fan. Besides stark physical differences in height[17] and skin tone, and a twenty-one-year age gap, the two both possess round faces with similar smiles and noses. The resemblance, though, is almost beside the point for the Japanese media, who like to generate excitement by introducing gaijin in fun and memorable ways—à la Tony Barnette, the fusion of Tom Cruise and Keanu Reeves.

During his time in the majors, Milledge became known for the long dreadlocks that extended below his neck. When he arrived, the dreadlocks were gone, his hair was fashioned into a sort of fauxhawk, with a buzz cut on each side and noticeably more hair on top. In Okinawa, Milledge was initially intimidated by the food offerings.[18] But at the end of the lunch line, there would always be fried Spam, which he typically added to his plate. That earned Milledge the nickname Spam, although Tony didn't remember it sticking for long.

In Yakult's season-opening win, Swallows bats produced 13 hits, but Milledge couldn't buy one. Batting third, the left fielder struck out twice. He singled the next night but also struck out three times.

Later in the week, Orlando Román debuted on a Friday April night, just as Tony had done two seasons earlier. Standing tall at six-foot-one and over 200 pounds, the righty boasted sideburns that extended to the bottom of his earlobes. He sported a goatee to go with his short brown hair. Facing the Dragons, Román performed admirably but lost 1–0. The following afternoon, Milledge wasted little time avenging Román's loss by smashing the second pitch he saw into the left-field seats, marking his inaugural NPB home run.

Two weeks in, the .500 Swallows looked unbalanced. Strong pitching and defense mitigated the trouble their lack of hitting caused. Then, on April 14, they erupted for 10 runs, triggering a 13–4–1 stretch. Meanwhile, Milledge was growing more comfortable.

Seven games later, Milledge helped Román achieve his first win in four tries. Earlier that night, he had grounded into a rally-killing double play. Undeterred, he smoked a fifth-inning double to break a 2–2 tie. A quartet of relievers, including Tony, held the one-run lead to secure a sweep over the Giants. During the postgame Hero interview, Wladimir Balentien nailed Milledge with a towel full of shaving cream, much like D'Antona did to Whitesell following his debut.

For all the concerns some had going into the season, Milledge proved to be a model citizen in Tokyo. There were a couple missteps over the course of the season but nothing too serious. Late in a tight May game, Milledge lost his temper after a disputed called third strike and appeared to curse,[19] a fairly automatic ejection, especially for gaijin who are given less latitude. He briefly had to be restrained.

A much more bizarre ejection happened two months later in Hiroshima. Displeased with a couple strike calls, Milledge said as much while walking back to the dugout following a strikeout. Despite avoiding any expletives or histrionics, he was summarily tossed. Ogawa had his back, both on the field and in postgame comments, but the second ejection automatically triggered a one-game suspension and a league-imposed ¥100,000 fine.

Back in May, the Swallows hoped to carry their winning ways into the Interleague period. In recent years, they'd struggled against opponents from the comparatively stronger Pacific League.[20] Following a trouncing of the Fukuoka SoftBank Hawks, they then fell into their worst funk of 2012, dropping ten straight, most of which were not close. During the period, their starting pitching suffered, and Tony finally surrendered his first runs of the season. By June 20, Yakult had fallen to .500 thanks to their 9–15 Interleague record.

By early July, the Giants had overtaken Chunichi for the Central League lead, and Yakult was within striking distance in third. Despite their middling first half, the Swallows earned seven All-Star selections, running the gamut from first-timers Katsuki Akagawa and Tony to forty-one-year-old Shinya Miyamoto. Balentien, the NPB home-run leader, earned a second All-Star nod in as many chances.[21] Conspicuously missing was Milledge, whose offensive punch and above-average defense had been invaluable.

Holding multiple All-Star Games has been an annual tradition since 1951, a year after NPB's inception. Since 2002, two All-Star Games had been scheduled on consecutive nights and hosted by different regions in an effort to reach more fans across the country. Since 3/11, though, the league added a third event and would be doing the same for the 2012 festivities.[22]

Tony was excited to be named to his first All-Star team and to have the opportunity to share it with Hillary, whom he brought along to Osaka (Game 1), Matsuyama (Game 2), and Morioka (Game 3). A private plane shuttled the players and coaches and their guests from city to city. Due to the frenetic schedule, Hillary didn't get to explore as much as she would have liked, but the Matsuyama portion was her highlight: "I went up this mountain and went walking around the city. Then after the game, Tony and I were able to walk through town in the dark back to our hotel, so that was really cool."

From a baseball perspective, Tony's first All-Star appearance underwhelmed him. He did record a save as the CL took the opening game 4–1. Tony was welcomed with a double by Nippon-Ham's Dai-Kang Yang, who had already homered in the game. Next, despite falling behind 3-0, Tony retired that batter and the next two, most notably getting former big leaguer Wily Mo Peña to fly out to the warning track to end the game. "I remember walking out of there. I was like, 'Wow. That was extremely unspectacular.'" A day and a half later, he felt discomfort in his back and was done for the rest of the break.

Fortunately, the strain was deemed to be minor and only sidelined Tony for less than three weeks. A pair of his Yakult All-Star teammates had much more memorable performances. In the finale, in Kazuhiro Hatakeyama's home prefecture of Iwate, an area badly damaged by the earthquake and tsunami, the first baseman homered,[23] though the PL won 6–2. That night, Akagawa, still twenty-one, impressed with three perfect innings against some of the league's best. The electrifying performance won him a car. He didn't have a driver's license but said he planned on getting one soon. In the meantime, his parents could have the Mazda.

Román proved to be a wise addition. A 9–11 record belied his 3.04 ERA. At times he struggled with control, but he was the workhorse Yakult desired, frequently pitching deep into games. Most impressively, emerging from the All-Star break, Román threw 380 pitches over three consecutive complete games, including two shutouts.[24]

Despite his steady start, he was demoted in mid-June due to Yakult's gaijin logjam. Román knew the team had more gaijin than spots for them and respectfully went down to Toda without as much as a negative word. His patience quickly paid off when Lim was shut down and the final gaijin spot opened up.

Boasting a three-game advantage over the Carp for the final playoff spot with the season winding down, the Swallows traveled to Hiroshima for a critical three-game series. Yomiuri had easily secured the top spot with a dominant second half,[25] and Chunichi all but locked up second place. As they prepared for Hiroshima, they learned that a left shoulder strain would sideline Milledge for weeks, likely ending his regular season. That night, a blown Carp save set the stage for a one-batter, two-pitch save for Tony in the bottom half.

In the middle game, Shohei Tateyama tossed a 146-pitch complete game for the winning Birds, who were conserving Tony's arm for the stretch run. He had pitched each of the previous four days and six of the last seven. And this wasn't the only time all year he'd pitched four straight days.[26]

Hungry to complete the sweep, Yakult came from behind again to do just that, dealing Hiroshima's playoff hopes a fatal blow. A 23–12–3 finish lifted the Swallows' spirits and provided confidence as they prepared for their first-round matchup with the Chunichi Dragons, a rematch of last postseason's epic battle. About half of the stellar closing stretch came without Milledge, who was expected back and healthy in time for the playoffs.

Tony ended the regular season as strong as he started, resulting in the best year of his career to date. From July 14 through October 5, the closer allowed one measly earned run and picked up 13 of his NPB-leading 33 saves.[27] If his microscopic 1.82 ERA wasn't his biggest accomplishment, he again improved his hits-allowed rate and more impressively managed to lower his walk rate to an elite 1.8 per nine innings. All the while, his strikeout-to-walk ratio improved to better than 4.7. Simply put, he was dominating the competition.

Tony is confident that transitioning into the closing role took his career to heights it never would have reached had he remained a setup man: "I probably still would've done well as a bullpen guy in the eighth inning, but the fact that I was a closer and I did so well, it definitely spring-boarded my career and gave me a little more of the attention and more of the spotlight." Ahead of the upcoming postseason, his success in the role also set into motion discussions of a sizable new contract. "Now everybody's eyes are on me, hoping that I continue the pitching I've done for the past couple years."

Notes

[1] The Golden Glove is Japan's version of MLB's Gold Glove.

[2] Daisuke Matsuzaka had held the record after the Red Sox paid the Seibu Lions a posting fee of approximately $51.1 million in late 2006. Matsuzaka was named after Swallows pitching coach Daisuke Araki, who at the time had just starred in the 1980 Summer Kōshien tournament as a sixteen-year-old.

[3] Aoki's 2011 base salary with Yakult was considerably higher at approximately $4 million, although his deal with Milwaukee was packed with performance incentives.

[4] Román had actually played with Milledge in the Mets farm system.

[5] Tony's first save capped off Yakult's season opener in which Masanori Ishikawa no-hit the Giants through eight and one-third but left with leg cramps after his no-hitter had been spoiled. The new closer needed only eight pitches to secure the two-out save.

[6] Tony claims he "didn't really have a full grasp" of his splitter until 2015.

[7] Eric Sogard, Tony's college teammate at ASU, had split the past season between the Oakland A's and their Triple-A affiliate in Sacramento. In 2023, he would represent the Czech Republic in the World Baseball Classic as its only player with MLB experience and collect seven hits in four games.

[8] Hall of Fame third baseman Chipper Jones once compared Rivera's cutter to a "buzz saw" for the devastation it had on left-handed batters in particular.

[9] Also known as ulnar collateral ligament reconstruction, this procedure was devised in 1974 when Dodgers team doctor Frank Jobe operated on pitcher Tommy John. It's especially common in baseball.

[10] By rule, only one interpreter per language per team could sit in the dugout or go onto the field each game. Therefore, Go remained in the bullpen with the pitchers, while the more senior English translator, Kondo, took the field when needed.

11   Pitchers use rosin bags to keep their hands dry and improve their grip on the baseball.

12   "I always gave 'em away," said Tony of his save balls. "You should've seen the faces when they'd get it. Handing it to a kid was the best, but watching the mad scramble for a ball tossed fifteen rows up was always a joy."

13   Both lived nearby. Although Seth left the Giants to join the Chiba Lotte Marines ahead of the 2012 season, he continued living in the Roppongi district.

14   These are essentially rice balls with fermented *ume* fruits served on top. *Umeboshi* is often translated into English as "Japanese salt plums" or "fermented plums," but they are technically a species of apricot.

15   Largely because her father worked in the oil industry, Joana had lived on four different continents by her early twenties, including, in order, South America, Africa, Europe, and North America. Following the 2013 season, travel enthusiasts Joana and Seth celebrated their upcoming nuptials with a trip through Vietnam, Cambodia, and Thailand.

16   Pellegrini also kept quiet about the possible appearance out of respect for Tony, whose Swallows were scheduled to play the following afternoon.

17   Degawa stands five-foot-three, around 8 inches shorter than Milledge.

18   Although Milledge disliked Japanese staples, like rice and noodles, he loved *yakiniku*, which he ate with Balentien on a number of occasions.

19   "That's a fucking joke," Milledge said, according to David Watkins' lip-reading.

20   The Swallows' most recent winning Interleague period came in 2009.

21   Pitcher Shohei Tateyama, first baseman Kazuhiro Hatakeyama, and catcher Ryoji Aikawa rounded out the Swallows' All-Star contingent. By virtue of Yakult finishing second in 2011, manager Junji Ogawa was chosen as an assistant coach for the Central League too.

22   For the previous year's Game 3 in Sendai, the players association hosted one thousand Japan Self-Defense Force—the name for Japan's military—troops who were involved in providing support to affected areas. The 2013 All-Star week would also hold three events.

23   This marked Hatakeyama's first Tōhoku region home run in 20 games played there. He hails from Hanamaki, about forty-five minutes south of Morioka Stadium, where the game was played.

24   Román had no other complete games in 2012. Still, only three Central League pitchers finished with more: Kazuki Yoshimi (6), Daisuke Miura (6), and Kenta Maeda (5).

25   Yomiuri would finish the 2012 regular season with an impressive 86–43–15 record.

26   Tony also did so August 29 through September 1, a stretch that strangely yielded zero saves in the midst of two team wins and two ties. In addition, the busy closer pitched four times in five days twice more earlier in the season, in late April and mid-June.

27   Hitoke Iwase also saved 33 games for the Dragons.

CHAPTER TWELVE
SHOW ME THE YEN

As of right now in my life, money is not going to be an issue.

This time around, Yakult drew Chunichi one round earlier. The Dragons' nine-and-a-half-game advantage earned them the privilege of hosting the best-of-three series. That aside, the Swallows took some solace in their 13–8–3 head-to-head record, including 6–3–1 at Nagoya Dome. And Lastings Milledge would be back.

Neither Milledge nor his teammates could do much offensively in the opener. They stranded the bases loaded in the eighth and subsequently lost 6–1. The defeat left Yakult with little margin for error.

Led by ace Shohei Tateyama, who delivered six scoreless innings, the Swallows fought back in Game 2. In the fourth, Wladimir Balentien's second homer of the series put them ahead 1–0. Picking up where Tateyama left off, two relievers patched together a scoreless seventh. Then, Junji Ogawa called upon his lights-out closer to slam the door. Not once all year had Tony been asked to pitch two full innings.[1] Yet Ogawa's faith was rewarded. On a 1-0 fastball, cleanup hitter Tony Blanco grounded to third. The next two batters flew out, and Tony followed the 1-2-3 inning with a 1-2-3 ninth, knotting the series at one game apiece.

With a final-stage date with the Giants on the line, all was riding on a decisive Game 3. Scheduled for the next night, there'd be no rest for the weary. Of course, the winner would advance. Unique to NPB rules, however, should a tie occur, the higher-seeded Dragons would win the series.

For the all-important game, Chunichi opted to start forty-seven-year-old Masahiro Yamamoto.[2] Boasting a deep and accomplished bullpen, the first-year Dragons manager was content to feature his relievers heavily as long as Yamamoto could keep them close. Game 3 unfolded similarly to Game 2. The Swallows manufactured a second-inning run and led 1–0 through seven and a half innings.

With the top of the Dragons' lineup due up, they weren't going to go away easily. Liking the idea of a lefty-lefty matchup, Ogawa permitted Katsuki Akagawa, a 2011 playoff standout, to face Yohei Oshima. The tiny center fielder reached with his ninth hit of the series. Employing typical Japanese station-to-station baseball, Chunichi bunted the speedy Oshima, the potential tying run, into scoring position.

Tetsuya Yamamoto relieved Akagawa, but lasted one batter after quickly walking the next Dragon. Despite Tony's Game 2 workload, Ogawa determined he needed his most reliable pitcher to extricate Yakult from the eighth-inning jam.

"I was gassed," Tony said later. "I remember my arm was hanging already." He had also warmed up twice before coming in. But it was playoff baseball, a win-or-go-home situation. Amped in such a critical moment and facing Kazuhiro Wada, who'd homered in Game 1, Tony quickly got ahead. At 1-2, he tried a slow curveball out of the zone. Wada didn't bite.

Each of the next two pitches also missed, leaving Tony in quite the pickle with the bases loaded and the dangerous Tony Blanco stepping to the plate for the Tony Bs' second encounter in as many nights. Though Blanco had gone hitless in eight series at-bats, he'd demonstrated his substantial power ever since he got to Japan in 2009.[3] Much to Tony's alarm, he could not locate any of his first three pitches. Not wanting a walk to force in the tying run, Tony "threw a fastball right down the middle, and he swung right through that damn thing. He swung and missed, and I was like, 'God.'"

There was no time to feel relief. Blanco was waiting for his 3-1 offering. "In hindsight, I should've thrown a cutter," he said, "but I've thrown three cutters for balls. I've gotta try to spot this next fastball. I've gotta get it in there. I tried to pound it down and away, and it just leaked up and over, and he hit the shit out of it." Blanco deposited the ball deep into Nagoya's left-field bleachers for a grand slam at the worst possible juncture for the visiting Swallows. "He did not miss it, man. He crushed it."

"My arm, it just hadn't rebounded." Tony's two-inning Game 2 save, coupled with heavy usage over the season's closing five weeks,[4] rendered him something other than the dominant closer Ogawa had come to expect every time he called his number. "You look to the dugout," continued Tony, "and they're not coming for you."

Mercifully, Tony was able to retire the next two Dragons. In the ninth, a last-second comeback was not to be, as Yakult went down in order, leaving Balentien in the on-deck circle[5] and Chunichi advancing to the next round. After the game, Ogawa admitted he "used [Tony] in an unfair situation."

"Deflation" was the term Tony kept coming back to when reliving the brutal loss. "Just the most utter deflation," he recounted. "I was so deflated. I remember sitting on my seat in the bus, and man, the sound of the stadium just doesn't leave you. Everything's over. That's the weird feeling about losing this way 'cuz it just sucks. You sit there, and there's nothing else to do except for just go home now. You don't get to celebrate. You don't really want to say goodbye to anybody. You don't say, 'Hey, good job this season,' whatever. There's nothing really else to do except for just get your shit and go home."

As the 2012 NPB playoffs approached, Tony and his agent felt good about his prospects for obtaining a lucrative new contract, which would include a handsome pay raise. Going into the season, he wanted a two-year deal. He felt he'd earned a little more security after impressing as a first-time reliever. Yakult didn't agree, instead offering another vesting option. Tony was not interested in a contract whose terms would so heavily be shaped by his statistical output.

"I hate playing baseball that way," he said. "Every time I give up a run, I'm almost having a heart attack because you have to be a stat rat. It sucks to play toward stats, so we told them that we're not going to do any type of option."

Thus, Tony signed a straight one-year deal, knowing he'd be entering restricted free agency ahead of 2013. He'd be free to negotiate with Yakult or any team in the world except for other NPB clubs. He was essentially betting on himself, banking on a productive 2012 campaign that would send the message, loud and clear, that he was worthy of a big-time contract at a critical moment in his career. The Lim injury provided Tony the golden opportunity to step into the coveted closing role, a spot where he flourished, elevating his game to new heights. Naturally, this strengthened agent Don Nomura's bargaining position.

Throughout the negotiating process, which began just before the postseason, Tony was pretty hands-off. While he prepared for what he hoped would become a deep playoff run, Nomura contacted the Swallows front office, asserting that his client would be seeking the two-year deal they refused to offer after 2011 and approximately $2 million per year. Privately, he told Tony that he'd consider anything above $1.25 million annually to be a good deal. Nomura was merely opening with a higher bid because that's what good negotiators do: They start high, their opponent usually starts low, and then, ideally, the two parties can find a mutually agreeable set of terms somewhere in the middle.

Periodically during the negotiations, Nomura would text or call Tony with updates. Initially, the Swallows countered Nomura's two-year, $4 million offer with a two-year, $2 million proposal that included additional performance incentives. He quickly declined the counteroffer, but discussions continued.

By mid-December, Nomura and Yakult agreed to a guaranteed $3.2 million over two years. On top of the $1.6 million of base salary for each of the next two seasons, a maximum of $800,000 in performance incentives would be available. The Swallows publicly shared the news, along with the revelation that they'd picked up the 2013 options of Balentien and Milledge. Additionally, they secured Balentien's services for three more seasons, through 2016, for $2.5 million annually and Milledge's for two more years for a total of $3.3 million.[6]

Sure, Hillary knew that top-tier professional baseball players could command a great deal of money. She also knew that her husband fit that mold after a spectacular season in the prime of his career. Still, "When they started talking about money," she said, "I had no idea, and I think his agent was kind of like, 'What did you expect?' And we really didn't know what to expect. But when they started throwing out numbers, I just couldn't even comprehend it anymore."

Over the previous three seasons in Japan, Tony made a tad over $1.5 million. With that income, he bought his and Hillary's dream home in Litchfield Park, he bought a car, and he started putting money away in investment and retirement savings accounts. Ahead of his 2009 Triple-A season, Tony had purchased a black Ford F-150 long bed, which allowed him to "basically pack my life with me everywhere I went." The next car, a gray F-150, didn't need to store all his earthly belongings and would presumably last a while, sitting unused in Arizona for large parts of every year.

According to Tony, he and Hillary are not "extravagant kind of people." Some of his teammates, particularly fellow gaijin, would needle him about being cheap or not spending more to enhance certain aspects of his outward appearance. They may as well have been howling at the moon. But did anything change after Tony received word of his sizable pay raise? "Nothing absurd," he said. "Not like Omar Epps in *Major League II*[7] when he rolls up in that huge limo. It's definitely nothing crazy. Obviously, I bought some nicer clothes. Back when I wasn't making money, I'd be wearing the same pair of jeans for five years. You go to the mall looking for those two-for-$20 jean sales."

Tony said he considers luxuries to be functional items they'll end up using and enjoying again and again, stuff like camping gear or a fishing boat. They much prefer such purchases to superficial items of status. "I don't need a Louis Vuitton travel bag or anything," clarified Tony. "I don't need a $3,000 bag that's going to be chucked around by an airport worker."

As he described months after signing the contract, he felt like a gigantic weight had been lifted: "Right now in my life, money is not going to be an issue. I'm obviously very thankful for that, me and Hillary both. The fact that I can provide Hillary with the type of life that I'm going to be able to, that alone just means the world to me." The following April, Hillary said, "I don't think it has sunken in yet for either of us or ever will. It's so surreal. That was life-changing."

Additionally, the nature of the contract allowed Tony to stop placing undue pressure upon himself to hit statistical benchmarks. "Now I can just concentrate on doing what I have to do to win a baseball game," he noted. "Obviously, there's still going to be pressure on me to win ball-games, to get saves, to get guys out, but I'm not going to be going home at night saying, 'Fuck, I'm not going to have a job next year if I don't pull my head out of my ass.' Now, if I have a bad game, I can catch my thoughts on the game—what did I do wrong and what do I have to fix so that it doesn't happen again as opposed to what the long-term repercussions of that one bad game are going to be."

Notes

[1]   In an early-June save at Orix, Tony retired four batters, the most he had in any one 2012 appearance.

[2]   Yamamoto broke his own record for oldest pitcher to start a Climax Series game. In 2006, the lefty no-hit the Giants at forty-one years old, another NPB record. In Game 3, he performed serviceably but was replaced after 55 pitches and three innings.

[3]   Blanco launched 71 home runs over his first two NPB seasons. Despite missing ample time the following two years, he managed to hit 40 more. Blanco would finish his Japanese career with 181 dingers and a .516 slugging percentage.

[4]   Tony made 17 appearances over that closing stretch, including two instances of four straight days on the mound.

[5]   Deliberately avoiding Balentien's bat, Chunichi walked him on all but one of his plate appearances from the sixth inning of Game 2 onward.

[6]   Yakult and Milledge also agreed on a mutual option for 2016. Both Milledge's and Balentien's deals included performance incentives.

[7]   Omar Epps played flashy center fielder Willie Mays Hayes after Wesley Snipes declined to reprise his role for the sequel.

CHAPTER THIRTEEN

WE JAPANESE LANGUAGE SCHOOL

Baseball players are baseball players no matter what country you're in. He teaches them dirty American words, and they teach dirty Japanese words.

From the moment Hillary moved to Tokyo, she'd been interested in formally learning the language spoken all around her, and by Year 3, she was. Clear-eyed about how difficult it would be, she endeavored to take an intensive course in order to best and most quickly achieve her goal.

Just before Tony left for the field, Hillary would take off on her bike to We Japanese Language School, often passing the famous Shibuya Crossing and the iconic Hachikō statue, and make her way up to the fourth floor.[1] The class ran four days each week from 12:30 till 5. Other than the half-hour break midway through, it was pretty much all Japanese, all the time. The timing worked perfectly, allowing Hillary to align her weekday schedule with Tony's. While he was at the field readying for the night's game, she was in school working hard. When the class ended, she'd rush home to change clothes for the game or settle in to watch on TV.

She benefited from learning from two instructors, a woman and man, with vastly different instructional styles. On Mondays and Thursdays, she'd have one, and on Tuesdays and Fridays, the other. Anzai-*sensei's*[2] approach centered around book learning, whereas Yamaguchi-*sensei* high-lighted conversational skill in an effort to accelerate fluency and comfort with the language. "He was a lot more like, 'Don't look at your notes,'" Hillary said of Yamaguchi, "'look me in the eye, I'm just gonna ask you a bunch of questions and pop quiz you. Just respond really fast.' He would try to trick me, and it would work every time." These moments often helped Hillary avoid repeating the same mistakes. By contrast, Anzai was more "nurturing," offering an encouraging word or warm smile if a student wasn't quite grasping the material. The two styles complemented each other, particularly coming in consecutive days.

Many of We's other classes, which spanned an hour per day over a longer stretch, predominantly featured American students and were larger in size. Hillary's class was cozy, providing the opportunity for considerable one-on-one teacher-to-student attention. Actually, just Hillary and two others comprised their first semester class, which rotated between the two *sensei*s for two and a half months.

When the class concluded, Hillary enrolled for the next semester, encouraged by her progress and determined to learn more. Both teachers retained their roles. By virtue of the back-to-back intensive courses, she developed a strong understanding of Japanese grammar, which, in turn, allowed her to comfortably formulate sentences, especially as she continued to expand her vocabulary.

"Oh, man. That's going take a while," Hillary said in April 2013 of acquiring a decent command of *kanji*, the only Japanese character set that gave her serious trouble.[3] "I'm nowhere close on that." Every word has a corresponding *kanji* character, which was derived from Chinese. The *kanji* symbols can resemble the words they represent, but their meanings aren't always so intuitive.

Further complicating matters, most *kanji* have multiple pronunciations, with the correct one depending on the context in which it appears. For example, Hillary's lone second-semester classmate could identify the meaning of a particular *kanji* character. That's because she spoke Chinese, and the symbol for the term was the same in both languages. She just had no idea how to say it in Japanese.

Learning *kanji* can be "quite intimidating," said David Watkins. "That's a pretty large undertaking, especially with someone coming over here." Hillary added, "They're just so daunting and so many of them." Writer Rob Smaal was selective about which *kanji* he learned because tackling so many at once simply wasn't feasible. Instead, he focused on baseball-related *kanji* and everyday "stuff you have to know," such as food *kanji* on restaurant menus.

Hillary's formal learning and Tony's colloquial exposure gave them the opportunity to help each other at times. Although Tony had a pretty robust vocabulary base by 2012, he would ask for help in putting certain phrases together. After Hillary demonstrated how to say something, he rarely needed to ask again. "Once Tony hears one phrase," said Hillary, "he remembers it forever, which is crazy." When needed, Tony sought Hillary's help with decoding Twitter mentions in Japanese.

While she was in school, Japanese speakers were all around Tony. Generally, these native speakers worked in baseball and naturally liked to goof around. Their language, often colorful in nature, reflected that. "He's exposed to a lot more of the slang and the casual jargon and probably curse words," said Hillary. At the field, Tony returned the cultural favor, teaching his Japanese teammates crude words from his own lexicon. Hillary, the daughter of a baseball player and wife of another, knew the drill: "Baseball players are baseball players no matter what country you're in."

Spending five years in Japan, Aaron Guiel "understood a fair amount of Japanese" by his own estimation, but following his retirement, he regretted not learning more. "Because I was in Tokyo and because I had an interpreter, I think I got a little bit lazy," he admitted. "It wasn't vital to speak Japanese the way it was maybe in Sendai or Sapporo or Hiroshima or any of those other cities." Where Guiel fell short, he noticed Hillary excelled, lauding her determination to learn the language: "She was just off the charts!"

Well after taking those courses, Hillary embraced a particular app as a useful and convenient language aide. Japanese for "memorization," *Anki* allows its users to import flash cards from textbooks and other sources into their phones. From 2013 onward, she liked to sit at Swallows games and reinforce old vocabulary. Other times, she'd import new flash cards to learn.

"I can get my point across if I need to, but I'm definitely not fluent," Hillary said in 2013. "If someone talking to me starts babbling off, I'll probably catch about a quarter of what they're trying to tell me. And I can usually tell them, 'If you talk slower, I'll understand you,' and they're pretty good about that." In retrospect, she's grateful for the approach she took to formally learning Japanese: "You just have to 100 percent go for it, just going all out, and that was enough for me to kind of build on that."

Notes

1   Round trip, it was just under two and a half miles.
2   *Sensei* is the Japanese honorific for teacher.
3   Syllabic scripts *katakana* and *hiragana* were relative easy to learn. Meanwhile, there are several thousand *kanji* in regular use and more than 50,000 in existence. The average educated Japanese speaker is familiar with approximately 3,000 *kanji*.

CHAPTER FOURTEEN
BABY GIRL AND BALENTIEN BOMBS

Every single at-bat of his, people would stand up and watch. And then when he either hit a home run or struck out or whatever happened, they'd sit down and just start talking to each other again.

As March began, Wladimir Balentien was away from the team, in Taichung, Taiwan, representing the Netherlands in his first World Baseball Classic. Entrusted with the cleanup role, one spot ahead of his idol, fellow Willemstad, Curaçao, native Andruw Jones,[1] he delivered. Only, in a second-round meeting with Cuba, he pulled his groin. Although he returned a week later to play in the Dutch's semifinal loss,[2] clearly Balentien needed more time to heal. He wouldn't be ready for opening day, just eleven nights away.

All of his teammates called him "Coco." He liked the nickname, which was forged in early childhood when a cousin teased him for wearing a baseball cap that made his head look like a coconut.

The Swallows sorely missed Coco's bat the opening two weeks. Four seasons earlier, in his penultimate MLB at-bat, he'd hit one of the farthest homers in recent history.[3] Back on the field by April 12, Balentien started slow as Yomiuri swept Yakult. Though, in his home debut, he teased his tantalizing power potential with two opposite-field home runs in consecutive innings.

Tony had begun as expected, with five saves in six appearances, building off what he'd done the prior two seasons. But the following night, his promising start was compromised when he felt "instant tightness" along his right side after delivering an otherwise ordinary pitch. He labored through a disastrous 11th inning and was ultimately tagged with the loss.

The next day's MRI confirmed Tony had strained his right oblique and would be out of commission, joining a growing list of sidelined key contributors, including three skilled everyday players and right-handed ace Shohei Tateyama, who'd be out for the rest of the season while recovering from reconstructive elbow surgery.[4]

Balentien did his best to single-handedly power the shorthanded offense. In late April, five Coco homers carried Yakult to six straight victories, including a 12–3 win in Yokohama that featured a trio of Balentien bombs. Despite missing twelve contests, he had amassed eight homers in 15 games and ranked third in the league.

By Tony's late-May return, the Swallows had fallen eight games below .500. In retrospect, he believes he returned prematurely, giving into pressure, largely self-imposed, to promptly reverse the team's misfortunes. He admitted, years later, that he should have focused on healing, however long it took.

The SoftBank Hawks' Bryan LaHair welcomed him back with a two-out RBI double. Each of his next two appearances resulted in deflating sayonara losses in Saitama. "I hate Seibu [Dome]," he joked. "That place is the bane of my existence."

First, he entered a ninth-inning tie. With one out, Seibu's red-hot lead-off batter doubled. Though the next batter grounded out, Tony was not yet out of trouble. With an open base, he intentionally walked a veteran lefty. Facing Hideto Asamura, who'd homered an inning earlier, he left a hanging curve over the plate. By the time it landed beyond the left-field wall,[5] Tony had already started walking toward the visiting clubhouse. Final: 4–1.

Next, the Swallows had an afternoon game before hitting the road for Chiba. This time, Tony and company fell 3–2, experiencing their demise an inning later, in the 10th. The decisive hit was struck hard off the center-field wall by the same lefty he had purposely walked one night earlier.

Weeks before, as Tony was rehabbing, he had an idea. Ever since switching to the pen, ZZ Top's "Sharp Dressed Man" had been his entrance song and served him well. But he felt like making a change and used the opportunity to get the TokyoSwallows.com guys involved. David Watkins and Chris Pellegrini had similar rock music sensibilities too. So he reached out to Pellegrini, requesting options for consideration. Chris emailed David, and the search was on. Honored to be asked, they spent an entire Tuesday evening formulating a list and sent it to Tony. Later, he replied, "I've made my choice. You'll have to wait till the stadium to find out."

Pellegrini, at Jingu Stadium, and Watkins, watching from home, listened intently as Tony's name was called on May 26. At 8:52 p.m., they emailed each other with the same one-word message: "Panama!" As they heard the Van Halen song blaring over the Jingu sound system, they grinned from ear to ear. "We were like, 'Wow, that's pretty cool,'" said Watkins. He'd kept his promise.

The song switch could only do so much for the still-injured pitcher. Although the playing of "Panama" did precede two strong outings, the healing effects of the new song, if there were any, could not be felt on the road, where he struggled twice more. Capped off by a four-run June 16 outing in which he notched just one out, his short-lived return had to be put on hold. Understanding that he was not healthy, the Swallows once again deregistered Tony.

The second sayonara loss did feature one silver lining. Balentien's game-tying home run halted a nine-game homerless drought, during which he batted .188 and Yakult went 2–6–1.

Even amid difficult slumps, Balentien's confidence never wavered, according to Tony: "I say it as a compliment, but he was definitely arrogant as a hitter. To be good, you have to be like that in a sense. . . . He would just step up to the plate, he would go to his leg kick, and then he would just get that foot down and crush baseballs."

Coco really began to catch fire the following Thursday against Rakuten, Andruw Jones's team, jumpstarting a torrid stretch. He then homered in four consecutive at-bats stretched over the next three games.[6] Emblematic of the 2013 season-long paradox that juxtaposed Coco's offensive dominance with his team's struggles, Yakult wound up losing all four games despite its cleanup hitter's exploits.[7]

"Every single at-bat of his, people would stand up and watch," observed Watkins. "And then when he either hit a home run or struck out or whatever happened, then they'd sit down and just start talking to each other again. He was like the sole attraction."

In late June, he found himself in a home-run derby of sorts as the NPB home-run leader, Dominican first baseman Tony Blanco, batted cleanup for the other side. Balentien trailed by one. In his first chance, he tied the race, while handing Yokohama a 3–0 deficit. As part of a six-run fourth, Blanco lurched ahead. Down 7–5, Balentien delivered a ninth-inning solo homer, knotting the gaijin at 25 apiece. Predictably, the next three Swallows went down in order.

While the duo battled each other for the 2013 home-run crown, they were acutely aware of the NPB history books and the three men they were chasing for the all-time single-season mark. In 1964, Sadaharu Oh first set the long-standing record with 55 home runs. Thirty-seven years later, Tuffy Rhodes matched the mark. Then, Alex Cabrera tied it the next season.[8] Now, Balentien was on pace for 61.

On July 13, Kan Otake's Carp held a one-run lead before he fell behind him, 3-0. Three weeks earlier, he burned him for the game-winning homer. This time, it would have been easy for Otake to put Balentien on base as opposed to risking something worse. Anyone familiar with NPB norms throughout its history would have expected as much. There had long been a tradition of protectionism in which Japanese players did their best to prevent gaijin competitors from breaking records held by Japanese. Often, this nationalistic pride manifested in pitchers not challenging non-Japanese power hitters with as many pitches in the strike zone or its vicinity.

Otake refused to give Balentien a free pass. Once the count became full, Otake challenged him inside and regretted it instantly. He wasn't done victimizing him, either.

An inning later, with the bases loaded and nowhere to put Balentien, Otake opted to go right after him. An offspeed payoff pitch hung up in the zone and then into the seats for Coco's first NPB grand slam. The ball was walloped with such force that the camera operator missed its path and left fielder Fred Lewis didn't move an inch. Over three weeks, three Balentien swings had produced eight runs against Otake.

"They want to protect the records," said Aaron Guiel, who experienced Japanese protectionism as a first-time gaijin. "They definitely do." He was competing with Shuichi Murata for the 2007 Central League home-run crown when he stopped seeing pitches to hit.

He reported first noticing the phenomenon a couple weeks before the season's end, but it increased considerably in the last two games, which naturally came against Murata's club. Amplifying the protectionist mindset, the BayStars had another vested interest in avoiding his bat—helping their teammate win the crown. Guiel walked twice in each game and finished one shy of Murata's Central-topping 36 home runs.[9]

The next season, a BayStar pitcher Guiel declined to name publicly confirmed what he essentially already knew: Yokohama's manager and pitching coach had instructed their pitchers not to deliver any strikes to him during the season-ending series. The pitcher apologized, though, of course, the damage had already been done.

The single-season home-run record was a special case. No man in NPB history was and is more respected than Oh, whose number-one jersey was retired after twenty-two brilliant years with the Giants. Though Oh's father was Chinese, the left-hander was born and raised in Japan and always embraced by the Japanese as one of their own. As a player, he won 11 championships and nine MVPs, while setting still-standing all-time records of 868 home runs and 2,170 RBIs.[10] Oh remained involved in the game, managing through his sixty-eighth birthday. Under his direction, Japan won the inaugural World Baseball Classic. He was a living legend. As the decades passed, some sluggers came close to surpassing his record, but none ever succeeded, sometimes with opposing pitchers all but making sure of it.

In 1985, Randy Bass had 54 going into the final game against Yomiuri, which was managed by Oh himself. The left-handed American walked four times. Appearing on *Late Night with David Letterman* after the season, Bass joked that breaking the record could have cost him his visa.

Something eerily similar happened to gaijin home-run hitters Rhodes and Cabrera in 2001 and 2002, respectively. Each tied the mark with several games left but still had to face an Oh-managed squad that would throw neither any reasonable pitches. By this time, the commissioner had deemed the tactic "unsportsmanlike," while the public and media were similarly opposed to it. Both years, Oh denied any involvement in protecting the record, but his public remarks did him no favors.[11]

One July Tokyo night, Tony and Hillary went out to dinner. A "starving" feeling struck Hillary before she scarfed down nearly four entrées. Something was off. The very next day, she bought a pregnancy test from the closest drugstore.

Barely able to decipher the directions in Japanese, she followed them and got multiple positive readings. When he got back from the field, "He thought I was joking. Well, he asked, 'Are you serious? Are you serious? Are you serious?'" Shortly thereafter, a doctor's ultrasound confirmed it. Hillary was pregnant with the couple's first child, and it was going to be a girl.

They had been trying but were hoping for an early offseason birth when Dad wouldn't be needed in Japan. When February and the ensuing months passed without a pregnancy, they thought waiting until the next year made the most sense. However, fate intervened and set Hillary on track for a due date that would coincide with 2014 spring training, meaning Tony would almost certainly have to fly in from Japan. Challenges aside, they felt grateful and determined to make it work.

The doctor handed Hillary a pocket-sized notebook, with which she was instructed to track her pregnancy. The office also gave her a pin. Affixed with the same Japanese maternity logo that appears on every train, the badge is designed to provide a layer of protection for pregnant women riding the subway. If a pregnant woman boards a train and all the priority seats are full, an able-bodied, non-elderly adult is expected to give up his or her seat.

Around the six-week mark, when Hillary first learned she was pregnant, the bottom half of her face broke out with "crazy, really bad acne." Other than that and occasional bouts of extreme fatigue, pregnancy didn't significantly curtail the frequency of her typical Japanese adventures.

In Litchfield Park, Arizona, she painted the nursery, bought a crib, and made sure the room was ready for its newest inhabitant. Much less would be needed before moving into their Tokyo apartment, given that the player apartments already provided a crib and most other baby necessities.

That offseason, Hillary's dad, Ken, and Tony worked together to build a large barbecue in the Arizona backyard. The project required many weeks of labor and plenty of cement and rebar. Tony's dad and brother helped to put giant wooden beams atop the pergola. By the first week of

January, the hard work was finally done, just in time for a barbecue party that doubled as a baby shower. For the occasion, hot dogs and hamburgers were served. Tony manned the grill.

Balentien entered the break with a league-leading 32 home runs, already eclipsing his career high.[12] A third-time All-Star in as many years, he topped the Central League fan vote. While Balentien's home-run prowess naturally dominated the headlines, his all-around hitting vastly improved as well.

Meanwhile, rookie Yasuhiro Ogawa was registering the team's best season aside from Balentien. He impressively burst onto the scene, allowing no earned runs through his first 17 innings, quickly earning the role of Junji Ogawa's (no relation) Saturday starter. The five-foot-seven right-hander overcame his diminutive stature and inability to throw hard with superb command and control and a powerful leg kick fashioned after Nolan Ryan's. Accordingly, he became known as "Ryan" Ogawa. By the break, injuries and inconsistency had forced Yakult to use a whopping 28 pitchers, including twelve starters. Despite the chaos around him, Ogawa was as reliable as they come.

Ogawa continued his brilliance in Game 2 of the showcase event with two scoreless innings.[13] After a first half marked by a significant offensive uptick—spearheaded by Balentien's record-setting home-run pace and the newly designed baseball—Coco ironically went hitless over the three games, and no one else homered.[14] At least he showed up in style with a large star cut into his hair.

In 2013, NPB run production rose dramatically, although not quite reaching 2010 levels. For months, the league denied any change in the specifications of the baseball. In June, NPB officials finally admitted to asking Mizuno to covertly increase its ball's jump off the bat. "The day after the revelation, commissioner Ryōzō Katō apologized for "causing such confusion as this" but continued to deny ever possessing knowledge of the latest ball adjustment. Three months later, he announced his resignation.

The break provided a six-day reprieve from an injury-ravaged season. At 32–49–1, the Swallows remained mired in the league's cellar.[15] Soon, they would have to return to the daily grind. Was there any chance they could turn the season around? If not, could Balentien's mesmerizing home-run feats make the losing palatable?

Entering August, Balentien was on pace for nearly 59, but anything could happen in the season's closing months. All he had to do was ask Cabrera, Rhodes, Bass, or any other gaijin who ever threatened to break Oh's sacred record. But even if the league didn't actively pitch around Coco, he'd have to both stay healthy and continue his scorching pace. Was it sustainable?

"Of course!" was the resounding answer. "I remember him hitting just everything that he swung at out of the yard," said Tony. "Some of the pitches he was hitting out were up in his eyeballs, and he was just so locked in, it was unbelievable."

On August's first Sunday, he homered[16] and reached base all five times, yet Yakult lost for the eighth time in 11 tries since the All-Star break and one of its few run producers, Lastings Milledge, fouled a ball off his left ankle. Days later, he further tweaked it. If an out-for-six-to-eight-weeks prognosis didn't put the nail in the last-place Swallows' coffin, their dropping six of the next nine all but did the trick.

On August 21 and 22, Balentien destroyed a quartet of pitches, achieving single-season records for Jingu Stadium and the franchise.[17] A homer the next night made 47 in 49 games, as Coco's unforgettable campaign somehow looked to be gathering even more steam.

After blast number 48 at Hiroshima, smoldering Balentien returned home to great fanfare. Coco's can't-miss at-bats and the weightier context behind them sent Jingu Stadium into overdrive, often generating more excitement than seen during either of the previous two stretch runs. Sometimes Hillary had been going home early to make dinner. Not anymore. Now she had to see every Balentien swing.

While it may have seemed odd—a last-place team's fans cheering in droves for a single player pursuing a single achievement—a long-suffering fan base was enjoying a spectacularly unprecedented season by one of its own and a chance to witness history. Attendance figures proved as much, as home attendance improved upon 2012 levels, when the team was actually good, by 8.3 percent. In his September 10 recap, David Watkins wrote, "Given the nature of the team . . . I wish I had the ability to fast forward time and just watch Coco's at-bats."

Back at Jingu on August 27, he entertained with a couple homers to left. Up to 50, 16 had come in August. Never had an NPB hitter stroked 17 in a month until Balentien accomplished the feat the next night.

In the series finale, Chunichi narrowly avoided another home run, intentionally walking him in the ninth after he'd just doubled off the wall. The following night, he clubbed another, his tenth in nine games.[18] Balentien stood three shy of tying the record, and the calendar still read August. He was enjoying one of the best months in league history.

At home, he tied Bass for second on the single-season list by hammering a shoulder-high fastball. The next one, a sixth-inning, opposite-field homer off poor Kan Otake, tied Balentien in the history books[19] with Cabrera, Rhodes, and the legendary Oh. With 22 games left, Coco needed just one more home run to secure sole possession of the record.

With her son primed to break the record, Astrid Balentien flew in from Curaçao to attend her first game at Jingu. Six home runs were slugged on September 12, but none by Coco. "It's a long season," he said postgame, "and there are times when you miss even hittable balls. It'd be a mistake to think I can hit one out every time." Nor did he hit one either of the next two days. Fortunately, Astrid was still in town on Sunday, September 15, when Balentien quickly halted any lingering suspense with a first-inning home run off Daiki Enokida's fastball.

After flipping his bat, Balentien triumphantly raised both arms as he watched the record-breaking ball sail over the left-field fence. The new NPB single-season home-run king pumped his fist as he rounded the bases. The Jingu crowd went crazy. As he touched the plate, he looked toward the sky and put his hands together to show gratefulness to God. Coach Tetsuya Iida was the first to hug Balentien, followed by Yasushi Iihara, the runner he had just brought home. Then, a Swallows cheerleader handed him a bouquet of flowers. In the dugout, Balentien received a hero's welcome with hugs and hand pounds aplenty. The game paused for ninety seconds so Balentien could receive a commemorative plaque from the team mascot, Tsubakuro, who then hugged him.

In the third, when Enokida fell behind Balentien 3-0, Tony heard the large visiting Tigers contingent booing along with the Swallows fans. Times had clearly changed from Japanese baseball's not-too-distant protectionist past. "They didn't want that shit," said Tony, who went on to channel their thinking: "We want to see home runs, damn it!" Taking full advantage of the green light he received, Balentien dispatched a 3-0 slider into the seats for another four-bagger, number 57.

One theory posits that the significant decrease in NPB record protectionism can be credited to Ichiro Suzuki's 2004 breaking of George Sisler's eighty-four-year-old single-season MLB hits record and his Hall of Fame–ensuring output since. Of his pursuit of the record, Ichiro said, "I felt that people were skeptical of me and that I had to prove myself, being from Japan, but people were fair to me. I did not see any discrimination." According to author Robert Whiting, "Everything [Ichiro accomplished] was widely welcomed. Nobody tried to stop him. . . . Nobody said, 'We're not going to let a Japanese break an American record.' Nobody said that."

Six years later, when Matt Murton broke Ichiro's NPB single-season hits record, he felt visiting "fans responded in a really positive manner." According to Whiting, there was also a gradual softening over the decades.

"The suspicious attitude they had toward Americans has diminished a lot since the 1980s," he said as Balentien neared the record, citing Japan's years of access to MLB content as well as the major-league success of players like Ichiro, Hideki Matsui, and Hideo Nomo. Then, in 2005, Bobby Valentine became the first foreign-born manager to win a Japan Series. When Bass, Rhodes, and Cabrera threatened to break Oh's record, it was a different world.

After the game, not one soul was surprised to see Coco standing on the field as the Hero of the Game. His mother, holding the 56th home-run ball, joined him at the podium for the interview. Later, Balentien posed with Tsubakuro, as they proudly raised two "New Japanese Record" plaques—for "56" and "57," respectively—offering those in the right-field cheering section an optimal view.

In mid-July, Tony returned to *ichi-gun* action after missing nearly four more weeks. His second game back, in Yokohama on the last day before the break, was a disaster, ballooning his ERA to a career-worst 12.86.[20] But things were about to take a turn for the better. Finally.

By August 4, after suffering a third sayonara loss since switching entrance songs,[21] Tony scrapped "Panama" and reverted back to "Sharp Dressed Man." Maybe the song change subconsciously reminded Tony of better times on the mound. More likely, the oblique had finally healed. Maybe both. Regardless, after looking like one of the worst pitchers in Japan through 16 outings, he dominated the season's final ten weeks, looking like the closer no sane hitter wanted to face a year prior.

The performance turnaround didn't earn him back the closer gig, although he was much more preoccupied with staying healthy and pitching well. On those counts, he succeeded, recording a 2.39 ERA from July 26 through the season finale.[22] Incredibly consistent, opponents scored against him in only four of his final 31 outings. Specifically, Tony grew even more dominant over the last six weeks, during which he accrued 27 strikeouts in just over 15 innings.[23]

Despite the stability his new contract offered, he remained just as competitive, and getting racked infuriated him. Alternatively, he relished squelching the competition appearance after appearance. As his dominance continued, he began paying attention to the progressive lowering of his ERA. How low could he finish? At home, he joked that he was going to be disappointed if he concluded the season at a clip over 6.00. Alas, Tony's scoreless third of an inning in the final game froze his ERA at 6.02. While he fell short of his goal, the twenty-nine-year-old hurler managed to slice his ungodly 12.86 ERA in half and then some.

Tony's recovery and Balentien's home-run heroics couldn't prevent the team's miserable, last-place finish (57–83–4). Closing at Tokyo Dome, the Swallows held a 3–2 ninth-inning lead but fittingly wound up with their ninth sayonara defeat.

Balentien established a new benchmark with a round 60 home runs.[24] Only two others slugged better than .570, while Balentien posted a mind-melting .779 mark, 145 points better than anyone else. Although he fell short of the Triple Crown—Tony Blanco's .333 batting average and 136 RBIs edged his .330 and 131 respective finishes—the historic season easily earned Coco the Central League MVP[25] and a maximum 99 rating in the forthcoming *Pro Yakyu Spirits* video game.

After the season, Balentien flew home with Andruw Jones on the latter's private jet and received a hero's welcome back in Willemstad, parade and all. His proud community even named a street after him. Balentien's off-season was far from one long celebration, however. In January 2014, he was arrested in Florida on domestic violence charges stemming from an incident with his estranged wife. After pleading not guilty, he was freed on bail and permitted to return to Japan, just in time for spring training.

Yakult held a press conference, which began with Balentien bowing deeply. Accompanied by Michael Okumura and the club president, Tsuyoshi Kinugasa, he proceeded to apologize to the fans, the organization, and his teammates. According to Swallows fans and NPB reporters interviewed, the offseason incident didn't do much to tarnish the gaijin's long-term reputation, although his beer commercials stopped airing for a time.

Madelyn would surely be arriving soon; her parents just didn't know when. "We really didn't have a very good plan," said Hillary. "Really, our plan was he just goes to spring training in Japan and we wait for me to basically go into labor naturally, and then he tries to come back. And if he makes it in time, then that's great, and if he doesn't, then that's fine, and he'll just be able to spend time with us after she's already born."

Late Wednesday night, February 26, the contractions began. From Arizona, Hillary called Tony. "I think it kind of freaked him out," she recalled. "I think he actually realized, 'Oh, my God, I might actually miss it.'" He informed Yakult. Over a period of several hours, as the sun was coming up in Arizona, he tried to help Hillary determine if the contractions were subsiding or growing stronger. Ultimately, after about five hours, they stopped. Hillary initially thought he should wait in Japan, but both quickly decided it would be better if he headed to her side as soon as possible.

Before Tony left, a thoughtful freelance reporter named Yasuhiko "Yas" Kikuta handed him a wooden box containing a rectangular pink bag adorned with vertical gold writing and white tassels at the top. It was a pregnancy charm. With this gesture, he was wishing Hillary a safe delivery.

Getting to Arizona would be tricky. When the frenetic journey started, Tony was with the team in Miyazaki, on the island of Kyushu in southwestern Japan. From there, he had to fly to Haneda Airport before taking a two-hour train from Haneda to Narita, the primary international airport. There, he boarded a flight to LAX, where he caught a connecting flight to Phoenix. Only the connecting flight was full, so Tony had to wait six hours for the next plane. In retrospect, he wishes he rented a car.

He eventually got to Phoenix, with total travel time exceeding twenty-one hours. By the time he arrived home around 11 p.m., Hillary was already on the hospital's waiting list for a delivery room. Exhausted, Tony made a sandwich, took a quick shower, and then went to sleep. Before 5 a.m., the hospital called with an available room. Hillary's parents and Tony's mom headed to the hospital too.

With Tony present and the due date near, they opted to induce labor. He downed coffee to ensure he remained awake and alert for the seminal moment, the birth of his first child. "I was just zeroing in on Hillary and that whole moment," he said. "I didn't know if I was tired or awake or sleeping because I was so jet lagged, and it was such a quick turnaround, and there was so much going on." Due to the inordinate volume of coffee consumed, he couldn't sleep much. Meanwhile, Hillary actually slept through most of her labor. By the time everything had aligned for them to officially become parents, it was already the next day, and a new month.

Madelyn Paige[26] Barnette was born on Saturday, March 1, 2014, at 3:50 a.m. local time with the pink pregnancy charm sitting beside the bed. Their firstborn weighed a robust 7 pounds and 6 ounces, measuring 20.5 inches long. Her dad remained in town for six more days, savoring his precious early time with Madelyn. In what felt like an instant, he had to return to his team in Japan. At thirty, a new chapter of Tony's life was just beginning, but, with repetition, his year-round Japanese baseball routine had already become second nature. Year 5 with the Swallows stood less than three weeks away.

A BASEBALL GAIJIN

Notes

1.   A twelve-year-old Balentien watched Andruw Jones, then nineteen, face the Yankees in the 1996 World Series. Jones played designated hitter for the Netherlands on the heels of his disappointing final MLB season and just ahead of his first season in Japan.

2.   Balentien helped guide the Dutch squad to a best-to-date fourth-place finish.

3.   Between 2009 and 2017, Balentien (Reds), Aaron Judge, and Giancarlo Stanton were the only major leaguers to hit a home run traveling at least 495 feet. Since, as measured by Statcast, Ronald Acuña Jr., C.J. Cron, Joey Gallo, Nomar Mazara, Ryan McMahon, Jesús Sánchez, Christian Yelich, and Miguel Sanó (twice) have also done it. Mazara's 505-foot 2019 shot is the farthest homer Statcast has ever recorded.

4.   From 2010 through 2012, Tateyama comfortably led the Swallows starting rotation in nearly every key metric. They won 57.1 percent of games he started over that period. When someone else started, they won just 47.0 percent. Over the stretch, he led Yakult starters in ERA, WHIP, wins, strikeout-to-walk ratio, and innings per start, among other stats.

5.   This was Hideto Asamura's first two-homer game of 2013, a breakout season in which the twenty-two-year-old hit 27 home runs and slugged .554.

6.   Two walks in the middle game do not count as at-bats and thus did not disrupt the streak. Only seventeen other NPB players had ever accomplished the four-straight-homer feat, including the most recent prior to Balentien, fellow Swallow Atsuya Furuta, ten years earlier.

7.   In the series finale with the Fighters, the Swallows squandered a pair of Balentien blasts by surrendering six unearned runs in a game they lost 10-4.

8.   Both nearing the end of their playing careers, Tuffy Rhodes and Alex Cabrera were actually teammates with the Orix Buffaloes in 2008 and 2009. In 2008, the duo combined to hit 76 home runs and drive in 222 runs.

9.   Neither Guiel nor Murata hit any homers in the games. Despite coming to the plate at about the same frequency in 2007, Guiel drew 23 more walks than the Japanese third baseman. Protectionism notwithstanding, Murata should have seen fewer pitches, given he went on to bat .287 and slug .553, noticeably more impressive than Guiel's respective .245 and .493. Statistically, Guiel was also easier to strike out.

10.   Oh's 1.08 OPS still stands as the best career mark in NPB history.

11.   In 2002, Oh went as far as to command his pitchers not to approach Cabrera differently than anyone else. But after the season, after they failed to heed his orders, he revealed his lack of remorse by telling the media, "If you're going to break the record, you should do it by more than one. Do it by a lot."

12.   Balentien hit 31 homers in each of his first two seasons with Yakult. By the 2013 All-Star break, the Swallows stood just 13–12 in games in which he homered, whereas in 2012, they had won 20 of 25 such games.

13.   Ogawa's catcher for the game, Motonobu Tanishige of the Dragons, was nearly nineteen and a half years older than the twenty-three-year-old pitcher.

14   The series went down as the first three-game All-Star set since 1953 to conclude with no home runs.

15   What's more, the Swallows lost their final four pre-All-Star-break games by a 41–11 margin.

16   The homer was his fourth in five games and the 100th of his NPB career, needing only 1,316 at-bats to achieve the feat.

17   Roberto Petagine (1999) and Akinori Iwamura (2004) had been tied for the Swallows single-season record at 44.

18   Illustrative of the type of season Balentien and the Swallows were having, Yakult won just four of nine, and six of the ten home runs were solos.

19   To make matters worse, this was the Hiroshima starter's fourth home run of 2013 allowed to Balentien. In 2012, Otake allowed six total home runs.

20   The only non-qualifying times when Tony's ERA was worse as a pro were during his rookie-ball debut (2006) and during parts of his first two games in Double A (2008). This, however, came 16 appearances in, in mid-July.

21   Although those three sayonara losses and two more road fiascoes occurred while "Panama" was Tony's song, a player's entrance song only plays at home. In the three games in which Tony actually trotted in as the song played, he allowed one run in three innings. Not bad. The road appearances were the issue. Still, on the October TokyoSwallows.com season review podcast, Watkins and Pellegrini joked about the havoc "Panama" wreaked on the pitcher's play and their role in the affair. Years later, Tony said of the initial song change: "Yeah, it was awful. It didn't work. . . . Good effort, good try."

22   The stretch would have looked even better if not for one outlier performance on August 31, when the same BayStars who pummeled Tony's pitching on July 17 touched him up for four runs in two-thirds of an inning.

23   By the final month, he'd regained his control too. Tony walked none over his last 23.2 innings after issuing 19 walks over his first nearly 28 innings.

24   Coming in Yakult's home finale, Balentien's sixtieth was a game-tying home run that landed in the *ōendan* section. Talk about putting an exclamation point on his season!

25   He received 200 of 273 first-place votes.

26   Madelyn has the same middle name as her mom.

CHAPTER FIFTEEN
MADELYN MEETS TOKYO

That was the first time I'd ever gotten emotional about baseball because I was so sick and tired of being sick and tired.

The Swallows opened 2014 with a bang—a special treat for their fans, who endured a difficult 2013—coasting to a home victory after compiling seven first-inning runs. The flashy start, unfortunately, would not be a sign of things to come. Five nights later, there would be another bang.

The moment before it happened Tony had ample reason to feel confident. He dominated the competition to conclude 2013, he made his season debut look easy, and the prior inning he successfully preserved a 3–3 tie with a timely double play. After a scoreless top of the 12th, Tony returned. The Swallows could only tie or lose.

Leading off, Hiroshima's pinch-hitter struck a high chopper about evenly between the mound and first baseman Yuichi Matsumoto. Somehow, they considered such a scenario before the inning began. Matsumoto suggested Tony try to make the tag as opposed to risking an on-the-move toss. When the hypothetical situation improbably unfolded shortly thereafter, Tony complied. Unsure of where he was relative to first base after corralling the ball, he took a couple steps before diving at the runner.

"Out," the umpire demonstrably signaled as the same word leapt from this throat. Tony had made a dazzling play, but he took a punishing fall in the process. In an interview with John E. Gibson on the *Japan Baseball Weekly* podcast a few months later, he detailed the play and the aftermath: "I came down pretty hard, but at the time, adrenaline pumping and all that, didn't really think anything of it. Just kind of thought, 'Man, diving hurts. It's been a while since I've done that.'" So he continued to pitch. In a flash, the next batter was circling the bases following a sayonara home run.

Tony seethed, but physically he thought he was fine until he got to the clubhouse. He took off his pants and saw a bloody and swollen left knee. The next day's MRI revealed a partially torn PCL, which instantly triggered a visceral reaction.

"I was so sick and tired of being sick and tired," said Tony. "I was so tired of being hurt. I was so tired of working so hard in the offseason to get myself right. And I know in the grand scheme of things, guys have come back from way worse injuries, but when you want to be on the field and you've got stuff to prove, it hurts. I was fighting back tears in the doctor's office because I was so upset. Even the trainers . . . were upset. Everybody knew how much I wanted to be out there and how much I cared, and the fact that I couldn't, I think it resonated with everybody else."

On the podcast, he further summarized his reaction: "After last year, I had really busted my tail in the offseason. . . . I came to spring training feeling great. We gave birth to our first daughter. So everything was pointing to this phenomenal year. And for that to happen in the second game of the season for me, I was pissed. I kind of wanted to punch through the monitor at the moment. It took a couple days for me to calm down."

Hillary was sitting with Madelyn in Arizona when Tony shared the bad news. "I hate being on the other side of the world when he's trying to deal with stuff," she said. Normally, she would have been in Tokyo, but Hillary was trying to obtain necessary paperwork to allow for their baby's exit from the United States and entry into Japan. She was six weeks old by the time her visa[1] and passport arrived. In the intervening weeks before they could join Tony, the newborn got a chance to meet all of her grandparents.[2]

With everything in order, it was time to leave, and maternal grandma Kim would accompany them. By Hillary's account, Madelyn, whom she described as a "very easy baby," barely made a sound during the long flight. Kim and Hillary alternated serving as a pillow for Madelyn, who slept and ate and ate and slept until she arrived in Tokyo, her new home.[3]

At 6–17, with nine straight losses, the Swallows already appeared destined for another losing season. Tony missed all of May as he continued to rehab his knee, but Yakult managed to stay afloat, going 13–11–1, as outfielder Yuhei Takai captured Central League MVP honors for the month.[4]

Originally a starting pitcher, a teenage Takai made his NPB debut in 2003. The five-foot-nine left-hander threw with decent speed and movement but was plagued by control issues that only worsened over time. Ultimately, his pitching career was beyond repair.

Inspired by American pitcher Rick Ankiel's redemption story, he began transitioning into an exclusive position player role after 2009. Ankiel had been a hot young southpaw before he infamously lost his control and successfully reinvented himself as a power hitter. Takai also knew of NPB contemporary Yoshio Itoi, among a couple others,[5] who switched to the outfield in his mid-twenties, just like him, and proceeded to become one of NPB's highest-paid players.

Yuhei Takai wasn't done making big changes. From 2011 onward, he'd simply be known as the mononymous "Yuhei." By 2012, Yuhei had earned one of six outfield spots on the opening-day *ichi-gun* roster and logged valuable time there. He began the next season with the top team too and stormed out of the gates with a .622 slugging percentage, thanks in part to his first two NPB homers since eight years prior when he was still pitching. Unfortunately, Yuhei's 2013 ended prematurely when he injured his knee during the same April game in which Tony got hurt.

During May 2014, he batted .364 and flexed his budding power. In a four-game stretch, he slugged four homers, including two in back-to-back innings of a May 5 win. Less than a month away from his thirtieth birthday, he was on fire.

The posterior cruciate ligament is the biggest and strongest of the four major ligaments in a human knee. Although ACL injuries are much more common and typically more severe, an injured PCL can cause significant pain because of its critical importance to the knee. Together, both ligaments, which cross each other in an "X" shape and connect the femur with the tibia, provide stability. Because there was no joint damage, the Swallows opted for a nonsurgical approach, which would return Tony to action, they hoped, within eight to ten weeks.

He rehabbed in Toda, the same place where he rehabbed the oblique strain and spent ample time during a tumultuous rookie season. A right-handed pitcher lands on his left knee, so Tony took a break from throwing. He was instructed to start slow, gradually building back strength in integral areas surrounding the knee. Leg lifts with ankle weights and other lower-body exercises were designed to strengthen his left hip, which would, in turn, put less strain on the recovering knee.

With throwing on hold, upper-body lifting could resume much sooner. Over the next few months, the weight room became Tony's office. He had nothing else he could do to improve, so he spent three to four hours there most days. Within days of the diagnosis, the devastation wore off and morphed into determination. Tony drew inspiration from envisioning what it would feel like to be back with his teammates.

Virtually any professional athlete who's rehabbed an injury will admit that the process can get awfully lonely. Typically, you're on a schedule unique from your teammates' and coaches', and in Tony's case, he was geographically removed from his usual colleagues. Helping to reduce his isolation, the *ni-gun* translator, an older gentleman named Shin Koyama, accompanied him in the weight room.

At that time, there were no other gaijin around. Therefore, his gym days were always blessed with Koyama's "goofball" antics, which involved American sarcasm, something Koyama learned to appreciate in the States. His occasional lack of seriousness may have annoyed some higher-ups, but Tony loved it. By virtue of all those hours spent together, the two grew pretty close over a short period.

Once Tony returned to throwing after about a month, he gradually started ramping up the length of his bullpen sessions and the intensity of his throws. Eventually, Yakult cleared its gaijin closer to make a few rehab appearances. Throughout the process, the team understandably took a cautious approach, especially after he returned from injury too early the prior season. In four *ni-gun* outings, Tony pitched an inning apiece and, most importantly, avoided any injury setbacks. Soon enough, he was back with his peers.

Yakult naturally adjusted his conditioning regimen, but he felt confident in his ability to pick up where he'd left off. On June 19, Tony entered his first *ichi-gun* game in two and a half months. The left PCL had completely grown back but wouldn't reach peak strength until the offseason.[6] Although the Fukuoka SoftBank Hawks pushed him to throw 28 pitches, he recorded a scoreless ninth.

The nature of the NPB schedule and the Swallows' prime Tokyo location afforded Tony more family time than he could have dreamed. Road series against Yomiuri, DeNA, Lotte, and Seibu involved "commuter trips," from which he'd return home each night, and while he was rehabbing, he merely shuttled to and from Toda. "He seemed like he was home all the time," said Hillary.

Once Madelyn turned three months old, Hillary could take her to the Tokyo American Club. Open daily from 5:45 a.m. until late, it was run out of an enormous eight-story building in the Minato ward and had virtually everything.[7] Most relevant to Hillary, the club enabled her to get back in the gym while the day care center watched her infant. Madelyn would frequent a play area in the middle of a big café that served American food. They also spent time together by the club's kiddie pool.

Hillary enjoyed the facilities, but biking nearly five miles round-trip while holding Madelyn no longer made sense after a couple months, and there was no train station nearby. She then switched to the more easily accessible My Gym, as recommended by many of their friends. Much less fancy than the club, it was simple—one large room containing play equipment—and offered structured weekly classes for Madelyn. Each class ran an hour, was conducted in English, and began with a song. Then, the babies, with help from their accompanying parent, would try to mimic the instructor at the front of the room. Scattered around the week, too, were "free play" hours in which Madelyn could play to her heart's content.

Hillary would take her to My Gym every single week. "I'm really glad we had four years [in Japan] before we had her, so when she did come around, it wasn't that big of a struggle at all," said Hillary. "We had the time to adjust there as a couple, to learn some of the language, to learn our way around. We knew where to get food for her. And it's nice that he never changed teams. We were always in the same apartment. We were always in the same area, the same people around us, many of the same teammates, some familiarity. That helped a lot." By spring 2014, the couple also had a reliable group of friends that could watch Madelyn or share tips on raising kids in Tokyo.

With all the scenic parks and gardens nestled in their buzzing urban environment, Madelyn had beautiful playground options. Now that Hillary knew the area inside and out, "Madelyn and I could zip our way around on the bike and get through everything." Traveling with her on the subway wasn't always ideal, but mother and daughter got by.[8]

Madelyn was one happy baby, crowded subway rides notwithstanding. She particularly loved going to Jingu Stadium to watch her dad play. By 2015, she'd always have a bag of popcorn in her hands as she soaked in the one-of-a-kind atmosphere. Whenever the Swallows scored and "Tokyo Ondo" played, Madelyn bobbed up and down with her own mini-umbrella. The commotion of the games could overwhelm someone her age. Instead, she couldn't be bothered. "Actually, I think the louder it was, the more she enjoyed it," said Hillary. Privileged with perpetual sensory stimulation—such as the crowd chanting and dancing, the crack of the bat, and vendors hawking beer—curious Madelyn observed it all. During July, she could view middle-of-the-seventh fireworks while still making it home for a reasonable bedtime.

Becoming a father had a tangible effect on Tony, Hillary felt: "It's toned him down a lot. He's definitely much more relaxed in general, and it's not just at home, but on the baseball field as well; he'll agree to that too. He's matured a lot. He can give up a home run now, and you can see it doesn't completely shake his foundation anymore." No reasonable observer could suggest he'd lost his fiery edge, but he clearly was adapting, showing a new consideration to when and how he showed emotion. "I don't think I've seen him yell at anybody since Madelyn was born," noted Hillary.

At thirty years old and with a child in tow, Tony was improving as a leader, according to Go Fujisawa, who already considered him a responsible teammate: "He was trying to be a leader for [the] pitchers." He also recognized a nurturing nature that was starting to take shape in the right-hander. "I think he got some kind of deep idea how to take care of people."

Tony liked to entertain Madelyn with goofy impressions. Actually, well before she was born, he liked to do voices. "He has pretty much no shame," Hillary said with a laugh. "He never has had really any shame, and probably more so now." It's a remarkable juxtaposition between the fierce-looking pitcher, glaring from the mound, and the doting father doing anything to make his daughter laugh. "That's Tony," said Hillary. "You'd kind of be surprised. You see him on TV. Somebody said he looks like a serial killer when he's pitching, just the long hair, and he looks so stern. And then you come home, and he's walking around, talking in an Elmo voice."

Upon Tony's mid-June return, the Swallows split their final six Interleague games, but any lingering playoff hopes disappeared when they dropped 16 of their next 20, oftentimes getting blown out. Balentien—essentially Yakult's entire 2013 offense—ultimately missed 29 games with a sore left Achilles tendon. Still, he arguably outhit everyone in the league.[9] Yuhei finished strong, his first full season as an *ichi-gun* hitter yielding a top-six ranking in batting average, slugging percentage, and OPS. Only three Central League players struck out more, but Yuhei's output more than made up for that.

Most impactful was Tetsuto Yamada, whom Yakult drafted out of high school in 2010, months after he impressed scouts at the ninety-second Summer Kōshien tournament. By nineteen, he was already starting NPB playoff games. Just twenty-one when the 2014 season began, the second baseman, who unleashed a forceful leg kick as each pitch approached, finished second in MVP voting. The phenom durably played all but one game and led the league in hits, runs, and plate appearances, all while posting elite power numbers rarely seen from a leadoff hitter.[10]

Largely back in the closing role, Tony was consistently mediocre, neither suffering close to his 2013 lows nor even remotely reaching the heights of his dominant two-month stretch to finish that season.[11] Showing flashes, he led the league in strikeout rate for the second consecutive season. In an August home series with Yomiuri, he appeared in all three games and strikeouts accounted for eight of his nine outs.

But in the first outing, Tony's couldn't secure a 4–3 lead due to three hits and an off-the-mark relay throw that could have ended the game and taken him off the hook. Instead, the game was tied. The next half-inning, tempers flared. Shortly after he grounded out, a frustrated Balentien threw his helmet at an empty part of the bench. He and Tony exchanged words before TV cameras briefly cut to several Swallows holding Balentien back.[12]

All the losing had taken a toll, and on this night, the Swallows had surrendered a late-game lead and were on their way to being the first to 60 defeats. The third straight loss dropped their record in extra-inning games to an abysmal 1–8–2. Despite the drama and despair, first-year pitching coach Shingo Takatsu adeptly diffused the dugout tension.

Takatsu's superb NPB career was spent entirely with Yakult. Along with manager Katsuya Nomura and catcher Atsuya Furuta, he elevated the franchise to unprecedented levels. All within a decade, the Swallows captured the 1992 Central League crown before doing one better and securing the 1993, 1995, 1997, and 2001 Japan Series titles. As closer, the unwavering Takatsu delivered each of the final outs in those championship seasons. Such clutch dominance—no runs allowed over 11 career Japan Series appearances—earned the six-time All-Star the "Mr. Zero" moniker.[13]

With Tony livid, coach Takatsu focused on calming a fellow closer. According to Tony, after he and Balentien were separated "when everybody was cooling off down underneath, there was Takatsu just standing there, smiling at me, just kind of like chuckling. I was pretty hot at the moment. Finally, I just kind of break, I smile, and I ask my translator. I'm like, 'What are you smiling about? What's so funny about this?' He looked at me, and he just goes, '*Daijobu?*' which is basically like 'You okay?' I was like, 'All right, all right. Yeah, I'm fine.' He enjoyed it. I think he enjoyed the fire of it."

Under the guidance of Takatsu, Yakult finished last in virtually every pitching category, while allowing 31 more homers than any other team. "Ryan" Ogawa took a sizable step back, and others regressed too.[14] After all that, the Swallows retained Takatsu, giving him another chance to inspire the glory he once helped conjure as their legendary closer. A managerial change, however, was overdue.

Junji Ogawa originally took over when Shigeru Takada resigned in May 2010 and turned things around, falling just short of the playoffs. Then, Ogawa guided the Swallows to the postseason each of the next two seasons, advancing one round in 2011. Since, Yakult had fallen on hard times, with colossal disappointments in 2013 and 2014.

Injuries dearly cost both teams.[15] Still, Ogawa knew that another last-place finish would be unacceptable. With 11 games left, he offered to resign upon season's end, and team management accepted. That day, at the official press conference, he acknowledged feeling a semblance of relief, before going on to share his regret for failing to bring Yakult a Central League title.

Many of the players weren't thrilled to see him go, but now the Swallows needed a replacement. Less than a day after the season wrapped, they installed a new manager, one they hoped would usher in a new era of winning. This man was a Swallow through and through, having been a member of the organization for more than half his life.

In 2014, Mitsuru Manaka served as chief hitting coach, overseeing an offense that led the league in runs scored and batting average. Until then, he'd served on the *ni-gun* staff, first as an assistant[16] before occupying the managerial post for three seasons. Years earlier, the lefty manned the outfield during Yakult's golden era and went on to set the single-season record for pinch hits in 2007.

Despite all the baseball experience, Manaka was only forty-three—and he wasn't just young in years. He'd be bringing with him a new-age, nontraditional approach when it came to strategy. Unlike the station-to-station baseball that continued to pervade NPB managerial thinking, including that of Manaka's predecessors, he was much less fond of the bunt, opting instead to let his offense go for larger scoring outbursts at a time.

Tony felt the standard NPB offensive orthodoxy that went back decades effectively kept managers from innovating. "They've been doing it that way for so long," said Tony. "'Well, they did it there, might as well not change.' But with our team, I think he knew we had to be different in order to compete. We couldn't be the same as other teams."

After Manaka was named manager, three young coaches were promoted from *ni-gun* to the *ichi-gun* staff. With Ogawa and his lead assistant gone, pitching coach Takatsu was suddenly the second-oldest on staff.[17] On average, under forty-three years old, the new *ichi-gun* coaching group became NPB's youngest.[18]

One of the promoted coaches, Katsunori Nomura, had been Toda's battery coach and would fill the same role at *ichi-gun*, tasked with working closely with the catchers and strategizing with the pitchers in scouting meetings. He was also the half-brother of Tony's agent.[19] According to Tony, "goofball" Katsunori could not have been any more different than his serious, straitlaced brother. "We'd teach him some cool phrases," said Tony, "and he would just wear 'em out and make 'em his own. He was a funny guy." In good-natured fun, they'd tease each other. "I'd always tell him, 'Leave me alone or I'll call my agent.' And he'd be like, 'It's my brother.' And I'm like, 'I don't care.' I'd tell him that he likes me more than him because I pay him."

In Manaka, Tony noticed a refreshing desire to delegate integral tasks to his trusted assistants. For one, he believed Manaka "gave full control of the bullpen" to Takatsu. "When the manager has confidence that the pitching coach is gonna make the right decisions and get the job done," said Tony, "it's one less thing for him to worry about. If you have a manager with too many things to worry about at once, it can cause a fire."

Over Go's numerous interactions with Manaka over the years, he found him to be "very funny, very talkative." The first time they spoke after Manaka's latest promotion, he seemed much more serious. One could hardly blame him. Bringing the Swallows back to the playoffs after two years in the Central League cellar figured to present quite the challenge. Manaka would be counted on to turn around a struggling, desperate franchise. Players like Tony, Balentien, and Yamada, and a small but loyal fan base were hankering to experience winning baseball again.

Notes

[1] A visa sponsor is required. Naturally, Tony's employer, the Tokyo Yakult Swallows, sponsored Madelyn as they had been doing for Tony and Hillary.

[2] Hillary's mom particularly spent quality time with her and Madelyn at nearby parks.

[3] Kim stayed with the family for a week before returning to Arizona.

[4] He homered eight times with 19 RBIs. Sponsored by the Japanese life insurance company, the monthly Nihon Seimei MVP Awards go to each league's best hitter and best pitcher.

[5] Paving the way for Itoi were pitchers-turned-infielders Takuro Ishii and Kazuya Fukuura. Each played until his forties and collected 2,000 hits and more than 100 homers.

[6] On an MRI, a fully healed PCL appears black. At the moment, Tony's weakened PCL still looked grayish and would show up that way, he was told, for another four to five months.

[7] In 2017, the USOC announced Team USA would be staying at the Tokyo American Club during the 2020 Summer Olympics, which were later postponed amid the coronavirus pandemic.

[8] With Madelyn attached to Hillary's chest in a baby pouch, she would start crying every time people bumped into her.

[9] Balentien finished 2014 with 31 home runs and a .301/.419/.587 slash line. His 1.007 OPS led NPB.

[10] Yamada tied for the league lead in doubles, ranked third in home runs, and placed fourth in RBIs with one fewer than Yuhei. Of qualifying Central League players, only Balentien and the Carp's Brad Eldred posted a better slugging percentage than the young leadoff hitter.

[11] From July 5 onward, Tony's ERA never rose above 5.00 or fell below 3.00. He finished the season with 14 saves and a 3.34 ERA.

[12] It's unclear what exactly was said between Tony and Balentien to spark the drama.

13 Takatsu went on to pitch briefly for the White Sox and Mets before returning to Yakult for two years. Chicago gave him a ring for his contributions to its 2005 World Series title.

14 Compared to his rookie season, Ogawa allowed four more home runs despite pitching nearly 70 fewer innings. In addition, Swallows lefties Masanori Ishikawa and gaijin Chris Narveson surrendered a combined 36 homers, and starter-reliever Taichi Ishiyama allowed a career-worst 15 dingers. Collectively, the staff allowed nearly five runs per game.

15 In addition to Tony and Balentien, Lastings Milledge also missed significant time in 2014. His injured right shoulder limited him to 10 games all season.

16 Manaka joined the coaching staff immediately after retiring from the Swallows as a player in 2008.

17 Only Shigeru Sugimura, who was promoted to chief hitting coach, was older.

18 The mean age of Hanshin's coaches was highest at just over fifty-one years old.

19 Not to mention the biological son of the late Hall of Fame catcher and longtime Swallows manager Katsuya Nomura

CHAPTER SIXTEEN
THE 2015 YAKULT SWALLOWS

That was one of the cooler things ever. I get chills just thinking about it now.

Madelyn Barnette is on the field, frolicking with Swallows mascot Tsubakuro at Mazda Stadium, home of the Hiroshima Toyo Carp. Twenty minutes earlier, the second of two 2015 All-Star Games had concluded. Madelyn's dad had made the Central League team for the second time, the first since 2012. Not coincidentally, 2015 saw Tony's first injury-free first half since then.

Most of the other All-Stars and their families had already dispersed. After games, Hillary and Madelyn would always head down to the field for a brief hello before Tony disappeared into the clubhouse. But those were fleeting encounters. This was a special occasion, and Tony wanted to savor it. So, once the final out was recorded, he summoned them down.

After posing for family photos, Hillary handed a not-yet-walking Madelyn over to Tony, who carried her around the field. Television cameras quickly took notice of the scene, the little girl donning a navy blue Yakult jersey with a red bow in her hair. Tsubakuro then joined in on the fun. Again, TV crews jumped at the chance to capture the considerable cuteness occurring as the fifteen-month-old euphorically played with the silly large bird. The parents beamed, watching the pure joy on her face.

Tetsuto Yamada, who was fast becoming one of the league's most feared hitters, went over to greet Madelyn, whom he'd seen around the team. Without warning, she suddenly bent over and vomited on the second baseman's shoes. "That was fun," said Tony, with a chuckle. "He played it off great."

During media availability, Tony was asked which Pacific Leaguer he most looked forward to facing. He chose speedy center fielder Yuki Yanagita, whose left-handed bat hit .367 with power. "I was at the top of my game," said Tony. "I was pretty cocky. I was like, 'Yeah, I want to face him. I want to give him my best, see what he does with it.' And we ended up getting to do it."

Yanagita led off the eighth. Tony wasted no time, going after him with his trademark cutter. He jammed him, as he'd hoped, but Yanagita got just enough for the ball to go through to center field. It was a good pitch, just not good enough. The next batter, Sho Nakata, grounded into a double play. To cap the quick but memorable inning, Tony fanned Nobuhiro Matsuda on three pitches.[1] The Central League, coached by Giants legend and usual rival Tatsunori Hara, would win 8–3, allowing Madelyn to celebrate on the field with a furry mascot and her All-Star dad.

Earlier that day, Tony rooted for Yamada as he won the Home Run Derby.[2] From right field, Tony took selfies while donning neon Oakley sunglasses and a black Central League cap, making sure to capture dozens of energetic fans in the background. He shared his favorite on Twitter, where it garnered more than a thousand retweets. One day earlier, he took a pregame picture with the other Yakult All-Stars, including Yamada, third baseman Shingo Kawabata, and both Yuheis, including catcher Yuhei Nakamura. When they won, Tony took and posted another selfie with fans.

Hillary's most cherished part of the festivities, on par with Madelyn's on-field fun, was getting the opportunity to spend the first game with Go and his family at Tokyo Dome. Tony secured five tickets behind the dugout.

Go, his wife, and their daughter, Emiri, sat next to Hillary and Madelyn. "It was one of the only times I was really able to hang out with his whole family," said Hillary. Go's wife didn't speak any English, and neither Emiri nor Madelyn was speaking yet, but everyone had a nice time together.

Going into the season, Go had been promoted to the front office to serve as head of business operations for the *ni-gun* squad, a role created just for him. Instead of traveling with the *ichi-gun* team, as he'd done since 2010, he was primarily based in Toda. The new role afforded Go the opportunity to tap into his economics background and creative ingenuity as he set the annual budget for the farm team, determined ticket prices, populated the team's schedule, and planned promotional events. But it kept him away from the hustle and bustle of NPB action, away from the bullpens and clubhouses, and away from Tony and other good friends and friendly faces in *ichi-gun*. He was now, for all intents and purposes, a businessman.

Tony had been in Japan for five full seasons and no longer needed to rely much on an interpreter. Still, Go was more than a translator or even a friend. Tony and Hillary considered him family. Fortunately, Tony had already developed a good rapport with Go's replacement, Shin Koyama, when he was rehabbing his knee, not that anyone could ever truly replace Go. Providing the tickets was one small way of thanking Go for everything he'd done for Tony since he arrived in 2010 as a first-time gaijin. Though his family left after the fifth inning to take Emiri to bed, the girls, separated by nine months, had enough time to enjoy each other's company. "His daughter and my daughter," recalled Go, "they were grabbing hands and trying to do things to each other, so that was cute."

With an unforgettable All-Star weekend in the books, Tony looked forward to continuing his pitching mastery. But because Yakult wouldn't resume its schedule for a couple days, they stayed in Hiroshima until the next day.

Although Yokohama's rookie closer, Yasuaki Yamasaki, ran away with the fan vote,[3] Tony was a shoo-in to make the team once Hara filled in the rest of the pitcher slots. "If I didn't make the All-Star team that year, then I didn't know what else I had to do to make it," said Tony. He had a point. Healthy and clearly on a mission, he began the season obliterating the competition. It was his 29th inning and two weeks into June before he gave up a single earned run.

By the July All-Star break, only one more earned run had been charged to the right-hander, who had a barely there 0.49 ERA and 21 saves in 21 chances. In contrast to his previous two seasons, he was pitching primarily to contact.[4] By strategically placing less emphasis on striking out batters, his efficiency improved sharply. His WHIP dropped down to an impressive 0.76 from 1.18 and 1.36 in 2014 and 2013, respectively.[5]

Sometimes teams with a gifted closer struggle to bridge the gap between their starters and their closer. This can lead to blown leads without the closer even getting a chance to strut his stuff. The 2015 Swallows did not have this problem, boasting a deep bullpen that was especially reliable on the back end.

Shortly into the season, they settled on a general formula that worked exceedingly well. Along with Tony, three right-handers, Orlando Román, Ryo Akiyoshi, and Logan Ondrusek, formed the backbone of the pen. While the order in which they were used varied from game to game, at least two of them pitched in nearly every narrow win. Román, a versatile pitcher accustomed to starting games, could go more than an inning when called upon. Akiyoshi could too, but two was his max. Meanwhile, Ondrusek was rarely asked to get more than three outs. In early May, Mitsuru Manaka added southpaw Kentaro Kyuko into the late-inning fold as an integral specialist for precarious situations where a capable left-handed hitter or two were due up. By the time those guys were done for the night, the stage was set for Tony to slam the door shut.

Yakult opened the Manaka era with a road victory, although it took nearly four and a half hours to accomplish. In a 10th-inning tie, Tony set down Hiroshima in order. After Lastings Milledge tripled in two, Manaka stuck with his closer, who sealed the deal with another 1-2-3 inning.[6]

Through Yakult's first 14 games, opponents rarely scored.[7] But when the starters began to slip, the bullpen didn't. Through the break, the Swallows won all but one of 37 games in which they led or were tied after seven innings. Over the period, the team bullpen recorded a 2.31 ERA, and on three occasions—once in each of the first three months—logged stretches of at least seven games and 25 innings without allowing an earned run.

The core reliever quartet alongside Tony collectively surpassed expectations by a landslide. Neither Román nor Kyuko even made the opening-day roster. At thirty-six and coming off elbow surgery the previous June, Román was called up in April to make his first *ichi-gun* start in nearly two years. He beat Hanshin and never went back down to Toda, although he'd only start twice more.

Kyuko spent a little longer at the farm, where he dominated over-matched batters. Swallows left-hander Masato Nakazawa's struggles around the same time made Manaka's decision an easy one.[8] Despite allowing a home run to the first *ichi-gun* hitter he faced, Kyuko bounced back, managing to surrender no more all season.

Ryo Akiyoshi's success was much more expected after he'd proven himself with a strong 2014 rookie campaign. While Ondrusek was a high-priced import with a demonstrated history of success at the major-league level,[9] there's always some risk when it comes to acquiring a gaijin who has never played overseas. The long-haired, six-foot-eight American began the season with a string of nine scoreless outings. During his subsequent appearance, a rule change prevented Ondrusek from convening with his catcher between pitches.[10] Shaken, he allowed a tie-breaking three-run homer on the very next pitch. However, indicative of the bullpen depth, Akiyoshi, Barnette, and Nakazawa combined to hold Yokohama scoreless over the next five innings, just long enough to tie the game and ultimately eke out a 9–8, extra-inning win.

The two-inning effort along with Tony's previous two outings show-cased his ability to help Yakult win in an array of ways. Most traditionally, on April 15, he smoothly protected a 1–0 lead, enabling the Swallows to overcome a complete game from Kenta Maeda.[11] Two nights later, he was inserted with two runners on and notched the save on a single pitch, a line-drive double play, to the pitcher no less.

By the break, no Central League team had created distance. The 40–43–1 Swallows stood in fourth place, but the standings were tight with only four games separating first and last. Yokohama narrowly led, one and a half games ahead of Yakult. For the Swallows, it was a far cry from their 2013 and 2014 starts, when, each season, they compiled precisely 32 pre-break wins and were nowhere near first or second place.

Injured Wladimir Balentien was a nonfactor, garnering just two first-half plate appearances. Beginning the season rehabbing his Achilles, he tried to return in April but reinjured it while running in the outfield, which sidelined him until mid-September. Picking up the slack, Yamada catapulted his game into superstardom, managing to improve upon his already strong 2014 power numbers and doubling his base-stealing frequency. For his part, Kawabata led the league in hits.

Kazuhiro Hatakeyama added considerable power. On April 3, Boo struck a first-inning grand slam, one night after Yamada hit one of his own.[12] By June 10, he had hit 18 home runs, including eight in a nine-game span. Despite being curiously omitted from the All-Star team, Hatakeyama earned Central League MVP honors for a spectacular June.

Emerging from the break, the Swallows looked like they could finally be ready to shed their mediocrity in place of consistent winning base-ball. Relying heavily on key bullpen contributors, they won their first six games,[13] but it would be nearly another month before the mediocrity had vanished once and for all.

Courtesy of Tony Barnette

Early in his senior season, Tony, essentially relegated to "alternate" status, contemplated redshirting so that he could transfer to a Division II school. Of course, he stuck it out in Tempe and got drafted that June.

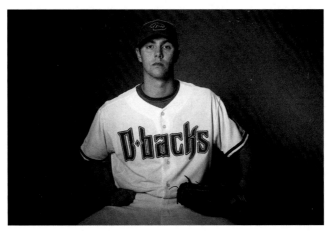

Getty Images

The twenty-five-year-old former tenth-round draft pick smiles for official team photos at the Diamondbacks spring camp. He would spend the entire season in Triple-A Reno before Don Nomura persuaded him to go to Japan.

All Arizona State alums, Hillary's parents, Kim and Ken, join her and Tony in November 2013 as the football team trounces its chief in-state rival, Arizona.

Ken (left) and Tony build the Litchfield Park backyard pergola ahead of the January 2014 barbecue-baby shower. Tony's dad, Phil, sans right arm, is just out of frame.

The first-time parents celebrate Madelyn's arrival on March 1, 2014.

The newborn steals some shut-eye on the subway.

Courtesy of Tony Barnette

The Brothers Barnette pose, a tie-less little Tony flanked by Cory (left) and Randy (right).

Courtesy of Hillary Barnette

Fellow Japan resident Jesse Dunbar savors a moment with his stepbrother and new niece.

Courtesy of Tony Barnette

Tony and interpreter Go Fujisawa are all smiles in their first season together.

Courtesy of Rob Smaal

The baseball friends (L–R: Tony, Aaron Guiel, Seth Greisinger, Rob Smaal) enjoy a round of golf in Arizona.

Trailblazing agent Don Nomura poses in his KDN Sports office in Los Angeles. His late friend, then–Red Sox coach Wendell Kim, is pictured over his left shoulder.

In Don's cherished mounted photo above the couch, a pair of clients, Mets pitchers Masato Yoshii (left) and Hideo Nomo (right), look on before a June 1998 game. The jerseys of clients Hisashi Iwakuma (left) and Kyuji Fujikawa (right) hang on the side.

Phil Barnette catches a Seahawks win in enemy (Arizona Cardinals) territory. Several weeks later, Seattle would make its second straight Super Bowl appearance and nearly win again.

The Swallows' "All for Win" campaign hits Tokyo ahead of the 2013 season. In the ad, Tony and second baseman Hiroyasu Tanaka accompany Wladimir Balentien, who will go on to shatter the single-season Japanese home-run record en route to winning 2013 Central League MVP.

A dreadful season started with optimism for manager Junji Ogawa (bottom center), Kazuhiro "Boo" Hatakeyama (bottom left), Shohei Tateyama (middle), Tony (top left) and company.

Hillary and friend Yuri get their hands (and feet) dirty planting rice in Tateyama in April 2013.

Three-week-old Madelyn joins her mom as they explore Sensō-ji, a Buddhist temple in Asakusa.

Kim and Hillary, donning the pink compass necklace that she wore everywhere in Japan, visit the annual Shibuya Kagoshima Ohara Festival.

A month after Tony returned from his April knee injury, No. 34 warms up for a save opportunity. He then retired the Carp in order to seal a 3–2 victory.

Tony says hello to his "All for Win" column in a local subway station.

Courtesy of Hillary Barnette

Courtesy of Tony Barnette

With Po by his side on a beautiful fall day in 2013, Tony fishes at Lynx Lake in Arizona's Prescott National Forest.

Making his second and final NPB All-Star appearance in the showcase event's Game 2 at Mazda Stadium on July 18, 2015, Tony couldn't resist taking a selfie with fans as he rooted for teammate Tetsuto Yamada to win the Home Run Derby.

Courtesy of Hillary Barnette

On one of the hottest days of the year, Tony accepts a ¥300,000 check for winning the Central League's Nihon Seimei July (2015) MVP Award.

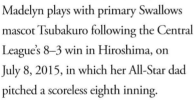

Madelyn plays with primary Swallows mascot Tsubakuro following the Central League's 8–3 win in Hiroshima, on July 8, 2015, in which her All-Star dad pitched a scoreless eighth inning.

Before Tsubakuro joined the party, the Barnettes pose for some postgame family photos.

With her trusty mini-umbrella in hand, Madelyn is ready to jump into action whenever the "good guys" score a run.

Kyodo / Kyodo News Images

Emblematic of Tony's disastrous rookie NPB season that resulted in multiple demotions and his release by season's end, he surrenders a first-inning, three-run homer to future Japanese Baseball Hall of Famer Alex Ramirez (right). The Yomiuri Giants would score nine earned runs against him in just three innings on May 5, 2010.

Courtesy of Hillary Barnette

Nearly five and a half years after Tony's ill-fated start pictured above, by this point an All-Star closer, he and the Swallows celebrate eliminating those same rival Giants in order to advance to the 2015 Japan Series. Tony's star jump captured here by *Sankei Sports* would spawn a viral meme.

The TokyoSwallows.com contingent (L–R: Dan Yoshimoto, David Watkins, Chris Pellegrini, Kozo Ota on the end) and three friends celebrate Yakult's 2015 Central League pennant, which was cemented by Yuhei's 11th-inning sayonara hit on October 2, 2015.

Dressed in Gomiuri/Anti-Giants shirts, the TokyoSwallows.com crew (Back row, L–R: Kozo and Garrett DeOrio; front row, L–R: David and Chris) congregate, along with their friend Mac Salman (back middle), behind the right-field cheering section of Jingu Stadium after the Swallows have eliminated the Giants in Game 3 of an opening-stage Climax Series on October 31, 2011.

On April 5, 2016, Tony's dream finally came true as he made his first appearance in "the show" for the Texas Rangers. He would notch his first career victory on May 2.

Not a bad day at work. At 2018 Rangers Family Day, Tony chases Loretta around the outfield with Madelyn not too far behind.

Robinson Chirinos helps a dazed Albert Pujols rise to his feet after Tony's 92-mile-per-hour fastball caught the all-time great in the helmet during a game on July 19, 2016. Home-plate umpire Mark Wegner stands between the two men, but there would be no issue as Pujols goes on to forgive an apologetic Tony.

Photo by Kathy Cole, courtesy of Hillary Barnette

Loretta Lee (left) and Madelyn Paige (right) Barnette each share a middle name with a parent, their dad and mom, respectively.

Courtesy of Tony Barnette

Now a West Coast–based scouting consultant for the Swallows, Tony speaks with his colleague and former bullpen coach Tomo Ito in Okinawa as the team readies for the 2023 campaign.

Following a late August home loss and their customary Monday off, the 56–57–1 Swallows went on a tear, proceeding to win 20 of their final 29 regular-season games. "There's nothing better than winning in sports," said Tony, reflecting on how he felt as the victories piled up. "It's fun to do, and it's fun to do a lot. And when you do it like that, it feels like everything rolls along quickly and like you just find a rhythm."

Back on June 28, the Swallows cautiously celebrated the return of longtime ace Shohei Tateyama after nearly 27 months away from *ichigun* action. He'd undergone surgeries on his throwing elbow two straight Aprils and had been making rehab starts for months. Yakult's methodical approach to his return worked. Excluding an understandably rusty debut, he impressed over his final ten starts, particularly starring during the stretch run.

Tony's closing mastery continued through the end of the season, as he notched goose-egg innings and saves with relative ease. He was so imposing that he allowed one run, total, on the road, and the only home run anyone hit off him came in September.[14] As autumn approached, Tony was nearing the single-season franchise record for saves. The record-holder, Shingo Takatsu,[15] achieved the distinction in 2001, the last time the Swallows won the Central League pennant. Fourteen years later, the team stood in prime position to take the pennant, again guided in large part by its lights-out closer.

From Tony's days as a fledgling NPB starter to his reign as one of the league's elite closers, David Watkins distinctly noticed that he had evolved: "He had much more belief in himself, a definite swagger, and a confidence. Earlier on in his career here, you just remember moments of something going wrong on the mound. He sometimes got distracted by stuff, and that just never happened [later], especially in [2015]. He was laser-focused. Nothing bothered him. If a man got on, he'd just keep it cool. He had that kind of confidence [that had] you really [believing] that he was gonna deal with any situation that was thrown at him."

In an uncharacteristically shaky outing on September 22, Tony tied Takatsu's mark of 37 saves. Strangely, the feat earned him his first Hero of the Game honor amid a spectacular season and the first since his NPB debut five and a half years earlier. Two nights later, he and the Swallows were back at it again at Jingu. Following their winning formula, Ogawa handed a 4–2 lead to the bullpen, which combined for three innings of one-hit ball, including Tony's record-setting 38th save.[16] Again, he was chosen as one of the team's "heroes," and for the only time in his Japanese career, he kept the save ball as a memento.

As he walked off the field, the pitching coach whose record had just been relegated to second-best gave him a huge hug. "He was so happy," recalled Tony. Takatsu had a sense of humor about the whole thing as well. "It was really funny," said Tony. "He was quoted in the paper, saying, 'In hindsight, I wish I would've used him less in save situations.'" Takatsu was a Swallows legend. Nevertheless, Tony's 2015 season easily eclipsed Takatsu's 2001 campaign in virtually every key metric, including innings, ERA, WHIP, and strikeout rate, among others.

The individual accomplishments were nice, but from Tony's perspective, Yakult had a grander purpose: "You could just kind of tell there was something different about the team. A lot of good things were happening that year, a lot of milestones, a lot of records, a lot of guys having really good years, and we weren't letting the celebration last. We were celebrating it real quick, and then we were moving on to the next game because I think there was a feeling around the team that that was our chance of going for it all."

The Swallows collectively had their eyes on the Central League pennant, which is awarded to the highest-finishing regular-season team. Other than a Japan Series title, it's the preeminent team prize in NPB. The pennant has been widely revered since 1950, the Central League's debut season, whereas the three-team playoff format known as the Climax Series stages was less than a decade old.[17] Furthermore, Central League pennants had been fairly rare for every franchise but Yomiuri, which ostensibly grew them on trees.[18] Yakult's most recent came fourteen years earlier, while the Giants had captured the last three.

In a critical September 27 game,[19] Tony clawed his way through a sloppy but inspired four-out save, twice stranding a pair of runners while holding a precarious 2–1 lead. After he struck out the final two batters, he exulted, further endearing him to Swallows fans watching at Tokyo Dome and on TV. For Watkins, Tony's raw emotion transparently showed how badly he wanted to win.

For game 140 of 143, fans packed into Jingu Stadium on a Tuesday night in anticipation of the Swallows' potential pennant clincher. But the Carp, who still had something to play for as they hoped to sneak into the third and final playoff spot, hung on for a 4–2 win. A scheduled off day and a rainy Thursday meant Yakult had to wait until Friday, October 2, before it could take another swing at the franchise's seventh league pennant. A win or tie would suffice, as ace "Ryan" Ogawa took the mound against Hanshin, another team still battling for a playoff spot.

A 1–0, first-inning lead held firm for a while, as Ogawa turned in six innings of two-hit ball. Ondrusek handled a 1-2-3 seventh. In the eighth, after a pair of two-out singles against Akiyoshi and Kyuko, Tony was summoned to strand the runners. He couldn't. On his first offering, a Tiger pushed the ball past the infield, through the middle. Tony got the next man, Matt Murton, to fly out, but the damage had been done. The 1–1 tie would persist into extras.

Though each team made noise, neither scored in the 10th. Román then retired all Tigers he faced in the 11th. In the home half, Yakult benefited from Central League batting champion Shingo Kawabata's lead-off single to left. With the potential winning run on first and nobody out, nearly every NPB manger would have wanted to move Kawabata over with a bunt. Manaka likely would have too had presumptive MVP Tetsuto Yamada not been stepping to the plate.

Not bunting, Yamada worked a full count. On the payoff pitch, he swung and missed. Kawabata, though, was on the move during the pitch,

223

and the catcher's wild throw allowed him to move to third. Hanshin intentionally walked Boo. Then, Hiroyasu Tanaka flew out, too shallow for Kawabata to try to score. Two outs, runners still on the corners.

Pitcher-turned-outfielder Yuhei embodied Yakult's next chance. Following a breakout 2014, his 2015 represented a significant step back.[20] Tigers left-hander Atsushi Nomi was in the midst of his first relief appearance in nearly three years. Yuhei laced his 2-1 pitch down the right-field line.[21] "It was one of the most amazing things," said David Watkins, who was in attendance, before interrupting himself. "Well, it was *the* most amazing thing I've seen as a Swallows fan."

As the ball rolled into the outfield and Kawabata jogged toward home plate, everybody knew what was happening. The Swallows-heavy Jingu Stadium crowd erupted, as Yuhei's teammates scrambled out of the dugout to mob him after he rounded first base. Keiji Obiki, who'd been waiting on deck, opened his arms as widely as he could to bring a scoring Kawabata in for a celebratory hug. Kawabata held his arms open too, so the two could embrace once he scored. The young coaching staff engaged in a group hug in the dugout. "Just the noise," Watkins reminisced, "and everyone was crying around us. All the fans essentially started crying. It was crazy because no one thought . . . It was a surprise championship."

"When we clinched that night," said Tony, "it was a big party." Shortly after the Yuhei sayonara hit, players and staff congregated in the middle of the field, where they began the *dōage* lifting ritual. First, teary-eyed rookie manager Mitsuru Manaka was tossed into the air, with Tony responsible for raising the skipper's left leg. Later, Tony and Yuhei, among others, received their own *dōage* treatment.

Then, the team embarked on a customary victory lap, eleven players leading the way with a "2015 Central League champions" banner. The rest who followed took turns raising the trophy as Yakult circled the field.

Flanked by key bullpen cogs, Tony received the trophy from Kyuko with both hands, extended his arms upward, tucked in his chin, and, for a split-second, placed it atop his navy cap. Then he raised it again, triumphantly with his right arm as he, in pure ecstasy, unleashed a primal scream.

Naturally, exuberant Tony's spotlight wasn't fading after he handed off the trophy. Not by a long shot. Feeding off the energy in the cheering section, he daringly and questionably scaled the right-field fence despite the objections of two stadium security guards who admonished him to climb down to safety. Upon his successful dismount, fans started "Baw-Net-Toh" chants, undoubtedly egged on by the closer's antics. He tipped his cap, acknowledging the adoring crowd.

Near the end of the lap, Tony borrowed mascot Torukuya's pink backpack, which is fashioned after the Yakult company's signature yogurt bottle. He strutted around with it, paused briefly to pose while pumping his fists, and then strutted some more. "He's a clown," said Hillary.

Then, the players ducked into the clubhouse, where they changed into their commemorative shirts and had some drinks. Some fastened GoPro cameras to their foreheads in order to forever document the shenanigans ahead.

While the team enjoyed its quick private celebration, the grounds crew laid out a large blue tarp, as kegs and bottles of beer were brought onto the field. When the players emerged, most wearing protective goggles, it seemed as though not a single fan had left his or her seat. Utility infielder Ryosuke Morioka stepped to the microphone and gave a quick yet impassioned speech, culminating with the cheer "*Yakuruto sutairu* ("Yakult style" in English), *Yakuruto sutairu*. Ay-ay-oh." "Then, everybody popped the beer, and it was crazy," said Hillary. "That was like the peak of the Ay-ay-oh chant."

According to Tony, catching coach Katsunori Nomura first started the cheer. When Tony broke Takatsu's saves mark, he fit "Ay-ay-oh" into his Hero interview, introducing the chant to the public. "The fans caught on to it," he said, "and [it was] just something that stuck. I'm not really sure what it meant. It's just that they loved it, and I loved it. It's a natural thing that happens around a winning team, and everyone has these little slogans or little chants or little jokes that they're running with, and that was just one of ours. That's the thing about the Japanese fans: They want to be on board, they want to see victories, and they want to see us having fun doing it."

Post-Morioka speech, craziness ensued. Delirious Swallows could be seen running around and tackling one another. They also poured beer on their teammates' heads and engaged in Slip 'N Slide runs on the slick tarp. Hillary and Madelyn had already made their way to the field, by the home bullpen, a tad removed from the unruly players. "It was just the most awesome thing," said Hillary, who remembered the field reeking of beer. Madelyn sat in the bullpen, attentively playing with the ribbon thrown down from the crowd as streamers.

The game ended just after 10 p.m., but the on-field celebration lasted until 11:30. Most Swallows went out drinking afterward. The next morning, the team would be leaving on a bullet train for Hiroshima. One could've forgiven a literal or figurative hangover among most of the players the next night,[22] yet Yakult managed to stage a three-run, eighth-inning comeback in order to force extras, where it ultimately won. Though the win was meaningless in terms of playoff positioning, it further exemplified the special collective spirit residing in the 2015 Swallows.

Go Fujisawa felt elated for Tony and the men he'd worked with daily before moving on to his front-office role. Still, it didn't feel right that he was not celebrating alongside Tony. Go was at Jingu, but other obligations kept his attention away from the game. That night, he took care of VIPs from sponsors and the parent company, and later, as the game wore on, he helped set up a stage in case Yakult won. "At the moment, to be honest, that was very awkward for me," he admitted. "I don't know if the word is right, but I felt like I was an outsider. I felt like I was not in the right spot. I didn't really feel like celebrating the team 100 percent. I wished I could be with the players as a teammate." In retrospect, Tony felt terrible for Go. "[It] sucked that he didn't really get to enjoy the fruits of his labor for his first [five] years in that position."

Go's demanding new role also prevented him from following Yakult's impressive second-half run. Overloaded with work and focused on the *ni-gun* team, Go rarely even checked the box scores. Had he been watching, he'd have witnessed the best season of Tony's career, a year in which the NPB veteran's numbers sparkled off the page. He tied for the league lead with 41 saves and didn't blow one all season until the pennant clincher, when an inherited runner scored. Tony's 1.29 ERA and 0.89 WHIP ranked first and second among Central League closers, respectively. His 5.3 hits allowed per nine innings easily bested all closers around the league.

Finishing atop the standings meant the Swallows had the luxury of awaiting—and then hosting—the winner of the Climax Series' first stage between the Yomiuri Giants and Hanshin Tigers.

Halfway through the season, the term "Triple 3" or *Toripuru Suri* began reverberating all over the baseball-crazed country. It referred to the rare and impressive phenomenon in which a player finishes a season with at least a .300 batting average, 30 home runs, and 30 stolen bases. Before Kazuo Matsui most recently accomplished it in 2002, there had been only seven such seasons. Further fueling the fire, two players were threatening Triple-3 campaigns: Tetsuto Yamada and the Fukuoka SoftBank Hawks' Yuki Yanagita,[23] the All-Star Tony told reporters he'd most like to face.

In a demonstrative nod to his versatility, Yamada wound up as league leader in homers (38) and stolen bases (34),[24] while batting .329. It's no wonder he'd been dubbed the "Mike Trout of Japan" that summer by NEIFI Analytics[25] with a few others following suit. Remarkable consistency earned him three straight monthly MVP Awards from July through September and four throughout the season.

He led the Central League in both runs and extra-base hits by a land-slide. For good measure, his OPS, 1.027, was more than 100 points better than the next guy, and only Boo narrowly bested him in RBIs. Yamada didn't miss a single game either.

Yamada's Triple 3 pursuit didn't feel assured until maybe mid-August. Stolen bases were the biggest sticking point,[26] and his .306 pre-break average left little margin for error. In late July, Yamada noticeably accelerated his base-swiping pace, stealing six over nine games. By September 6, with nearly a full month remaining, he'd stolen his thirtieth base and was comfortably batting above .300. He'd already reached 30 home runs weeks earlier when he had hit numbers 29, 30, and 31—all in the same game.[27]

The term *Toripuru Suri* achieved such wide-reaching popularity that the *Jiyu Kokuminsha* publishing house named it one of the year's most memorable buzzwords.[28] Yamada and Yanagita—the latter finished at .363 with 34 homers and 32 steals—appeared at the award ceremony together to collect their prize. More exciting for them, they'd earned Most Valuable Player Awards. Months earlier, on the heels of a season for the ages, it was time for the Swallows star to strive for playoff glory. In their 2011 and 2012 playoff stints, Yamada appeared just three times. In the 2015 postseason, as unquestionably Yakult's best hitter, all eyes would be fixated on him.

With Yakult keeping tabs, Yomiuri squeaked by Hanshin in a low-scoring series. The forthcoming Giants-Swallows Climax Series would mark the first postseason meeting between the Tokyo teams since 2011, when Yakult edged Yomiuri in the opening stage. Since then, the Swallows hadn't won a playoff series, with two eliminations at the hands of the Dragons followed by two playoff-less seasons. Meanwhile, the Giants had excelled, appearing in three Climax Series final stages (2012–2014) and two Japan Series, winning one.

The Giants' recent success, coupled with their long-standing dominance, fostered a competitive animus that turbocharged the Swallows' motivation to beat their intracity rivals. Personally, Tony had never forgotten how the 2010 Giants ruthlessly welcomed him into the league. During the 2015 season, the teams nearly split 25 meetings, with Yomiuri winning 13.

Following Yakult's nine-day hiatus, the series was set to begin October 14. Per NPB protocol, the higher-seeded Swallows automatically started with a 1–0 series lead. Yomiuri quickly evened the series with a 4–1 win, scoring two runs apiece in the fifth and sixth. After the loss, Yakult could reflect upon a couple of missed opportunities. Most costly, Balentien squandered a first-inning, bases-loaded chance by grounding into an inning-ending double play.

Undeterred, the Swallows scored four runs off talented Miles Mikolas[29] the next night and shut out the Giants with eight innings from Ogawa and another from Tony. In the victory, Balentien made amends with three hits and two RBIs, a rare good game amid an injury-ravaged season that limited him to 15 games. Then, they blanked Yomiuri again to take a commanding 3–1 series lead, combining six stellar innings from Shohei Tateyama with the lethal Akiyoshi-Kyuko-Ondrusek-Barnette quartet.

Within a week of the *ni-gun* season ending, Go left on a work trip to Miyazaki, where he remained for the Climax Series. "All I remember is I felt like I was a fan," he said with a laugh. "I remember the moment that I was having dinner by myself at the team hotel and watching [Tony on] TV, and it was like, 'What the heck?'"

Saturday night's Game 4 presented the Swallows with their first chance to punch their ticket to a Japan Series since 2001. Sensing its imminence, they capitalized early. In the first couple frames, they scored three, aided in part by a defensive miscue. In the fifth, a Shinnosuke Abe single trimmed Yakult's lead to 3–2 and halted Yomiuri's 25-inning scoreless streak that began midway through Game 1.

But whatever relief the Giants felt from finally getting runs on the board, it began to vanish inning by inning as the vaunted Swallows bullpen kept stifling them. A microcosm of the season the pen had, it was reliably doing its job yet again. The one-run lead looked a little dicey with Abe coming up with two on in the seventh. His 11 hits had already set an NPB record for the most in a single playoff stage, yet Ondrusek remained unfazed as he escaped the jam by inducing a rally-killing double play.

If Tony could preserve the one-run lead, Yakult would soon be celebrating. "I remember when I was leaving the bullpen to go into the game," he said. "It was a sellout crowd of 35,000 people that night, and they were all just going, 'Let's go Tony!' You get 35,000 people doing that, standing on their feet, that was awesome. That was one of the cooler things ever. I get chills just thinking about it now."

Not about to let the crowd down, he began the final inning with a strikeout. He secured the second out by adeptly locating a high chopper, bare-handing the ball, and rifling it to first base, just in time. Then, as if the drama needed to reach a fever pitch, Tony and Giants veteran lefty Yoshinobu Takahashi battled each other all the way to a full count. "Me and him had battles throughout my entire career," contextualized Tony. "Me and him were very familiar with each other."

Their paths had most recently crossed in the previous night's game, which ended with a Takahashi strikeout. During the regular season, Tony had his number, picking up four saves that culminated in a Takahashi out. But back on August 1, 2013, Takahashi electrified a 44,508-strong Tokyo Dome crowd with a two-out sayonara single off Tony, whose record dropped to 0–6 with a 12.60 ERA. Here he was, a little more than two years out from the nadir of his career, facing the same man, one strike away from achieving the ultimate redemption for himself and his team.

On the payoff pitch, Takahashi whiffed, prompting another well-earned celebration and a forthcoming Japan Series appearance. "Beating the Giants on that stage, that was gratification," said Tony. "Knowing that from the very beginning, they kicked me around. I remember they just pounded me. And to come out on top at the very end of my stint there was really rewarding. It was something that you look back on. You're like, 'That's where I started against them, and they were just a powerhouse. I got better, and I ended up beating them in the end.'"

A special era was ending for the Giants, and the Swallows helped accelerate its termination. Legendary manager Tatsunori Hara abruptly resigned at the age of fifty-seven.[30] Over twelve years, he'd guided the Giants to seven pennants and three Japan Series titles. Giants lifer Takahashi, the man who made the final out, would be taking over. Teammate Hirokazu Ibata also retired to join his staff.

"For the longest time, you sit there and live underneath the shadow of the Giants," Tony said. "There's a big-money team that they market, and we're just the other Tokyo team trying to contend. So you live in that shadow. Being there for six years, I felt the rivalry, and I embraced it. To beat them like that on that stage, that was awesome for me. That was the best feeling."

Once again, they began their *dōage* celebration with Manaka. Each of the seven times the rookie manager was elevated by his players, Tony did a star jump, squatting down before exploding upward while spreading his arms and legs. The large monitor in right field captured every jump, as he was positioned directly in front of Manaka. Before long, his antics went viral. On Twitter, a hashtag began to spread with the rough translation of "Tony Barnette crappy Photoshop contest."

"The Japanese internet went wild with it, putting him in all kinds of situations," said David Watkins. While only a search of the particular Japanese hashtag can do the meme justice, it should be noted that Tony's star-jumping likeness was shrunk, rotated, and stitched together multiple times to form a chain-link fence and placed in disparate settings such as outer space, Leonardo da Vinci's "Vitruvian Man," over the ocean after being launched by a tidal wave, volcanoes, Japanese game shows, dance routines, anime, the Super Mario Bros. video game, and naturally in various baseball scenarios. In other images, he was transformed into rockets, fireworks, wind turbines, a keychain, and a calculator's multiplication sign. Ten TBs even formed their own cheerleading pyramid.

Online, people had Tony climbing jungle-gym monkey bars, performing a gymnastics floor exercise, breakdancing, and celebrating Tokyo's winning 2020 Olympics bid alongside prime minister Shinzo Abe and other leaders. Pokémon and a restaurant chain inspired the most widely shared images. One depicted Tony emerging from a Poké ball with the caption "Barnette, I choose you!" The other showed Tony and Hiroshima's Takahiro Arai giddily awaiting their order at a Shanghai Yoshinoya.

"Oh, my God, that was so funny," Hillary said of Tony's viral moment. "I was loving every second of it, especially because they were so creative. To take that one photo and the things they were putting it into, I was laughing all night."

Following Manaka's aerial adventure, the stellar bullpen was paid its due, as Tony was lifted into the air three times, followed by three more tosses of Ondrusek and Román each. Other integral players, including series MVP Shingo Kawabata—who batted .467 and scored four times— were lifted too.

Mitsuru Manaka had taken the Swallows from last to first and to the Japan Series in his first year at the helm. In the other dugout, manning the Fukuoka SoftBank Hawks, would be another rookie manager in Kimiyasu Kudo. The former star pitcher, who enjoyed a decorated career,[31] inherited a championship team and evoked the self-assurance to match that. Ahead of the Japan Series, he revealed that he told his players on the first day of spring camp that they'd win another title.

His confidence wasn't misplaced. An NPB-best offense, coupled with the Pacific League's best pitching unit, made SoftBank the prohibitive favorite. The talented and balanced reigning champions dominated with a 90–49–4 record. Once the Hawks held a late-inning lead, they handed the ball to six-foot-four Dennis "the King of Closers" Sarfate, and opposing teams were all but finished. Compared to SoftBank, Yakult lost 16 more games and needed two more weeks to clinch its pennant. Still, anything could happen, and the Swallows had their own MVP and dominant closer, along with a formidable offense and red-hot, dependable bullpen.

Yakult received a break when Hawks captain and noted clutch performer Seiichi Uchikawa[32] was scratched from Game 1 with broken ribs and appeared likely to miss the series. But their lineup still boasted the likes of MVP Yanagita and right-handed mashers Dae-ho Lee, who historically killed Yakult,[33] and Nobuhiro Matsuda. In addition to achieving the Triple 3, Yanagita posted an otherworldly 1.100 OPS. As if that wasn't enough firepower, Lee and Matsuda provided protection behind him, slugging .533 and .524, respectively. Plus, Akira Nakamura batted .300 for the third straight year.

The Hawks jumped out to a two-game series lead by dominating from the rubber. Two pitching gems—from young Shota Takeda and Dutch gaijin Rick van den Hurk[34]—limited the Swallows to two runs and seven hits across both games. In the deflating Game 2 loss, they batted only two more than the 27-hitter minimum.

After a day off, the series shifted to Jingu, where Yamada not only reminded everyone why he won MVP, but he also made a compelling case for being a transcendent homegrown offensive talent, the likes of which Japan had rarely ever seen. The twenty-three-old wunderkind put Yakult's offense squarely on his back as he struck three home runs in his first three chances.

Even with Yamada's insane Game 3 heroics, the Swallows couldn't coast to victory, given the Hawks' relentless ability to fight back at nearly every critical juncture. Directly after each of Yamada's first two home runs gave them a lead, SoftBank tied the game. The Hawks then took a one-run lead in the fifth before Yamada launched a two-run, go-ahead homer, a lead that finally held once the bullpen got involved. Later, Yakult added three runs off one-time Swallows closer Ryota Igarashi, without, believe it or not, Yamada's help. Following the 8–4 win, Yamada was awarded Hero of the Game honors; it was either that or crowning him emperor.[35]

A rotund six-foot-four Korean who migrated to NPB at thirty, Dae-ho Lee quickly put the Hawks in control of Game 4 by driving in four over the first three innings. Yakult battled Sarfate in the ninth but ultimately stranded a couple, including the potential game-tying run.

On the brink of elimination, Yakult had another quiet night, courtesy of gaijin Jason Standridge,[36] who delivered six strong innings. Lee launched a two-run homer, which provided the Hawks with a lead they never relinquished. Though Lee supplied much of the run production all series, infielder Kenji Akashi, along with a different teammate or two each night, contributed immensely, while the vaunted Yanagita badly struggled[37] and Uchikawa never played. Although SoftBank led 5–0, Kudo gave Sarfate the honor of clinching the championship. Once he made quick work of Yakult, the 2015 season was officially in the books, and the Fukuoka SoftBank Hawks were champions.

Once thirty-year-old Dennis Sarfate left for Japan, the New York native registered three strong seasons for the Carp and Lions. But he didn't truly leave his mark until after joining the Hawks in 2014. The lights-out closer helped guide them to consecutive titles right away. In 2017, they'd win another, with him earning MVP, Japan Series MVP, and the Shoriki Award, a rare gaijin honor.[38] Although the hip problems that would force his retirement kept the right-hander off the mound for much of 2018 and all of 2019, his Hawks won two more rings. In previous years, Sarfate spurned various opportunities to return to the big leagues. Instead, he built an NPB legacy, becoming one of the highest-paid gaijin of all time, while notching 234 saves. No gaijin and only six others have ever recorded more.

The Swallows could only watch as the Hawks gleefully lifted their manager, owner, Japan Series MVP Lee,[39] and others—on Yakult's turf no less. Owner Masayoshi Son, who also chaired the Sprint Corporation headquartered in Kansas City, joked that his team should have a chance at facing the Royals in a "real World Series" if they finished off the Mets. Kansas City did, but the cross-league matchup never transpired.

The Swallows bullpen posted a 1.99 Japan Series ERA, yet it rarely had a lead because the starting pitching didn't live up to the challenge posed by SoftBank's lineup. Including the clincher in which Yakult already trailed 4–0, Tony appeared only twice, and not one starter got through five innings. "Our biggest asset was our bullpen," the closer said, "and we weren't able to get to our bullpen. Going into the Japan Series, we knew that if our starters were able to get through the fifth and sixth with one, two runs scored, then we were gonna have a chance, but that just wasn't the case. They ended up overpowering us from the very get-go."

The series lasted only five games, and the Swallows never led in any of the games they lost. The final round was a disappointment, to be sure, but it paled in comparison to the joy derived from winning the Central League pennant or taking down the Giants. "I don't know a single person in the Yakult organization that saw the Japan Series as a total loss," said Tony. "We won the Central League. We won the Climax Series."

Notes

[1]   After two cutters away, Tony went up and in. "He just swung through and hit the dirt," he said. "I apologized to him after the game, and he was like, 'No, no, no. It's a good pitch.'"

[2]   Yamada won by tiebreaker, but not via swing-off. Instead, the win was awarded to the player who received more fan votes to appear in the contest. Thus, Yamada topped Takeya Nakamura for the Derby crown.

[3]   Yokohama's Yasuaki Yamasaki received 357,396 votes, more than double Tony's total of 150,729. Giants closer Hirokazu Sawamura finished second in fan voting.

[4]   At the 2015 All-Star break, Tony had struck out 6.6 batters per nine innings, much lower than his respective 2013 and 2014 K-per-nine rates of 13.8 and 11.7.

[5]   To put 0.76 in better perspective, in Tony's best previous season, 2012, he had a 1.01 WHIP (walks plus hits per innings pitched). Of course, the lower the WHIP, the better a pitcher tends to be doing.

[6]   Tony efficiently retired all six batters in 13 pitches.

[7]   Yakult allowed more than two runs just once over the first 14 games, and that happened in a 4–3 win over Hanshin.

8   Upon the May 4 Kyuko promotion, Nakazawa wasn't actually deregistered, but Kyuko's consistently stellar play relegated Nakazawa to a much less important bullpen role.

9   Yakult was paying Ondrusek, who'd amassed 271 major-league innings between 2010 and 2014 with the Reds, $1.2 million plus incentives for the season.

10   Ondrusek had been unaware that mound visits were restricted to three per team within the first nine innings and that Yakult had none left.

11   After the season, the Dodgers would pay a $20 million posting fee for the right to sign Maeda to an eight-year deal.

12   Swallows teammates hadn't recorded grand slams in back-to-back games since May 1993 when Jack Howell and Takahiro Ikeyama did it.

13   Tony, Ondrusek, and Román each appeared in five of the six games, while Akiyoshi logged three outings that week.

14   Ironically, the lone 2015 home run against Tony was slugged by Yokohama's Toshiro Miyazaki, a five-foot-seven pinch-hitter who hit no others all year. It was also just his third career homer, though he did go on to hit 28 as a full-time starter three seasons later.

15   Less notably, Ryota Igarashi and Hirotoshi Ishii shared the record with Takatsu, closing 37 games for Yakult in 2004 and 2005, respectively. All three record-holders pitched for the 2001 Central League–winning Swallows. Nicknamed "Rocket Boy" for his blazing-quick fastballs, Igarashi later rejoined the franchise in 2019.

16   Coincidentally, Tony's stepbrother, Jesse, officially got married on September 24, 2015, the same day Tony set the single-season franchise record for saves. Jesse and Etsuko's ceremony and reception weren't held until 2017.

17   The Central League began with eight teams. One disbanded after a year. By 1953, two others merged, bringing the CL down to the six-team count that has long endured. Before 2007, the Central team with the best record merely earned an automatic place in the Japan Series.

18   Although the Swallows ranked third of six Central League teams with six all-time pennants, the output came over a period of sixty years. Meanwhile, Yomiuri had six times as many pennants. That's thirty-six.

19   The Swallows came in leading Yomiuri by a single game. As such, a loss would have evened the rivals in the standings with a week to go, whereas a win would've brought Yakult's Central League magic number down to three.

20   Yuhei's 2015 .695 OPS was a stark regression from his .877 mark in 2014. More specifically, his slugging percentage dipped from .505 to .388.

21   As fate would have it, the career-defining sayonara hit came against Nomi, the very same pitcher who, as a rookie ten years earlier, surrendered Yuhei's first career homer. At the time, Yuhei was a twenty-year-old pitcher who'd go on to record just one other hit that season.

22   There was at least one exception. As the next day's starter, Taichi Ishiyama left Jingu for Hiroshima before the game ended and thus did not party with the team. Wanting to include him in the experience, Yakult's bullpen catcher actually wore Ishiyama's uniform during the celebration.

23   By the time July started, Yanagita was batting .381 with 16 homers and 14 stolen bases. Meanwhile, Yamada was hitting .303 with 14 and 12, respectively.

24 Caught stealing just four times, Yamada boasted an 89.5 percent success rate.

25 An acronym for Normalized Empirical Individual Forecasting Index, the proprietary player evaluation service works with clients at the major-league, minor-league, and collegiate levels.

26 Yamada had only 15 stolen bases at the All-Star break.

27 That August 22 masterpiece marked Yamada's third straight game with at least one homer.

28 The other term, *Bakugai*, was defined by Quartz, a business-focused international news site, as an "explosive shopping spree carried out by Chinese tourists."

29 Mikolas enjoyed a 1.92 ERA in 2015, his first NPB season. After two more superb seasons with Yomiuri, the "Lizard King" returned to the majors by signing a two-year deal with the Cardinals. He was so excellent that just one season in, St. Louis gave the righty a four-year, $68 million extension.

30 Some speculated Hara's resignation was influenced by a gambling scandal that rocked the Giants this year, and his previous brush with organized crime only fueled rumors. Still, Hara was never implicated in the gambling scandal, and he cited declining on-field results, and nothing else, as his rationale for stepping down. Hara would ultimately return to manage the Giants in 2019.

31 The left-handed Kudo, who would be inducted into the Japanese Baseball Hall of Fame in 2016, played twenty-nine NPB seasons. An eight-time All-Star, he won eleven titles, 224 games, two league MVPs, and two Japan Series MVP Awards.

32 Uchikawa, a career .300 hitter, had a penchant for playoff success, earning 2014 Japan Series MVP, as well as Pacific League Climax Series MVP in 2011 and 2015.

33 Between 2012 and 2015, Lee batted .368 against Yakult with five home runs and 14 RBIs in 15 regular-season games. As a member of the Buffaloes in 2012, Lee's monstrous, mid-May two-run home run spoiled Tony's save and were the first runs scored off the new closer. The following year, Lee's two-run single off Tony helped Orix storm back from a five-run deficit to win 10-8. Tony was tagged with the loss.

34 Van den Hurk spent the previous two seasons in South Korea following parts of six seasons with the Marlins, Orioles, and Pirates. For the 2015 Hawks, he went 9–0 in 15 starts, striking out 120 batters in 93 innings.

35 Never before (and never since) had a player hit three home runs in a Japan Series game, let alone in three straight plate appearances in the same game.

36 The expansion Devil Rays' first-round pick out of high school, Standridge played parts of seven seasons in the majors. After spending two stints and ten years in Japan, his playing career concluded following the 2017 season.

37 One of Yanagita's three Japan Series hits came in the last inning of Game 5 off an inside Tony Barnette cutter that, like in the All-Star Game, he was able to muscle just over the shortstop's head.

38 Bobby Valentine (2005) was and remains the only other gaijin to have won it. Named after Matsutarō Shōriki, an early pioneering owner of the *Yomiuri Shimbun*, the award annually goes to the player or manager who contributes most to Japanese baseball.

39 The first-ever Korean-born MVP totaled eight hits, eight RBIs, and two homers in the series.

CHAPTER SEVENTEEN
BIG-LEAGUE DREAMS

---

*He can give up a home run now, and you see it doesn't completely
shake his foundation anymore.*

In 1964, the Nankai Hawks loaned Masanori Murakami and two other
prospects to the San Francisco Giants organization. By September, the
left-handed reliever became the first-ever Japanese-born person to play in
the major leagues. There, his instant success spurred Giants executives to
seek to exercise a clause in his contract that would enable them to buy his
rights from Nankai. The Hawks were opposed, arguing Murakami was
exclusively on loan for the 1964 season. Following a two-month stale-
mate, San Francisco agreed to return him to Nankai after 1965. This incident led to the 1967 United States–Japanese Player Contract Agreement,
more commonly known as the "working agreement," wherein neither
MLB nor NPB would interfere with the other side's rights to players.[1]

Accordingly, no Japanese-born player appeared in the majors again
for another three decades. Then, in 1994, Don Nomura got involved,
forever changing the face of Japanese and American baseball, as well as the
flow of talent from NPB to MLB. It was understood that an NPB player
could not sign with a major-league team unless he reached free agency

after ten years of service or his contract was sold to the new team. But in fact, as Nomura would momentously discover, the Japanese Uniform Players Contract's reserve clause contained a loophole that meant a player who "voluntarily retired" from NPB could then legally sign with a major-league team. Once his client Hideo Nomo failed to come to terms with the Kintetsu Buffaloes, Nomura advised him to retire. A "free" Nomo subsequently signed with the Dodgers, and although Kintetsu protested, it had no recourse. No rules were violated.

In 1997 and 1998, respectively, Nomura had his fingerprints all over moves that resulted in pitcher Hideki Irabu[2] and young infielder Alfonso Soriano[3] leaving their NPB teams and landing with the New York Yankees. Many parties seethed, including all non-Yankee MLB teams who were not given a chance to bid on Irabu, and the Japanese teams that lost Nomo and Soriano. The remaining NPB teams feared their players could soon be poached. With change sorely needed, the posting system was created when the Orix BlueWave's general manager rewrote the working agreement, and the MLB and NPB commissioners signed the pact in December 1998. Although the specific rules have changed over the years, the broad framework, with a posting or transfer fee at the system's core, has remained in place ever since.

The original posting system featured blind bids over a four-day period. Through the 2012–2013 offseason, teams were still blindly bidding against one another for exclusive negotiating rights with the posted player, but over a thirty-day window. Up until late 2013, including the 2011 postings of Nori Aoki and Yu Darvish, there was no cap on posting fees. Ever since, $20 million has been the maximum allowed per bid. The new agreement also removed the exclusive negotiating element and altered how posting amounts were determined. Under the new rules, MLB teams would no longer be bidding against one another when it came to the fee. Rather, the posting NPB team would designate a specific amount. Then, any MLB team willing to pay the posting amount could come to terms on a contract with the player.[4]

Nomura makes no secret about his utter disdain for the posting process he inadvertently helped to create. In an interview with author Robert Whiting, Nomura once referred to posting as a "slave auction," and he stands by his use of the metaphorical term today. Most troubling to Nomura, the system provides Japanese players little to no autonomy. Under the rules, NPB teams can refuse to post any player indefinitely. The system most prominently benefits Major League Baseball, and NPB next; the Japanese player is a distant third. Even if a player is permitted by his team to post, his earning power is theoretically limited because his MLB team must also compensate his former team. Thus, players often agree to contracts below their true market value. Despite the system's flaws, Nomura doesn't see it changing significantly any time soon. There are too many vested interests.

Growing up in Tokyo, Nomura was a rebel from the start. He was born in 1957 with the name Donald Engel, to a Japanese mother and a Jewish-American father. He attended a private, English-speaking Catholic school until he was expelled for fighting at sixteen. A few years earlier, he began seeing his mom again, years after she left their family. By then, she'd changed her name to Sachiyo and was living with NPB catcher and manager Katsuya Nomura.[5] Katsuya's connections would allow Don to participate annually in a rigorous summer baseball program, an experience he would later credit for changing his life.

For college, he moved to California to enroll at Cal Poly Pomona and play baseball there. But by 1977, Japan was no longer allowing Nomura to hold dual citizenship in both countries. He had to choose. He went with Japan, in part because he wanted to play in NPB, which had a strict gaijin quota that could benefit him.[6] He briefly assumed the name Katsuaki Itō until his stepfather adopted him, giving him the name Don Katsuki Nomura.[7] The next year, he began a four-year stint with the Toda Swallows, which ended with the infielder's release. In a 1996 *Sports Illustrated* profile, he told Franz Lidz, "I left the game thinking I never wanted to pick up a baseball again."[8]

Nomura returned to the United States, looking for a baseball job. He still loved the sport and would have been a coach, a scout, or virtually anything in a front office. There were no takers. "No teams were looking for bilingual guys," said Nomura. He worked various odd jobs and, for a time, had to send his wife and young daughter back to Japan while he lived out of his car in Los Angeles. By the mid-1980s, the Swallows brought him back as a part-time scout. Shortly thereafter, he learned the Kintetsu Buffaloes were looking for English speakers and began serving as a Japanese-English interpreter in the US, Mexico, and the Dominican Republic.

By 1989, sizable earnings from various real-estate deals enabled Nomura to get involved in American baseball in an exciting new way. When he learned that Joe Buzas[9] was looking for a co-owner of the Salinas Spurs, an unaffiliated High-A team,[10] he jumped at the chance. Beginning with Nomura's first season in ownership, the Spurs went international, welcoming eight Japanese players—four from the Swallows and four from the Daiei Hawks—to their roster.

During the 1991 season, a friend called Nomura, asking him, "Can you take care of Mac in Salinas?" Mac was Makoto Suzuki, a Japanese sixteen-year-old whom Nomura had met a few years earlier. Mac had just been expelled from high school, and his parents wanted to send him to the United States. "I brought him under my wing," said Nomura, who assigned Mac to work in Salinas's clubhouse, primarily laundry duties. On the final day of the 1992 season, he asked the kid if he wanted to pitch. He did, so Nomura signed him to a minor-league contract. Mac pitched an inning and looked phenomenal out there.

In 1991, Nomura bought out Buzas's 50 percent stake, becoming the sole owner of the Spurs. Ahead of 1993, amid pushback on his plan to move the Spurs to San Bernardino, he decided it was best to sell the team. The transaction was made with the agreement that the Spurs would reserve a roster spot for Mac that season.[11]

Originally, he had planned to try to get Mac a job in Japan following the 1993 season. That calculus changed midseason when Mac's fastball

rose to 96 miles per hour, and more than a dozen major-league organizations became interested in signing him. Mac trusted Nomura and
knew teams were suddenly after him, so he asked him to represent him.
Unflinchingly, Nomura accepted the challenge and began educating himself on the business.

By early September, they settled on the Mariners,[12] and Mac agreed
to a contract. By the next season, Nomura had to become certified as an
agent if Mac were to be allowed on Seattle's 40-man roster. This entailed
requesting an application form from the Major League Baseball Players
Association, returning it completed, and then passing a grilling by Gene
Orza, second-in-command at the association.

Nomura got certified by the MLBPA, and by 2008, he founded KDN
Sports, his own management company. Among a handful of mementos
in his Los Angeles office, Nomura displays a photograph from 1994 in
which Mac is shaking hands with then–Birmingham Barons outfielder
Michael Jordan. Mac is the one who got Nomura into player representation, and Jordan is, well, Michael Jordan.

After the 2009 season, Nomura had been trying to get Bobby Korecky
a job in Japan. Although a deal never materialized, he asked the Aces
reliever for his teammate's number. He liked that Tony had won 14 games
and been a workhorse in his lone Triple-A season. Also, "[Japanese] teams
specifically were looking for a starting pitcher, and he was fairly young,"
said Nomura. Of course, Tony was ultimately persuaded to take advantage of the opportunity in Japan.

Although Nomura and Tony's American agent, Dean Steinbeck, then
signed documentation stipulating that representation would revert back
to Steinbeck if and when Tony returned to North America, Steinbeck left
the industry entirely in the intervening years. This made the legendary
Nomura Tony's sole agent. Following an epic 2015, a consequential offseason loomed ahead.

Coming off another spectacular month, Tony accepted the Central League's July MVP Award[13] before a game against Hanshin on one of 2015's hottest days. For the occasion, Hillary arrived before first pitch.[14] Carrying Madelyn, she moved behind the backstop for a better vantage point to take photos of Tony receiving the award.

Nearby, a man sprung up from his seat, amazed that the "closer's wife," as he called her, would already be at Jingu Stadium. He introduced himself as a Texas Rangers scout. Wasting little time, he asked, "Do you think Tony would want to go back to the States?" "That's the question that took me aback," said Hillary, reflecting back years later. She recalls responding diplomatically, conveying Tony's interest in a potential big-league opportunity, while making it clear that he was content in Japan. "You don't ever want to say, 'Yeah, he can't wait to leave Japan,' 'cuz we were happy there." After the game, she told Tony, "Hey, there was a guy watching you from the Texas Rangers." His response? "I hope he liked you."

The encounter caught both off guard. "It wasn't even on my radar," said Hillary, "or Tony's radar to think that scouts might be looking at him. We had been in Japan for so long that I think we thought that he had passed the point of gaining interest in the United States. So when the Rangers scout said to me, 'Oh, I'm here watching Tony,' I was [thinking] like, 'What? Are you sure you're here for the right person?' I was surprised, for sure." Soon, more major-league scouts began to reach out.

Considering Tony's 2015 pitching mastery, which began early and never wavered, his agent, Don Nomura, purposely avoided discussing any contract extension with Yakult. Impending free agency would provide his client a golden opportunity to finally make good on his long-held dream of pitching in the majors. In late summer, Nomura notified Tony of the growing interest among big-league scouts. "He kept it from me for a while," said Tony. "He knew a lot of people were interested, but he didn't want me to focus anywhere else but the task at hand, which was what I needed at the time."

Also around then, an American League (non-Rangers) scout responsible for key Asian hot spots, including Japan, asked Rob Smaal, the Canadian sportswriter, for Tony's contact information. In fact, Hillary had seen him at games but hadn't put together that he, too, had interest until her memorable meeting with the Rangers scout.

On October 14, as the Swallows prepared for their Climax Series with Yomiuri, Nomura requested that they post Tony upon season's end. He didn't have to go through the posting system in order to leave Japan, as he was set to become an international free agent on December 1, like he'd been the previous offseason.[15] Still, he and his agent had two primary reasons to give posting a try.

First, going through the process would grant Tony a chance to give back to the Swallows after all they had given him over the previous six years. It was the right thing to do, he felt. Plus, it made sense to maintain goodwill with the organization.

Secondly, posting would provide valuable intel. "I wanted to know for my sake what the market was for Tony," said Nomura. "How many teams [were interested]? And if he doesn't get posted or nobody signs him there, at least I would know who was interested. That would help us find what his marketability would be versus just going out cold in the free-agent market. And if we had no bite—I was pretty confident that we would—we didn't want to come back to Japan in late December saying we couldn't find a job and then the team in Japan would say, 'Well, we already signed somebody. We don't have anything left.' Or 'We only have, you know, peanuts here.' So I wanted to be on the safe side, and that's why we went through the posting."

Technically, the Swallows didn't have to cooperate. According to Nomura, a few organizations were philosophically opposed to posting any of their players.[16] The Swallows were not one of those teams, and due to Tony's impending free agency they knew he could still leave by other means, in which case they would get nothing in return. Therefore, they assented to Nomura's request. Naturally, the Swallows preferred to retain their closer's services, but if that weren't going to happen, receiving a posting fee would be the next-best thing.

Four days after the Swallows' Japan Series elimination, they held a press conference to publicly announce Tony's posting and the attached $500,000 release fee.[17] Within days, Yakult filed the paperwork, officially starting the posting period in early November. Interested major-league teams had thirty days to negotiate directly with Nomura.[18]

Toward the tail end of the period, teams began calling. Neither the Cubs nor the Rangers made an offer. Neither did the Diamondbacks, the organization that drafted Tony and for whom he played through 2009. But Arizona was easily the most bullish of the three.

Shortly after its outreach, Arizona determined it was willing to pay the posting fee, which was negotiated down to $250,000, and struck a deal with Nomura[19] . . . or so he thought. "We basically had an agreement, we shook hands on the deal, and it was just the signing of the contract and all that, but I mean, we were there." They verbally agreed to terms near the start of the week. Nomura called back Wednesday and Thursday but couldn't reach anyone. On Friday morning, the Diamondbacks called to deliver the bad news. Before their partnership was consummated, they'd signed superstar right-hander Zack Greinke to a massive deal that would tie up their entire payroll.[20] "At the eleventh hour," said Nomura, "they backed out. They said, 'We don't have money. We just signed Greinke. I'm sorry.'"

Though Arizona's reneging stung, Nomura was not headed back to the drawing board. After a brief flirtation from the Padres, Orioles, and Rangers again, the posting period elapsed without a bid. He had planned for this contingency. "At least I know who's interested," Nomura thought. Continuing to negotiate with teams, he required nothing short of a major-league deal, while strongly preferring two or three years in length.

When Tony's posting period expired, Nomura was already in Nashville, Tennessee, for MLB's winter meetings held at the Gaylord Opryland Resort and Convention Center. Teams were on the prowl for pitchers who could add depth to their roster. Accordingly, a number of teams contacted Nomura,[21] although many didn't make offers. "They were kind of digging for information," he said. "They had an interest. They knew how well he pitched in Japan, [but] there was other competitors in the market, so I guess they were talking simultaneously with other pitchers."

Tony remembers "always constantly texting" with Nomura. He wouldn't relay to Hillary every single piece of information he learned. Rather, he reserved for her the "stuff that was life-changing that was gonna come down the line." As a result, "I thought it was just dead quiet until winter meetings happened," said Hillary, "and then it was just chaos from there." She was half-right. Although teams had reached out earlier, once Nomura got to Nashville, a version of chaos did ensue as a slew of teams contacted Nomura, who, in turn, alerted Tony.

For Tony, there were long periods of radio silence when the process felt agonizingly dull. Other times, so much was happening that the pitcher could barely take a breath. "It was sitting and watching and waiting," detailed Tony. "You get stuck in this time warp. You don't really know what day's what and where you're at and what you're doing. You're just kind of sitting there, looking at your phone, waiting." Then, seemingly on a dime, everything changes. "'One team's in. Okay, now they're out. Hey, this team's in. Okay, now they're out. This team offered this. Nope. They offered this now.' So, I mean, it's just chaos."

Toward the end of the short week, as the winter meetings wound down, Baltimore reached out with a tentative offer,[22] and San Diego got in touch again, as did the Cubs. The Rangers called repeatedly, sticking in Nomura's mind as "more aggressive" than any other organization in their pursuit.

The Rangers could be the "right fit," Tony thought. "It seemed like they were serious and very willing to give me an opportunity and kinda give me the chance that I deserved and earned, whereas a lot of the other teams, they were just kind of skeptical, where you weren't really sure if you were gonna go in and just be a depth piece or if you were gonna go in and actually compete for a spot or what was going on. To be honest with you, everybody else was trying to lowball me. They were thinking that they could get me for the bare minimum. And nobody was really taking me seriously outside of the Texas Rangers and a couple other organizations. Texas, I think, really valued who I was."

He added, "The name that kept coming up was the Texas Rangers." During the winter meetings, Rangers manager Jeff Banister called Tony over the phone, and the two talked for an hour and a half. "It was something that just felt right," Tony said. "I felt needed. I felt wanted."

In a Nashville hotel suite, general manager Jon Daniels and a few of his associates, including assistant GM Josh Boyd,[23] sat down with Nomura and his right-hand man, Shaun Inouye. The sides neared a potential agreement. From Arizona, Tony expressed his enthusiastic approval regarding the proposed terms. "When Texas came through with the offer that they did, it was one of those days where me and my agent [proverbially] whispered in the corner, saying, 'Is this it?' He was like, 'I think this is it.' And I was like, 'This feels right. Let's not even screw around anymore. Let's just get pen on paper, and let's get going. I want to be a Texas Ranger now.'"

The following day, a deal was struck for two years and $3.5 million guaranteed. Specifically, Tony would be paid $1.5 million in 2016 and $1.75 million the next year. A 2018 club option would be worth $4 million. If the Rangers were to decline it, they would owe Tony a $250,000 buyout.

"Everything was awesome," said Hillary of her and Tony's situation as the 2015 season concluded. "He loved his team, we loved the city, loved the people, so it was almost weird to be so happy where we were and to be looking to go somewhere else." For the first time, Tony stood on the doorstep of signing a major-league contract. While Hillary undoubtedly felt every bit as excited as he felt, she later acknowledged the presence of "bittersweet" emotions about what was to come.

"We were really starting to get comfortable with Japan in general," she noted. "The difference between the first year and the sixth year was huge. The first year, you're awkward, you don't know what you're doing, you don't know where you are. It's an uncomfortable situation. And then by the sixth year, it was very stable. We had a lot of good friends. It just felt like home, felt like a home away from home."

In addition to the safety blanket provided by their friends, Tony benefited immensely from playing for the same franchise the entire time. Although Shigeru Takada resigned from his managerial post early in 2010, the *ichi-gun* managerial slot remained fairly consistent through 2015. Even when Junji Ogawa stepped down as manager after 2014, he didn't go too far, moving on to join Yakult's front office. The pitching and bullpen coaches, Swallows staff Tony interacted with most, remained steady during his six years in town,[24] a fact not lost upon Hillary, who believed such stability made a huge difference: "I think it was really, really important for him in his development. That totally changed the kind of pitcher he was, and who he is now as a pitcher for sure."

It was the Swallows organization that provided Tony a second chance after a miserable Year 1, bringing him back with a 50 percent pay cut. There, he worked closely with bullpen coach Tomohito Ito, who helped Tony, mentally and tactically, acclimate to his new role as a reliever. Ito placed full confidence in him as he essentially overhauled his pitch repertoire. Over his time in Tokyo, Tony was also blessed with a slew of hardworking, supportive teammates, who made it a pleasure to come to work every day.

There was also the relationship with Go, Tony's interpreter for his first five NPB seasons and a bona fide friend. Their bond stayed strong even after Go moved into a front-office role that took him away from the team on a day-to-day basis. They ensured it did by keeping in regular touch and exchanging gifts between each other and their families.

For Christmas 2015, Go would send Madelyn a toy *Shinkansen* train.[25] Of course, that summer, Tony had gotten All-Star Game tickets for Go's family, who sat with Hillary and Madelyn. The year before, Go lent the Barnettes a Japanese-style swing and sold them his daughter's former stroller. Over his latter years in Japan, including after 2015, Tony was quite generous with Go when it came to financial bonuses, his preferred way of showing appreciation. Because Go felt he was merely doing his job, he always politely declined such money. Tony, always adamant when he feels strongly about something, never took no for an answer.[26] Despite the above accounting, there was never a scorecard, only a mutual love and respect for each other that persists to this day.

Boasting all that support from his organization and interpreter gave Tony the wherewithal to make dramatic changes to his skill set. Aaron Guiel, Tony's teammate and mentor for 2010 and 2011,[27] saw most of these improvements from afar but was impressed by the transformation: "Tony didn't come to Japan one player and then come back to the States the same player. He came to Japan, transformed himself, [and] to his credit, gave himself a new pitch. So, when he came back, so much was different."

Guiel recalled the starting pitcher throwing virtually the same pitches as most other right-handers. Little set him apart. But then he got to know Tony and experienced three primary characteristics that enabled his seismic transformation. He was an "extremely hard worker," Guiel learned. He was also "humble" and a "fighter." Beginning in spring 2011, Tony utilized these qualities to develop his patented cutter. "When he did that, he put a weapon into his arsenal that he didn't have when he came," Guiel said. "And it was devastating. That pitch all of a sudden was an equalizer for everything else, so it was something he could lean on. It was 100 percent him in how he changed his game and his weapons, and that's the reason why he was able to come back."

Tony felt no shortage of love and support from Swallows fans over his time in Tokyo. For instance, every November 9, without fail, fans mailed him birthday greetings via the team.

Early in his Swallows tenure, one fan sent a good-luck charm specific to athletic performance. It was black and adorned with vertical gold writing, as well as various symbols in gold and two shades of green. An attached white string enabled the carrier to easily transport it from place to place. Hillary decided to make good use out of it. "I carried that sucker to every game until the last game in Japan that he played in," she said, "so, I don't know. Maybe it worked."

According to David Watkins, the fan base really started to consider Tony a de facto member of the crew at some point during 2012, his first year closing games. "The thing about foreign players in Japan," said Watkins, "is that a lot of them come for a year and kind of disappear. They're here as hired hands. They have no real connection or affinity for the team. The kind of player that Tony became, i.e., a player that stays over a prolonged period of time and very much becomes part of the identity of the team . . . When you think of that team, he's one of the faces that you think of. For a foreigner, it's fairly tough to do over here, especially maybe for the Swallows."

As Tony grew from an inconsistent starting pitcher to a reliable reliever into a shutdown closer and his prominence increased, more and more fans recognized him in public, typically smiling without bombarding him with requests.[28] Whenever possible, he stopped to sign autographs; it was flattering and something he enjoyed doing.

Later, when he helped guide Yakult to its first pennant since 2001, he reserved a special place in the hearts of the franchise's more diehard supporters. "He seemed to be kind of like one of the fans," Watkins continued. "He seemed to have a disdain for the Giants quite a lot, and he seemed to have a real love and appreciation for the organization and the team itself. He really, really was a part of the team and was very passionate about it, which helped people really bond to him."

Yakult faithful knows how to take care of its own. "I have bins full of stuff," said Hillary, in reference to the letters, drawings, and other gifts Swallows fans sent Tony and his family. Tony got a particular kick out of the caricatures they'd send. As a wedding gift, they received two small cro-cheted bears. When their daughter was born, they were given a Swallows onesie with "Madelyn" on the back. Other gifts included functional handmade crafts such as key chains, as well as more decorative tchotch-kes. They've kept them all.

From reading one of the pamphlets circulated at games, one fan named Nao learned that Tony was fond of Oreos. "Yeah, got a lot of free Oreos," recalled Tony, "lot of free Oreos!" Although Nao was the most consistent Oreo giver, others, too, would occasionally bring their favorite closer a sleeve of the classic black and white cream-filled cookies. "People would just give 'em to me, so I would eat them," Tony said, absolving himself of any guilt.

Granted, reporter Yas Kikuta's pregnancy charm gift well exceeded expectations of how media members should treat players, but it's also true that Tony rarely came into conflict with the press, especially once he began to navigate the language barrier and acclimate to the cultural differ-ences of Japan. Initially, he found some of the local journalists to display a sort of tabloid style he disliked.[29] He would quickly learn, however, that the more baseball-focused reporters flat-out knew their stuff and loved the sport to boot.

Going into the 2015–2016 offseason, Tony all but knew he'd have to accept less money in order to prove his worth in the big leagues. Had he wanted to continue earning a higher salary, he would have remained in Japan.

His friend Rob Smaal delineated the trade-off he'd be making with his move to the States: "I think the question for a guy like Tony would be: I mean, he could make a ton of money over there because of the success he was having as a closer, and he's probably gonna have to take a pay cut and possibly end up in the minors if he goes back to the US. That's his dream to play Major League Baseball, but it is a risk, right? You leave guaranteed, good money on the table by tossing it in and coming back."

Although Texas presented a better offer than any other major-league team, and one which Tony and his agent were happy to accept, Tony did feel the Rangers got him for a bargain: "In comparison to what other guys around the league are getting with my experience, they got me on the cheap. My experience happened to be somewhere else in the world, so that hurt me in the market." Still, Tony beamed with enthusiasm about the next stage of his career in the States, where he planned to accomplish his lifelong dream of pitching in the big leagues.

Plus, pursuing the major-league opportunity didn't really pose much of a risk, according to Hillary, who deemed it a "win-win situation. It was 'Wow, if you get a chance to play in the big leagues, that's awesome. If you don't get a chance to play in the big leagues and we come back to Japan, that's awesome.' We really were in a great place. I think we were more like, 'Let's see what happens.'" This rationale enabled Hillary to overcome what she described as "that little flip of the stomach of being uncomfortable for a second of just doing something different." She concluded, "It was definitely a risk worth taking."

As much as Tony loved so many aspects of the Japanese experience, including the exceptional people who made it all possible, he confirmed it was essentially a "no-brainer" to accept the Rangers' ultimate offer. "I was gonna come back to the States," Tony said. "This was my time to do it."

"You see our guy [Rangers rookie] Nomar Mazara," he continued. "He's up here at twenty-one. He just got here a lot faster than I did. It took me a long time to get to the level where people here at the major-league level say, 'Hey, he can help us.' I think I was there before. Like 2012, 2013, I think I was ready then. It just didn't work out contract-wise. Japan was offering me the moon at the time, it seemed, and I wasn't gonna get anything over here. But this was the moment. This year was my last chance at it. If it didn't happen this year, if I didn't take the leap and once again bet on myself to come to the big leagues and try to be successful, then I probably never would have gotten this opportunity again."

Notes

1. The pact came at a time when neither league had free agency, enabling team owners to control their players' rights indefinitely.

2. First, the Chiba Lotte Marines sold the six-foot-four, 240-pound Irabu to the Padres in January, but he refused to sign with any team other than the Yankees. Three months later, San Diego traded his rights to New York. Before playing a single major-league game, Irabu was signed by the Yankees for four years and $12.8 million.

3. The Hiroshima Toyo Carp's refusal to raise Soriano's salary from the league minimum rate to $180,000 per year played a large role in his departure. As with Nomo, Nomura advised Soriano to retire, which allowed him to earn an initial four-year, $3.1 million contract with the Yankees.

4. Presently, NPB teams no longer designate the posting amount they'll receive. Instead, the sum is based off the contract the player signs with his new team: 20 percent of the first $25 million, 17.5 percent of the next $25 million, and 15 percent of any amount above the first $50 million. After the 2022 season, the window was expanded from thirty to forty-five days.

5. Katsuya Nomura was a player-manager for the Nankai Hawks between 1970 and 1977.

6. Then, each *ichi-gun* team was limited to two foreigners at once, meaning ample spots for Japanese-born players like Nomura.

7. Of the new name, Nomura once said, "It helped me get into places and meet people."

8. Ever the critical thinker, Nomura "clashed with coaches, ballplayers, even the team's bus driver" during his time in Toda, according to Lidz.

9. At one point or another, Buzas, once the opening-day shortstop for the 1945 Yankees, owned a total of eighty-two minor-league franchises.

10. Although they were technically unaffiliated, the Spurs had partial working agreements with various teams, including the Brewers, Giants, and White Sox, while they also welcomed players owned by Japanese teams.

11. As owner, Nomura had promised Mac a roster spot, and he did not want to break his promise.

12. Among other teams, the mighty Blue Jays, who had won the 1992 World Series and would go on to win the 1993 title as well, were in the mix. However, Nomura felt the Mariners presented his client the best chance of reaching the majors the quickest.

13. Tony was given a check for ¥300,000, which was roughly equivalent to $2,450 at the time.

14. By 2015, arriving so early was a rarity for Hillary. Typically, she and Madelyn walked to the field, appearing by the seventh inning, in time to potentially see Tony pitch the ninth. Sometimes they left the stadium early so Madelyn could sleep at home while Hillary prepared dinner for Tony—Hillary watched the rest of the game on TV—but on these nights, they hardly ever arrived before first pitch.

15. There was one major difference between Tony's free-agency status after 2014 and after 2015, although the distinction wouldn't ultimately matter. After 2014, he was not entitled to sign

with any NPB team other than the Swallows. After 2015, due to language Nomura negotiated into Tony's 2015 contract with Yakult, he could have theoretically signed elsewhere in Japan.

[16] Nomura cited Yomiuri, Hanshin, and SoftBank as the three franchises categorically opposed to posting their players. Yomiuri may be changing its philosophy on this, however. Since Nomura's remarks, the Giants posted their first two players, both pitchers, in consecutive seasons: In 2019, it was Shun Yamaguchi, followed by Tomoyuki Sugano in 2020, although Sugano remained with Yomiuri after failing to come to terms with any MLB team and Yamaguchi struggled with the Blue Jays and returned to Yomiuri after just one season away. Until late 2022, when Hanshin posted pitcher Shintaro Fujinami, it had only ever posted left-handed hurler Kei Igawa (2006). No Hawk has ever been posted.

[17] Although negotiable to a certain extent, any major-league team interested in signing Tony during the posting period would have to pay Yakult roughly this amount.

[18] The posting period began November 7 at 8 a.m. on the East Coast (10 p.m. in Japan) and ran until December 6 at 7 a.m. Eastern Standard Time.

[19] The verbally agreed-upon deal would have paid Tony $2.25 million in Year 1 and a potential $3 million on a second-year club option.

[20] Coming off a 19-win 2015, in which he registered a 1.66 ERA and finished second in the NL Cy Young race and seventh in MVP balloting, the thirty-two-year-old Greinke was given a whopping six-year, $206.5 million contract.

[21] Nomura estimated hearing from seven or eight teams, including the Angels, Cubs, Mariners, Orioles, Padres, and Rangers, among others.

[22] The Orioles, particularly, were offering much less than what the Rangers were discussing, according to Nomura.

[23] As Texas's director of pro and Pacific Rim scouting, Josh Boyd was responsible for bringing over Yu Darvish ahead of the 2012 season. A former writer for *Baseball America*, Boyd first joined the Rangers front office in 2007 and he hasn't left since.

[24] Bullpen coach Tomo Ito served in that role all six seasons. Over the same stretch, Tony worked alongside just two pitching coaches in Araki and Takatsu.

[25] The bullet train replica spoke Japanese, made lots of noise, and above all succeeded in capturing the little one's attention.

[26] Some years, he left the money in Go's locker so that his friend wouldn't discover it until after Tony had already left Japan for the year.

[27] Due to Guiel's lingering back injury, he was barely around the *ichi-gun* team in 2011, his final NPB season.

[28] Early in his NPB career, before he was Yakult's closer, Tony was misidentified as virtually every Swallow gaijin from the present and recent past, somehow including Wladimir Balentien. He disliked being called by the wrong name.

[29] Because he was born in Alaska, a reporter wanted to know if he was an Eskimo who lived in an igloo. When it was learned that he worked at a restaurant one minor-league offseason to make ends meet, he was dubbed a baseball-playing master chef.

CHAPTER EIGHTEEN
THE THIRTY-TWO-YEAR-OLD ROOKIE

He's a rookie on paper, but he doesn't act like a rookie. He doesn't really pitch like a rookie.

Tony had just registered the best season of his career, his performance surpassing even his own expectations and directly leading to his first major-league contract. Still, he felt the need to prove himself to his new team. "I had to show everybody," Tony said of his mindset heading into spring training. "I had to come in with a chip on my shoulder because I was getting side-eyed in the clubhouse. Guys are like, 'Who's this guy? Who's this thirty-two-year-old from Japan that's never been in the big leagues? What's happening here?'"

There were two teammates whom Tony didn't need to convince. One was Yu Darvish, who missed all of 2015 after Tommy John surgery and focused on returning as soon as possible. Although Darvish pitched in the Pacific League, he knew of Tony's NPB success in 2011[1] and since. During the spring, the two talked occasionally, in both languages. Tony also recognized Darvish's new interpreter, Hideaki Sato, who had been working for Toda in 2015.

Ike Davis knew Tony much better. They overlapped at Arizona State and trained together every offseason. On the heels of Tony's wedding, which Davis attended, he had a career year for the 2012 Mets with 32 home runs.[2] Since, he never came close to matching that number, bouncing from team to team. In August 2015, Davis tore his labrum, ending his Oakland tenure.

Nine days before Texas's first full-squad workout, Davis agreed to terms with the organization. Unfortunately, just as spring was ramping up, he sprained his right knee. The incident, which Davis characterized as "terrible timing," sidelined him for a few weeks. As a result, he didn't make the opening-day roster and began the year in Triple A. But he remained confident, telling reporters, "Eventually, I'll be back in the big leagues." Davis's prediction would prove correct, but not as a member of the Rangers, who released him in June.[3]

Although Tony hadn't met Colby Lewis,[4] Lewis's Japanese experience had resembled his own. After 2007, Lewis was twenty-eight and a fringe major leaguer when he left for Japan, where he'd spend two successful years starting games for Hiroshima. His wife, Jenny, would later bond with Hillary over their shared experiences living in Japan and raising newborns there.[5] Upon returning, Lewis effectively carved a stable spot for himself in the majors, quickly becoming a key contributor for consecutive World Series teams. Save for a few rehab stints, he remained with the big-league Rangers ever since.

Lewis came into spring camp nearly 30 pounds lighter after falling in love with long-distance cycling. A torn meniscus the preceding May had prevented him from running between starts,[6] and cycling became a fun, low-impact method of shedding the extra pounds he'd put on. Lewis was thirty-six and going into the season with a one-year contract, a long-standing tradition between him and the Rangers.

Tony couldn't wear thirty-four because Nolan Ryan's Rangers jersey had long been retired. The reverse, forty-three, would be fine with Tony, who was happy to emulate Dennis Eckersley, another fiery, long-haired starter turned reliever. Once spring games began, Tony consistently pitched so masterfully that he felt "there was no reason for me not to make that team." Virtually no opposing batter had faced him before. This lack of familiarity, he believed, gave him a competitive advantage. And he was throwing the ball well, which bolstered his confidence and helped breed more success.

He also seemed to think he was the recipient of a few lucky breaks. A week and a half in, he hit a Brewers batter with a fastball, just below the ribs. Only later than usual, the batter had requested "time," which the umpire apparently granted. So, Tony hit a player, and, for his troubles, the poor guy didn't even earn a trip to first base; just a nice bruise. "Stuff like that was happening for me," said Tony. "It was a good spring."

As the regular season beckoned, Tony assumed he'd soon earn a roster spot. Even so, "You really don't know until you know, I guess." Any traces of doubt were dispelled when manager Jeff Banister finally delivered the good news less than a week before opening day.

Sitting at his locker in Surprise, Arizona, Tony eagerly awaited the start of his inaugural big-league season. But there was something else at the forefront of his mind: Baby number two was expected any day, or as he put it, "[Hillary was] ready to blow." When she went into active labor, she called Tony. With phone in hand, he darted into the office of his manager, who already knew the day was fast approaching. "All right, see you in Arlington," said Banister.

The timing appeared to be pretty fortunate. Shortly after Tony got word, the Rangers left for Arlington to host a two-game weekend exhibition before opening the season there the following Monday. Meanwhile, the rookie was allowed to remain in Arizona to experience one of life's most cherished moments, the birth of a child.

Loretta Lee[7] Barnette was born on Thursday, March 31, at 4:51 a.m., measuring 18.5 inches long and 7 pounds and 3 ounces. "Everything went perfect with the birth," said the proud father.

"Loretta came out kicking, screaming, happy, healthy, and [Hillary] looked at me and she was like, 'Go. Just go do your major-league debut. Don't be late. Don't miss opening day.'" As with Madelyn's birth, Hillary brought the pink pregnancy charm in its fancy wooden box. Her dad came, while her mom watched Madelyn in Litchfield Park. Once Loretta was born, a babysitter took over so Hillary's mom could see her newest granddaughter. Madelyn would meet her sister at home shortly thereafter.

Following Hillary's orders, Tony quickly headed for Texas, arriving in time for the opener. Back in Arizona, when Hillary got home from the hospital, she suddenly realized everything was going to be different: "I came home, both kids by myself, and I got freaked out."

Hillary and the girls wouldn't make it to Arlington for another couple weeks. In fact, she and Tony were talking to real-estate agents from the hospital. With no place yet to live, Tony spent the first three days of the season in a hotel. After that, the team ventured to Anaheim and then Seattle for a seven-game road trip, allowing them extra time to find a place.

On April 4, the Rangers opened with a 3–2 win, edging Seattle in a speedy affair.[8] Tony did not pitch.[9] The very next day, with the game tied 2–2 through six, Banister signaled it was time for the thirty-two-year-old rookie to grace a big-league mound for a game that counted.

According to Tony, although he strived to become a major leaguer for so long and there he was finally about to pitch as one, he approached the debut as he would any other ordinary game: "It really was like, 'All right, here we go.' It was a normal feeling for me. It was a baseball game. I don't want to downplay how large of a thing it is to pitch in the major leagues and to finally get there and be one of 750, the top guys amongst the world at that time. It's something special. It's something I'll look back on probably years later and be like, 'That was pretty cool.' But for the moment being, I had a job to do. Let's go do it." Tony had already been through so much as a pro, it's no wonder there weren't extra nerves.

He started strong, getting pinch-hitting lefty Seth Smith to whiff on an inside fastball clocked at 92 miles per hour. After missing low and away with a splitter, he, again, pounded Smith inside with a fastball, this one out of the zone. Smith managed to line it into center field for a single. Bouncing back, Tony retired the next two Mariners on a line out to center and a three-pitch strikeout,[10] respectively.

Tony was not yet out of the woods. Facing a third lefty in Leonys Martín, he dug in, needing one more out to complete his MLB debut. On a 1-1 count, a slider caught too much of the plate as Martín struck an RBI double to deep right. Coincidentally, the next batter would be former Swallow Nori Aoki.[11] Alas, Aoki couldn't go easy on his friend, singling to right, halting Tony's outing and extending Seattle's lead to 4–2.

"Got it out of the way," Tony, the losing pitcher, wryly and succinctly told reporters after the game. Later that night, he spoke with his manager. At one point, Banister stopped and looked at him. "There's nothing like the big leagues. Is there?" he asked. It was his way of putting into perspective Tony's minor stumble amid the larger achievement of proving himself worthy of making the roster. After his first official game, he knew what his manager was getting at, but it didn't exactly sink in. Upon compiling a dozen more outings, he had a definitive answer for the looming question: "Looking back, 'No, there's not. There really isn't a bad day up here.'"

A month later, he had much more to say about the disappointing debut: "It was a little bittersweet, considering I didn't even get out of the inning. That kinda sucked for me. I'm not a young guy, twenty, twenty-one, getting called up for the first time; you get all that excitement, whatever. I'm thirty-two, and I've been doing this for a while. I kinda look back on it now, and I'm like, 'Yeah, it was cool to finally pitch in the big leagues, but I didn't get my job done.' So it wasn't really a moment that I look back on all that fondly."

Part of the beauty of professional baseball lies in the opportunity for players to go out after a subpar performance, optimally the following day, and put forward a better one, placing their struggles further in the past.

It's a game with a large sample size and ample opportunities to make amends. The next night's game afforded Tony that chance, which he made good on, retiring three of four batters and putting a zero on the board.[12]

After Tony's debut, he logged in to his Twitter account and read some of his mentions. According to his recollection, he saw statements to the effect of "The Barnette experiment's failed," as well as "Get him out of here." This was after a single game pitched. "It's unbelievable," said Tony. "The reactionary . . . just with social media and everything out there, just being able to be so knee-jerk reaction with opinions and things, it's fun."

Fun? Really? For Tony and some of his peers, "It's actually pretty interesting" and "quite funny" to read mean tweets about themselves. He detailed the mindset behind his approach of being in on the joke as something of a protective shield: "You can't look at your Twitter and take it seriously because as a professional athlete, you're gonna cry yourself to sleep. People are ruthless, man. If you're worried about what some guy on Twitter says, then you've got larger issues that you need to take care of." Lazy or derogatory tweets typically didn't grab his attention, but "we try to look for the good ones—the ones that are actually clever. Like, last night, I looked at one, and it said, 'Barnette looks like the high school smoke pit kid.'"

In Anaheim, Banister called his number twice, each time in a critical situation. "Coming from Japan and pitching in the ninth inning all the time, the more high-leverage situations there are, the better I feel about it," said Tony. On April 8, Texas's four-run advantage was in jeopardy with two outs in the eighth and the bases loaded. In Tom Wilhelmsen's second inning, he was losing control and Banister had seen enough. He brought in Tony, who, despite falling behind 3-1, proceeded to get the Angels' catcher to line out to center. He registered his first career hold, and Texas hung on to win 7–3.

Two nights later, Tony helped the Rangers avert another crisis, although they ultimately lost. Again, the bases were loaded as he trotted in from the pen mid-inning. Only this time, arguably the best hitter in the game,

Mike Trout, waited at the plate. Meanwhile, surefire Hall of Famer Albert Pujols stood on deck. Throwing only fastballs to Trout, Tony could exhale a little when Trout's deep fly to right-center field was secured. The runner scored from third, but there were much worse alternatives. With the count full to Pujols, Tony rose to the occasion, executing a near-perfect low-and-inside slider. Pujols weakly grounded the pitch to shortstop. Just like that, he had again persevered through difficult circumstances.

Not only did he appreciate his manager's utmost faith in him, but he also recognized its rarity among first-year major leaguers coming from overseas. "I've proven myself in Japan, but I haven't proven myself here yet," said Tony, plainly. "And usually the leash is pretty short with guys like that over here. And Banny's been giving me so many opportunities to succeed. It's a great feeling as a ballplayer when they don't have to tell you that they have some trust in you. Just by their actions and when they want to use you, that speaks volumes."

Tony had the team's next stop, Seattle, circled on his calendar ever since the schedule was released. Although he grew up a Mariners fan, "It really didn't do anything for me when we opened up against them," he admitted. Playing at Safeco Field was completely different. Hailing from Federal Way, a town located thirty minutes south on I-5, it represented a homecoming. He'd be the local "kid" returning to the city and infrastructure that cultivated his baseball talents and helped launch him onto stages such as Safeco. He'd be returning to the family, friends, and coaches who supported and pushed him during that critical developmental stage.

Naturally, family came to revel in the homecoming. Tony was pleasantly surprised, however, to see so many familiar faces from high school, given he'd lost touch with the majority of them after deleting his Facebook account years earlier. What particularly struck the reliever was that they didn't ask for tickets or anything else from him. Throughout the game, they merely stopped by the Rangers bullpen, one after another, to salute an old friend and note that they'd been rooting for him throughout his long, winding journey. "For them to come out and give me the support and say how happy they are for me after so long, that was really neat," said Tony. "Everybody was so happy."[13]

Tony's best major-league performance to date came in the afternoon series finale, which he entered with two outs and two on, trailing 2–1. He promptly struck out the dangerous Nelson Cruz[14] on five pitches to get out of the seventh-inning jam. The timely out held the score in place, long enough for Texas to open the eighth with a game-tying solo shot. Tony breezed by the eighth and ninth for a career-high two and one-third innings of scoreless ball.[15] He was so locked in that only five pitches missed the strike zone.

Like Tony, Japan Series MVP Dae-ho Lee was a thirty-something former NPB gaijin debuting in the American League West.[16] The biggest difference? Tony signed a big-league deal in December, whereas Lee wasn't added until February with Seattle offering only a minor-league contract. While Lee managed to make the opening-day roster, regular at-bats were hard to come by. Initially, he served as a pinch-hitter unless a lefty was starting, and his coaches questioned his ability to handle major-league pitching. The reasoning went this way: Lee could thrive in Japan with his batting leg kick, but the kick could become a problem against big league–speed fastballs by slowing down his reaction time.

In the series finale, Lee batted with two outs in the 10th. On an 0-2 pitch, Lee turned on a 97-mile-per-hour fastball from left-hander Jake Diekman, dispatching it into the left-field seats. This, Lee's second big-league homer, a walk-off no less, proved to the doubters that he could, indeed, hit major-league speed, and hit it far.

With the walk-off loss, the Rangers prepared to bring a 5–5 record back to Globe Life Park at Arlington. Questions about their bullpen remained, but Tony was beginning to fall into a groove with four straight scoreless appearances following the underwhelming debut. As the road trip concluded, he inched closer to moving into the rental house, which was now ready. His wife and daughters would not be too far behind.

Various firsts continued rolling in. Number forty-three surrendered his first homer on April 21. Nursing a 6–2 lead, he relieved starter A.J. Griffin with a 1-2-3 seventh. There was some confusion as to whether he was going to return for another inning. According to Tony, he was told that he was done for the night, but then a little later Banister asked if he could continue. "Yeah, I feel good," he told him. "Let's do it."

After he retired José Altuve and George Springer, Carlos Correa reached on a bloop single. Colby Rasmus fell behind 0-2 before fouling off a fastball. Tony felt an inside slider would be ideal, but he missed the target. "If I would have executed my pitch, I'm sure as shit I probably would have got him out right there. But I left the slider out over the plate, and that was right in his bat speed that day.[17] That's just the game we play up here, cat and mouse. It's a game of chess. Stuff like that happens. Hindsight, they probably should have gone to a lefty that was hot in the bullpen, but that's gonna happen in baseball."

True to form, the experienced rookie shook off Rasmus taking him yard and got back on track in subsequent outings—first in Chicago and then back in Arlington before heading north of the border to Toronto. Fittingly, there, on foreign soil, an American who pitched six years in Japan before entering the majors would achieve his initial major-league victory. In the clubhouse, his teammates celebrated the moment. "They ambushed me with a bunch of ice-cold Bud Lights," said Tony, who had no previous knowledge of the tradition. "The big leagues are fun, man."

In postgame, he didn't shy away from expressing the gravity of the accomplishment. A few days later, he reiterated the message he'd relayed to reporters: "It's one of those things that nobody can take from me now. I'm a winning pitcher at the MLB level. That's mine. I own it."

Specifically, Tony weathered a mini-storm of his own making to keep the score tied at one. Leading off the eighth, fellow Rangers rookie Nomar Mazara broke the tie with a home run to straightaway center.[18] The 2–1 score later turned final, and Tony and Texas had their win. "It was cool to see your name on the board as the winning pitcher," said Tony, "but the more exciting thing was that it was a tight game, and it was against the

265

Blue Jays, where there's some bad blood." The previous postseason, the Rangers and Jays had battled in the divisional round. In Toronto's series-clinching Game 5 victory, José Bautista hit the game-winning homer off Sam Dyson, who along with much of the rest of the team didn't appreciate Bautista's flamboyant bat flip. The mutual animosity continued into the following season, with it reaching its crescendo a few weeks after Tony's first win when Rougned Odor infamously punched Bautista in the face, triggering a brawl.

Banister kept Tony busy, using him in all but one of the four games at Rogers Centre. Pitching for the third consecutive day and the fourth time in five days, Tony suffered his first major-league walk-off loss on May 4. He had entered a 3–3 tie to begin Toronto's ninth. Following a single, two walks, and a pop out, Russell Martin delivered the hit that sent the Toronto crowd into a frenzy and the Rangers off the field.[19]

Determined, Tony refused to let the unfavorable experience derail his strong rookie campaign. He responded with eight straight scoreless appearances, stretching over more than three weeks. As a scorching Texas summer approached, bets began to be made as to when Tony would trim his shoulder-length locks.

The 2016 Texas Rangers built their bullpen with a diverse array of characters, including Tom Wilhelmsen, Shawn Tolleson, Keone Kela, Sam Dyson, Jake Diekman, Matt Bush, and of course Tony Barnette. Each pitcher took his own bizarre route to Texas, leading ESPN writer David Schoenfield to call the group a "motley collection of relievers" in an April piece for his now-defunct *SweetSpot* blog. Boasting an average of about two seasons of major-league experience, they were a collective bargain too. Their modest salaries enabled Texas, with its top-ten payroll, to afford the likes of Cole Hamels, Shin-Soo Choo, Prince Fielder, and Adrián Beltré, while still retaining flexibility. Among the motley crew, only Tolleson,

Wilhelmsen, Diekman, and Tony were earning more than $1 million, with Tolleson and Wilhelmsen easily the high men at $3.3 and $3.1 million, respectively.[20]

Wilhelmsen, a free-spirited, six-foot-six righty, backpacked through Europe, Mexico, and the United States after twice testing positive for marijuana in 2004 and quitting the sport the next year. He'd spend six full seasons away from the minors and five out of baseball entirely.[21] Before his return, he worked at a tiki bar in Tucson, Arizona, earning him the nickname "The Bartender." Wilhelmsen wouldn't appear in the majors until he was twenty-seven. After the last game of the 2014 season in which the Mariners were eliminated from playoff contention, quirky Wilhelmsen helped the home crowd cope by vigorously dancing to "Turn Down for What." In late 2015, Texas acquired the thirty-two-year-old in a trade from Seattle, where he spent the previous five seasons.

Tolleson's presence on a major-league roster would not have been easily predicted as recently as 2010, when the Dodgers drafted him in the thirtieth round. The stocky, smiley right-hander had dominated Texas high school baseball until Tommy John surgery derailed most of his senior season, leading him to redshirt as a Baylor freshman. Over the next three seasons, Tolleson showed glimpses of brilliance, but control issues and inconsistency hurt his draft stock. Defying the odds, he ascended through the minors at warp speed, reaching the majors by 2012. After 2013, which he largely missed due to back surgery, the Rangers claimed him off waivers. With Texas, Tolleson turned in a pair of stellar seasons, including 2015, when he took over the closer role and notched 35 saves.

When Kela was born, neither parent was older than sixteen. He split his childhood between Southern California and Seattle and hoped to get drafted as a hitter. When it didn't happen, he went to Everett Community College and developed a mid 90s fastball. Texas liked what it saw and drafted him in the twelfth round. He performed so well at various minor-league stops that his MLB debut arrived nine days before his twenty-second birthday. That 2015 rookie season, he excelled, most often pitching in the seventh or eighth with the score tied or Texas clinging to a narrow lead. At times, Kela's brusque, combative personality irritated teammates and media members, even leading to team-imposed discipline, but his talent and potential were never in doubt.

Although Dyson was a 2010 fourth-round pick, he faced no small measure of adversity right off the bat, immediately undergoing Tommy John surgery and not returning until 2012. He truly established himself as a major leaguer in 2014. Just ahead of the 2015 trade deadline, the Rangers acquired Dyson from Miami. In 31 games with Texas, the dominant right-hander posted a 1.15 ERA, along with 30 strikeouts, four walks, and one home run allowed.

Tony was nine years old and rooting for the hometown Mariners when Rangers bullpen coach Brad Holman pitched his only nineteen major-league games for Seattle. When asked to describe Tony's personality, Holman said, "Quirky, left-handed." He laughed. "Yeah, he's supposed to be a lefty," he continued. "Just his personality. Most lefties have a little bit of a squirrelly way about them, and he really fits that mold."

Quickly, Tony became closest friends with an actual left-handed pitcher in Jake Diekman. Maybe Holman was on to something. Diekman's unique journey took him from a small town in Nebraska[22] to an NAIA school to a community college all the way to the Philadelphia Phillies organization. Like Tolleson, he was a thirtieth-round pick.

The lanky, six-foot-four sidearmer debuted in 2012 but accrued ample Triple-A time until 2014. At the 2015 deadline, Philadelphia dealt Diekman to Texas, alongside 2008 World Series and NLCS MVP Cole Hamels,[23] in exchange for six players. Since childhood, he's battled ulcerative colitis, which can cause abdominal pain, fatigue, and weight loss, among other symptoms.[24]

Soon after meeting Tony, Diekman felt they operated on similar wavelengths: "He has a very, very good sense of humor. I feel like we all fit along really, really well. We try to keep each other in check, but yet we like to have a good time. Tony's a guy that likes to keep it loose down there, which is good. Sometimes things can get stressful and everything, but if you just take a breath and have fun and relax, it's pretty easy."

Away from the field, the two would spend some time with Dyson, who could also exhibit somewhat of a zany personality. Before the season, when David Schoenfield asked Dyson to name the league's most intimidating pitcher, without skipping a beat, he deadpanned, "Shawn Tolleson because of his tight pants. And I think he's going to wear them even tighter this year."

The bullpen enjoyed playing table tennis in the clubhouse and spent more time than any other group engaged in games. "There's some good [non-bullpen] players,"[25] said Tolleson, "but I would take us against anybody." He added, "There's definitely a lot of competition within the bullpen, but it's all friendly." When asked, Diekman cited Tolleson and Dyson as ranking among the best table-tennis players on the squad.

At a certain point, the bullpen guys will buckle down, but games are long and if the starting pitcher is doing his job, the bullpen won't be needed for a while. So, the eclectic bunch fills the void with fun. "We play a lot of games and make a lot of silly bets," said Tolleson. "Everything's a contest." Case in point: The previous night in Anaheim, $20 was awarded to the relief pitcher who could best estimate how many sunflower seeds were in a cup. "We just don't play baseball," Diekman said of the bullpen's camaraderie. "We sit down, and we bullshit with each other."

In assessing the young, inexpensive, and largely unproven bullpen, coach Holman noted the interchangeability of various roles within the group. "I think versatility is just a good attribute to have," he said. "All those guys[26] could close a game out."

Thirty-year-old Matt Bush's journey to the Rangers bullpen is unparalleled in both its darkest and most redemptive elements. In 2004, the hometown Padres made him the first high-school shortstop selected first overall since Alex Rodriguez.[27] While his talent was undeniable, Bush struggled with substance abuse and anger issues that would lead to multiple serious off-the-field incidents over the coming years. By 2007, the organization converted the underwhelming batter into a pitcher. Bush instantly excelled, his fastball reaching 98, but a torn ligament in his pitching elbow necessitated Tommy John surgery, giving a man with troubling inner demons far too much idle time.[28]

His problems only worsened, causing Bush to bounce around. With the Rays, everything came to a head on March 22, 2012, when an alcohol-induced hit-and-run accident nearly killed a motorcyclist named Tony Tufano. The twenty-six-year-old Bush was sentenced to fifty-one months in prison, Bush's third DUI conviction and his rock bottom. "I forced myself to think about it every day in prison," he said of the damage he inflicted on that catastrophic night, "because I deserved to suffer." Tufano's life changed drastically. The one-time avid runner requires a walker. He battles depression, has to take at least two-dozen pills daily, sleeps often, and rarely leaves his home.

Ultimately, an initially skeptical Roy Silver[29] and an even more wary Rangers general manager Jon Daniels helped make Bush's controversial redemption story possible. In December 2015, two months after his sentence concluded, Daniels summoned him and his dad to Texas for a tryout and interview. Three days later, Bush signed a minor-league deal, which stipulated that he couldn't drink, drive, walk into a bar, or even carry over $20 in cash at any time. At his first spring camp with Texas, he told reporters, "To me, drinking alcohol is a matter of life and death or prison. I want to live."

Nearly four years to the day of the tragic accident, Bush took the mound again.[30] Afterward, Banister gushed about the spring performance. The next week, he hit 100 on the radar gun. The Rangers cautiously started him in Double A, but by mid-May, he'd already reached the big leagues.

For home games, Tony quickly developed a daily routine. First, he tried to sleep in as much as possible, although his eldest daughter regularly had other ideas; usually, he got up when she did. After that, said Tony, "I try to relax as much as I can, just kinda hang out and keep things as calm and collected as possible."

They lived in Grapevine,[31] a suburb of Dallas and Fort Worth located about 17 miles from Arlington. For the typical night game, he left home between 12:45 and 1 p.m., heading south on Texas State Highway 360. Tony knew he was getting close when he saw Six Flags Over Texas on his right. No later than 1:30—oftentimes, closer to 1—he arrived. "I'll get to the field," said Tony, "and we're joking around with the guys and playing Ping-Pong and stuff. I gotta be relaxed."

In the early weeks and months in Grapevine, Madelyn struggled with suddenly having to share her parents' attention with a baby sister. As her final baby teeth grew in and she experienced a sudden growth spurt, she felt pain all over. Madelyn also had to contend with acclimating to a new city, a new climate, and a new, later bedtime triggered by the start to the baseball season. Both parents desperately wished they could do more to help. "As a parent," said Tony, "it's so frustrating because you just want them to talk to you. You want her to point and tell me exactly where it hurts, and I promise [I'm] 99-percent positive I can fix it. 'Just tell me. Just please, God, tell me.' I'm pleading with my daughter." Thankfully, Madelyn overcame those challenges in short order, in part thanks to resources in their community.[32]

According to her mom, "Madelyn loves going to the stadium." She particularly enjoyed the nursery, located in the park's basement, where she played with other players' kids. After she was dropped off, Hillary could choose between a couple seating options for Loretta and herself. Each had its benefits. The wives' suite, with its refreshing air conditioning, provided them a chance to escape the Texas heat. It also included access to a TV broadcast of the game. Still, Hillary preferred the family section by a hair. "It's closer to the field," she said, "and I can see everything better. So when Tony comes in to pitch, it's nice to be able to see where his pitches are."

From the suite, she found TV pitch displays like FoxTrax and K-Zone to be useful. Although Tony cautioned her to take the placements and resulting calls with a grain of salt, the tools vastly enhanced her viewing experience. Plus, it helped her get a sense of the particular home-plate umpire's strike zone and whether Tony was likely to get calls on certain borderline pitches.

Tony was always the first player at the field, according to Shawn Tolleson, who added, "He treats himself like a rookie." He liked to get to the stadium a few hours before the pitchers began stretching to aid his preparation for the workday ahead. That gave him more time to enjoy the kitchen anyway. "They'd cook you whatever you wanted," said a marveling Tony. "It was fantastic. Why wouldn't I show up for this?"

He also brought water to his teammates and carried one of the two rookie bullpen bags. "It's just kind of the approach he's taken with it," said Tolleson. "He's not taking anything for granted. Even though he's been playing for a long time and been really good for a long time, he realizes that he's a rookie here, and he's not letting his experience get past that."

Tony transported an assortment of snacks to the bullpen in a *Frozen*-themed suitcase, while right-handed flamethrower Matt Bush carried a pink suitcase containing bullpen and training equipment, such as catcher's gear, headache medication, bandages, and nail clippers, for instance. "We both carry our girly-looking suitcases out to the field," said Bush, who claimed not to mind in the slightest. Similarly, Tony had no problem with the daily task, even though the popular animated Disney film was far less geared to a stereotypical baseball audience: "What do I care? I have two daughters. My life is being inundated with pink backpacks. I might as well just get a jumpstart right here."

"I was in charge of keeping everybody on the borderline of diabetes," he joked. Even with regard to a duty as seemingly small as stocking the bullpen snack bag, Tony treated it with the utmost seriousness. "I made sure that it was the best snack bag that these guys had ever seen." This involved looking for the best candy stores in the area, buying a variety of types, and then experimenting with which held up in the heat and which didn't.[33] "It's not a chore," he remarked. "It's fun to do."

Traditionally, the rookie buys all the snacks but is reimbursed by the more financially comfortable veterans. Everyone plays a role. But Tony believes his veteran teammates took advantage of his vast professional experience, using it as a justification for not reimbursing him for the candy purchases.[34] Depending on which was more convenient in a given situation, they either treated him as a rookie or a veteran. That frustrated him, but he never complained.

When young José Leclerc was promoted in early July, he took over Tony's rookie assignment. The reprieve lasted only a couple weeks before Leclerc was demoted to Triple A. With Tony back on bag duty, the bullpen's snack game returned to its previous glory.[35]

On a Wednesday night in May between two home series, the team held its annual Rangers Triple Play fundraising gala, best known for its game shows that pit the players against one another. Per tradition, the rookies were expected to entertain the veterans midway through. Donning a Kiss shirt, emcee A.J. Griffin welcomed his newest teammates onstage. Then, four rookies, three in their early twenties, along with older rookies Tony and Bush, came out dressed as members of the rock band, in mostly black with a little silver, tight pants, six-inch platform shoes, and Kiss masks.[36] Impersonating lead singer Gene Simmons, Tony belted out "Rock and Roll All Nite" and moved confidently onstage, as Hillary watched from the crowd. He loved the experience and is sure he would've gone further than Adrián Beltré did as event organizer and hired makeup artists to maximize the authenticity. "That would have just been the next level," said Tony.

Despite the humility he brought, he was decidedly not your typical first-year player. He was a professional baseball veteran who'd been *there* before and acted like it. From bullpen coach Brad Holman's perspective, "He just melded right in with the veteran guys especially."

Texas's veteran of all veterans, the thirty-seven-year-old Beltré went one step further, claiming Tony "looks like a true veteran." "He's a rookie on paper, but he doesn't act like a rookie," added Beltré, the four-time All-Star and five-time Gold Glove winner who brought 2,767 career hits and 413 home runs into 2016, his nineteenth MLB season.[37] "You can tell he has experience. He knows how to pitch. He's been there. Obviously he pitched in Japan, so he has the way he carries himself; he's preparing himself for the game."

From a future Hall of Famer, like Beltré, to a fellow rookie in Bush, Tony seemed to belong ever since he reported to camp. "When I met Tony in spring training, I never really looked at him as a rookie," Bush said. "It's a little bit strange being a rookie at our age," the former top pick continued, "but definitely when you think of typical rookie, [you think] 'young guy, doesn't know what he's doing, doesn't really have shit figured out.'" For Bush, Tony's even-keeled approach to pitching belonged on the opposite end of the experience spectrum: "His demeanor on the mound, I think he turns that on when the time's right, but even from some of the outings that he's had that haven't been the best, Tony's the same guy. He doesn't change his personality or attitude if things haven't gone his way. To me, that's a veteran."

It was this maturity, largely derived from going through six years of myriad ups and downs in Japan, that closer Sam Dyson believed thoroughly prepared Tony for his rookie season. Dyson said, "I think he's well-equipped to go out there on and off the field, deal with all the stresses of life."

Catcher Bobby Wilson particularly enjoyed his presence, echoing Holman's assertion that Tony had effortlessly assimilated from an interpersonal standpoint. "The most important thing is he's been a really good clubhouse guy," said Wilson, who was traded to Detroit in late March but, in a rare move, reacquired from the Tigers a month later. "He's come in and meshed really well with the core group that we've already had here." Wilson had spent parts of seven big-league seasons with four different organizations, so he'd seen a great deal. "He's a guy," added Wilson, "that you walk in the clubhouse and you smile at just 'cuz you know he's gonna be in a good mood, and everything he does is always uplifting to everybody. In this business, it's tough to be that way every day, but he seems to really, really have that mastered."

"[Tony]'s been pitching for a long time," said Tolleson, "so he obviously has his routine, and he knows what works for him, and he hasn't strayed away from that." Playing catch after stretch time was one integral element. Typically, each pitcher has a catch partner assigned by the season's start. Unlike position players warming up, pitchers have a much more difficult balance to strike in which they must consider their recent workload. Tony initially paired with rookie Andrew Faulkner, but by mid-April, Faulkner was sent to the minors.

About a week later, another lefty, César Ramos, joined Texas and instantly became a "great catch partner" because he didn't throw hard and was deftly accurate. "With César, it was always a nice relaxed game of catch," said Tony. "We'd get the work in we needed. Our ankles and our shins and our thumbs were for the most part safe from each other. You looked down the line, and there's Johnny Big Fastball just throwing 102 miles an hour with a relief guy who's down there squatting for him 'cuz he's like, 'Hey man, can you get down?' Like, 'No, I'm not gonna get down while you throw 100 miles an hour at me. Absolutely not. I got a wife and kids, man.'"

Tony may use colorful and a tad hyperbolic language, but he's not joking. At the major-league level, with pitchers approaching or topping speeds of 100 miles per hour and deploying a number of pitches with considerable late movement, receiving such throws can be a safety hazard.[38] To make matters worse, catch time is often a prime opportunity for players to experiment throwing pitches they either haven't used in games or haven't quite perfected.

Once Tony finished playing catch, typically during the first round of batting practice, he ran laps with the other pitchers. Then, he shagged baseballs for the remainder of BP, which generally lasted until 5:15 to 5:30. "It's a hundred degrees out there, so you're sweating bullets, and it's miserable," he shared. "You're just sitting there in the sun, working from 3 to 5:30, and then they expect you to come in, relax, cool off, and then, 'Okay, we're gonna be ready for a 7 game.'" Finding a way to cool down before game time became his primary motivation: "After a shag, you get in as fast as you can. You're so hot. You just want to cool off."

For his body to perform at the level required, Tony constantly needed to be eating. Only he never had the appetite to eat when coming into the clubhouse after exerting himself for hours in the extreme heat. So, first, he'd replace his sweaty clothes with something dry. Next, he'd typically consume something cold or in liquid form, such as a Popsicle or smoothie, to increase his appetite. "And then," said Tony, "I would try to get some food in my belly and then go get ready for the game." Cold sandwiches often worked well for the svelte reliever because there wasn't usually enough time to work up to feeling like eating a hot meal.

From there, he showered and dressed for the game, did a little more stretching, saw the athletic trainer if he needed any work done, and then sometimes grabbed a quick snack before heading to the bullpen. Without fail, he made sure to situate himself there in time for the game's first pitch.

Notes

1 Darvish's final two seasons in Japan coincided with Tony's first two. Tony pitched against Darvish's Fighters twice in 2011, on June 3 and June 4.

2 Davis logged 156 games that season. He struck out often and posted a low .308 on-base percentage, but, thanks to his sheer power, he managed to drive in 90 runs.

3 A day later, Davis was signed by the Yankees, who provided a brief opportunity at the big-league level until they demoted him to Triple A. They ultimately released him in August. That would mark the end of Davis's MLB career, although he did star for Israel in the 2017 World Baseball Classic, posting a .471/.571/.706 slash line in 17 at-bats in the international competition. Finally, in 2017, Davis appeared as a two-way player for the Dodgers' Triple-A affiliate.

4 Colby Lewis's first year back was Tony's first year abroad, so the players' paths never crossed in Japan.

5 Cade Lewis was born before the 2007 season, so he was one year old when Lewis debuted for Hiroshima.

6   Despite the right knee injury, Lewis played through the pain the rest of the year and wore a knee brace whenever he pitched. In the process, he set career highs in wins and innings pitched, leading the 2015 Rangers in both categories.

7   Like Madelyn and Hillary, Loretta and Tony share a middle name.

8   Longtime Swallows nemesis and 2015 Japan Series MVP Dae-ho Lee made his big-league debut, striking out in a late-game pinch-hitting appearance.

9   Agent Don Nomura and his wife came to Texas to watch Tony's debut. His dad, Phil, made the trip too. Unfortunately, due to other commitments, the Nomuras had to leave town after the Rangers' first game and didn't get to see Tony pitch the next day.

10   He set down twenty-two-year-old Venezuelan infielder Luis Sardiñas on an up-and-in cutter.

11   The longtime Swallow was now playing for his fourth team in five major-league seasons.

12   Technically, Seattle scored five in the inning, but all runs were charged to Shawn Tolleson before Tony entered the game.

13   Supportive sentiments didn't stop the good-natured trash talking that commenced, given that his old friends were Mariners fans and Seattle and Texas were divisional rivals.

14   In 2016, Cruz would finish with 43 home runs, his third straight 40-plus season, and a .915 OPS. In the second game of the shortened 2020 season, Cruz topped the 400-homer career mark.

15   In the ninth, he retired old friend Aoki on a fly ball to left-center, a small dose of payback for Aoki's RBI single during Tony's debut.

16   Over in the NL Central, Seung-hwan Oh was another MLB rookie in his thirties after pitching as a gaijin in Japan. He was Korean like Lee, and a former Central League closer like Tony. For the Cardinals, Oh went on to have a spectacular season, recording a sub-2.00 ERA in 76 appearances. He also saved 19 games for a team that fell one game short of a postseason berth.

17   Two at-bats earlier, Rasmus homered off a pitch of the same speed.

18   In the bottom of the same inning, in one fluid motion, young Mazara caught a fly ball on the run before nailing Michael Saunders, the potential tying run, at home plate. This memorable inning happened less than a month into Mazara's MLB career.

19   It was Toronto's second walk-off win in as many days. The previous night, Justin Smoak ended things with a two-run homer. Less than thirty seconds earlier and under half a mile away, the Raptors' Kyle Lowry had converted a buzzer-beating half-court shot to force overtime in Game 1 of the Eastern Conference semifinals. Although the Heat would take the game, the Raptors went on to win the series in seven.

20   Kela, Dyson, and Bush would make no more than $526,000 apiece, while $507,500 was the minimum annual salary for a major leaguer.

21   In 2009, Wilhelmsen appeared in 11 games for the now-defunct Golden Baseball League's Tucson Toros.

22   Diekman's high school was too small to field a baseball team so he played for an American Legion team in the summers.

23   Strangely enough, Hamels threw a no-hitter in his final start with the Phillies. What's more, Diekman was involved in Hamels's only other career no-hitter, a combined no-no against

the Braves on Labor Day the previous season. Then-rookie Ken Giles and closer Jonathan Papelbon pitched the final two innings for Philadelphia, respectively.

24 According to Diekman, his condition "didn't really flare up" until he became a pro baseball player. He had to have his colon removed in early 2017. Before returning for the final month of the season, he and his fiancée, Amanda, started a nonprofit foundation called Gut It Out in order to help others afflicted with the disease.

25 Tolleson singled out Elvis Andrus as being especially good. Diekman concurred and also mentioned catcher Bryan Holaday.

26 Holman was not including Wilhelmsen, who was no longer part of the organization after refusing to go down to Triple A a month earlier and becoming a free agent. He then signed with his old team, the Mariners.

27 Going in, shortstop Stephen Drew (Florida State) and pitcher Jered Weaver (Long Beach State) were the consensus top picks, but the Padres opted not to deal with superagent Scott Boras, who represented both. After Bush, Old Dominion's Justin Verlander went to the Tigers with the second pick.

28 In 2016, Bush told ESPN, "I was so depressed . . . [and] hollow inside." He cited "money, fame, and expectations" as his "devils" during those painful years.

29 Silver previously ran the Winning Inning Baseball Academy, where Bush lived for a couple months while with the Rays, and was now a Rangers player development assistant. Silver had played a key role in aiding fellow first-overall pick Josh Hamilton's substance abuse rehabilitation years earlier.

30 The family of the maimed motorcyclist filed a $5 million civil suit but settled in 2013 for a reported $200,000. In August 2016, Tufano candidly told the *Tampa Bay Times*, "How ironic is it that his life was turned around, which is good, but now my life was turned into something bad? When Bush was in jail, he had a chance to think about his life, reflect on his choices. If only I got another chance. I didn't get those choices."

31 As children, musicians Norah Jones, Demi Lovato, and Post Malone were all raised in Grapevine. More into history? A marker remains just outside of Grapevine, at the intersection of Dove Road and State Highway 114, where an associate of Bonnie and Clyde killed two police officers on Easter Sunday in 1934.

32 "The amount of money they put into their community is pretty awesome," said Tony. "There's a lot of stuff for my wife to take her to that's free of charge or really cheap."

33 Tony especially liked purchasing candy that reminded his teammates of their childhood. For example, he bought ZotZ, AirHeads, Laffy Taffy candy, and Bazooka gum, although he quickly learned Bazooka was an "awful choice." Meanwhile, AirHeads were most popular.

34 Essentially, Tony believed, his veteran teammates reasoned that because he made a certain amount of money in Japan, they didn't need to refund him for the candy he bought.

35 According to Tony, once he was no longer in charge, the bullpen snacks "kind of fell apart." He added, "It was just like the luster was gone. Nobody really took it seriously. I remember some guys came in and thought they were too cool for it or whatever."

36   Alongside Tony and Bush, the rookie contingent included the freshly promoted Joey Gallo and Jared Hoying, Luke Jackson, and Nomar Mazara. At one point, twenty-three-year-old Hanser Alberto, who had exceeded his rookie limits the previous season, jumped onstage and tried to rip off Tony's shirt until he was chased away by a security guard who was also playing along.

37   Less than two months after the 2018 regular season concluded, Beltré announced his retirement. He'd surpassed 3,000 hits in the summer of 2017 and was just 23 home runs short of 500 when he decided to end his playing career.

38   In June 2019, the Cubs' Brandon Kintzler hit teammate Steve Cishek in the inside of his right knee when the former's sinker failed to sink in the thin Denver air. Luckily, it only produced a bruise, and Cishek pitched again within a week.

CHAPTER NINETEEN
WHY'D YOU BEAN PUJOLS?

He's not afraid to break the mold. A little funk is good if it's not dangerous.

Tony really began hitting his stride midway through June. His most dominant and consistent stretch, June 19 through August 10, directly followed three poor performances.[1] During those superb seven-plus weeks, which included 18 outings and a tad over 25 innings, Tony was charged with zero earned runs and pitching as efficiently as ever.

"He's already pretty polished," coach Brad Holman said of Tony's skill set before a July game. "My experience in the past with guys that have come over from other countries is limited, but from Japan to United States, there seems to be very little growth need. You're pretty much already there." That didn't mean there weren't "little things" he felt the pitcher could work to improve.

And he was. For example, Tony reintegrated a curveball into his regular repertoire. Relative to 2015, he used the curve much more, primarily to show opposing batters a markedly slower pitch, given four of Tony's other pitches were of similar speeds.[2] This recent adjustment, Holman believed, would particularly come in handy against lefties, to whom Tony was, at times, appearing a tad predictable.

Catcher Bobby Wilson noticed a particular "refreshing" quality that enabled Tony to achieve success on this new stage much quicker than he otherwise may have. "As a thirty-two-year-old rookie, he's still trying to learn new things every day," Wilson said. "He's not closed off to different thought processes, different ways of doing things. He's not set in his ways. And when you have those kind of guys that you can approach and say, 'Hey, I think this might work better,' he receives it well."

Of course, he was no tabula rasa when he began his MLB career. Rather, he brought with him loads of experience that taught him, over time, what worked and what didn't. "I'm pretty much throwing everything that I've thrown in Japan. Still throwing it here," emphasized Tony.

"One of the hard parts for me is getting the catchers to know that I'm not your typical relief guy. I've got a five-pitch arsenal; feel free to use it. These guys are only gonna see me one time. If they're sitting on one pitch, and I've got five in the bag, [I might as well use the others]. If I can throw all five pitches for strikes and mix them in, leaving these hitters going, 'I have no idea what this guy's gonna throw.' If I can do that consistently, then I think I'm gonna have a lot of success here."

"He has four plus pitches," said Wilson, "and he's not scared to throw any pitch at any time. He obviously has the stuff, he has the makeup, everything that you need to be a top-of-the-line reliever. It's just understanding your stuff, really." Through the season's first three months, Wilson noticed progress: "He's starting to understand more about what he can do and sticking with his strengths."

Tony's delivery exhibited a noticeable pause, which he developed two seasons earlier after tearing his PCL. "He hangs a little bit at the top of his balance point, and that becomes hard to time," said Holman. Stylistically, another distinct characteristic stood out. Before beginning his windup, Tony's right elbow protruded, pointing toward center field, as he gripped the pitch in his glove. According to Holman, "It's just kind of a quirky thing that he does. Largely what makes him good is he's not afraid to be different. He's not afraid to break the mold. A little funk is good if it's not dangerous."

Hosting the slugging Red Sox on June 24, he entered with Texas leading 7–4. Although Boston wound up coming back to win, Tony retired all six batters he faced, including Mookie Betts, Dustin Pedroia, Xander Bogaerts, David Ortiz, and Hanley Ramírez.[3] The outing did come with a couple scares. In the seventh, Betts drilled a low fastball on one hop directly at shortstop Elvis Andrus. The next inning, Ramírez struck a 3-1 fastball at 109.1 miles per hour[4] and for a distance of 360 feet. Fortunately, the rocketed ball found its way into Ian Desmond's glove in deep right-center field.

Earlier that week, on a hot Sunday afternoon in St. Louis, the Rangers entered their series finale with wins in five straight and seven of their last eight. So whom were they going to call upon with one out, the bases loaded, and the score tied? Tony Barnette, of course. With his strikeout of large lefty Matt Adams, he inched closer to escaping the jam. However, he faltered, walking the next Cardinal on four pitches. The bases still loaded, Tony accurately placed a fastball low and in, jamming Kolten Wong on a weak fly out to end the sixth.

Jeff Banister's double-switch effectively allowed Tony to remain in the game without having to bat as soon. Although Texas came up empty in the seventh, Tony delivered a lightning-quick inning against the top of the Cardinals lineup.[5] In the eighth, when his spot finally came up, pinch-hitter Jurickson Profar produced a clutch two-run single. After Matt Bush and closer Sam Dyson did their jobs, Texas had its sixth straight victory and Tony improved to 4–2.

"He seems to be our guy that Banister trusts to come in with runners on base, which is never an easy situation to come into," said Shawn Tolleson. "I can't tell you how many times he's come in with the bases loaded this year." Dyson added, "Him being a closer in Japan kind of allows him to go into any inning that he's pitching in and kind of simplify it, attack, and do what he has to do to get out of the inning. I think he slows his game down very well."

Tony had long before grown accustomed to filling a variety of roles depending on what his team needed from him. When the longtime starting pitcher struggled mightily as an NPB rookie and was just barely given a second chance, he embraced switching to a bullpen role the following season. As he improved and further showed what he could do, he became a dominant closer. With the Rangers, he often threw multiple innings. He occasionally relieved struggling starters early in games, but other times, he filled more of a middle-relief role in tight games.

"He's been crucial to our bullpen obviously," Tolleson said. "He's got to be up there with the number of innings thrown for our bullpen and appearances too. And it's huge because it can save a bullpen. He's just very versatile. There's not really a situation that I don't think the team would feel comfortable him coming into." Added Nomar Mazara, "He's always available. He's ready to go every day. It really doesn't matter. It could be back-to-back innings, back-to-back days, three innings. Whatever the manager decides, he's gonna be ready for it."

On the second Friday of July, the Rangers were mired in a rare rough patch. Losers of seven of their last nine, they had lost 10–1 to the lowly Twins the night before. On this night in Arlington, Tony registered yet another valiant performance that helped guide the Rangers to victory. In the game, Cole Hamels's start was deteriorating rapidly after he surrendered a three-run, fifth-inning home run and then walked two of the next three Twins. Trailing 5–4 with two men on, Banister called for Tony, who validated the decision by skillfully inducing a pair of ground balls to squelch any further damage. He then tallied two more scoreless, drama-free innings.[6] Before his third inning of work, Texas regained the lead, ultimately resulting in Tony's sixth win after Bush and Dyson combined to slam the door.

On August 6, a Saturday night in Houston, Texas needed Tony earlier than ever before, with two outs in the fourth. Despite falling down 3-0 to eventual 2016 American League batting champion José Altuve,[7] he outdueled him on a cutter that the diminutive second baseman rolled to shortstop. It kept Texas's deficit at one. Tony's next and last inning did the same, though he needed an inning-ending double play to overcome two singles. The Rangers went on to win 3–2.

Wilson referred to Tony as a "bulldog when he gets on the mound." Holman and Tolleson concurred, juxtaposing the pitcher's killer intensity on the rubber with his softer, lighter, calmer side virtually everywhere else. "He knows when to stop having fun and when to turn to business," said Holman. "On the mound, he's a little psycho, but off the mound he's a family man and a likable guy. From crossword puzzles to his witty sense of humor, just everything about him, he's hard not to like."

"He has a really good ability to focus once he's in the game," Tolleson said of his fellow reliever. "He's definitely a high-intensity pitcher. Once he steps in between the lines, he kind of turns into another guy."

In his first-ever action at Yankee Stadium, Tony featured prominently in the bookend games of a late July four-game series. Both would be memorable, but for very different reasons. Gloomy weather slightly delayed the series opener, yet at the time, rain hadn't begun to fall and tarp wasn't placed onto the field. In retrospect, the game shouldn't have been delayed initially. It wouldn't begin drizzling until the middle innings. Out after out, inning after inning, the field conditions worsened.

Tony entered in the seventh with one out, a runner on second, and Texas trailing 6–4. "It was dumping when I was pitching," he recalled. "The mound was a little wet, but I've pitched in worse before." He retired two Yankees to end the inning. Starting a fresh eighth, now down by just one, Tony walked Jacoby Ellsbury, and the next hitter singled. Two outs later, a pitch in the dirt hit the catcher's glove and rolled away, moving Ellsbury to third. No sweat. Tony's cutter was fouled off before he unleashed a curve that Mark Teixeira swung through and missed. Tony's night was done, but the game was far from it.

Ultimately, a three-and-a-half-hour rain delay and a middle-of-the-night rally transformed the Rangers' deficit into a controversial 9–6 victory.[8] By the 2:44 a.m. finish, maybe only 100 fans remained in the crowd.[9] Tony was credited as the winning pitcher of the unforgettable game he dubbed "insane."

In the finale, on the last day of June, Tony suffered an infuriating walk-off loss without any one of his pitches leaving the infield. After walking two, Starlin Castro's weak roller to first moved the potential winning run 90 feet away. Three pitches later, the delivery to Ellsbury got by catcher Robinson Chirinos. Scurrying home, Chase Headley made it safely, just under Tony's tag. After the game, Chirinos took responsibility, plainly stating, "It's my fault." Tony also admitted guilt. "It's unacceptable," he told reporters of his lack of control in the critical situation. "You walk a guy to start an inning, most of the time he's going to score." The loss represented Texas's second consecutive walk-off defeat in Yankee Stadium and, in retrospect, signaled a difficult July ahead.

Although July wasn't a good month for Texas,[10] it was easily Tony's best of 2016. In 13.2 innings, opposing batters mustered just three hits and two walks. Over the broader, nearly two-month period cited earlier, Tony notched three wins and five holds, as his ERA practically reduced by half, from 3.81 to 1.93.

Bobby Wilson observed what the good run of games was doing for Tony's mindset: "You can see him pitching with more confidence every time he gets out there. The confidence from where's he at now to where he was at in the beginning of spring training is completely different."

Less than a handful of miles from "The Happiest Place on Earth," the Angels were hosting first-place Texas for the middle contest of a three-game set. For the Rangers, the series was sandwiched between three games at Wrigley Field and three more at Kaufmann Stadium that would cap their road trip. Yakult, Tony's employer for the prior six seasons, advertised its brand with a prominent red sign adjacent to Angel Stadium's recognizable waterfall in center field.[11]

The night before, Banister summoned Tony to clean up a sixth-inning mess, as Texas held a precarious 4–3 lead. There were no outs and two runners on. A wild pitch moved both runners into scoring position. Tony dug deep and struck out Albert Pujols on a 2-2 slider. But Texas's lead wouldn't last after a Rougned Odor error tied the game, and the next batter singled in the go-ahead run. Tony escaped further damage with an inning-ending double play, but the Angels ultimately hung on for a 9–5 win and Tony was tagged with a blown save.

On Tuesday, Tony was called upon again, but, this time, if there were going to be a mess, it would be of his own making. Opening the seventh may have seemed nice if it weren't for the unenviable task of first facing a pair of future Hall of Famers. On the third pitch to Mike Trout, Tony utilized a well-placed cutter, low and inside, to elicit a fly out to right.

Pujols was no longer the perennial All-Star he'd been in his prime. Still, at thirty-six and seven years removed from his third and final MVP season, the ten-time All-Star had plenty of pop left. As part of a very good last month,[12] he homered twice against the White Sox two nights earlier. Raising his play to even greater heights, Pujols entered the Tuesday matchup with Tony a perfect 3-for-3, including a pair of three-run homers.[13] Never one to back down from a challenge, Tony tested the two-time World Series champion with two heaters on the inner part of the plate. He whiffed on both, giving Tony the upper hand at 0-2.

Tony went even more inside on the next pitch, but Pujols stayed alive, fouling it off. As he came set and readied another 0-2 offering, Pujols waited with his trademark deep knee bend and gently swaying bat.

In an instant, Pujols was lying on the dirt, face down. Thankfully, this lasted less than a second, before Pujols rolled over and gingerly rose to his feet. He looked a little dazed, as Robinson Chirinos grasped his right shoulder and started walking with him to first base, making sure he was okay. On the pitch, Tony had inadvertently hit the all-time great, and with a 92-mile-per-hour fastball no less. Chirinos had called for a high-and-inside fastball, but obviously not that high or inside. Sensing imminent danger, Pujols managed to tuck his chin into his chest at the last possible split second, allowing the baseball to hit the bill of his helmet. It then grazed the slugger's cheek and deflected off his hands before coming to rest on the grass, a few feet from home plate.

Virtually as soon as the pitch hit Pujols's helmet, he fell. Immediately, a concerned Tony rushed in from the mound, realizing what he'd done and hoping the batter wasn't badly hurt. Simultaneously, home-plate umpire Mark Wegner, after the obligatory point to first base to award Pujols the bag, quickly waved the Angels medical and coaching staff onto the field to check on their player. A tick after, the on-deck hitter, Daniel Nava, also looking uneasy, collected the helmet from the ground and went to assess the situation.

Heeding the umpire's signal, manager Mike Scioscia and the Angels' head trainer left their dugout to tend to Pujols. The first- and third-base coaches joined them just a handful of steps down the first-base line. Pujols took a knee as the trainer performed a standard concussion protocol test. Tony watched from five feet away, as did Chirinos and Wegner.

Amazingly, within forty seconds of being hit in the helmet by a major-league fastball, Pujols was upright, ready to take his base. But first he needed his helmet, which Nava handed to him. After one more test—a smiling Pujols followed the trainer's moving finger with his eyes—he was on his way to first and extremely fortunate to have eluded serious injury. "You always worry about a concussion," said Scioscia following the game, "but he felt fine, and he was laughing."

Before the series finale, Tony self-deprecatingly joked, "It helps that I don't throw hard." When reminded that the pitch was still 92, Tony cracked, "That's most of these guys in this room's changeups." But he knew how serious it was. "It's a scary thing, hitting a guy in the head," he said to reporters after Tuesday's game, "especially up and tight like that. It can do some damage. I've got a family, he's got family, and it can be scary stuff for them. I'm glad he's okay." Anyone watching the game could plainly see how remorseful Tony was by his on-field demeanor. The pitcher profusely apologized. In fact, he apologized twice immediately. He somehow recovered from the frightening moment and Nava's ensuing single to escape unscathed.[14] Before running into the dugout, Tony called out to Pujols, apologizing again. Following the game, he made sure to issue a fourth apology between the two clubhouses.

He had no reason to purposely hit him. Late in the game, putting any runner on base could have been costly. Secondly, if a pitcher wants to bean a batter, it makes no sense to wait until the fourth pitch to do it, especially after throwing the first three for strikes.[15] It didn't matter that Pujols had homered in each of his last two at-bats or that he was one of the most prolific home-run hitters of all time. Tony was challenging him. Finally, from a reputational standpoint, Pujols was known as a consummate professional who wouldn't disrespect his opponent. Typically, if a pitcher is throwing at someone, there's bad blood lingering from a previous situation. In this case, the players had none of that, and neither did their teams.

But in tumultuous scenarios like this, emotions can pretty quickly overshadow logic. Following standard procedure, the home-plate umpire positioned himself between pitcher and hitter right after Pujols stood up, just in case the hit-by-pitch precipitated some after-the-play fireworks. Pujols wasn't mad, just a little shaken, and Tony was apologetic, so there was little surprise when no drama followed. Still, the Angels bench naturally snapped to attention when they saw their beloved teammate hit the dirt. "It was obviously adrenaline," said Tony. "Emotions were running high. I can't imagine we would react any differently after he just got done pounding us all game, and then the guy gets hit up and tight. But obviously there was no intent. I was just trying to get him to chase up and ran into his head."

Brad Holman knew from his playing days and capacity as bullpen coach the virtues of pitching inside. Primarily, when they repeatedly go inside, pitchers are either trying to jam an opposing batter, back him off the plate in an effort to paint the outer edge later, or some combination of the two. "As pitchers, you gotta pitch inside," said Holman, "and sometimes in doing that, one's gonna get away from you, especially righty on righty because the ball tends to run arm side."

When the players met after the game, they spoke briefly and respectfully. According to Tony, there were "no hard feelings. Everything was kosher. Albert was great about it." Pujols confirmed as much when he spoke to the media: "I'm pretty sure that's the last thing that he wants to do on an 0-2 count, but it's one of those things that happens in a game. I just told him, 'It happens. It's baseball.'"

The two Yankee Stadium walk-offs may have triggered the 2016 Rangers' worst stretch, which saw losses in 15 of 19 games.[16] The starting rotation was awfully shorthanded, with Colby Lewis, Derek Holland, and Yu Darvish missing time. Meanwhile, the offense sputtered without Prince Fielder, who hadn't appeared in a game since mid-July and had struggled for weeks before then. An MRI revealed bad news. The big-swinging, highly priced left-hander[17] had a herniation of disks in his neck, just above an area that was repaired two years earlier. The front office worried Fielder would not be back for quite some time, if at all.

They were losing their grip of the divisional lead, slipping to two and a half games ahead of the hard-charging Astros. Their sweep of the Royals added some distance, but an ever-growing sense of urgency remained. General manager Jon Daniels was ready to make bold moves. Despite the Yankees' and Brewers' high prospect asking price, he showed no fear in completing a notable deadline deal with each. In so doing, he unmistakably went all in on the season in the interest of bolstering his first-place squad's offense and back-end bullpen depth. Specifically, he acquired three skilled veterans, Carlos Beltrán, Jonathan Lucroy, and right-handed reliever Jeremy Jeffress, all in one day, in exchange for a slew of highly touted prospects.[18]

Upon Jeffress's arrival, two days after he was acquired from Milwaukee along with Lucroy, he became Tony's new catch partner. By mid-June, previous partner César Ramos's performance had regressed dramatically. On three occasions over a four-week period, the former first-round pick surrendered at least five runs. Ramos was officially released July 25.

This was Tony's first time seeing a friend cut at the major-league level. "You get to know guys," he said, "and when they're good people with good families, and then all of a sudden because so many exponential factors [are] happening they've got to let you go, whatever. These things happen so you've got to move on. You just hope they land on their feet, in a good situation that can possibly help them move forward as a family."

Catch-partner pairings usually persist throughout the season unless one of the players is moved, like Ramos, or demoted. Until Jeffress joined the team in Baltimore, Tony had a different partner most nights. Jeffress had been masterfully closing games for Milwaukee, but the team opted to "sell" at the deadline, given its unlikelihood of finishing anywhere near a playoff spot.[19] Texas slotted him in as Dyson's primary setup man.

Jeffress, always rocking a fierce scowl while he pitched, could understandably come off as one of the league's more intimidating pitchers.[20] With teammates, he usually wasn't that intense.[21] Tony liked Jeffress, but he did miss his days warming up with the deftly accurate, softer-throwing Ramos. Jeffress's power sinker was thrown hard and with late movement. "It's a hard ball to hit, and it's a hard ball to catch," Tony said. "That sinker is gonna move downwards and also to my left. So if you turn your glove over, you run the risk of getting smoked right in your palm if the ball doesn't sink, and that hurts."

While Jeffress wasn't his sharpest right away, veteran hitters Lucroy and Beltrán made an immediate impact. Four months older than the GM who traded for him, Beltrán appeared determined to prove he could still be a key contributor on a championship contender. Within the switch hitter's first five games, he clubbed four extra-base hits and drove in three. He displayed his home-run prowess early in his second game when he pulled a fastball at Camden Yards. Over Lucroy's first four starts, the catcher launched three homers of his own—two coming in a critical 3–2 road win over Houston in which Beltrán also starred.[22]

The August 6 win preceded an even more thrilling victory the next afternoon. A late-inning collapse by Jeffress and Dyson spoiled a stellar Darvish start, necessitating extra innings to settle a 3–3 tie. But a two-run 11th and six outs supplied by Bush carried the Rangers past Houston. Then, they reeled off three narrow wins against Colorado. First, at Coors Field, they found themselves down 3–1 heading into the ninth. The fearless visitors used a two-run single to tie it before Mitch Moreland delivered the game-winning double. The next game, Texas trailed 5–1 through six. Not a problem. One run in the seventh, four in the eighth,[23] and one in the ninth led to a 7–5 win.

The comeback kids were at it again on the 10th, this time hosting Colorado. Facing a late 4–3 deficit, the Rangers did what they do. In the eighth, they found a way to scrape together a couple runs. Next, Bush retired the Rockies in order, and Texas had its fifth straight win, all of them exhilarating.

With the victory, it improved its record in one-run games to an almost unfathomable 26–8. With win after win by some of the slimmest of margins, Texas was quickly developing the reputation of a team that simply found a way to win—through skill, strategy, luck, whatever—regardless of circumstance. Were the Rangers a "team of destiny," as David Schoenfield speculated on his ESPN blog? For some, it was starting to feel that way.

Despite the never-say-die aura building around the club, Wednesday, August 10, began in somber fashion. At a 4 p.m. press conference, Prince Fielder announced his retirement from pro baseball,[24] confirming leaked reports from the prior night. "The doctors told me since [I had] two spinal fusions," he said to the assembled group of media and Rangers personnel, "I can't play Major League Baseball anymore." Just thirty-two with All-Star appearances in four of the previous five seasons, the development was obviously hitting Fielder hard. "I've just been in a big-league clubhouse since I was their age,"[25] Fielder said, gesturing to his sons by his side, "so to not be able to play is gonna be tough, but I'm happy I got to enjoy my career."

Lucroy continued thriving, doing more than his fair share to compensate for the loss of Fielder. By August 12, he'd recorded two multi-homer games in eight starts for his new team. In a home win over Detroit, the sixth-hitting Lucroy compiled three hits and five RBIs. Batting third, Beltrán homered and scored three times.

Although Texas's divisional lead appeared fairly secure as August wound down, the front office refused to bypass an opportunity to further strengthen the team's lineup. Two days after rival Houston released outfielder Carlos Gómez, Texas pounced. Batting eighth in his August 25 team debut, he homered on the second pitch he saw. The three-run drive to left traveled 415 feet at an exit velocity of 107.2 miles per hour. It would be a sign of excellent things to come. After badly struggling with Houston,[26] Gómez finished the regular season with 24 RBIs in 33 games. With Texas, he batted .284 with a .543 slugging percentage. Similarly, Beltrán closed strong, slugging .511 in September.

From the mound, Jeffress began to rebound, although he still wasn't dominating like he had in Milwaukee. Despite his cheery clubhouse nature and respectable in-game performances, he was hurting on a daily basis. He admitted as much in a surprisingly candid interview with MLB .com's T. R. Sullivan, in which he bravely shed light on his ongoing battle with epilepsy and extreme anxiety. "I have a lot of anxiety each and every day," he said. "Every day I wake up, I've got so much. I have a hard time waking up. Sometimes it's hard to go to sleep. Most of the time I'm by myself, I'm scared and nervous." He added that he's taking measures to ensure he's "well taken care of." He also said, "But there are certain things I can't do. I can't self-medicate. I have to follow the rules and respect authority and other people."

Jeffress had self-medicated over the years, testing positive for marijuana three times while in the minors, most recently in 2009. Unfortunately, he was still using in the summer of 2016. The same week Sullivan's story came out, Jeffress was arrested for DWI early Friday morning, mere hours after Gómez's debut. At the scene, Jeffress's blood-alcohol concentration level tested over the legal limit, and police found weed in his glove compartment.[27] Given the choice between an MLB suspension and treatment, he chose the latter. To the Rangers' credit, they allowed him to enter an inpatient rehab clinic near Houston, prioritizing Jeffress, the person, over Jeffress, the setup man, amid their quest for a pennant.

With Jeffress off to rehab, Tony resumed playing catch-partner musical chairs, though Bush tended to be his partner more often than not. "Again, didn't really help there, either," Tony joked about playing catch with the rookie who threw gas. "Texas liked to fill their bullpen with guys that throw a billion [miles per hour]. I missed my days with César."

Near the end of Tony's September 4 outing, he pulled a muscle pitching to José Altuve. He felt discomfort on his left side and underwent a postgame MRI. Nothing serious was found, but given Texas's strong position in the standings, management elected to play it safe, allowing him to carefully rehab the strained oblique without rushing him back. According to Tony, he could have played through the pain if needed.

Because the roster had already expanded to forty, the team didn't need to place him on the disabled list. As a result, the injury flew under the radar for a week until a reporter asked about it. "We noticed you haven't pitched in a while," the reporter said. "Jesus, you guys are astute," he wryly retorted, finding humor in the fact that the media hadn't inquired sooner. Meanwhile, he was recovering well, on track for a return before the playoffs began. Although he couldn't rehab in the minors because all affiliates' seasons had ended, the Rangers creatively found ways for Tony to get in work. In Oakland, he threw live batting practice to Shin-Soo Choo, who was also rehabbing from injury.

As the Rangers closed in on their divisional crown, they continued to thrive despite the absence of Jeffress and Tony from their bullpen. Specifically, they excelled in winning close games, often in dramatic fashion, as they'd done all year. But especially since the trade deadline, tight wins became commonplace. Between then and their clinching of the AL West on September 23, the Rangers won 13 of 17 one-run games in which they were involved. In the two weeks that immediately preceded the clincher, six of Texas's seven wins came by a single run.

The final six one-run wins included two walk-offs and a 12-inning contest in Houston in which a game-winning Rougned Odor home run helped Texas overcome a Dyson blown save. Riding high, Texas produced more magic the next night by ruining Ken Giles's save for a 3–2 win.

The Rangers would ultimately post an otherworldly 36–11 record in one-run games despite losing nine of the first 11 walk-offs of which they were a part with Tony's June 30 loss at Yankee Stadium going down as the final one they'd suffer all season. Their final two walk-off wins came three nights apart with Lucroy and Ian Desmond playing hero.

In Oakland, on the ensuing Friday night, once Odor flipped the ball to Elvis Andrus at second base, the AL West champs were crowned. Hillary, her girls, and their grandma had all made the trip for the clincher even though Tony hadn't yet returned to play.[28] The 3–0 victory, which featured Hamels's 15th win, improved Texas to 91–63, the league's best record by a hair over Cleveland and Boston. In the Coliseum's cramped visitors' clubhouse, the team popped champagne bottles, but out of respect for Bush and Jeffress, the guys began with a Canada Dry ginger ale toast.[29]

With a week to spare, Banister quickly reincorporated Jeffress and Tony. He wanted the bullpen ready to go by playoff time. That last week, the two relievers combined for five scoreless, albeit mostly rusty, appearances. It was better to dust off the cobwebs then than in the postseason, when one mistake could result in elimination.

By season's end, Tony's numbers undoubtedly showed what he'd proven time and again: He belonged in the major leagues, and not for a brief cameo but for years to come. He finished with a 2.09 ERA and was even better after the All-Star break, an 18-game stretch during which he recorded a 1.37 ERA. All season, a consistently long-haired Tony[30] tormented right-handed hitters, who batted .205 and slugged .262 against him.[31] He was trusted and for good reason. No other Ranger inherited more runners, and he managed to strand nearly 73 percent of them. He wound up entering about 38 percent of his appearances in a high-leverage situation, which was more often than three-quarters of 102 qualifying non-closers.[32]

Tony leaned heavily on his famous cutter, throwing it more than two-fifths of the time, but it was actually his curveball and splitter—used a little more than 10 percent apiece—that were most effective in terms of batter outcomes. The curveball was particularly difficult to handle. Much like with his cutter, when unleashing a curveball, he could generate significant horizontal movement.[33]

Never had Tony thrown the ball fast, at least by big-league standards, but he possessed a skill increasingly coveted by franchises. He could spin his fastball and cutter at elite levels, approaching an average of 2,500 revolutions per minute with each. Fully aware of this ability and his velocity limitations, number forty-three largely pitched to contact and was able to drastically curtail the power of opposing batters. Among qualifying pitchers, he placed in the 89th and 86th percentile in (slowest) exit velocity and (lowest) hard-hit rate,[34] respectively. Fittingly, quite low rates of extra-base hits and home runs followed. For good measure, he induced ground balls for double plays at a well-above-average rate. Over the years, Tony had marvelously complemented his physical tools with ingenuity. Clearly, his rookie season embodied a natural progression of that melding.

Once the Rangers officially clinched, they set their sights on securing the league's best record, which would mean home-field advantage throughout the playoffs by virtue of the AL's All-Star Game win at Petco Park.[35] Only the Cubs finished with more home wins than Texas, which won 53 games in Arlington.

Through September 23, it was a three-team race for the best record, pitting Texas, Cleveland, and Boston against one another. When the Yankees, who were essentially playing the role of spoiler, swept the Red Sox in Boston's penultimate series, the Rangers led Boston by two games with three remaining for each and Texas owned the potential tiebreaker.[36] Like Boston, in order to overtake Texas, Cleveland needed Texas to lose all three games while it ran the table. On the last night of September, the Rangers clinched the best record by beating the Rays as Darvish struck out 12. After two perfunctory games, they'd be hosting a best-of-five series against the victor of the winner-take-all wild-card game.

Soon, Baltimore and Toronto secured the two wild-card spots. The Blue Jays managed to catch the Orioles at 89–73 by winning their last two, while the Orioles split theirs.[37] On paper, the AL East teams looked evenly matched. True to form, the game was a doozy that concluded when Edwin Encarnación dramatically hit an 11th-inning, three-run homer off Ubaldo Jiménez. Toronto was moving on for a playoff rematch with the Rangers.

The previous postseason, Toronto had eliminated Texas in the divisional round, three games to two, in excruciating fashion. The Rangers had led the series 2–0 following a pair of wins in Canada. Home-field advantage shifted back to Toronto after Texas failed to end the series in Arlington. Texas didn't just lose the decisive Game 5; it was *how* it lost Game 5. In the rubber match, the Rangers held an early 2–0 lead and, later, led 3–2 through six and a half innings. Then, they suffered through a brutal seventh that featured errors on the first three plays and four Blue Jays runs. Following the errors, José Bautista's bat flip–inducing, 442-foot home run off Sam Dyson broke the tie and ultimately sent Texas packing. More recently, the teams brawled after Odor punched Bautista.[38]

So, the teams were scheduled to meet for the first time since the May incident and in a playoff series no less. Despite the budding rivalry and Texas's AL-best record, MLB placed the first two Boston-Cleveland games in prime time, following each of the first two Toronto-Texas matches. As a result, the Rangers had to host weekday games on Thursday and Friday at 3:39 and 12:08 p.m., respectively. They weren't thrilled.

The series opened with the sun out and the temperature a toasty 90 degrees. Hamels took the hill for the home team. In the third, a hard-hit Josh Donaldson ball deflected off Beltré's glove and headed for left field. The two-out hit led to a five-run inning for the Blue Jays, who coasted to a Game 1 victory. Villainous Bautista, who was roundly booed during pre-game and every one of his at-bats, responded by treating the crowd to two hits and four RBIs, including a three-run, ninth-inning homer off Jake Diekman sans bat flip. Donaldson and Troy Tulowitzki added a combined seven hits and five RBIs for a high-powered offense that hung 10 runs on the Rangers. Meanwhile, Marco Estrada, the same pitcher who beat Texas in the previous postseason's critical ALDS Game 3, silenced Rangers bats with a four-hit gem. In the 10–1 loss, Tony pitched a quick eighth inning in which all three outs featured cutters that never left the infield.

The next afternoon's game looked a lot different from the start. The field was wet as a slight drizzle fell from the sky. This time, Texas came to hit. In the second, Toronto jumped ahead on a two-run Tulowitzki homer. Nine Rangers reached base through the first four innings, yet only one scored. Despite all the stranded runners, Texas continued fighting. In the eighth, Texas sliced its 5–1 deficit in half. With two outs, a passed ball moved Carlos Gómez to third, but Roberto Osuna got Carlos Beltrán to strike out swinging. Continuing the troubling pattern, Texas wasted Beltré's ninth-inning leadoff double after the next three hitters were retired by Osuna.[39] In all, the Rangers stranded 13 runners, outhitting the Blue Jays 13 to six in the 5–3 Game 2 loss.

Four home runs—all against Yu Darvish,[40] who was starting his second career playoff game—accounted for all of Toronto's runs. "When I left it on the plate, they got it," Darvish said through his interpreter. Tony threw two scoreless innings, most notably inducing ground outs from Tulowitzki and Donaldson, but the Rangers had squandered another golden opportunity, losing again at home.[41] Suddenly, they found themselves with no room for error as the series moved to Canada.

On the brink of elimination, Texas manufactured a first-inning run on a Gómez walk, a stolen base, and two grounders. But Encarnación erased the short-lived lead with a two-run homer off Colby Lewis in the home half, and Russell Martin added a solo shot two batters later. Still, Texas kept coming for Toronto. Andrus opened the third with a solo home run. In the third, Donaldson and Encarnación did more damage to take a 5–2 lead, but the Rangers answered right back with two runs on an Odor home run. In the sixth, Mitch Moreland's two-run double gave Texas its first lead since the opening frame. Only a two-out passed ball knotted the score at six runs apiece. Then, the game entered a holding pattern. Not one player reached base over the next three innings.

The pattern continued into extras, as Osuna, in his second inning, set down Texas in order. Jeff Banister saw Matt Bush retire all six batters he faced over the previous two innings. He'd never been asked to get more than six outs, but the Rangers bullpen was overworked and Bush assured Banister he felt strong and up to the task.

With one out, Donaldson doubled to center, putting the potential series-winning run in scoring position. Following an Encarnación intentional walk, Bush struck out Bautista on a high-stakes 3-2 fastball, up and away, that was measured at 98 miles per hour. On another payoff pitch, this time to Martin, it looked as if Bush found a way to escape the scoring threat. But what seemed to be a routine inning-ending double play was no such thing when Odor erred on his throw to first. Donaldson came around to score, marking the first time in big-league history a playoff series ended on a walk-off error. The TV broadcast showed a fan-made sign that read, "I would rather get punched in May than get knocked out in October." The rookie, Bush, had given a hell of an effort, throwing a season-high 42 pitches, but he was drained, physically and emotionally. As Toronto celebrated its series victory, Bush kneeled in the infield.

"We got cold at the worst moment," Beltré said after the series-ending loss. The explosive Jays offense, which produced eight home runs and 22 runs over three games, proved too much for the Rangers. Key Texas hitters, primarily the newcomers acquired in August, also mightily struggled. Beltrán, Gómez, and Jonathan Lucroy combined to bat 5-for-36 with no extra-base hits and two RBIs. Cleanup batter Beltré managed just two total hits.

Tony ultimately pitched in every game of the series. In Game 3, he entered with a runner on second and nobody out in the third. Although he promptly allowed the inherited runner to score on an Encarnación single, he then outdueled Bautista, Martin, and Tulowitzki, and was done for the night.

Lewis's disastrous outing would be his final major-league start. The veteran, who'd make his retirement official the following January, was charged with five earned runs in two-plus innings. Sunday's dreadful start notwithstanding, he achieved tremendous postseason success over the course of his Rangers career after returning from Japan[42] and will surely be remembered for that. Most famously, Lewis won the 2010 ALCS clincher that propelled Texas to its first World Series appearance. Later, he won Game 3 of that World Series, though the Giants would take the Series.

Granted, the unceremoniously fast exit from the playoffs hurt, particularly after such an inspired season. But Tony possessed perspective. He had just pitched well in his first year and postseason in the Show. Even more importantly, he'd be home with his wife and daughters soon. He yearned to be back with his young family. They had memories to build together.

Notes

1   The three-outing rut was capped off by a game against the hometown Mariners, in which he surrendered two runs and could retire only one of four batters faced.

2   Four of Tony's pitches clocked in within an 88-to-93-mile-per-hour window. By comparison, his curveball averaged 77.9 miles per hour.

3   These were the first five batters in a Red Sox lineup that, in 2016, led the majors in a slew of categories, including runs, batting average, slugging percentage, and OPS.

4   Only two balls were hit harder off Tony all season. Both went for singles and were hit by Miguel Cabrera and Abraham Almonte, respectively.

5   All he needed were four pitches. Tony's quickest three-out appearance of the season, seven pitches, came on July 31 when he preserved a 4–3 lead over the Royals.

6   Amid a prolific season, it would go down as Tony's longest appearance at two and two-thirds innings. In terms of pitches thrown, Tony's season high came on September 4 against the Astros when he threw 35. On three different occasions, including the game against Minnesota, his pitch count tallied 30.

7   The American League also crowned Altuve batting champion in 2014 and 2017 and league-wide MVP in 2017 as well.

8   According to league rules, the umpires could have called the game earlier, giving the Yankees the win. In postgame remarks, Yankees manager Joe Girardi made no effort to hide his frustration that the game was allowed to continue for as long as it did.

9   After the game, Adrián Beltré confirmed it was so quiet that he could hear his nine-year-old son cheering for him during his last at-bat. Apparently, the boy had no summer bedtime, or his dad was willing to make an exception.

10   They finished 11–15 and would have had an even worse record had they not swept the Royals in four games to conclude the month.

11   Due to Yakult's sponsorship with the Angels, it provides free samples before games. Since 2014, the company has had a factory in Fountain Valley that manufactures for the United States and Canada. It's located 10 miles southwest of Angel Stadium.

12   Going into the Tuesday-night game, Pujols had driven in 22 runs over his previous 23 games.

13   Pujols had chased starter Kyle Lohse from the game by slugging a homer in consecutive innings. Interestingly, it would go down as the final game of Lohse's 16-year major-league career.

14   Tony got Andrelton Simmons to ground into an inning-ending double play.

15   Additionally, it's doubtful a pitcher would aim for an opponent's head except under extreme circumstances, which these were not.

16   Directly before the walk-off defeats, Texas stood at an impressive 51–27. The team's loss on July 22 dropped it to 55–42.

17   Through 2020, Fielder's contract paid him approximately $24 million per year.

18   The prospects dealt included three former first-round picks, outfielder Lewis Brinson and right-handed pitchers Luis Ortiz and Dillon Tate.

19   Brewers general manager David Stearns's team stood in last place in the NL Central. He had become the youngest active GM when he was hired at thirty years old as the 2015 season wound down. Ten years earlier, Jon Daniels had been twenty-eight when Texas made him the youngest GM in big-league history.

20   "I'm a warrior at battle once I get up on that mound," Jeffress told TexasRangers.com reporter Emily Jones soon after joining the team. "I always told people, 'If my mom was in the box, I would do the same thing. I'm sorry. . . . If she gets in that box, she's gonna have to feel my wrath."

21   For example, Jeffress liked to joke around in the clubhouse and dance to hip-hop music.

22   Beltrán delivered three hits, including the tiebreaking RBI single in the seventh.

23   The four eighth-inning runs included a mammoth, 405-foot game-tying double from Adrián Beltré.

24   By not officially retiring—he was declared "medically disabled"—Fielder was owed roughly $104 million through 2020. Of the total, Detroit would contribute $24 million, Texas would pay $44 million, and insurance would take care of the remaining $36 million.

25   By sheer coincidence, Fielder finished with 319 major-league home runs, precisely the same number as his father, Cecil, whose last season came in 1998. Cecil spent 1989 playing in Japan, as mentioned in Chapter 1.

26   With the Astros in 2016, Carlos Gómez posted a dreadful .210/.272/.322 slash line in 85 games.

27   Jeffress reportedly denied the drugs were his and ultimately was not charged with possession.

28   Once Hillary got down to the clubhouse with her stroller, which was quite a challenge, the room was filled with cigar smoke. Accordingly, they stayed just long enough to give Tony congratulatory hugs and take a few pictures together. After they returned to the hotel, Hillary's mom offered to watch the girls so Tony and Hillary could go out for a quick celebration, which they did.

29   After both pitchers were drenched in ginger ale, they retreated to their lockers. Hanging plastic sheets protected them from spraying champagne and beer as they watched the rest of the celebration. The ginger ale toasts began in 2010 when Josh Hamilton and "straight edge" C.J. Wilson played for Texas.

30   Occasionally, he got slight trims, but the Samson-inspired question of whether losing the hair would drain his strength was never tested.

31   Out of 134 plate appearances, not a single righty took Tony deep. To his detriment, however, left-handers batted .287 with a .426 slugging percentage.

32   In order to qualify, a pitcher needed at least 40 relief appearances and fewer than six save opportunities. A high-leverage situation occurs with a leverage index of 1.5 or higher, where 1 is the average LI and a neutral situation.

33   Per Statcast, among all 2016 MLB pitchers, the median horizontal movement average for curves was just over 8 inches, while Tony's topped 14. Even more impressively, his

average horizontal movement on the cutter, 6.2 inches, came in at more than 2.5 times the league median.

34 Hard-hit rate measures the relative frequency of a baseball hit 95 miles per hour or faster. Just 29.4 percent of batted balls against Tony reached the threshold. His average exit velocity? 86.7 miles per hour. On both metrics, he outperformed a slew of superstar pitchers, including offseason workout buddy Max Scherzer.

35 This was the last year of this arrangement. For 2017 onward, MLB switched to winning percentage as the determining factor for World Series home-field advantage.

36 Head-to-head record would have been the first tiebreaker used, but the Red Sox and Rangers split six games. The second tiebreaker then would've considered intra-divisional record, a category where Texas was superior. Texas also held the tiebreaker with Cleveland, given its 5–2 head-to-head record.

37 This was critical for the Blue Jays, who narrowly won the head-to-head season series, 10 games to nine. Thus, they'd be hosting the wild-card game.

38 Odor was handed an eight-game suspension that was reduced to seven games after appeal. Six were ultimately suspended as a result of the incident, including Bautista for one game and Blue Jays manager John Gibbons for three. Moments before the punch, Bush, who was pitching in his second MLB game, hit Bautista with a fastball to open the eighth inning. Later, he was fined for the incident but not suspended. Interestingly, Bush notched his first big-league win in the same unforgettable game.

39 Osuna's five-out save marked his return from the shoulder soreness that cut short his appearance in Toronto's wild-card win over Baltimore. Osuna initially entered Game 2 in the eighth when Francisco Liriano exited after being hit near the back of the head by a Gómez liner. After the game, the lefty was checked out at a hospital and subsequently cleared to fly with the team to Toronto.

40 The difficult outing meant the Japanese-born right-hander became the first MLB pitcher since Rick Reed in 2002 to allow four home runs in a postseason game.

41 The Game 2 loss remarkably dropped the Rangers franchise to 1–11 in home ALDS games. Its only home divisional series win came against the Rays in 2011, the season Texas fell one win shy of a World Series title.

42 Before the playoff start in Toronto, Lewis boasted a 2.38 ERA in nine postseason games, which included eight starts.

EPILOGUE
FULL CIRCLE

I lived a dream.

In the second and final year of Tony's deal, he was pitching fine until the Rangers visited their in-state divisional rivals to begin May. In 2017, the Astros would emerge as one of MLB's elite clubs. They'd go on to win 101 games and the World Series, and then appear in three of the following five World Series to boot. In their first head-to-head meeting of the season, Jeff Banister called for Tony to protect a 2–1 lead with no outs in the seventh and two Astros in scoring position. On his fourth pitch, a George Springer infield single tied the game. Then, a fielder's choice was followed by doubles from Altuve and Correa, and just like that, Banister came to get Tony. Later in the inning, Correa came around to score, and the Rangers ultimately lost 6–2. In the series finale, although Texas won, all three batters Tony faced reached base.

On June 14, back in Houston, the same thing happened, where Tony retired none of the four batters he faced, this time allowing three earned runs. Two days later, Texas sent him to the disabled list. Tony had hurt his right ring finger, but he admitted to reporters that the move had more to do with providing a mental reset than healing anything physical: "You can call it a [reset] or whatever you want. It's about me needing to get outs. I have a job to do and haven't been getting it done. It absolutely makes sense [to do], but you never want to admit that. I accept what has happened, and I'll try to get with the people who can help me get going in the right direction." In 14 appearances between May 1 and June 14, the second-year big leaguer suffered a 9.19 ERA, as opposing batters hit .359 against him with a .984 OPS.[1]

Back on June 11, a day before the Astros hosted Tony and the Rangers, former Swallows teammate Nori Aoki recorded his 2,000th professional hit (NPB and MLB hits combined). Fans supplied a boisterous ovation, Astros teammates and coaches gifted the outfielder fine wine, and Aoki gained exclusive entry into the Meikyukai, one of Japan's two baseball halls of fame. After the game, he received an honorary jacket from one of its members, Tokuhiro Komada, who was on hand to welcome the club's newest member.

The 2017 Rangers had their moments, like a ten-game winning streak in May that included a pair of consecutive walk-offs, but over the course of the season, they displayed neither the excellence nor the consistency of the AL regular-season champs from the prior year. This year's team performed poorly in close games, never led its division, and at best stood three games over .500. Overall, Tony was not great either, finishing with a 5.49 ERA and 1.50 WHIP, and particularly struggled on the road, against left-handed hitting, and with runners on base. He pitched respectably upon his July 3 return but still well short of his own expectations.

A closer look at his Fielding-Independent Pitching (4.01, per Baseball-Reference) and expected ERA (3.95, according to Statcast), however, reveals that Tony didn't pitch nearly as badly as his ERA would suggest. And then there was the whole Astros cheating scandal. Confirmed by MLB in January 2020, the 2017 and 2018 Astros illegally stole pitch signs from opposing catchers through the use of technology. Tony may have been particularly damaged by Houston's actions. Here are his 2017 split stats against the Astros and everyone else:

- Against the Houston Astros: 7 apps, 4.2 IP, 13 H, 13 ER, 25.07 ERA, 3.86 WHIP, 3 HR, 5 BB, .481 BA, .889 SLG.

- Against everyone else: 43 apps, 52.2 IP, 51 H, 22 ER, 3.76 ERA, 1.29 WHIP, 4 HR, 17 BB, .262 BA, .400 SLG.

Following the season, Tony agreed to a slight pay cut to remain with Texas for another year. By 2018, Colby Lewis, who retired after the 2016 season, had joined the front office as a special assistant to the general manager, a role he retains to this day. While the 2018 Rangers featured a few more young players, aging veterans like Adrián Beltré, Cole Hamels, and Shin-Soo Choo returned, and forty-four-year-old Bartolo Colón was even added to the mix. In retrospect, they were likely a team that should have more fully embraced a rebuild but struggled to given certain existing large contracts.

From late May through the end of June, Tony got into an excellent groove, although he was rarely granted the opportunity to pitch in close games.[2] Granted, the 2018 Rangers occupied the AL West cellar for the vast majority of the season, but their prospects particularly turned bleak after an 8–17 July effectively eliminated all remaining hope. On the month's third day, Tony injured his right shoulder. He would be sidelined for the rest of the season and never again appear in a Rangers uniform. In 22 games, he posted a 2.39 ERA and 0.91 WHIP.

With its season headed nowhere and an eye to the future, Texas traded Hamels ahead of the deadline. On September 21, following several days of swirling rumors and speculation, Banister was fired after a surprise meeting with the front office. His 2016 Rangers had it, whatever "it" was. If you recall, they somehow finished 36–11 (.766) in one-run games. In 2017 and 2018 combined, the Rangers went the exact opposite direction with a 25–43 record (.368) in such games. Of course, in 2018, they also suffered a dismal record in games decided by five runs or more. After the season, cornerstone Beltré retired, and the franchise began to rebuild in earnest.

In the two seasons since Tony left for Texas, Yakult struggled to win games, placing dead last and eleventh of twelve in ERA in 2016 and 2017, respectively. In 2016, Logan Ondrusek stepped into closer duties but was released and left Japan midseason a few weeks after a spat with coaches.[3] Tetsuto Yamada recorded another Triple-3 season (.304, 38 HRs, 30 SB) and Wladimir Balentien struck 31 home runs, but no one else did much offensively. In 2017, the Swallows' hitting significantly worsened. Even 32 more home runs from Balentien couldn't save Yakult from finishing 45–96–2, one of its worst records of all time.

For 2018, the Swallows may have enjoyed a nostalgic lift by bringing back two beloved figures from their not-too-distant, much-less-depressing past, Nori Aoki and Junji Ogawa. Another friendly face returned in the form of Go Fujisawa, who moved back to Tokyo from his role in Toda in order to establish a data analytics division for the *ichi-gun* team. That season, they managed to boost their previous win total by 30 and place second in the Central League. Although the rival Giants would sweep them in the playoffs, the Swallows' season was deemed an incontrovertible success. And Aoki was back. After his MLB career ran its course, he opted to return to the Swallows to finish his career where it began. Donning his original number, 23, the thirty-six-year-old picked up where he left off with a terrific season, slashing .327/.409/.475 with 67 RBIs. The only real difference was that Aoki no longer was a prolific base stealer. Yamada led the offensive attack with yet another Triple-3 season (.315, 34 HRs, 33 SB), as Ogawa moved from the front office back to the dugout.

Aaron Guiel was busy running a landscaping company in Arizona when his former organization contacted him after the season about coming on board as a scouting consultant. Since his 2011 retirement, Guiel had stayed in touch with Swallows International Director Michael Okumura, routinely expressing his interest in a scouting job should one become available. For years, Yakult hadn't employed any US-based scouts, with Okumura largely handling Stateside scouting duties with the help of a few others. By 2019, the Swallows finally made the investment, as other organizations already had, to add a former player to scout for them in the United States. Guiel enthusiastically accepted the offer, relishing the opportunity to return to professional baseball.

The position would take him to Japan at least once each year until a once-in-a-century pandemic hit.[4] Most notably, the fans' selection of Guiel to appear in the Swallows Dream Game on July 11, 2019, presented a special opportunity for something of a redo after his abrupt departure in 2011. The game, which assembled some of the best Swallows of yesteryear to commemorate Yakult's fiftieth-anniversary season, allowed Guiel to properly thank the fans and many of his former teammates and coaches who also appeared in the game. In front of a sold-out Jingu Stadium and in a steady drizzle, Guiel's Swallows Legends (managed by his last manager, Ogawa) defeated the Golden '90s squad (managed by his first NPB manager, Atsuya Furuta) 6–3 in a star-studded six-inning affair. Chang-Yong Lim and Guiel proudly comprised the gaijin player contingent, with the latter also competing in the event's Home Run Derby.[5]

Most thrilling for Swallows fans, eighty-four-year-old Katsuya Nomura, Don's stepfather who guided the franchise to four Central League titles and three Japan Series championships as its manager in the 1990s, made an unforgettable, heartwarming appearance. He spoke to the crowd, and at one point took a ceremonial swing at home plate. Sadly, the elder Nomura would pass away exactly seven months later, making the Dream Game his final public appearance.

In August 2019, Tony's stepbrother, Jesse Dunbar, and Jesse's wife, Etsuko, welcomed Sawyer, a baby boy, into the world. They are living happily in Ibaraki prefecture, northeast of Tokyo, and are fresh off a five-month return to the States. Excluding as an infant, it was Sawyer's first time seeing where his dad was born and raised.

Unfortunately, a large regression cut Ogawa's second stint as manager to two seasons. One positive development from 2019 was Go's installation of Hawk-Eye, the visual tracking system that MLB utilizes to compile its Statcast data. In doing so, Yakult became the first NPB club to use the technology. After the season, Swallows mainstay Balentien became a free agent and bolted for the Hawks. By virtue of his nine years of *ichi-gun* service, he simultaneously shed his foreigner status and would not count against SoftBank's four-gaijin quota.

As a free agent ahead of 2019, Tony spoke with multiple teams. Desiring a legitimate shot at winning a World Series, the thirty-five-year-old pitcher chose to join the Cubs,[6] where familiar faces Cole Hamels and Yu Darvish were already on the roster. Tony began the season rehabbing his injured shoulder. By late April, he was sent to Iowa, the Cubs' Triple-A affiliate. Within a week and a half, it became obvious that his shoulder needed more strengthening, so he returned to much warmer Arizona to rehab more. By June 1, he was back in Triple A, where he dominated the competition over three weeks.[7] Then, the Cubs promoted him. Only, his time in the big leagues would be short-lived, and it wasn't Tony's fault. The Cubs had signed big-name free agent Craig Kimbrel a few weeks earlier. Once Chicago deemed Kimbrel ready, after a four-game stint in Iowa,[8] it optioned Tony back to Triple A to make room.

He believed the Cubs had no more options on him, so when they demoted him again, he was shocked. So was his agent. At that stage of his career, after just two big-league appearances with Chicago, Tony didn't want to go. He refused the assignment, thus landing him on the Cubs' restricted list. Don Nomura immediately contacted the players association, which confirmed that Chicago had the right to option Tony to Triple A because he hadn't reached five years of major-league service time. Nomura had mistakenly thought the rule was three years. Understandably, as a true professional, he deeply regretted (and still regrets) his costly error. "That's my mistake," Nomura admitted. "I screwed up."[9]

For over a year, Tony had been battling digestive problems he'd later largely attribute to anxiety, and he was exhausted. By simplifying his diet—he moved to a dairy-, gluten-, and sugar-free diet shaped by the results from a food sensitivity test—his issues could be managed at the major-league level, nice restaurants and hotels and all. But they wouldn't have been back in Iowa or on the road in the minors. So Tony returned home to contemplate his baseball future. As the offseason progressed, he increasingly leaned toward retirement. Tony wanted to be home more with his young daughters, and he wanted to take care of his physical and mental health. So, naturally, when Okumura reached out about the same US-based scouting position Guiel had taken a year before, Tony needed no convincing. "That was the opportunity where I was like, 'You know what? It's time for me to go be Dad," said Tony. "It's time for me to go take my kid to kindergarten and be home for my kids and give everything that I have for them now. They earned it. My wife and my kids, they chased me around the world playing this game, supporting me. And that was the moment where I was like, 'It's my time to give it back to them.'"

On January 28, Tony officially announced his retirement with a heartfelt and grateful Instagram post that ended with "I had the privilege of playing the greatest game in the world for a living, I lived a dream. Being a ballplayer has been an honor. I've thrown my last pitch." Tony and Guiel then left for their first Okinawa trip together in their new roles. Once the pandemic's deathly toll came into clearer focus within the next several weeks, the nature of their jobs changed dramatically. Fortunately, though, they could evaluate talent from home.

In Japan, following Ogawa's departure as manager, Shingo Takatsu took over. By 2021, Year 2 under Takatsu, everything clicked for the Swallows as they bounced back from a poor 2020 season to earn their first Japan Series berth since Tony's final season. As a bonus, Yakult had swiftly eliminated Yomiuri to get there too. Back in 2018, a strapping teenager named Munetaka Murakami debuted for the *ichi-gun* Swallows and could barely buy a hit in limited time, though he did homer for his lone hit of the season. By 2021, his third full *ichi-gun* season, the lefty slugger topped 100 RBIs for the first time and was named Central League MVP. Yamada did his usual thing as well. Below are some of the others who played an outsized role in Yakult's 2021 regular-season success, along with a few other telling facts:

- The Swallows easily scored the most runs (625) of any NPB team.
- Exclusively a pinch-hitter by this point in his career, old friend Shingo Kawabata excelled (.372 BA, .908 OPS).
- Rookie right-hander Yasunobu Okugawa, who was nineteen when the season began, pitched like a vet (9–4, 3.26 ERA in 18 starts).
- First-year gaijin Domingo Santana proved his worth (.877 OPS).
- Gone since 2017, Tony's beloved longtime bullpen coach Tomohito Ito returned to the franchise as its *ichi-gun* pitching coach.
- Returning gaijin Scott McGough masterfully stepped into the full-time closing role in late May (31 saves, 76 Ks).
- Young Noboru Shimizu's 72 appearances led NPB (2.39 ERA).
- Leadoff man Yasutaka Shiomi got on base and moved well (.357 OBP, 21 SB, 80 runs).
- At forty-one, Masanori Ishikawa turned back the clock (3.07 ERA, 16 starts). Although he only appeared once before June, he didn't miss a single post-All-Star-break start.
- Yakult played its best baseball between September 7 and October 17, going 23–8–5 (.708) while outscoring opponents 173–93.

During his six-year major-league stint, Aoki kept narrowly missing a championship. In the 2014 World Series, he played for the Royals, who took the Giants the distance before falling short in Game 7, 3–2. Then, while Aoki was in San Francisco, Kansas City won it all the very next year. In 2017, he played 71 games for the eventual champion Astros before being dealt away at the deadline. Fortunately, for his contributions, the Astros gave him a World Series ring. Although a thirty-nine-year-old Aoki saw a steep offensive decline in 2021, he started 120 contests plus every playoff game, playing left field and usually batting second, and he finally found the championship that eluded him for so long! It's funny. Seiichi Uchikawa had grown unaccustomed to *not* winning titles. Coming into the season, he had won seven championships, including six of the last seven Japan Series and four straight. Upon joining Yakult, although he played poorly, only starting six games including none after May, Uchikawa promptly won another championship.

In the top of the 12th of Game 6, it was only fitting that Kawabata, a hitter who came through in countless clutch situations throughout the season,[10] notched the game- and series-winning single. McGough featured prominently throughout a tightly contested Japan Series. Although he blew a save in Game 1 and surrendered Game 5's winning run, he was spectacular in the championship-clinching victory, in which he threw the final two innings and a third and allowed only one runner to reach. Yuhei Nakamura earned Japan Series MVP honors. A still-developing young catcher when he caught Tony, by 2021, he was as polished as they come. Credited for expertly handling the Yakult staff and throwing out two base stealers, Nakamura also recorded seven Japan Series hits and three RBIs.

When McGough recorded the final out and the Swallows' celebration began in Osaka, David Watkins was watching the action on his phone, on his way to a train station after leaving the Takadanobaba bar where he had deejayed that night. Naturally, they knew he was a diehard Swallows fan and had set him up with a comfortable way to view the game. But as extra innings dragged on, he had to leave to catch the last train of the night. Once Yakult clinched its first championship in twenty years, "I started jumping up and down and screaming on the street," said Watkins, "and everyone thought I was weird." Then he boarded the train, sat down, and grew emotional from watching the postgame celebration and ceremony. Watkins began to cry.

The 2021 season was unconventional in a few noticeable ways, although that reality did nothing to diminish the Swallows' exhilarating championship run. For one, COVID-19 restrictions continued, preventing Jingu Stadium from operating at full capacity and fans from audibly cheering.[11] Additionally, coming out of the All-Star break, NPB took a three-and-a-half-week hiatus, while Tokyo hosted the rescheduled Summer Olympics, which included baseball for the first time since 2008. Finally, as a result of the schedule being pushed back, all of the Yakult's Japan Series "home" games were played in Tokyo Dome as opposed to Jingu, where amateur baseball tournaments were promised use of the field.[12] Accordingly, Watkins avoided his least-favorite stadium and watched Games 3 through 5 at home with his daughters, a decision he does "not regret one bit."

And those 2021 Swallows were no aberration. They reached the Japan Series again the next year, powered by unanimous Central League MVP Munetaka Murakami, who won the Triple Crown.[13] In the process, the impressive twenty-two-year-old broke Sadaharu Oh's sacred single-season home-run record among Japanese-born players, falling just four short of tying Wladimir Balentien's 60 home runs. On the pitching side, Tony's former teammate Yasuhiro "Ryan" Ogawa put together one of his best seasons in years. Only once before, in 1992 and 1993, had Yakult appeared in consecutive Japan Series, as Takatsu and Murakami appeared to be ushering in a second golden age for the Swallows, the first coming before the latter was even born.

Even in the early 1990s, they hadn't been able to secure two NPB championships in a row. In pursuit of their first-ever two straight, the Swallows won two games and tied another through their first three games in a Series rematch with the Orix Buffaloes. Despite the strong start, they failed to win any of the following four games, doomed by offensive struggles from Murakami and Yamada and a slew of errors leading to costly unearned runs. In each of their narrow losses in Games 5 through 7, the Swallows surrendered at least one unearned run. In Game 5, McGough, who was coming off another terrific season as closer, inherited a 4–3, ninth-inning lead. Following a walk and an infield single, a McGough throwing error tied the game. Two batters later, Masataka Yoshida delivered a two-run sayonara home run.

In Game 7, it was a two-out, fifth-inning line drive misplayed by Shiomi that allowed three unearned runs to score. Even after that, the Swallows didn't go down without a fight. Trailing 5–0, Murakami singled in one before first baseman José Osuna fully resuscitated the sold-out Jingu crowd with a three-run shot to cut the Yakult deficit to one. Naturally, the TokyoSwallows.com guys were in attendance and out of their seats, hoping for a comeback, which would have extended the Japan Series to an eighth game for the first time since 1986. Unfortunately, it was not to be, as Orix smoothly escaped the eighth with its lead intact before Jacob Waguespack retired the side in the ninth to clinch the championship and deprive Yakult.[14] Despite the runner-up finish, second-year gaijin Osuna played an excellent postseason, deserving every bit of his Climax Series MVP and Japan Series Fighting Spirit Awards.

Tony, who was serving in his second and third years as a scouting consultant, derived great joy from his franchise's renewed success. He attributed such success to a looser, more fun-loving vibe around the team. In 2020, when he and Guiel spent time with the club in spring training, they noticed the organizational approach beginning to shift immediately as Shingo Takatsu took over. "Man, the culture's different here," they thought, according to Tony. "It's like the culture that I thought that we were building in '15."

When they returned to Japan for the first time in three years, they recognized that the figurative seeds Takatsu had planted had grown into trees. Tony also credited veterans like Aoki, Ishikawa, Nakamura, and Ogawa for the atmospheric evolution. "You could just feel it, and you could see," said Tony. "We talk about it, like, 'There's something different here. It's definitely lighter. It wasn't like this when we were here.' You see that they allow that youthfulness to come out of the guys, and the guys can just be those young guys that they are and not be so nervous about stepping on eggshells in front of anybody. It's just a very welcoming clubhouse atmosphere." Tony wouldn't be surprised if other organizations "latch on to a more relaxed atmosphere" in hopes of achieving similar success.

Of course, the gaijin running TokyoSwallows.com thoroughly enjoyed their view of the team's best period since they became fans. In recent years, as they grew older and began to amass more work and family commitments began to mount, posts appeared less frequently. Still, they continued to release their regular monthly podcast through August 2022. Then, in the spring of 2023, the English-language Swallows website's impressive run sadly reached its end. Over nearly fifteen years, TokyoSwallows.com spread joy, laughter, and information to Swallows fans worldwide. Although all good things supposedly must come to an end, much of the website is intact by virtue of the Wayback Machine.[15]

Specifically, Watkins's life away from the website has kept him plenty busy. When the pandemic hit in 2020, the language school he founded in 2013 was hit hard. No classes meant no income. Ultimately, however, the school, which also includes training for teachers, moved to an exclusively virtual format, allowing Watkins to assist a wider array of people in new ways. Unsurprisingly, both of his daughters are "100-percent bilingual" after he and his wife made a conscious decision to raise them with only English at home. In 2020, Watkins took up deejaying. Vinyl records are "just taking over the house," he noted, amusingly. At least twice every month, he deejays at the same place where he watched most of the 2021 championship clincher.

Although Scott McGough cost Yakult in Game 5, he unquestionably played a key role for those Japan Series teams and earned a two-year, $6.25 million contract with the Arizona Diamondbacks as a result.[16] His career trajectory is eerily similar to that of Tony Barnette. Hailing from the same conference,[17] McGough was drafted five rounds earlier and moved up to Triple A a little faster. But ultimately, like Tony, McGough's career was stagnating in the States.[18] He wasn't called up to the big-league Marlins until 2015, but with Miami he pitched just six times, accruing a 9.45 ERA. By 2019, at twenty-nine, the right-hander headed to Japan. There, over four seasons, he spent time as a reliever before developing into a skilled closer. The NPB experience resurrected his career. Sound familiar? Then, in 2023, McGough returned to MLB at thirty-three, just a year older than Tony was when he debuted with the Rangers.

The Rangers hadn't won too much since Tony's debut season. Over the first four seasons since his departure, they finished fourth or last in the

AL West three times, suffering a combined 228–318 record (.418). In late 2020, former pitcher Chris Young was named general manager, while Jon Daniels remained as the President of Baseball Operations. Two summers later, Daniels was fired after six consecutive losing seasons. Daniels now serves as a senior advisor for the Rays.

Soon, Young brought in veteran manager Bruce Bochy, and Texas was back! Led by former Yomiuri Giant Adolis García, the 90-win 2023 Rangers went on to vanquish the rival Astros in a seven-game ALCS, winning four road games to advance.[19] Coincidentally, in the World Series, they met Tony's only other primary franchise, Arizona, which was without McGough whose season ended in September with right shoulder inflammation. Texas made quick work of the Diamondbacks, winning its first-ever World Series, with Corey Seager taking MVP honors. Still left from 2018 were José Leclerc, Martín Pérez, Matt Bush,[20] and coach Tony Beasley. Offseason workout buddy and midseason acquisition Max Scherzer also won a ring,[21] as did Bobby Wilson, who was now serving as the catching coach.

Balentien retired from Japanese baseball ahead of the 2022 season after two abysmal seasons with SoftBank. Ironically enough, in a June 13, 2021, game against his old team, he recorded both the 1,000th hit and 300th homer of his NPB career.[22] Only three gaijin, Tuffy Rhodes, Alex Ramírez, and Alex Cabrera, slugged more home runs. After spending 2022 in the Mexican League, followed by unsuccessful appearances in the Dominican Winter League and the Caribbean Series, Balentien decided to hang it up.

In 2022, former Swallows interpreter Shin Koyama received a devastating diagnosis. It was colon cancer. Tragically, he was not able to overcome the disease and passed away by year's end. Tony will forever remember Koyama as a "good dude" who helped brighten his days, especially in Toda in 2014 when Tony longed to be healthy and back in Tokyo.

Renowned and popular gaijin Alex Ramírez, who became a Japanese citizen in January 2019, was elected into the Japanese Baseball Hall of

Fame in early 2023, along with Randy Bass. In doing so, they became the third and fourth gaijin to ever receive such an honor.[23] In his acceptance speech, Ramírez thanked all of his interpreters by name. "[Initially], I wanted to go to Japan, make good money, play baseball a year or two, and come back to the minor leagues or the major leagues," he said, "but I fell in love. I fell in love with Japan, and the way the Japanese people treated me was number one. This was the place for me."

When the highly anticipated World Baseball Classic finally returned in 2023, Japan's national team blew through most of the competition on its way to gold. Samurai Japan, as they're nicknamed, swept the group stage, winning all four games by a 38–8 margin before taking down Italy and Mexico in the quarterfinals and semifinals, respectively. They then edged the Americans 3–2 in the championship game in Miami. Although Swallows Japan Series antagonist and current Red Sox outfielder Masataka Yoshida and two-way superstar and two-time AL MVP Shohei Ohtani spearheaded Japan's attack, Tony's former teammates Nakamura, Yamada, and Yu Darvish all played helpful supporting roles. Young Swallows cornerstone Murakami was especially impactful, launching a massive fourth-inning homer to tie the championship game at one and driving in five runs over the previous six games.

Four of the team's pitchers weren't done making waves in the States. Within nine months of Samurai Japan's win, the Dodgers had signed both Ohtani and right-hander Yoshinobu Yamamoto to a total exceeding $1 billion. Ohtani's ten-year, $700 million contract was particularly noteworthy, shattering the previous MLB record by over $250 million and including an unprecedented amount of deferred money.[24] Southpaw closer Yuki Matsui, a twenty-eight-year-old international free agent after ten NPB seasons, signed a five-year deal with the Padres. Meanwhile, the Cubs inked their own Japanese left-hander, Shōta Imanaga, to a long-term contract after he was posted by Yokohama.

If you wanted certain advanced analytics on, say, Murakami's WBC blast (115.1 miles-per-hour exit velocity, 432 feet, 25-degree launch angle) and the game were at Jingu, you'd consult the Swallows' Baseball Research and Development group, which Go still runs today. At home, Go's family is keeping busy. The WBC actually got his five-year-old son, Kei, interested in baseball, meaning it's no longer just soccer for him. Additionally, Emiri has learned to dance, swim, and play the piano, but these days she's most interested in learning English. Her dad, a skilled former interpreter who never enjoyed learning English, finds it amusing. As a family, occasional visits to an *onsen* (hot springs) are some of their most cherished excursions together.

Midway through 2022, Tony and Hillary separated but continued to amicably co-parent their girls. Madelyn and Loretta occupy the center of their worlds. Madelyn has taken an interest in fashion and theater. Meanwhile, her sister will play virtually any sport, including flag football, basketball, and gymnastics, her current favorites. Sadly, Po suddenly passed away in June 2016 when Madelyn was two and already inseparable from her furry friend "Popo." Though they will never forget Po, Penny joined the family a few months later. The following year, they added Banjo, who quickly became the girls' favorite playmate. Professionally, Hillary has transitioned into education in recent years, giving her a chance to work at her daughters' school and develop her career. She began as a technology teacher, switched to STEM more broadly, and then moved into the behavioral specialist role in which she currently serves.

Upon returning from Chicago, Tony was cooking "all the time." Drawing from his genes—his brother Randy, his father, and a grandfather were all skilled cooks—he began to experiment. Particularly, baking became his favorite activity. He does all of his own grocery shopping and loves spending time in the kitchen. Sometimes the girls join him.

Now, it's all about family for Tony, who has made a concerted effort to grow closer to his only living biological sibling, Cory. To ensure that and that his daughters know their Wisconsin cousins and uncle well, he's planned numerous family trips and gone hunting with Cory after actively avoiding guns for his entire baseball career.

Tony holds Cory in high regard, finding inspiration from the path of service that his oldest brother has taken in life. Following the 9/11 attacks, Cory enlisted in the Marines and fought for his country in Afghanistan and Iraq. When he came home and took a job with 3M, he began volunteering with a local firefighting program. After years of hard work, he ultimately became fire chief of his county. "We have become better friends than anything," said Tony.

In his scouting work with the Swallows, Tony continues to learn, while embracing being on the other side of the backstop after decades as a competitor. Though he and Aaron Guiel almost never appear at the same field—that would be inefficient when they could see more players by dividing and conquering—they both thoroughly enjoy working together again. They do periodically meet for lunch to go over players they've been watching and to discuss the state of the Swallows and any timely organizational directives. The friends share the latest about their kids too, such as how Guiel is delighting in coaching his son's club baseball team while rooting for his soccer-playing daughters from the sidelines.

With his return to the Swallows in 2020, Tony's story had come full circle. The same organization that provided Tony the opportunity to transform himself, on and off the field, has given him the chance to grow and evolve in the second act of his baseball career. "I obviously love Yakult," said Tony, fully aware that Yakult loves him right back. By identifying the prospective players to serve as the Swallows' future gaijin, Tony and Guiel can continue to give back to the organization that has given them so much while potentially playing a critical role in prolonging or even revitalizing some players' careers. Each view their Japanese playing experience as a gift. Now they can pay it forward.

Notes

1   Four of those outings came against Houston, which scored in each. Across those appearances, Tony surrendered eight earned runs in two and one-third innings.

2   In 2018, Tony entered a mere four of 22 appearances when Texas was within two runs in either direction. According to Baseball-Reference, over 88 percent of his appearances were low-leverage, a far cry from 2016 when 32 percent were considered high-leverage and another 22 percent were deemed medium-leverage.

3   Ondrusek was initially suspended for engaging in abusive postgame behavior toward coaches, his manager said. Ondrusek seemed to be incensed that his left fielder's error led to a blown save. He apologized behind closed doors and was permitted to practice with the farm team, but he ultimately requested his release. Then, the Orioles quickly scooped him up on a major-league deal.

4   The 2021 and 2022 Okinawa trips were canceled.

5   Out of ten swings, Guiel was pleased to hit a home run eight years after his retirement. Two others, Akinori Iwamura and Naoyuki Naito, tied him for a share of the derby win.

6   Tony would receive a guaranteed $750,000 with a second-year team option for $3 million.

7   In nine scoreless appearances, just two batters reached.

8   Craig Kimbrel and Tony actually both pitched for Iowa on June 18 and 21.

9   "It is my job to protect the players from certain events on the contract," Nomura said candidly. "He even told me, 'I don't want to be optioned to the minor leagues,' and I said, 'Yeah, I know. I'll make sure we have that in.' And then in the course of negotiation I did talk about it with the club, but I did not have that in writing. . . . It was totally my fault. I mean, I have no excuse. It's a learning process for me, to dot the i's and cross the t's. And it was a wake-up call for me as well."

10   During the regular season, when Kawabata drove in a run or more, the Swallows went 10–4–1, and 15 of those 18 pinch-hit RBIs came in tight games.

11   The ōendan's trumpet-powered tunes were prerecorded and piped through the stadium. Clapping along was allowed, but fans were prohibited from singing or shouting.

12   The Swallows were also forced to play several August and September home games at Tokyo Dome because of Jingu's proximity to the Olympic and Paralympic games being held at the time.

13   In 2022, Murakami became the first unanimous CL MVP since 1977 when Sadaharu Oh won the award. He was so dominant that he slugged .711, reached base nearly 46 percent of the time, and drove in 134 runs, 44 more than any one of his peers. Even more telling, Murakami hit 26 more homers than the Central League player placing second in the category.

14   Orix's Jacob Waguespack was the only active foreigner on its title-winning team. That was the first time that happened since 2002 when the Yomiuri Giants won it all with only one gaijin, pitcher Héctor Almonte, on their active roster.

15   You can find many of those pages at the following link: https://web.archive.org/web/20191106220639/https://tokyoswallows.com/.

16   Tony's former Rangers manager, Jeff Banister, happens to be the Diamondbacks bench coach, taking the position ahead of the 2022 season.

17   McGough was an Oregon Duck; Tony, a Sun Devil.

18   McGough had to undergo Tommy John surgery, which sidelined him for all of 2014. The time missed certainly didn't help his progression.

19   García, the ALCS MVP, set a playoff record with 15 RBIs in a single series. His 22 RBIs over the course of the postseason would also set a record. His time in Japan was brief, and he spent the bulk of it on the farm, logging just seven plate appearances with the *ichi-gun* Giants in 2016.

20   Technically, Pérez and Bush were reacquired. In the interim, Pérez pitched for both the Twins and Red Sox after signing as a free agent. Bush, however, was traded to the Brewers on August 1, 2022. When Bush was released the following July, Texas signed him to a minor-league contract before adding him to its major-league roster just in time for the playoffs. Although he didn't end up pitching, he made the wild-card and ALDS rosters and was ultimately given a ring.

21   Each of Scherzer's two championships was the first for a particular franchise, the Washington Nationals (2019) being the other one.

22   Balentien compiled just 10 hits and four home runs in that final NPB season and was deregistered for good on June 25.

23   Wally Yonamine (1994) and Victor Starffin (1960) were the first two gaijin to make the Japanese Baseball Hall of Fame.

24   More than 97 percent of Ohtani's total salary from the deal won't be paid to him until July 1, 2034. And the money owed won't include interest either. Ohtani merely wanted to help the Dodgers build the best championship-contending teams they could.

ACKNOWLEDGMENTS

First and foremost, I have to thank Tony for openly sharing his inspirational story with me and for doing so with such enthusiasm and passion. We became connected in the spring of 2008, when he was a minor-league pitcher who'd amassed a ton of strikeouts and innings pitched at the Double-A level. That was all I knew about him.

Over the decade and a half since, I've come to regard Tony as a friend. When I first contacted him about blogging for my small, independent website, I had no idea he'd prove to be such a charismatic and fascinating figure. Of course, I also had no idea—and neither did he—of the cinematic twists and turns his career would take, beginning with his decision to leave for Tokyo after the 2009 season.

In the winter of 2015–2016, Tony's already fascinating story became much more relevant to a broader American audience after he signed with the Texas Rangers. At thirty-two years old, after navigating a challenging yet exhilarating six-year Japanese odyssey, he would finally be making his major-league debut—a decade after being drafted—and I wanted to turn his story into a full-length book. I cannot thank Tony enough for allowing me to do that, and for being so helpful throughout the process. To this point, it's been the honor of my life.

Thank you so much to Hillary as well. Whatever I needed, whenever I needed it, she was always there to provide invaluable support. Her kindness and perpetual enthusiasm for the project will never be forgotten.

During each busy baseball season, Tony and his teammates could under-standably be difficult to pin down at times. With Hillary, that never was the case. I also deeply appreciate her openness throughout the reporting process, which allowed for a nuanced, unvarnished retelling of her and Tony's story.

During my outreach to prospective agents, my pitch caught the atten-tion of Ayesha Pande Literary's Stephany Evans, who wanted to see the full manuscript. After determining that the book was simply too long, she recommended that I reach out to Mark Weinstein whom she claimed was excellent with helping nonfiction sports authors tighten their narratives. For that referral, I'm extremely grateful.

By that point, I had been researching, reporting, and writing the story for years and felt extremely protective over it. Naturally, I felt wary of cutting a significant amount. Given Mark's track record of success in the world of book publishing, I trusted him and his feedback that finding a quality publisher and/or agent would be quite difficult at the book's present length. He also convinced me that shortening the story wouldn't harm its effectiveness.

So I decided to have his firm, Kevin Anderson & Associates, conduct a "critical review and analysis" of the manuscript, where they provided detailed editorial feedback to help me identify the best parts to remove. Matt Silverman, the particular editor Mark assigned to my project, proved Mark correct. Cutting a decent amount of content not only didn't hurt the quality of the narrative, but instead helped make it even more powerful. Although the new and improved version of the book didn't end up being the right fit for Stephany, Mark and Matt's assistance empowered me to fearlessly make further word-count reductions and other improvements on my own, which ultimately led to my deal with Skyhorse Publishing. Thank you, Mark and Matt.

Additionally, Mark played a more direct role in making the deal with Skyhorse possible by giving me Jason Katzman's information as well as that of two other acquisitions editors he believed might be interested in the manuscript. Several months after first contact, the partnership with Skyhorse was made official. Working with Jason and his team has been a pleasure. Through the myriad ups and inevitable downs, I've always respected Jason's vision, expertise, and editorial eye. If not for his good, hard work on the book, I'm not sure you'd even be reading this right now. Most simply, I'm appreciative that he believes in me.

For two and a half weeks, during the spring of 2018, I took a trip to various parts of Tokyo that will forever stay with me. My good friend Jonathan Santiago, whom I met through our campus radio work at KDVS in Davis, was the primary driving force behind the experience in the first place. Having frequently traveled and lived in international settings in the preceding years, he encouraged me to leave my comfort zone and just go with him . . . and man, did we make the most of it. We packed myriad diverse activities into our trip which was, for me, a hybrid of work and leisure. Most importantly, getting to physically be in Tokyo, precisely where most of the book's scenes unfolded (including Jingu Stadium, Tokyo Dome, Legends Sports Bar, Aoyama Cemetery, and the Imperial Palace, to name a handful), made a story that already captivated my attention absolutely come to life.

And it wasn't just the places; it was the people, too! After I'd interviewed David Watkins numerous times from across the Pacific via Skype and Facebook call, he graciously agreed to serve as an informal guide at various junctures. No surprise, he was extremely kind and knowledgeable in person and wound up taking me to two games at Jingu—he hilariously refused to set foot in Tokyo Dome—where I experienced the one-of-a-kind umbrella dance up close. He also treated Jonathan and me to unbelievably good *okonomiyaki* in some nondescript basement restaurant in Shinjuku and joined me for conveyor-belt sushi another day. I couldn't have asked for a better guide.

Throughout this process, David's contributions were critical to my ability to write this book, at every stage going above and beyond whatever I asked of him. I'll never forget repeatedly waking up at something like

5:30 a.m. to catch him at a good time and never minding in the least because of how impeccable of a source he was. Also, given that I couldn't read Japanese, his website and Yakyu Baka (thanks, Gen Sueyoshi!) were certainly the two most used and important online resources as my research was just beginning, and probably over the ensuing years as well.

Additionally, it was a joy meeting interpreter Go Fujisawa, who happily joined Jonathan and me at a TGI Fridays just outside Tokyo Dome before the Giants hosted the Swallows. In the flesh, Go is the same wonderful person whose goodness shines through in the book. He and Tony's stepbrother, Jesse Dunbar, with whom I also had lunch while in Tokyo, served as invaluable, consistent, and reliable sources over a span of multiple years. In interviews, Jesse generously shared much of his own illuminating experiences, including a great deal I asked about that ultimately wound up beyond the scope of the book.

Don Nomura's contributions are immensely appreciated as well. In addition to delivering a beautiful foreword, he brought me into his LA office for an in-depth discussion and has always been responsive and amenable when asked to talk. I'll always appreciate his candor when discussing the most sensitive of topics. His enthusiasm for the project will never be forgotten either.

Aaron Guiel and Rob Smaal belong in the same category as David, Go, and Don with regard to how helpful and accessible they've been. Their unique insight as longtime gaijin in Tokyo, as player and reporter, respectively, was integral to the story. They're such nice guys, too, which made it an absolute pleasure any time I had to reach out to either. I'm glad some of Rob's inspirational health journey could be documented inside these pages and wish him nothing but the best.

English-speaking Japanese baseball writers Jim Allen, Jason Coskrey, and Kazuto Yamazaki made themselves available to talk and also assisted me with research and rules questions whenever I reached out. Kudos to them for being so helpful without asking for anything in return. Those generous gestures meant the world to me.

Jerome Behar's profound impact on me and this project is impossible to adequately articulate in this space, but I'll do my best. From close to the very start of this journey, he perpetually motivated and inspired me. Oftentimes, I benefited immeasurably from the confidence boost he provided. Simultaneously or on other occasions, he held me to account on various aspects of the book and was never afraid to tell me what I *needed* to hear even if it wasn't what I *wanted* to hear. You always need someone like that in your life. As the founding CEO of Workiva (WebFilings at the time), Jerry generously set me up with a complimentary account so that I could much more easily and efficiently store and improve the manuscript over time. It's a tragedy that cancer robbed his family and friends of many more years with him and that he never got to hold this book in his hands, but his legacy will live on through everyone he continues to inspire. Of course, that long list includes me.

My late beloved maternal grandmother (my mom's stepmom) also passed away before publication, but her imprint is all over this book. She served as one of my biggest champions throughout my life, and even took the time to read early versions of certain chapters, marking those pages with questions, constructive feedback, and the occasional kind word. For a writer, when someone takes the time to do that it means much more than a generic "good job" or pat on the back. As a girl, her father took her to Ebbets Field to see Jackie Robinson and the Brooklyn Dodgers play. I miss her and our long, deep phone conversations about politics and society, but I'm heartened that I had so much time with her.

There are two other people I appreciated and loved who unexpectedly passed away before this book could come to fruition: basketball journalist and all-around-amazing guy Sekou Smith, and my selfless, loving, empathetic aunt Brenda Starks. Sekou and I never actually met in person, yet every time I updated him on the book, he responded like we were old friends or close colleagues, expressing his excitement and encouraging me to push forward. Once, the busy man even reached out to inquire about my progress, which was a rarity even among people I knew well. There's a lot I could say about Aunt Brenda. As a diehard Dodgers fan who attended games as often as she could with Uncle Tony, I could feel how proud she was that I was making this happen. She always cared about how and what I was doing even when she was battling her own various health ailments. Much like Jerome, that's how she was. Putting other people's happiness on par with or even above her own wasn't a strategic choice; she simply knew no other way.

Talented basketball reporter and author Jake Fischer, now with Yahoo! Sports, deserves a huge thanks for attentively reading multiple chapters and generously providing detailed feedback. It says a lot about his character that he would take the time to help on that scale.

My dad, Joel, and brother, Joshua, similarly read everything I asked them to read—often multiple times—and never ceased to provide smart and useful comments that I took into account when revising. Both also routinely helped me cope with the challenges of writing a book from an emotional and mental-health perspective. Additionally, I owe my mom, Jeannette, immense praise for her unconditional love and support. She and Bubbe Janet (my dad's mom) have always believed in me, which goes a long way. And thank you to my former partner, Jessica Lettich, for lovingly standing in my corner for years. I'm sorry for the strain this project put on our relationship.

Barbara Stark-Nemon deserves my heartfelt gratitude as well. She became an author later in life, yet it's clear that her passion has always been there. She's such a terrific and creative storyteller who never fails to write with heart. Given how I feel about Barbara, it's been an honor and privilege to share an open line of communication with her about various aspects of the writing and publishing process.

Special thanks to Andrew Keating for selecting an early excerpt, "The Gaijin Reliever: Tony Barnette Takes Tokyo" as a finalist for Cobalt Press's 2018 Earl Weaver Baseball Writing prize. In a cool twist, fellow finalist Sandra Marchetti asked to include more of my work in Boog City's 2020 baseball magazine. The resulting piece, "Tony Barnette Leaves Tokyo on

Top," a much tighter, 1,000-word excerpt, combined a few vivid scenes from mid-to-late 2016 in a way that I believe encapsulated the heart of the book. Thank you to Sandra for that opportunity.

I'd be remiss not to thank every single remaining source I haven't yet listed, including Seth Greisinger, Phil Barnette, Josh Whitesell, Jamie D'Antona, Adrián Beltré, Matt Bush, Jake Diekman, Sam Dyson, Brad Holman, Nomar Mazara, Shawn Tolleson, Bobby Wilson, Marty Kuehnert, and the American League scout who made time for me. I also would love to thank everyone else not mentioned who was kind and helpful to me during the 2018 Tokyo trip, including but not limited to our two incredible Couchsurfing hosts, Elena (Setagaya) and Phillip (Minato).

Writing a book, especially one's first, can often feel like a lonely and scary endeavor. For largely that reason, the incredible support from my "village" has been immensely important and sustaining throughout the process. Genuinely, it's difficult to overstate how much it's lifted me up when people I trust and respect have expressed enthusiasm for the project.

Though there are too many to list, current and former journalists whom I met at USC or UC Davis, through my two podcasts, via social media, and at various other stops over the years have shown great enthusiasm for the book. I've worked closely, at one point or another, with the following wise people who have not only shaped the journalist I've become but have also perpetually rooted for and encouraged me during this journey: James Ham, Danny Lee, Paresh Dave, James Santelli, Jacob Freedman, Jacqueline Monet Blessing, Sarah McWilliams Guerra, Ian Levy, Nick Denning, Kate Rooney, Julio Moran, and my friend and longtime *On the NBA Beat* co-host Loren Lee Chen. These supportive fellow authors with whom I've spoken about the project are more than deserving of a shout-out here too: Jonathan Abrams, Gabriel Allen, Ethan Scheiner, Ben Reiter, Brad Balukjian, Howard Beck, Paul Knepper, David Ostrowsky, Mick Minas, Brad Botkin, Tonya McKenzie, Melissa Isaacson, Alan Abrahamson, Eno Sarris, Pete Croatto, Marc Cooper, Agu Ibañez-Baldor, Ari Herstand, Rafe Bartholomew, and Lang Whitaker.

Thrillingly, a number of friends and family members have already pre-ordered multiple copies too. Four I'd love to highlight for their immense generosity are Sarah Becker, Bobbi Salcido, my uncle Ross Fischman, and Leslie Behar, Jerome's wife. Due to space concerns, there are too many whom I'm unable to thank, but here are some of the thoughtful others: Anthony/Vicky Digiulio, Brian Sameshima, Michael Barnett, Parur/Romella Topchyan, Daniel/Briana Barkin, Shea/Genevieve Huffman, David Kohan, and Heidi/Hoyt Holmes. Certainly, the above list is not exhaustive, as so many have been and will continue to be tremendously supportive.

I'm grateful to friend and former KDVS radio colleague Ben Taylor for hosting me at a San Jose Giants game, where I promoted the book on June 1. It figures to be a busy summer and beyond of promo, so I want to preemptively thank everyone else who will help me spread the word about *A Baseball Gaijin*.

I'll end where this whole thing likely began. Before I even knew Tony Barnette's name or story, I was particularly inspired by Rafe Bartholomew's *Pacific Rims*, which chronicled the Philippines's love affair with the game of basketball. Upon reading it, I felt I could do what Rafe did, and I'd like to think I have.

A final thank you to each and every one of you who picked this up and started reading. If any piece of it has resonated with you or made you smile, laugh, or cry, then I'm satisfied.

WORKS CITED

@FIFA. "2011 Women's World Cup Final: Japan 2-2 USA (3-1 PSO)." YouTube, July 16, 2012. https://www.youtube.com/watch?v=FNMTCT1lyhs.

@hillarypjones. "Central League Champions." YouTube, October 2, 2015. https://www.youtube.com/watch?v=syTvYEXgthw.

@hillarypjones. "Climax Series Champions." YouTube, October 17, 2015. https://www.youtube.com/watch?v=f-2TaxDiLNI.

@johnaguilar4198. "Nori Aoki DOES Speak English!" YouTube, May 4, 2015. https://www.youtube.com/watch?v=-0nzLMhmTyE.

@MLB. "6/27/16: Beltre Delivers Go-Ahead Hit after Delay." YouTube, June 27, 2016. https://www.youtube.com/watch?v=gh-8eJb4ozc.

@MLB. "TEX@LAA: Pujols Hit on the Helmet, Stays in Game." YouTube, July 19, 2016. https://www.youtube.com/watch?v=q_amft6IqCA.

@NBA. "Join Kobe Bryant in Support of Tsunami Victims in Japan." YouTube, March 23, 2011. https://www.youtube.com/watch?v=BXUmHA9xmhs.

@otoutama. "Swallows Dream Game ハイライト&ノムさん挨拶 #swallows." YouTube, July 27, 2019. https://www.youtube.com/watch?v=4GN6xjX8QYo.

@SNFaizalKhamisa. "Kyle Lowry's Game-Tying 3, and Justin Smoak's Walk-off HR Were Less than 30 Seconds Apart." X, May 4, 2016. https://twitter.com/SNFaizalKhamisa/status/727910961282207744.

@Tony.Barnette. "If You Cheered for Me, Thank You. ..." Instagram, January 28, 2020. https://www.instagram.com/p/B74ey48AbJA/?igshid =azougqgr60sr.

@yakyutvenglish5055. "Wladimir Balentien Breaks the NPB Home Run Record." YouTube, November 8, 2019. https://www.youtube.com /watch?v=352muhJlTQk.

"Aaron Judge Hits 496-Foot HR, Longest since Tracking Began." ESPN, June 11, 2017. https://www.espn.com/mlb/story/_/id/19608144/aaron-judge -hits-longest-home-runs-tracking-began-2009.

"AC/DC Setlist at Saitama Super Arena, Saitama." Set List, March 14, 2010. https://www.setlist.fm/setlist/acdc/2010/saitama-super-arena-saitama-japan -43d4b30f.html.

Adams, Steve. "Jeremy Jeffress Enters Rehab, Will Not Be Suspended by MLB." MLB Trade Rumors, August 31, 2016. https://www.mlbtraderumors .com/2016/08/jeremy-jeffress-enters-rehab-will-not-be-suspended-by-mlb .html.

AFP. "Giants Manager Sorry for Blackmail Scandal ." Arab News, June 22, 2012. https://www.arabnews.com/giants-manager-sorry-blackmail-scandal.

AFP. "Underdogs Japan Ready to Topple Giants US." The Local Germany, July 17, 2011. https://www.thelocal.de/20110717/36341.

Allen, Jim. "Dennis Sarfate in Japan." JBallAllen.com, August 9, 2020. https ://jballallen.com/dennis-sarfate-in-japan/.

Allen, Jim. "NPB's Free Agent System." JBallAllen.com, November 15, 2018. https://jballallen.com/npbs-free-agent-system/.

Allen, Jim. "The Hot Corner: Battle Just Beginning in Tohoku." Japanese Baseball (originally the *Daily Yomiuri*), May 5, 2011. https://www .japanesebaseball.com/writers/display.gsp?id=37568.

Allen, Jim. "The Hot Corner: Battle Just Beginning in Tohoku." Japanese Baseball (originally the *Daily Yomiuri*), May 5, 2011. https://www .japanesebaseball.com/writers/display.gsp?id=37568.

Allen, Jim. "The Hot Corner: Debate Ends as Baseball Begins." Japanese Baseball (originally the *Daily Yomiuri*), April 14, 2011. https://www .japanesebaseball.com/writers/display.gsp?id=37232.

Allen, Jim. "The Hot Corner: Disaster Hits Home for Eagles." Japanese
Baseball (originally the *Daily Yomiuri*), March 17, 2011. https://www
.japanesebaseball.com/writers/display.gsp?id=36781.

Allen, Jim. "The Hot Corner: 'Boo' Time Comes Again for Swallows." Japanese
Baseball (originally the *Daily Yomiuri*), April 28, 2011. https://www
.japanesebaseball.com/writers/display.gsp?id=37460.

Andracki, Tony. "While They Wait for Kimbrel, Cubs Add Another Intriguing
Option to Bullpen." NBC Sports Chicago, June 23, 2019. https://www
.nbcsportschicago.com/mlb/chicago-cubs/while-they-wait-for-kimbrel-cubs
-add-another-intriguing-option-to-bullpen/312679/.

Arba, Alexandru. "NPB: Leading Save Record Holders as of November 2023."
Statista, January 8, 2024. https://www.statista.com/statistics/1173431
/japan-leading-save-record-holders-npb/.

Associated Press. "2004 MLB Draft: June 7 Picks." *USA Today*, June 7, 2004.
https://usatoday30.usatoday.com/sports/baseball/draft/2004-06-07-picks
_x.htm.

Associated Press. "Balentien Ties Japanese Home Run Record." *The New York
Times*, September 11, 2013. https://www.nytimes.com/2013/09/12/sports
/baseball/balentien-ties-japanese-home-run-record.html.

Associated Press. "Brewers Give Norichika Aoki Incentives." ESPN, January 23,
2012. http://www.espn.com/mlb/story/_/id/7494442/milwaukee
-brewers-norichika-aoki-set-earn-1m-2012-125m-2013.

Associated Press. "Former Royals Pitcher Bannister Signs with Yomiuri."
Charleston Gazette-Mail, January 11, 2011. https://www.wvgazettemail
.com/former-royals-pitcher-bannister-signs-with-yomiuri/article_df8c8b79
-c507-56c4-b8cd-f4caccfb918c.html .

Associated Press. "Matt Murton Breaks Japan Hits Mark." ESPN, October 5,
2010. http://www.espn.com/mlb/news/story?id=5650587.

Associated Press. "M's Suzuki Will Start in Jacksonville." *Moscow-Pullman
Daily News*, March 22, 1994. https://news.google.com/newspapers?id
=1rwjAAAAIBAJ&sjid=rtAFAAAAIBAJ&pg=6645,2386760&dq
=mac+suzuki&hl=en.

Associated Press. "Outfielder Shogo Akiyama Wanted to Make History with Reds." ESPN, January 8, 2020. https://www.espn.com/mlb/story/_/id/28448363/outfielder-shogo-akiyama-wanted-make-history-reds.

Associated Press. "Rangers Fire Manager Jeff Banister after 4 Seasons." ESPN, September 21, 2018. https://www.espn.com/mlb/story/_/id/24754826/texas-rangers-fire-manager-jeff-banister-4-seasons.

Associated Press. "Yuki Matsui Can Earn $33.6m If He Becomes Padres Closer." ESPN, January 2, 2024. https://www.espn.com/mlb/story/_/id/39230484/yuki-matsui-earn-336m-becomes-padres-closer.

Axisa, Mike. "Fukuoka Softbank Hawks Win Japan Series Title, Want to Play Royals." CBS Sports, October 30, 2015. https://www.cbssports.com/mlb/news/fukuoka-softbank-hawks-win-japan-series-title-want-to-play-royals/.

Axisa, Mike. "Rangers' Jake Diekman to Miss First Half of 2017 after Surgery to Remove Colon." CBS Sports, January 26, 2017. https://www.cbssports.com/mlb/news/rangers-jake-diekman-to-miss-first-half-of-2017-after-surgery-to-remove-colon/.

Baer, Bill. "Yankees Sign Ike Davis to a Major League Contract." NBC Sports, June 12, 2016. https://www.nbcsports.com/mlb/news/yankees-sign-ike-davis-to-a-major-league-contract.

Baker, Geoff. "Former Brewers Pitching Prospect Tom Wilhelmsen Gets Another Chance with Mariners." *Seattle Times*, March 1, 2010. https://www.seattletimes.com/sports/mariners/former-brewers-pitching-prospect-tom-wilhelmsen-gets-another-chance-with-mariners/.

Barnette, Tony. "The Gaijin Pitcher: Nature's Fury." Davis Sports Deli (via the Wayback Machine), March 14, 2011. https://web.archive.org/web/20110724162138/http://davissportsdeli.com/?p=2438.

Bastian, Jordan. "Cubs Finalize 4-Year Deal with Japanese Lefty Imanaga." MLB.com, January 11, 2024. https://www.mlb.com/news/shota-imanaga-cubs-deal.

Bell, Jack. "Japan Earthquake Relief Soccer Match." *The New York Times*, March 28, 2011. https://goal.blogs.nytimes.com/2011/03/28/japan-earthquake-relief-soccer-match/.

bostonsportsguy17. "Daisuke Matsuzaka Donates One Million Dollars to
Help Japan." Over the Monster, March 26, 2011. https://www
.overthemonster.com/2011/3/26/2073819/daisuke-matsuzaka
-donates-one-million-dollars-to-help-japan.

Brown, Jim. "What Is a Torn PCL?" University Health News, August 1, 2018.
https://universityhealthnews.com/daily/bones-joints/what-is-a-torn-pcl/.

Burly (pseudonym). "Dennis Sarfate May Now Be the Highest Paid Player in
NPB History." Burly's Baseball Musings, March 28, 2018. https
://notanotherbaseballblog.wordpress.com/2018/03/28/dennis-sarfate
-may-now-be-highest-paid-player-in-npb-history/.

Butler, Sam. "Rehabbing Diekman Launches Foundation." MLB.com, August
6, 2017. https://www.mlb.com/news/rangers-jake-diekman-launches
-foundation-c248874172.

Calcaterra, Craig. "NPB Commissioner Ryozo Kato Apologizes for Altering
the Baseball." NBC Sports, June 14, 2013. http://hardballtalk.nbcsports.
com/2013/06/14/npb-commissioner-ryozo-kato-apologizes-for-altering
-the-baseball/.

Calcaterra, Craig. "Roughed Odor Gets an Eight-Game Suspension, Jose Bautista
Gets One Game." NBC Sports, May 17, 2016. https://www.nbcsports.com
/mlb/news/rougned-odor-given-an-eight-game-suspension-for-his-fight
-with-jose-bautista.

"Cardinals, Ace Mikolas Agree on 4-Year Extension." ESPN, February 26,
2019. https://www.espn.com/mlb/story/_/id/26085891/sourcecards
-mikolas-agree-68m-extension.

Castrovince, Anthony. "These MLB Legends Were Trailblazers in Japan." MLB.com,
February 4, 2024. https://www.mlb.com/news/larry-doby-don-newcombe
-first-major-leaguers-to-play-in-npb.

"A Chronological Table of Daisuke Matsuzaka." Nikkan Sports, n.d.
https://web.archive.org/web/20080609173205/http://matsuzaka
.nikkansports.com/en/history/top-history.html.

Collins, Jim. *The Last Best League: One Summer, One Season, One Dream.* 1st
ed. Cambridge, MA: Da Capo Press, 2004.

Coskrey, Jason. "All-around Talents Tetsuto Yamada, Yuki Yangita Deserving of Spotlight." The *Japan Times*, July 30, 2018. https://www.japantimes.co.jp /sports/2018/07/30/baseball/japanese-baseball/around-talents-tetsuto -yamada-yuki-yangita-deserving-spotlight/.

Coskrey, Jason. "Bannister in No Man's Land after Move by Giants." The *Japan Times*, April 10, 2011. https://www.japantimes.co.jp/sports/2011/04/10 /baseball/japanese-baseball/bannister-in-no-mans-land-after-move-by -giants/#.XvMBEZNKhD0.

Coskrey, Jason. "Bass Says Balentien Won't Get Easy Path to Oh's Record." The *Japan Times*, September 6, 2013. https://www.japantimes.co.jp /sports/2013/09/06/baseball/japanese-baseball/bass-says-balentien -wont-get-easy-path-to-ohs-record/.

Coskrey, Jason. "Fateful Decision in Japan Put Soriano on Path to MLB." The *Japan Times*, November 8, 2014. http://www.japantimes.co.jp /sports/2014/11/08/baseball/japanese-baseball/fateful-decision-japan -put-soriano-path-mlb/#.WGo3GWQrI01.

Coskrey, Jason. "Fateful Decision in Japan Put Soriano on Path to MLB." The *Japan Times*, November 8, 2014. http://www.japantimes.co.jp /sports/2014/11/08/baseball/japanese-baseball/fateful-decision -japan-put-soriano-path-mlb/.

Coskrey, Jason. "Hara Leaves Big Shoes for next Giants Manager to Fill." The *Japan Times*, October 19, 2015. https://www.japantimes.co.jp/sports /2015/10/19/baseball/japanese-baseball/hara-leaves-big-shoes -for-next-giants-manager-to-fill/.

Coskrey, Jason. "Hawks Pitcher Dennis Sarfate Facing up to Reality Career May Be over Due to Injury." The *Japan Times*, September 10, 2020. https://www.japantimes.co.jp/sports/2020/09/10/baseball/japanese-baseball /hawks-pitcher-dennis-sarfate-facing-reality-career-may-due-injury/.

Coskrey, Jason. "Leach Happy to Get Second Chance with BayStars." The *Japan Times*, July 31, 2011. https://www.japantimes.co.jp/sports /2011/07/31/baseball/japanese-baseball/leach-happy-to-get-second -chance-with-baystars/.

Coskrey, Jason. "Led by First-Year Managers, Hawks, Swallows Chasing Japan Series Title." The *Japan Times*, October 23, 2015. https ://www.japantimes.co.jp/sports/2015/10/23/baseball/japanese-baseball /led-by-first-year-managers-hawks-swallows-chasing-japan-series-title/.

Coskrey, Jason. "Ramirez to Salute Disaster Victims after HRs." The *Japan Times*, March 25, 2011. https://web.archive.org/web/20110401020029 /http://search.japantimes.co.jp/cgi-bin/sb20110325j1.html.

Coskrey, Jason. "Swallows Pitchers off to Hot Start on Mound This Year." The *Japan Times*, April 13, 2015. https://www.japantimes.co.jp/sports /2015/04/13/baseball/japanese-baseball/swallows-pitchers-hot-start-mound-year/#.WizvUbQ-dD1.

Coskrey, Jason. "Swallows' Balentien Reflects on All-Star Fun, Superb Start to Season." The *Japan Times*, July 20, 2013. https://www.japantimes.co.jp /sports/2013/07/20/baseball/japanese-baseball/swallows-balentien-reflects -on-all-star-fun-superb-start-to-season-2/.

Cromwell, Carter. "Randy Bass, Alex Ramirez Earn Rare Status of Foreign-Born Japanese Baseball Hall of Famers." Japan Ball, January 14, 2023. https://japanball.com/articles-features/japanese-baseball-news/randy-bass -alex-ramirez-earn-rare-status-of-foreign-born-japanese-baseball-hall-of -famers/.

Darvish, Yu. "What You Can Do." Web log. *Ameba* (blog), March 16, 2011. https://ameblo.jp/darvish-yu-blog/entry-10832628850.html.

DeOrio, Garrett. "Welcome to the Tokyo Yakult Swallows English Website." TokyoSwallows.com (via the Wayback Machine), June 5, 2008. https ://web.archive.org/web/20151228055737/https://tokyoswallows. com/2008/06/hello-world/.

Derysh, Igor. "2013 World Baseball Classic Stats Leaders." XN Sports, April 4, 2013. https://xnsports.com/2013/03/20/2013-world-baseball-classic-stats -leaders-top-performers/.

Dick, Ken. "Stars of Senbatsu." NPB Tracker, April 3, 2011. http://www .npbtracker.com/2011/04/stars-of-senbatsu/.

Divish, Ryan. "Keone Kela Goes from Seattle High Schools to Living the Dream of Playing in the Big Leagues." The *Seattle Times*, April 18, 2015. https://www.seattletimes.com/sports/mariners/keone-kela-goes-from-seattle-high-schools-to-living-the-dream-of-playing-in-the-big-leagues/.

Fischer-Baum, Reuben. "Is Wladimir Balentien Having the Most Dominant Baseball Season Ever?" *Deadspin*, September 4, 2013. https://deadspin.com/infographic-wladimir-balentien-is-murdering-baseballs-1248082048.

Fraley, Gerry. "Rangers Notebook: What Trick Did Tony Barnette Learn in Japan That's Already Paying Dividends This Spring?" The *Dallas Morning News*, February 26, 2018. https://www.dallasnews.com/sports/rangers/2018/02/27/rangers-notebook-what-trick-did-tony-barnette-learn-in-japan-that-s-already-paying-dividends-this-spring/.

Freeman, Joe. "Blazers' LaMarcus Aldridge to Donate $1,000 per Point to Japan Tonight." *Oregon Live*, March 27, 2011. https://www.oregonlive.com/blazers/2011/03/blazers_lamarcus_aldridge_to_d.html.

Fukue, Natsuko. "Urayasu Still Dealing with Liquefaction." The *Japan Times*, April 8, 2011. https://www.japantimes.co.jp/news/2011/04/08/national/urayasu-still-dealing-with-liquefaction/.

"Giants Pitcher Bannister to Retire." The *Japan Times*, April 27, 2011. https://www.japantimes.co.jp/sports/2011/04/27/baseball/japanese-baseball/giants-pitcher-bannister-to-retire/.

"The Giants-Hanshin Game on the 14th Will Be Held...Proceeds Will Go to the Disaster Area." Yomiuri Shimbun (via the Wayback Machine), March 13, 2011. https://web.archive.org/web/20110315024948/http://www.yomiuri.co.jp/sports/npb/news/20110313-OYT1T00425.htm.

Gibson, John E. "Hard Drives: Sports, Public Share Mutual Inspiration." Japanese Baseball (originally the *Daily Yomiuri*), March 30, 2011. https://www.japanesebaseball.com/writers/display.gsp?id=36993.

Gibson, John E. "Whitesell Provides Big Boost for Swallows." Japanese Baseball (originally the *Daily Yomiuri*), August 11, 2010. https://www.japanesebaseball.com/writers/display.gsp?id=33681.

Gibson, John E., and Jim Allen. "JBWP Vol. 4.21: Jim Allen and John E. Gibson Discuss a Chat with Tony Barnette..." *Japan Baseball Weekly* Podcast, June 30, 2014. https://japanesebaseball.com/audio/JBP_Pod _Vol._4.21.Barnette,_Swallows,_Interleague,_Notes,_Question.mp3.

Gilbert, Steve. "D-Zacks! Arizona Gets Greinke: 6-Year, Wild-West Deal." MLB.com, December 4, 2015. https://www.mlb.com/news /zack-greinke-signs-with-d-backs/c-158861948.

Graczyk, Wayne. "Aoki's Departure Leaves Big Void for Swallows." The *Japan Times*, March 25, 2012. https://www.japantimes.co.jp/sports/2012/03/25 /baseball/aokis-departure-leaves-big-void-for-swallows/#.W00jP9hKhsM.

Graczyk, Wayne. "Disaster Had Major Impact on NPB." The *Japan Times*, March 11, 2012. https://www.japantimes.co.jp/sports/2012/03/11/baseball /disaster-had-major-impact-on-npb/.

Graczyk, Wayne. "Pro Baseball Hopes to Inspire Fukushima in Return." The *Japan Times*, July 10, 2011. https://www.japantimes.co.jp/sports/2011/07 /10/baseball/pro-baseball-hopes-to-inspire-fukushima-in-return/.

Grant, Evan. "As Winter Meetings Come to a Close, Rangers Have yet to Address Biggest Offseason Need." The *Dallas Morning News*, December 10, 2015. https://www.dallasnews.com/sports/rangers/2015/12/11/as-winter -meetings-come-to-a-close-rangers-have-yet-to-address-biggest-offseason -need/.

Grant, Evan. "How Matt Bush, Jeremy Jeffress Were Able to Partake in Rangers Post-Clinching Celebration." The *Dallas Morning News*, September 24, 2016. https://www.dallasnews.com/sports/rangers/2016/09/24/how-matt -bush-jeremy-jeffress-were-able-to-partake-in-rangers-post-clinching -celebration/.

Grant, Evan. "Rangers Notebook: Shin-Soo Choo Takes Live Batting Practice off Texas Pitchers; Playoff Ticket Update." The *Dallas Morning News*, September 25, 2016. https://www.dallasnews.com/sports/rangers /2016/09/25/rangers-notebook-shin-soo-choo-takes-live-batting-practice -off-texas-pitchers-playoff-ticket-update/.

Grosbard, Adam. "Watch: Rangers Rookies Dress up like Kiss and Perform at Charity Event." The *Dallas Morning News*, May 26, 2016. https://www.dallasnews.com/sports/rangers/2016/05/26/watch-rangers-rookies-dress-up-like-kiss-and-perform-at-charity-event/.

Grow, Nathaniel. "Insuring Prince Fielder." FanGraphs, August 11, 2016. https://blogs.fangraphs.com/insuring-prince-fielder/.

Hibbett, Maia. "In Their Fight to Stop a New US Military Base, Okinawans Confront Two Colonizers." *The Nation*, May 17, 2019. https://www.thenation.com/article/archive/okinawa-japan-us-military/.

Hunter, Ian. "A History of the Feud between the Blue Jays and the Texas Rangers." *Toronto Life*, May 26, 2017. https://torontolife.com/city/toronto-sports/history-feud-blue-jays-texas-rangers/.

"Ike Davis and This Thing ." WFAA.com, March 23, 2016. https://www.wfaa.com/article/sports/mlb/rangers/ike-davis-and-this-thing/98649178.

Jacoby, Steve. "Rising Son: West High Grad Tuffy Rhodes Is a Star in the Firmament of Japanese Baseball." *Cincinnati Magazine* May 2002, May 1, 2002.

Jaffe, Jay. "Yankees-Rangers Rain Delay Should Lead to Rule Change ." *Sports Illustrated*, June 28, 2016. https://www.si.com/mlb/2016/06/28/yankees-rangers-rain-delay-umpires-curfew.

Johns, Greg. "Mariners Ink Korean Slugger Lee to Minors Deal." MLB.com, February 3, 2016. https://www.mlb.com/news/korean-star-dae-ho-lee-signs-with-mariners-c163553984.

Kanemoto, Tomoaki. "Kanemoto: 'It's Not a Situation to Give Courage.'" Nikkan Sports, March 17, 2011. https://www.nikkansports.com/baseball/news/p-bb-tp0-20110317-749357.html.

Karraker, Patrick. "Cubs Sign Tony Barnette to One-Year Deal with Club Option for 2020." MLB Daily Dish, February 1, 2019. https://www.mlbdailydish.com/2019/2/1/18207442/cubs-sign-tony-barnette.

Kikuta, Yasuhiko. "Balentien's 'Usual' Smile after the Apology Press Conference." Yahoo! Japan, January 30, 2014. https://news.yahoo.co.jp/byline/kikutayasuhiko/20140130-00032124/.

Kikuta, Yasuhiko. "The Parade Is 'the Best Time of My Life': Balentien's Visit to His Hometown." *Yahoo! Japan*, November 19, 2013. https://news.yahoo.co.jp/expert/articles/8ec0b99194ae19f8708592002bfc77bc8ef7f1eb.

Kim, Albert. "Remade in Japan." *Sports Illustrated*, May 14, 1990. https://vault.si.com/vault/1990/05/14/remade-in-japan.

Kim, Se-jeong. "Bears' Pitcher Bae Announces Retirement." *Korea Times*, October 29, 2019. https://www.koreatimes.co.kr/www/sports/2020/09/662_277871.html.

Kingston, Jeff, ed. *Natural disaster and nuclear crisis in Japan: Response and recovery after Japan's 3/11.* of *Nissan Institue/Routledge Japanese Studies Series.* London: Routledge, 2012.

Krauthammer, Charles. "The Natural Returns to St. Louis." RCP (originally the *Washington Post*), August 17, 2007. https://www.realclearpolitics.com/articles/2007/08/the_natural_returns_to_st_loui.html.

"Lakers Star Raises Money for Japan Relief with Every Point Scored." CBS News, March 26, 2011. https://www.cbsnews.com/losangeles/news/lakers-star-raises-money-for-japan-relief-with-every-point-scored/.

Lidz, Franz. "Fly Often and Carry a Big Stick: Agent Don Nomura Is Trying to Introduce U.S.-Style Player Representation to Japan." *Sports Illustrated* May 1996, May 27, 1996. http://www.si.com/vault/1996/05/27/213322/fly-often-and-carry-a-big-stick-agent-don-nomura-is-trying-to-introduce-us-style-player-representation-to-japan.

MacGregor, Hillary E. "A Hit With Players, Agent Is Screwball to Owners in Japan." *Los Angeles Times*, October 9, 1995. http://articles.latimes.com/1995-10-09/sports/sp-54976_1_japanese-player.

Mack, Eric. "Highlighting Top Diamondbacks Prospects for '09." CBS Sports, October 12, 2008. http://www.cbssports.com/fantasy/baseball/news/highlighting-top-diamondbacks-prospects-for-09/.

Marc, Stein. "Tabuse Hoping To Give Japan Big Assist." ESPN, March 27, 2011. https://www.espn.com/nba/dailydime/_/page/dime-110325-27/tabuse-making-play-japan.

Margalus, Jim. "Lastings Effects: Milledge Signing Has Minor Implications." South Side Sox, February 4, 2011. https://www.southsidesox.com /2011/2/4/1974011/lastings-effects-milledge-signing-has -minor-implications.

Martin, Dan. "Ike Davis Reflects on Magical Team Israel Run He Nearly Missed." *New York Post*, May 28, 2018. https://nypost.com/2018/05/28 /ike-davis-reflects-on-magical-team-israel-run-he-nearly-missed/.

Maymi, Javier. "Winter Leagues Roundup: Milledge Thriving." ESPN, November 23, 2011. http://www.espn.com/blog/sweetspot/post /_/id/18687/winter-leagues-roundup-milledge-thriving.

McDonald, Darragh. "NPB Posting Window Expanded from 30 to 45 Days." MLB Trade Rumors, December 6, 2022. https://www.mlbtraderumors .com/2022/12/npb-posting-window-reportedly-expanded-from-30-to-45 -days.html.

Merron, Jeff. "The Phoniest Records in Sports." ESPN, February 25, 2003. https://web.archive.org/web/20040621155959/http://sports.espn.go.com /chat/sportsnation/story?page=phonyrecords-030225.

Mooney, Patrick. "How a Rangers Executive Can See Everything Coming Together for Yu Darvish and the Cubs." *The Athletic*, February 27, 2018. https://theathletic.com/255896/2018/02/27/how-a-rangers-executive-can -see-everything-coming-together-for-yu-darvish-and-the-cubs/.

Morris, Adam J. "Texas Rangers 2016 Spring Training Schedule." Lone Star Ball, December 1, 2015. https://www.lonestarball.com/2015/12/1/9828880 /texas-rangers-2016-spring-training-schedule.

Morrissey, Michael. "At Last, Milledge Signs: 5-Tool Prospect Gets $2 Million after Controversy." *New York Post*, August 20, 2003. https://nypost. com/2003/08/20/at-last-milledge-signs-5-tool-prospect-gets-2-million -after-controversy/.

Mullen, Liz. "Octagon to Acquire CSMG Biz." *Sports Business Journal*, October 27, 2008. https://www.sportsbusinessjournal.com/Journal/Issues/2008/10/27/ This-Weeks-News/Octagon-To-Acquire-CSMG-Biz.aspx.

Murakami, Haruki. "About Haruki Murakami." HarukiMurakami.com, n.d. https://www.harukimurakami.com/author.

"Murphy Resigns at Arizona State." ESPN, November 20, 2009. https://www .espn.com/college-sports/news/story?id=4676055.

"NBA Basketball Stars Score for the People of Japan ." *Direct Relief,* March 24, 2011. Direct Relief. https://www.directrelief.org/2011/03/nba-basketball -stars-score-for-the-people-of-japan/ .

Nbakki (pseudonym). "Salaries of NPB Yakult Swallows Players in 2015." How much is it in Tokyo?, May 12, 2015. http://nbakki.hatenablog.com/entry /Salaries_yakult_swallows_2015.

NEIFI Analytics. "How Good Is Shohei Otani?" FanGraphs , August 31, 2016. https://blogs.fangraphs.com/how-good-is-shohei-otani/.

Newman, Patrick. "Balentien's Hot Start." NPB Tracker, May 21, 2011. http ://www.npbtracker.com/2011/05/balentiens-hot-start/.

Newman, Patrick. "Ganbarou Tohoku, Ganbarou Nihon." NPB Tracker, April 4, 2011. http://www.npbtracker.com/2011/04/ganbarou-tohoku/.

"NPB Scraps Extra-Innings Time Limit." The *Japan Times*, March 9, 2013. https://www.japantimes.co.jp/sports/2013/03/09/baseball/japanese-baseball /npb-scraps-extra-innings-time-limit/.

Olson, Casey. "Baseball: Barnette Signs Two-Year Contract to Return to Yakult Tokyo Swallows." Federal Way Mirror, December 17, 2012. http://www .federalwaymirror.com/sports/baseball-barnette-signs-two-year-contract-to -return-to-yakult-tokyo-swallows/.

"Open House Presents Swallows Dream Game." YakultSwallows.co.jp, n.d. https://www.yakult-swallows.co.jp/pages/info/event/dream_game/.

Ota, Kozo. "Remembering Masayasu Okada." TokyoSwallows.com (via the Wayback Machine), July 30, 2010. https://web.archive.org/web /20191106220644/https://tokyoswallows.com/2010/07 /remembering-masayasu-okada/.

Ota, Kozo, David Watkins, and Chris Pellegrini. "Tokyo Swallows Podcast 51 (October, 2019)." TokyoSwallows.com (via the Wayback Machine),

October 14, 2019. https://web.archive.org/web/20191106220641/https://tokyoswallows.com/2019/10/tokyo-swallows-podcast-51-october-2019/.

Ota, Kozo. "5/5/14 Monday Bullet #4 (Creepy Mascot Edition)." TokyoSwallows.com (via the Wayback Machine), May 5, 2014. https://web.archive.org/web/20210313080227/https://tokyoswallows.com/2014/05/monday-bullets-4/.

Otake, Tomoko, and Shusuke Murai. "'Bakugai,' 'Toripuru Suri' Share Top Honors as Year's Most Memorable Buzzwords in Japan." The *Japan Times*, December 1, 2015. https://www.japantimes.co.jp/news/2015/12/01/national/bakugai-toripuru-suri-share-top-honors-years-memorable-buzzwords-japan.

Panoringan, Anne Marie. "11 Healthy(Ish) Facts from Touring Yakult." OC Weekly, December 17, 2018. https://www.ocweekly.com/11-healthyish-facts-from-touring-yakult/.

Passan, Jeff. "Sources: Rangers Reliever Jeremy Jeffress Enters Rehab." *Yahoo! Sports*, August 31, 2016. https://sports.yahoo.com/news/sources-rangers-reliever-jeremy-jeffress-enters-rehab-wont-be-suspended-after-dwi-201610426.html.

Paterik, Brice. "Rangers Assemble Cheap, Unorthodox Bullpen." Shreveport Times (originally WFAA), March 29, 2016. https://www.shreveporttimes.com/story/sports/mlb/2016/03/29/rangers-build-strong-bullpen-cheaply/82394942/.

Piecoro, Nick. "Diamondbacks Agree to Terms with Reliever Scott McGough." The *Arizona Republic*, December 15, 2022. https://www.azcentral.com/story/sports/mlb/diamondbacks/2022/12/15/arizona-diamondbacks-to-sign-reliever-scott-mcgough/69731344007/.

"Police Countermeasures and Damage Situation Associated with 2011 Tohoku District - off the Pacific Ocean Earthquake." National Police Agency of Japan, March 10, 2021. https://www.npa.go.jp/news/other/earthquake2011/pdf/higaijokyo_e.pdf.

"Rangers Acquire C Lucroy and RHP Jeffress from Brewers." MLB.com, August 1, 2016. https://www.mlb.com/rangers/news/rangers-acquire -c-lucroy-and-rhp-jeffress-from-brewers/c-193027700.

Read, Richard. "Delta Air Lines Passengers Weather Japan Earthquake, Narrowly Escape Tokyo for Portland." Oregon Live, March 12, 2011. https://www.oregonlive.com/pacific-northwest-news/2011/03/portland _arrivals_recall_worries_waits_for_flights_out_of_japan.html.

Reiter, Ben. "The Complicated Life and Death of Hideki Irabu." *Sports Illustrated*, August 17, 2017. https://www.si.com/mlb/2017/08/01 /hideki-irabu.

"Report: Ichiro Suzuki Donates 100m Yen." ESPN, March 18, 2011. https ://www.espn.com/mlb/news/story?id=6234412.

Rubin, Deanna. "A Look at the Japanese Leagues -- Part 2: Eastern and Western, or Down on the Farm." Marinerds, December 10, 2008. http ://marinerds.blogspot.com/2008/12/look-at-japanese-leagues-part-2-eastern .html.

Sabin, Rainer. "Following Knee Surgery, Rangers Pitcher Colby Lewis Becomes Avid Cyclist." The *Dallas Morning News*, January 23, 2016. https://www .dallasnews.com/sports/rangers/2016/01/23/following-knee-surgery-rangers -pitcher-colby-lewis-becomes-avid-cyclist/.

Saslow, Eli. "'Matt Bush? That Matt Bush?'" *ESPN The Magazine* April 2016, April 7, 2016. https://www.espn.com/mlb/story/_/id/15147918 /the-story-texas-rangers-prospect-matt-bush-rediscovery-unlikely-comeback.

Schoenfield, David. "Five Things We Learned Wednesday: Maybe the Rangers Are Team of Destiny." ESPN, August 11, 2016. https://www.espn.com /blog/sweetspot/post/_/id/73062/five-things-we-learned-wednesday -maybe-the-rangers-are-team-of-destiny.

Schoenfield, David. "Rangers' Motley Crew of Relievers Has a Chance to Be One of the Best." ESPN, April 10, 2016. http://www.espn.com.au/blog /sweetspot/post/_/id/69625/rangers-motley-crew-of-relievers-has-a-chance -to-be-one-of-the-best.

Schoenfield, David. "Ten Sleeper Relief Pitchers to Watch for in 2016." ESPN, March 30, 2016. https://www.espn.com/blog/sweetspot/post/_/id/69279 /ten-sleeper-relief-pitchers-to-watch-for-2016.

Sharkey-Gotlieb, Simon. "Astros' Aoki Joins Japan's 'Golden Players Club' with 2,000th Pro Hit." The Score, June 11, 2017. https://www.thescore.com /mlb/news/1317064.

Shigeno, Goro (pseudonym). "Day 12 - Championship - Toukaidai Sagami (Kanagawa) vs. Kyushu Kokusaidai Fuzoku (Fukuoka)." Kokoyakyu in English, April 3, 2011. http://goroshigeno.blogspot.com/2011/04/day-12 -championship-toukaidai-sagami.html.

Shigeno, Goro (pseudonym). "Senbatsu Is On, but with a Few Changes." Kokoyakyu in English, March 19, 2011. http://goroshigeno.blogspot .com/2011/03/senbatsu-is-on-but-with-few-changes.html.

"Shohei Ohtani, Formally Introduced by Dodgers, Avoids Surgery Talk." ESPN, December 14, 2023. https://www.espn.com/mlb/story /_/id/39114951/shohei-ohtani-formally-unveiled-dodgers-wait-get-going.

"Sister Partnerships by US State." Asia Matters for America, n.d. https ://asiamattersforamerica.org/japan/data/sister-partnerships/united-states.

Smaal, Rob. "Baseball Legends Say Farewell to Wally." Japanese Baseball (originally The Asahi Shimbun), June 1, 2011. https://www .japanesebaseball.com/writers/display.gsp?id=37985.

Smaal, Rob. "Central League Pushes Back Opening Day to April 12." Japanese Baseball (originally The Asahi Shimbun), March 26, 2011. https://www .japanesebaseball.com/writers/display.gsp?id=36937.

Smaal, Rob. "Central League Pushes Back Season to Conserve Energy." Japanese Baseball (originally The Asahi Shimbun), March 22, 2011. https:// www.japanesebaseball.com/writers/display.gsp?id=36869.

Smaal, Rob. "Fukushima Games Have Some Players on Edge." Japanese Baseball (originally The Asahi Shimbun), June 22, 2011. https://www .japanesebaseball.com/writers/display.gsp?id=38337.

Smaal, Rob. "Guiel to Return to Swallows." Japanese Baseball (originally The Asahi Shimbun), December 16, 2009. http://www.japanesebaseball.com /writers/display.gsp?id=28576.

Smaal, Rob. "Hitters No Friends of New Baseballs but Pitchers Love 'em." Japanese Baseball (originally The Asahi Shimbun), June 25, 2011. http://www.japanesebaseball.com/writers/display.gsp?id=38388.

Smaal, Rob. "NPB Clubs Pitch in for Earthquake Relief Efforts." Japanese Baseball (originally The Asahi Shimbun), April 5, 2011. http://www.japanesebaseball.com/writers/display.gsp?id=37086.

Smaal, Rob. "PL Delays Opening Day, CL Sticks with March 25." Japanese Baseball (originally The Asahi Shimbun), March 19, 2011. https://www.japanesebaseball.com/writers/display.gsp?id=36818.

Smaal, Rob. "Swallows' Guiel Calls It Quits after 19 Years." Japanese Baseball (originally The Asahi Shimbun), September 22, 2011. http://www.japanesebaseball.com/writers/display.gsp?id=39740.

Smaal, Rob. "Swallows' Killer Bs Helping the Cause." Japanese Baseball (originally The Asahi Shimbun), May 8, 2011. http://www.japanesebaseball.com/writers/display.gsp?id=37608.

Smaal, Rob. "Teams, Players at Odds on Start of Regular Season." Japanese Baseball (originally The Asahi Shimbun), March 18, 2011. https://www.japanesebaseball.com/writers/display.gsp?id=36799.

Smaal, Rob. "The Departed: Reactions May Vary to NPB Players Who Left Japan." Japanese Baseball (originally The Asahi Shimbun), March 20, 2011. http://www.japanesebaseball.com/writers/display.gsp?id=36837.

Smaal, Rob. "The Pros and Cons." Japanese Baseball (originally The Asahi Shimbun), October 1, 2010. http://www.japanesebaseball.com/writers/display.gsp?id=34735.

Smaal, Rob. "'Typhoon' Energizes Swallows." Japanese Baseball (originally The Asahi Shimbun), September 3, 2010. http://www.japanesebaseball.com/writers/display.gsp?id=34214.

Smith, Joe. "Civil Case Settled for Ex-Ray RHP Matt Bush and Brandon Guyer." *Tampa Bay Times*, May 15, 2013. https://www.tampabay.com/civil-case-settled-for-ex-ray-rhp-matt-bush-and-brandon-guyer/2121171/.

Snyder, Matt. "Wladimir Balentien Arrested on Domestic Violence Charges." CBS Sports, January 13, 2014. https://www.cbssports.com/mlb/news/wladimir-balentien-arrested-on-domestic-violence-charges/.

"The State of Tsubamegun." TokyoSwallows.com (via the Wayback Machine), December 4, 2018. https://web.archive.org/web/20220420220201/https ://tokyoswallows.com/2018/12/the-state-of-tsubamegun/.

Stella, Jason. "D'Antona Wins Home Run Derby in Triple Overtime." MiLB .com, July 14, 2008. https://www.milb.com/news/gcs-432589.

Stevens, Matthew. "Ex-ASU Softball Coach Quits Auburn after Son Accused of 'Inappropriate Relationships.'" The *Arizona Republic*, August 29, 2017. https://www.azcentral.com/story/sports/college/asu/2017/08/29 /corey-myers-auburn-softball-accused-affair-student-athletes-z/612473001/.

Stevenson, Stefan. "Rangers' Barnette Has Strained Oblique, Holland in Bullpen for Now." *Fort Worth Star-Telegram*, September 11, 2016. https:// www.star-telegram.com/sports/mlb/texas-rangers/article101230292.html.

Stone, Larry. "Mel Stottlemyre on Father's Day: Courage, Tragedy, Baseball and an Unbreakable Family Bond." The *Seattle Times*, June 17, 2016. https ://www.seattletimes.com/sports/mariners/mel-stottlemyre-on-fathers-day -courage-tragedy-and-an-unbreakable-family-bond/.

Stottlemyre, Mel, Jr. "Fishing with Baseball Legends." Stotts Fishing Adventures, n.d. https://fishstotts.com/about/.

Sueyoshi, Gen. "Junji Ogawa Signs a 2-Year Deal with the Swallows." Yakyu Baka (via the Wayback Machine), October 12, 2010. https://web.archive .org/web/20101021045140/http://yakyubaka.com:80/2010/10/12 /junji-ogawa-signs-a-2-year-deal-with-the-swallows/.

Sueyoshi, Gen. "The NPB after the Big Quake, Day 1 [March 12, 2011]." Yakyu Baka (via the Wayback Machine), March 12, 2011. https://web .archive.org/web/20110316172001/http://yakyubaka.com/2011/03/12 /the-npb-a-day-after-the-big-quake-march-12-2011/.

Sueyoshi, Gen. "[7/18/2015] Mazda All-Star Series 2015: Game 2 Home Run Derby Results." Yakyu Baka, July 18, 2015. https://web.archive.org /web/20190629010637/http://yakyubaka.com/2015/07/18/7182015 -mazda-all-star-series-2015-game-2-home-run-derby-results/.

Sullivan, T.R. "Bush Grateful for Second Chance after Prison Term." MLB. com, February 23, 2016. https://www.mlb.com/news/former-no-1 -pick-matt-bush-at-rangers-camp-c165260280.

Sullivan, T.R. "Jeffress Makes Strides While Taking on Epilepsy." MLB.com, August 22, 2016. https://www.mlb.com/news/rangers-jeremy-jeffress -battles-epilepsy/c-197023442.

Sullivan, T.R., and Justin Wise. "Hamels, Beltre Help Rangers Punch Their Ticket." MLB.com, September 23, 2016. https://www.mlb.com/news /cole-hamels-leads-rangers-to-al-west-title-c202970432.

Summers, Jeff. "No Sale on Whitesell with Non-Tender." *Bleacher Report*, December 13, 2009. https://bleacherreport.com/articles/308420-no-sale-on -whitesell-with-non-tender.

"Swallows Agree to Post All-Star Outfielder Aoki." The *Japan Times*, November 11, 2011. https://www.japantimes.co.jp/sports/2011/11/11 /baseball/japanese-baseball/swallows-agree-to-post-all-star-outfielder-aoki /#.WzaouhJKhD0.

Swallows Army/Troop. "Cheering Song for Each Player." TSUBAMEGUNDAN .com, n.d. http://tsubamegundan.com/information.html.

Sypa, Steve. "Lastings Milledge: Where Is He Now?" *Amazin' Avenue*, January 8, 2014. https://www.amazinavenue.com/2014/1/8/5130900 /new-york-mets-lastings-milledge-japan.

Taylor, Jean-Jacques. "Prince Fielder: 'Can't Play Major League Baseball Anymore.'" ESPN, August 10, 2016. https://www.espn.com/mlb/story /_/id/17267384/prince-fielder-texas-rangers-emotional-doctors-told-play.

"Tetsuro Degawa Was in Yakult!" Nikkan Sports, February 9, 2012. https ://www.nikkansports.com/baseball/news/p-bb-tp0-20120209-901121.html.

"Tim Esmay Named Interim Head Baseball Coach." Tim Esmay Named Interim Head Baseball Coach | ASU News, December 3, 2009. https ://asunow.asu.edu/content/tim-esmay-named-interim-head-baseball-coach.

Todd, Jeff. "Rangers Designate Cesar Ramos." MLB Trade Rumors, July 22, 2016. https://www.mlbtraderumors.com/2016/07/rangers-designate-cesar -ramos.html.

Tokyo American Club, n.d. https://www.tokyoamericanclub.org/.

"TOMODACHI Partnership with Major League Baseball." *US-Japan Tomodachi*, n.d. Tomodachi. https://usjapantomodachi.org/programs-activities /cultural-programs/tomodachi-partnership-with-major-league-baseball/.

"Tony Barnette Held Back in Dugout." Imgur, August 19, 2014. https://imgur
.com/dx3zrKi.

"U.S. Dollar / Japanese Yen Historical Reference Rates from Bank of England
for 1975 to 2024." Pound Sterling Live, n.d. https://www.poundsterlinglive
.com/bank-of-england-spot/historical-spot-exchange-rates/usd/USD-to-JPY.

"US Team HQ to Be Based at Tokyo American Club in 2020." *Sports
Illustrated*, August 2, 2017. https://www.si.com/olympics/2017/08/02
/ap-oly-tokyo-2020-usa-house.

Various Twitter users. "'Tony Barnette Crappy Photoshop Contest' Hashtag
Search Results." Twitter, October 17, 2015. https://twitter.com/
hashtag/%E3%83%90%E3%83%BC%E3%83%8D%E3%83%83%E3
%83%88%E3%82%AF%E3%82%BD%E3%82%B3%E3%83%A9
%E3%82%B0%E3%83%A9%E3%83%B3%E3%83%97%E3%83%AA.

Wakabayashi, Daisuke, and Daniel Barbarisi. "Balentien Passes Legendary Oh
to Break Japan Home-Run Record ." The *Wall Street Journal*, September 15,
2013. https://www.wsj.com/articles/BL-JRTB-14960.

Watkins, David. "How a Brummie Got Into Baseball." TokyoSwallows
.com (via the Wayback Machine), March 11, 2009. https://web.archive
.org/web/20191106220740/https://tokyoswallows.com/2009/03
/how-a-brummie-got-into-baseball/.

Whiting, Robert. "Spring Koshien Cancellation Crushes Baseball Players'
Dreams." Nikkei Asia, March 13, 2020. https://asia.nikkei.com/Life-Arts
/Life/Spring-Koshien-cancellation-crushes-baseball-players-dreams.

Whiting, Robert. *You Gotta Have Wa*. New York, NY: Vintage Departures,
2009.

Wittenmyer, Gordon. "Cubs Reliever Steve Cishek Suffers Bruised Knee before
Wednesday's Game in Colorado." *Chicago Sun-Times*, June 12, 2019.
https://chicago.suntimes.com/cubs/2019/6/12/18663187/cubs-reliever
-steve-cishek-injures-knee-before-wednesdays-game-in-colorado.

"Women's Ranking." FIFA.com, March 18, 2011. https://www.fifa.com/fifa
-world-ranking/women?dateId=ranking_20110318.

"Yakult Gets New Helper! Triple-A Whitesell ." Sankei Sports (Via the Wayback Machine), June 8, 2010. https://web.archive.org/web/20100715225157 /http://www.sanspo.com/baseball/news/100608/bsf1006080505001-n1.htm.

"Yamada Beginning to Flex Muscles for Swallows." The *Japan Times*, July 23, 2014. https://www.japantimes.co.jp/sports/2014/07/23/baseball /japanese-baseball/yamada-beginning-flex-muscles-swallows/.

"Yankees Trade OF Carlos Beltran to Rangers for Pitching Prospects." ESPN, August 1, 2016. https://www.espn.com/mlb/story/_/id/17194381 /new-york-yankees-trade-outfielder-carlos-beltran-texas-rangers.

Yasuka. "Senpai and Kōhai Relationships in Japanese Culture." KCP International, April 14, 2021. https://www.kcpinternational.com/2021/04 /senpai-kohai-relationships-japanese-culture/.

"Yokohama's Leach Won't Return - First Restricted Player in History." Nikkan Sports, April 2, 2011. https://www.nikkansports.com/baseball/news/p -bb-tp0-20110402-755794.html.

Zencka, TC. "Wladimir Balentien Announces Retirement from NPB." MLB Trade Rumors, January 22, 2022. https://www.mlbtraderumors .com/2022/01/wladimir-balentien-announces-retirement-from-npb.html.

井上エイド. "Baseball Legend Alex Ramírez Becomes Legally Japanese." Becoming Legally Japanese, January 30, 2019. https://www.turning -japanese.info/2019/01/ramichan.html.

"由規、遺体で発見の元女房役に捧げる白星…ヤクルト." Yahoo! Japan (via the Wayback Machine), April 28, 2011. https://web.archive.org /web/20110430170550/http://headlines.yahoo.co.jp/hl?a=20110428 -00000034-sph-base.

Additional reference links below:

For NPB stats and information:
- DeltaGraphs - https://1point02.jp/op/index.aspx
- https://nf3.sakura.ne.jp/
- https://npb.jp/eng/

- http://www.npbtracker.com/
- TokyoSwallows.com via the Wayback Machine - https://web.archive.org/web/20220331113800/https://tokyoswallows.com/
- Yakyu Baka via the Wayback Machine - https://web.archive.org/web/20200423024755/http://yakyubaka.com/

For MLB and/or NPB stats and information:
- https://www.baseball-reference.com/

For MLB and/or WBC stats and information:
- https://baseballsavant.mlb.com/
- https://www.brooksbaseball.net/
- https://www.espn.com/
- https://www.mlb.com/

For minor league stats and information:
- https://www.milb.com/

For collegiate stats and information:
- http://www.thebaseballcube.com
- http://www.thesundevils.com/

INDEX